מסורה

ArtScroll Mesorah Series

Rabbi Nosson Scherman/Rabbi Meir Zlotowitz
General Editors

SUCCOS

SUCCOS — ITS SIGNIFICANCE, LAWS, AND **PRAYERS** / A PRESENTATION ANTHOLOGIZED FROM TALMUDIC AND TRADITIONAL SOURCES.

Published by

Mesorah Publications, ltd

Laws by
Rabbi Hersh Goldwurm

Background and Insights by
Rabbi Meir Zlotowitz

Prayers and Ritual by
Rabbi Avie Gold

Overview by
Rabbi Nosson Scherman

FIRST EDITION
First Impression . . . September, 1992

SECOND EDITION
Revised and expanded
First Impression . . . September, 1989
Second Impression . . . September, 1995

Published and Distributed by
MESORAH PUBLICATIONS, Ltd.
4401 Second Avenue
Brooklyn, New York 11232

Distributed in Europe by
J. LEHMANN HEBREW BOOKSELLERS
20 Cambridge Terrace
Gateshead, Tyne and Wear
England NE8 1RP

Distributed in Israel by
SIFRIATI / A. GITLER—BOOKS
4 Bilu Street
P.O.B. 14075
Tel Aviv 61140

Distributed in Australia & New Zealand by
GOLDS BOOK & GIFT CO.
36 William Street
Balaclava 3183, Vic., Australia

Distributed in South Africa by
KOLLEL BOOKSHOP
22 Muller Street
Yeoville 2198, Johannesburg, South Africa

ARTSCROLL MESORAH SERIES ®
"SUCCOS" / Its Significance, Laws, and Prayers
© Copyright 1982, 1989, by MESORAH PUBLICATIONS, Ltd.
4401 Second Avenue / Brooklyn, N.Y. 11232 / (718) 921-9000

ISBN
0-89906-166-4 (hard cover)
0-89906-167-2 (paperback)

Typography by Compuscribe at ArtScroll Studios, Ltd.

Printed in the United States of America by Moriah Offset
Bound by Sefercraft, Quality Bookbinders, Ltd. Brooklyn, N.Y.

ᴥᔰ Table of Contents

ᴥᔰ An Overview / Succah — Booths and Clouds

I. Cycles — Physical and Spiritual	9
II. The Succah on Two Levels	18
IV. The Double Role of Succos	26
III. The Leviathan and Fulfillment	34

ᴥᔰ Background and Insights

The Biblical Commands	39
The Festival	41
The Season	44
The Succah	49
Ushpizin	53
The Four Species	54
The Water-Drawing	59
Hallel	64
Hakhel	65
Koheles on Succos	66
Hoshanos and Hoshana Rabbah	67

ᴥᔰ Observance/The Laws

The Days before Succos	74
The Sabbath	75
The Succah	76
The Four Species	82

ᴥᔰ Observance/Prayers and Ritual

Kindling Yom Tov Lights	92
Ushpizin	94
Kiddush	102
Bircas Hamazon / Grace After Meals	104
The Three-Faceted Blessing	112
The Four Species	114
Kiddusha Rabba	116
Farewell to the Succah	118

ᴥᔰ Torah Study

Mishnayos Succah	122
Koheles / Ecclesiastes	158

We gratefully acknowledge the efforts of our dear friend, MR. AARON L. HEIMOWITZ, a tireless askan and man of rare vision and sensitivity. It is to him that the publication of this volume must be credited, for it is he who conceived of its creation, and has personally undertaken personal responsibility for its wide dissemination through an impressive list of Yeshivos and Torah institutions throughout the country. His only goal is to bring knowledge and appreciation of Torah — often for the first time — to thousands of his fellow Jews.

הקב"ה ישלם שכרו

—*The Publishers*

⩯ An Overview /
Succos—Booths and Clouds

Cycles—Physical and Spiritual
The Succah on Two Levels
The Double Role of Succos
The Leviathan and Fulfillment

—Rabbi Nosson Scherman

An Overview /
Succos—Booths and Clouds

תַּנְיָא. ,כִּי בַסֻּכּוֹת הוֹשַׁבְתִּי אֶת בְּנֵי יִשְׂרָאֵל
בְּהוֹצִיאִי אוֹתָם מֵאֶרֶץ מִצְרַיִם.' עַנְנֵי הַכָּבוֹד הָיוּ,
דִּבְרֵי ר' אֱלִיעֶזֶר. ר' עֲקִיבָא אוֹמֵר: סֻכּוֹת מַמָּשׁ
עָשׂוּ לָהֶם.

*We have learned [regarding the verse]: For
in succah-booths did I settle the Children
of Israel when I removed them from the
land of Egypt (Leviticus 23:43). [The
'succah-booths'] were the clouds of glory,
these are the words of R' Eliezer. R' Akiva
says, 'They made themselves actual
succah-booths' (Succah 11b).*

I. Cycles — Physical and Spiritual*

*Periphery
and
Essence*

The three
pilgrimage festivals
have two roles,
roles that are not
only different but
seem almost
contradictory.

The cycle of the three pilgrimage festivals,
Passover, Shavuos, and Succos, have two
Scripturally assigned roles, roles that are not only
different but seem almost contradictory. On the one
hand, they recall the formative miraculous events of
Jewish history and are constant reminders of the
reasons for Israel's being and its continued existence.
In this sense, the festivals are cosmic, lofty, intensely
spiritual phenomena that bind the Jewish calendar
with the Creator and Moving Force of the universe.

*The first section of the Overview is based primarily on *Maharal's Gevuros Hashem* ch. 46.

On the other hand, Scripture relates the festivals to the seasonal agricultural cycle of springtime, harvest, and ingathering of crops. On this level, the festivals seem "diminished," as it were, from sublime guideposts on a heavenly thoroughfare to mere commemorative, seemingly mundane celebrations of the agricultural cycle. They seem to surrender their grasp on eternity and become a mere reminder that seasons come and go and the land never yields its hold on those who work it and are in turn its servants.

Maharal notes this apparent discrepancy and explains how the two roles of the festivals are closely related.

Human existence involves a constant tension between what man is and the environment in which he lives.

Human existence involves a constant tension between what man is — his values, goals, concepts, visions, self — and the environment in which he lives. He is affected by everything around him: How much effort must he exert and how far must he go to earn his livelihood? What sort of people must he deal with? Are his neighbors and conditions of life compatible with his own sense of what he is and what he wishes to make of himself? How much should he learn from his neighbors and how much should he shun their influence, even if he cannot leave their company? This is but a small part of the infinite list that confronts every human being as he makes his way through life. In short, man is at the center of an often turbulent, always confusing, set of elements that entice and threaten, convince and reject, submit and rebel.

Man is at the center of an often turbulent, always confusing, set of elements.

Figuratively this condition is likened to the six directions — east, south, west, north, above, and below — that surround every human being wherever he is. The directions are the influences that work on him incessantly. They are outside of man, at a distance from his essence, but he is never free of them, always surrounded by them. The seventh factor is the placid center of it all — the inner man who is the object of all the forces, but is not part of them. How well he succeeds in shaping and maintaining his identity in accordance with the

spiritual dictates of his soul is the challenge and purpose of life.

In the realm of time, this concept is represented by the six days of the week and the Sabbath.

In the realm of time, this concept is represented by the six days of the week and the Sabbath. During the six days of creation, God fashioned all the divergent aspects of the universe from the gravitational forces that hold it together to the furiously speeding forces that tear at every atom and solar system. From mountain to amoeba, from the most spiritual to the most slothful and voracious, all was created during the six days. Those creatures represent the infinite variety of forces and values that constantly struggle for control of the universe and of man, who is its masterpiece and ultimate purpose. They are symbolized by the six "days" that surround the "inner self" of creation, for on each day new beings, forces and concepts were created, each of them removing man and his universe further from a true perception of the Creator and His will. What is the

What is the "inner self" within those external factors? The Sabbath.

"inner self" within those external factors? The Sabbath. For on the seventh day, God rested, as it were, to prove that Creation had not been, could never be, divorced from Him and His holiness. After every six days of turbulence the reminder returns: the holiest of days proclaims that in six days God created the untiring mainspring of activity, but on the seventh day, He called a halt to the sprawl of productive labor and reminded man that there is a point, a center, a purpose to it all — so that man would remember that God lavished blessing and potential upon him, so that he would utilize the universe to do His will and make it a reflection of His glory. It is in this sense that the Torah says, 'God blessed the seventh day and hallowed it, because on

God created the world so that man could make it a physical reflection of His holiness, and the Sabbath is the conduit through which sanctity and blessing come to earth.

it God abstained from all His work' (Genesis 2:3). As the Midrash and commentators explain, the Sabbath is the source from which all blessings come to the universe. God created the world so that man could make it a physical reflection of His holiness, and the Sabbath is the conduit through which sanctity and blessing come to earth.

The Seasons Reflect Man

The seven-day cycle of the Sabbath represents only one aspect of time. As inhabitants of the solar system, we are unalterably influenced by the solar day and the solar year, the changing months and seasons through which the year flits, as earth, moon, and sun perform their unvarying minuet through space and time. It is as if each year with its cycles were a new creation. Indeed, man must recognize that every year has its own potential for good and ill, and he is responsible to utilize it properly as another tool in the service of God. In the total sweep of history — from creation through the rise and fall of countless cultures, civilizations, and units of government, until the prophesied End of Days and Messianic times — there is a pattern of development: birth to growth to fulfillment. So it is every year in microcosm. "Time" is an essential dimension of the universe; from the start, God created a day to comprise an evening and a morning, and He created the heavenly bodies to 'serve as signs and for festivals and for days and years' (Genesis 1:14). Just as the universe we know is inseparable from the dimension of space, so it is inseparable from the dimension of time.

In the total sweep of history there is a pattern of development — birth to growth to fulfillment.

As an identifiable unit of time, each year is like a new creation. This idea is most pronounced in the cycle of seasons. "Creation" begins after the dreary respite of winter. In the spring the fields come to life and the trees blossom. Birds chirp and children romp on the new grass. The earth has come to life again. Slowly, the crops grow until they are ready for harvesting. A season of joy approaches as the first fruits mature and ripen. The harbinger of prosperity and success becomes ready under the benevolent smile of the sun. Finally, the earth's wealth is ready to be gathered from the fields and brought into homes, barns, and silos. The seasons of growth and harvest are over, and man is ready to let the products of his sweat provide for him until the next season of rebirth and growth begins. But the seasonal progression is wasted unless the farmer takes

The seasonal progression is wasted unless the farmer takes advantage of it.

advantage of it. Spring, harvest, and gathering have no meaning unless man turns his wit and muscle to capitalize on the opportunities nature gives him.

It is axiomatic in the Torah's perspective that the visible, tangible manifestations of nature are indicative of spiritual phenomena; indeed, the true *source* of events is Divine [see Overview to ArtScroll *Song of Songs*]. Seen from this viewpoint, the coming of spring is an indication that God smiles at man and offers him an opportunity to free himelf from the shackles of his wintry discontent. The time is opportune for man to aspire to freedom and a new beginning — just as Israel did centuries ago when it burst free from the physical and spiritual bondage of Egypt and just as the earth does every year when it shrugs free from the frost and lethargy of winter.

Like a teleprinter translating electrical impulses from a continent away, "nature" translates the phenomenon of spiritual rejuvenation into the physical manifestations of springtime.

Like a teleprinter translating electrical impulses from a continent away into a series of microscopic dots that form a recognizable picture of a far-off event, so "nature" translates the phenomenon of spiritual rejuvenation into the physical manifestations of springtime. What do the longer days and returning birds tell us? To lubricate the tractor, make vacation plans, begin strolling in the park — and to recognize spring for what it *truly* is: a signal that the time is ripe for spiritual renewal.

So it is with the season of harvest, the time that, in *Eretz Yisrael*, coincides with Shavuos, when the Torah was given. Springtime works wonders on the fields, but it would all be a waste unless the crops are harvested. To describe the foolishness of one who creates an opportunity but fails to follow through on it, the Talmud likens him to someone who plants seeds but fails to harvest the crop. The crop of human freedom is more precious than any found on field or tree, but it too will do no good unless it is harvested. On Shavuos, God told His foundling nation Israel the purpose of its freedom. Because Israel had accepted the Torah, the seeds planted in the springtime of the Exodus were harvested for a useful purpose. Otherwise, the crop of freedom would have become the rot of license and self-

The crop of human freedom is more precious than any found on field or tree, but it too will do no good unless it is harvested.

indulgence that has corrupted and destroyed so many civilizations.

The direction indicated by the harvest season is only the beginning, however. Gratifying it is that the farmer has the good sense to cut his crop and pick his fruit instead of admiring their height and luxuriance until they ripen, rot, and die — but what then? During the summer there is still much left to do. The grain must dry in the sun and then be bundled, threshed, winnowed, gathered. The fruit must be processed and prepared for storage or market. Not until the end of this productive and exhausting season can the farmer gather in his produce and truly rejoice in the success of his strivings. Only then can he say that he has completed the cycle set for him when spring began. Here, too, nature is but a reflection of the reality above. Man's freedom and dedication to a higher purpose reach their desired climax only when he gathers up his finished spiritual crop from his fields of endeavor. When his personal cycle of accomplishment is complete, he presents its *'You gave me life* end-product to God as if to say, "You gave me life *and direction — this* and direction — this is what I have made of Your *is what I have made* gifts."
of Your gifts.'

Birth and These three agricultural periods — spring, harvest,
Mission and ingathering — are paralleled in the spiritual development of man and his nation. A person blossoms into awareness as a thinking productive creature. But what should he do with his life? He searches for a philosophy, a code of conduct, a system of values. Shaping himself in accordance with them and following the path on which they lead him, he fashions a life — and, for better or worse, presents it to his Maker as the end product of the potential, opportunities, and resources given him. Every human being goes through the process, but no two results are the same. Some people complete the seasons of their lives with a harvest of virtuous greatness, others with one of cruel wickedness; such people have utilized every opportunity for the good or evil paths they have chosen. Most of us fall

Our lives are mixtures of leaps and falls, fulfilled and missed chances, gratifying and disappointing ventures.

somewhere in between. Our lives are mixtures of leaps and falls, fulfilled and missed chances, gratifying and disappointing ventures. Similarly, Israel's role and the festivals that recall the national genesis and continuous destiny are symbolized by the seasons of the sun and the cosmic forces they reflect.

Israel's national springtime of new life came in the month of Nissan when the Exodus from Egypt took place. Portentously does the Torah emphasize and reemphasize that it happened in חֹדֶשׁ הָאָבִיב, *the month of springtime.* Spring is the time of revival, of renewed potential after months of distressing inactivity. Just as the earth comes to life, so must Israel rejuvenate its resolve every year, as it did in that first Nissan (the *month of spring*) when it was elevated to nationhood. So vital is this characteristic to the message of Passover that the Sanhedrin was made responsible to adjust the lunar calendar regularly to assure that Nissan would always fall in the season of springtime.* So essential is the Exodus in its character of an act of national creation that the Torah commands Jews to remember it constantly *(Exodus 13:3)* just as it commands Jews always to remember the Sabbath, the symbol of God's creation of the universe itself *(Exodus 20:8).* The Sabbath and Exodus stand on the same plane; each reminds us that God made an entirely new and unprecedented phenomenon — the universe and the nation that was assigned to bring to fruition the reason for creation.

Just as the earth comes to life, so must Israel rejuvenate its resolve every year, as it did in that first Nissan.

Clearly, the birth of Israel achieved heightened significance when the Torah was given on Shavuos, for without that most magnanimous of heavenly gifts, Israel's freedom would have remained an unharvested bumper crop of unrealized potential. So both elements were present — the nation and its challenge. How would God help Israel find the way to a successful ingathering of its spiritual crop?

The birth of Israel achieved heightened significance when the Torah was given on Shavuos.

*In order to make this happen, a thirteenth month is added to the lunar year at periodic intervals; otherwise Passover would drift into the winter and would fail to deliver its proper spiritual message. For an explanation of the Hebrew calendar, see *Yad Avraham* commentary to ArtScroll Mishnah *Rosh Hashanah* and ArtScroll *Bircas HaChammah.*

Portent of Future Revivals

In the wilderness God enveloped and sheltered Israel in His עֲנָנֵי הַכָּבוֹד, *Clouds of Glory*, to show them His way and protect them as they followed it. The clouds were not a gift, they were a reward. The Midrash teaches that people who were undeserving of them — such as the insincere horde of Egyptians [עֵרֶב רַב] who accompanied the Jews into the Wilderness — did not enjoy the clouds' protection. Clearly, the presence of the clouds was a sign that Israel had risen to the spiritual plateau implied by God's all-enveloping protection. They had shown themselves worthy to be "gathered-in" by God in a national feat that would be commemorated eternally by the Succos festival. '*For in succah-booths did I settle the Children of Israel,*' God said. No other nation had ever earned such protection. Israel had completed the cycle. It had "farmed" spiritual nobility into its national essence. The promise of its springtime and the challenge of its harvest had been fulfilled as the nation was gathered into God's exalting, protecting, inspiring clouds.

That year became a watershed and a model in Israel's history. What had happened once became the goal of every future year, every future historical cycle, for what had been accomplished once *could* be done again. As we shall see below, Israel did not long maintain itself at that pinnacle — what nation or generation ever did? — but it clawed its way back in an example of repentance that, in itself, became a model for all time. As *Sfas Emes* and others point out, whenever an individual or nation scales a spiritual height, it becomes easier to regain even after it has been lost. It is similar to something that has been learned once and then forgotten. It is far easier to relearn it than to acquire new knowledge. Having become worthy of God's protection and of being gathered into His spiritual bosom, as it were, Israel bequeathed to its posterity the potential to do so again.

Many times in Jewish history, we have been forced to begin again in a new wilderness. Babylonia,

North Africa, Spain, Western Europe, Eastern Europe, *Eretz Yisrael*, America — all became reluctant hosts to Jewish migrations in the last 2500 years. In each, the process began of planting and nurturing a Jewish community solidly based on the Torah and developing a superior level of Torah scholarship. Nowhere was it easy. Some of the stories are enshrined in the history of Israel's golden eras; others are still being written. But of all these epochs we can say with assurance that the task of building anew was easier because the way had once been shown, the height had once been scaled.

Although most commentators identify the Clouds of Glory as the pillar of cloud that led the Jews by day and the pillar of fire that lit their way at night, *Midrash Tanchuma* gives a further definition. There were *seven* clouds, the Midrash records, one for each of the six directions — east, south, west, north, above and below — and the seventh which led them by day and by night. The similarity to the six days and the Sabbath and to the six directions surrounding man and his inner self is not coincidental. Just as the Sabbath is the essence of time and man's self is his essence within the surrounding turmoil of clashing interests on all sides, so too there is a difference between the protective clouds on six sides of Israel and the seventh which led them.

There is a difference between the protective clouds on six sides of Israel and the seventh which led them. God can protect him as He protected Israel in the Wilderness. But only man can save himself from temptation.

From every direction, man is simultaneously seduced and threatened; from the physical dangers, God can protect him as He protected Israel in the Wilderness. But only man can save *himself* from temptation. Only his inner self can provide the desire and the strength to live up to God's expectations. Man's inner self can climb to the goal set by its heavenly soul or tumble after the desires cultivated by its animal nature. In its infancy, Israel was shown sacred guides: a pillar of cloud by day and a pillar of fire by night. That such guides were provided did not compel Israel to follow them, any more than the offer of the Ten Commandments forced Israel to accept them. To the contrary, Israel received the Law because it wanted to and it followed God's Clouds of

Glory, because it wanted to assimilate into its being everything that those clouds represented.

II. The Succah on Two Levels

Parallel Truths

Strangely enough, many if not most commentators discuss the commandment of dwelling in a *succah* as if it symbolized only the Divine clouds of the Wilderness, yet the Sages of the Talmud — and *Mechilta* and *Sifra* as well — differ regarding the symbolism. According to one version, the *succah* does indeed recall the protection of the clouds, but another viewpoint holds that the Jews actually built makeshift booths to protect themselves from the daytime sun and nighttime chill of the Wilderness. Are the two versions mutually exclusive? Apparently they are not.

Rabbeinu Bachya (Kad HaKemach, *Succah*) and *Sfas Emes*, among others, assume that both interpretations are true. As *Michtav MeEliyahu* explains, when the Sages of the Talmud disagree regarding homiletical interpretations of Scripture, we must assume that both viewpoints are true, each in its own way. It is like different scholars analyzing the population trend of a large nation. One will focus on the military implications, another on the problems of education, law enforcement and so on, and yet another on the provision of physical and health services. All analyses are relevant although they branch off into different directions. Similarly, each sage expresses a different spiritual aspect of the verse or event under discussion.

When the Sages of the Talmud disagree regarding homiletical interpretations of Scripture, we must assume that both viewpoints are true.

Accordingly, we may assume that the Jewish people built themselves little huts, despite the presence of heavenly protective clouds. It is quite logical that they should not have relied on miracles, especially since they knew that only righteous people merited such Divine protection.

R' Bachya cites this as another of the many

instances where the truest, most significant sense of an event is clothed in a simpler, literally true, but more superficial narrative. In everyday life and discourse, such expressions are quite common. We are accustomed to hearing landslide election victories described in such obviously figurative terms as "an electoral tidal wave swept away all opposition" or "fifty years of ideology was guillotined by the swipe of a voting lever." The metaphors provide a vividness and a level of understanding that quite transcend a simple recitation of electoral statistics. On an infinitely more profound level,, the Sages sometimes express themselves in figurative allegory — as in the tales of the monster fish Leviathan that will be discussed below — that are intelligible only to those who are privy to the purposely vague esoteric vocabulary of the Sages. Not always did they consider it wise to express profound spiritual truths in terms that would be understood superficially by the unlearned and unsophisticated, but not truly comprehended; therefore they often used expressions that would be understood only by those with sufficient background. Similarly, Israel's sojourn in *succah*-booths occurred on both levels — the literal one and the deeper one — and both levels of the wilderness experience are relevant to all Jews in every generation.

Metaphors provide a vividness and a level of understanding that quite transcend a simple recitation of electoral statistics.

Israel's sojourn in succah-booths occurred on both levels — the literal one and the deeper one.

Lessons of the Booth

The commandment of *succah* tells Jews צֵא מִדִּירַת קֶבַע וְשֵׁב בְּדִירַת עֲרַאי, *leave the permanent dwelling and settle in a temporary dwelling* (*Succah* 2a). In the context of the desert experience, even a *succah* offered little security. The vast, baked, sandy expanse where there was neither food nor water, where snakes and scorpions were a constant danger (see *Deuteronomy* 8:15), could not have been made hospitable by makeshift walls and a thatched shade. The Torah gives a detailed listing of the forty-two almost uniformly desolate encampments (*Numbers* ch. 33) and of the frequent danger of thirst and starvation in order to make plain that Israel's comfortable survival for forty years was possible

only because of God's constant mercy, as demonstrated in the daily provision of food and water *(Moreh Nevuchim)*. When leaving his home in favor of his *succah*, the Jew remembers that his survival, like that of his forefathers, ultimately depends on forces beyond his personal control. Even in modern times with its massive construction and elaborate safety techniques, the combination of human destructiveness and the ever-present threat of natural disaster make plain that man has no safer refuge than his fragile *succah*, provided he is deserving of the Heavenly protection it represents:

HASHEM is with me, I have no fear;
how can man affect me?
HASHEM is with me through my helpers;
therefore I can face my foes.
It is better to take refuge in HASHEM
than to rely on man.
It is better to take refuge in HASHEM
than to rely on nobles (Psalms 118:6-9).

R' Samson Raphael Hirsch *(Horeb)* finds this aspect of *succah* to be both sobering and encouraging. To the powerful and wealthy, the *succah* says, 'Do not rely on your fortune; it is transitory; it can leave you more quickly than it came. Even your castle is no more secure than a *succah*. If you are safe, it is because God shelters you as He did your ancestors when they had but a booth to protect them against one of earth's harshest environments. Let the starry sky you see through your *s'chach* teach you to build your castle upon a firm foundation of faith in God and see the benevolent gaze of God even when you look at its sturdy, insulated roof. If you can do that, opulence will not blind you to the glow of God's beneficence.'

To the poor and downtrodden, the *succah* says, 'Are you more helpless than millions of your ancestors in the Wilderness, without food, water, or permanent shelter? What sustained them? Who provided for them? Whose benevolent hand wiped their brow and soothed their worry? Look around you at your *succah's* frail walls and at the stars you

When leaving his home in favor of his succah, the Jew remembers that his survival depends on forces beyond his personal control.

To the powerful and wealthy, the succah says, 'Do not rely on your fortune; it is transitory; it can leave you more quickly than it came.'

To the poor and downtrodden, the succah says, 'Are you more helpless than your ancestors in the Wilderness?'

see through its rustling roof. Let it remind you that Israel became a nation living in such 'mansions.' Those were the palaces of the *kingdom of priests and holy nation (Exodus 19:6)*, the homes where they became a great and Godly nation, where they developed the faith that overcame fear, and the knowledge that God's word was their guarantor for tomorrow — every tomorrow.'

R' Bachya carries this theme a step further. The temporary dwelling of our forefathers was, as they knew, intended to be a prelude to the most glorious of permanent dwellings: their own land where God's Presence would dwell among them in His Temple. Thus, the *succah* was an allusion to the impending greatness of the future. In this sense, our own *succah* reminds us that the suffering of exile is itself temporary, that it, too, will give way to the Redemption and the Third Temple.

Our own succah reminds us that the suffering of exile will give way to the Redemption and the Third Temple.

Undoubtedly, the Tabernacle of the Wilderness contributed to this allusion, for it too was a makeshift, portable building that was dismantled whenever the nation traveled. It was the Divine Presence's "temporary dwelling," until the permanent Temple would be erected in *Eretz Yisrael*.

Shelter of Faith

In the above literal interpretation, the Jewish nation sheltered itself with booths. The interpretation is true, of course, but it has a hidden, deeper meaning. The Torah customarily clothes supernatural concepts in words and deeds that can be spoken, understood, and felt by ordinary people. For instance, in the familar formulation of *Ramban*, the *tefillin* placed on the upper arm opposite the heart symbolizes the Jew's subjugation of his heart's desires and passions to do God's will, while the *tefillin* on the head symbolizes the dedication of one's intellectual ability to God's service. Thus, *tefillin* has a two-fold content: in the tangible sense, it involves properly written chapters of the Torah, black leather boxes and straps, their placement on the arm and head, and all the other detailed halachic requirements without which the performance of the

The Torah customarily clothes supernatural concepts in words and deeds that can be spoken, understood, and felt by ordinary people.

mitzvah cannot be considered valid. On another plane, it has the connotation of dedicating to God all of the wearer's emotional and intellectual capacities. The *mitzvah* is not complete unless both facets — physical and spiritual — are included in its performance. This is a point many commentators take pains to stress, lest people be deluded by the notion that the physical performance of a *mitzvah* is unnecessary for someone who absorbs its inner meaning.

In the case of *succah* the two aspects of the *mitzvah* reflect the phenomena experienced by Israel in the Wilderness. The people built booths, and so do we. But they were also privileged to enjoy an even greater protection, one that surpassed not only booths but fortresses. Israel was enveloped by God's Clouds of Glory. This was totally unlike the protection provided by steel and solid rock. An immovable object can repel an irresistible force, but Heavenly clouds transport a people into a spiritual environment where they are impervious to the stings and barbs of earthly danger. Israel in the desert was in a higher world, a world where earthly dangers had no power. The entire nation was like Abraham, Chananiah, Mishael and Azariah, none of whom could be even singed by the roaring fires of their would be executioners.

They were also privileged to enjoy an even greater protection, one that surpassed not only booths but fortresses.

The *Zohar* refers to the *succah* phenomenon as צִלָּא דִמְהֵימְנוּתָא, *the shelter of faith*. People can be surrounded by divinity, but unless they believe in God's protection they are naked to their enemies, exposed to every marauder. R' *Bachya* notes that the very word *succah* [סֻכָּה] alludes to the higher degree of spiritual perception acquired by Israel in the wilderness. In interpreting the name יִסְכָּה, *Yiscah* — the other name of the Matriarch Sarah — the Sages say:

People can be surrounded by divinity, but unless they believe in God's protection they are naked to their enemies.

לָמָּה נִקְרָא שְׁמָהּ יִסְכָּה, שֶׁסּוֹכָה בְּרוּחַ הַקֹּדֶשׁ

Why was she [Sarah] called Yiscah, because she saw [יסכה from the root סכה, to see] with the Holy Spirit (Sanhedrin 69b).

The word *succah* can be related to the same root, and indeed the ancient *succah* formed by God's Clouds of Glory, the one *Zohar* calls "the Shelter of Faith," was one of history's outstanding manifestations of an entire multitude gaining a superhuman insight into God's guidance of human affairs.

Bond with the Past

זֵכֶר עָשָׂה לְנִפְלְאֹתָיו חַנּוּן וְרַחוּם ה'

He made a memorial for His wonders, compassionate and merciful is HASHEM (Psalms 111:4).

In His compassion and mercy, God provided us with memorials to the miracles He performed for our forefathers. How can we get an inkling of His miracles of yore? How can we who have never seen and who cannot conceive of Clouds of Glory, achieve an attachment to the sublime experiences of our ancestors? There in the Wilderness, Israel was enveloped in Clouds of Glory; today we can wrap ourselves, as it were, in their memorial: the *succah*. Out of our homes, stripped of our security, without the accouterments that spell safety all year round, we sit in our *succah*, completely enwrapped in it. If we wish to perceive them, we can sense the glimmers of holiness. In the twinkling stars that intrude through the s'chach, we can see the One Above making us aware of His presence.

It is true, of course, that a homemade hut of canvas or plywood topped by bamboo or pine branches is hardly the equivalent of miraculous pillars of fire and cloud. On the other hand our ancestors built themselves *ordinary succah*-booths as well — so we, in whatever *succah* structures we sit, can feel a kinship with them. We can project ourselves across the millennia and unite with those who built *succos* then, and — if our faith is strong enough — we can feel the Divine Presence that remains with Israel wherever it is. As God promised, He is the One הַשֹּׁכֵן אִתָּם בְּתוֹךְ טֻמְאֹתָם, *Who dwells with them [even] amid their contamination (Leviticus 16:16).*

As the Chassidic masters taught, it is better to

In the twinkling stars that intrude through the s'chach, we can see the One Above making us aware of His presence.

perceive through faith than to see or feel with the senses. A person without faith is limited to what tangible evidence shows him, even though human beings are all too often misled by their senses or they misinterpret events that assault their eyes and bombard their ears. How else can we explain why those with the benefit of hindsight — and especially those whose faith in the Torah gives them a perspective on life and history — understand so clearly what confused and befuddled statesmen and pundits? But the man of faith has broader, deeper knowledge, because he integrates into his own experience the teachings and experiences of the Patriarchs, Moses and Aaron, the prophets, and all the teachers whose words still live for him and within him. When such a person sits in his *succah* — he may even be hunched into a barely valid structure only ten handbreadths high and seven square — he remembers that his ancestors sat in essentially similar booths. They had the benefit of Clouds of Glory, and so does he, because he, too, is under the protection of צְלָא דִּמְהֵימְנוּתָא, *the shelter of faith*. This is why Succos is called "the festival of our joy" — who would not be joyous to know that God envelops him and shelters him?

A person without faith is limited to what tangible evidence shows him.

Succos is called "the festival of our joy" — who would not be joyous to know that God envelops him and shelters him?

During the Russo-Japanese war in 1904-5, many young disciples of Ger were conscripted into the Russian army and sent to the Japanese front. The underfed, underclothed, undertrained young Torah scholars maintained a brisk correspondence — including the Talmudic novellae they composed at or near the front — with their *Rebbe*, Rabbi Yehudah Aryeh Leib Alter, known as the *Sfas Emes*, who grieved and allowed himself no rest as long as his disciples were in danger. Once they wrote him how, on the nights of Succos, those at the front dug a deep foxhole and covered it with branches, so that it would be a halachically valid *succah*. All through the night, they took turns scurrying to the *succah* with their rations so that they could fulfill the *mitzvah* of the festival.

Of people like you God says, "I have adorned heaven and earth with you today."

The *Sfas Emes* wrote them back, 'Of people like

you God says, "הַעִידֹתִי בָכֶם הַיּוֹם אֶת הַשָּׁמַיִם וְאֶת הָאָרֶץ,
I have adorned [homiletically deriving הַעִידֹתִי from
the word עֲדִי, jewelry] heaven and earth with you
today" (Deuteronomy 4:26). You are the jewelry that
beautifies heaven and earth!'

Didn't people of such faith see Clouds of Glory?
Did they feel less safe than a magnate in a safe
neighborhood who pushes a button and rolls away
the roof covering the s'chach in his luxurious dining
room? Wasn't their Succos a festival of joy for
themselves and their Maker Who adorned creation
with them?

Completion   As we have seen above, the Three Pilgrimage
Festivals form a progression: from the birth of the
nation on Pesach, to the assumption of its mission on
Shavuos, to the successful completion of its task on
Succos. This ascending order of achievement is
reflected in the Torah's description of the observance

Nowhere is the   of the respective festivals. Nowhere is the term
term שִׂמְחָה,   שִׂמְחָה, *gladness*, used with regard to Pesach
gladness, used with   specifically [although Pesach is included in the
regard to Pesach —   *general* commandment to rejoice on the festivals].
but no less than
three times is Israel   Only once does the Torah command Israel to rejoice
enjoined to   on Shavuos (Deuteronomy 16:11) — but no less than
celebrate on   three times is Israel enjoined to celebrate on Succos
Succos.   (Leviticus 23:40 and Deuteronomy 16:14,15). The
implication is plain. The birth of a nation is
meaningless without a sense of purpose. The
mission, the direction, the challenge, was given on
Shavuos; that is a cause for celebration. As the
Talmudic Sage R' Yoseif said in explaining why he
danced for joy on Shavuos, 'If not for what this day
had caused, I would be one of many ordinary Yoseifs
in the marketplace' (Pesachim 68b). But Succos
symbolizes the successful completion and ingathering of the harvest. Israel has attained its goal. That is
the greatest cause for rejoicing and surely ample
reason for the Torah to stress, three times, that it is
the time to rejoice and for the Sages to incorporate
into the prayers of the day that only Succos is
זְמַן שִׂמְחָתֵנוּ, *the season of our gladness* (Sfas Emes).

Completion has another connotation as well. In the process of learning and developing knowledge, the final stage of wisdom is called דַּעַת. First comes the spark of an idea, חָכְמָה. Then the idea is developed and applied, its ramifications and implications are compared with known facts and other hypotheses. This process of research, development, and refinement is called בִּינָה, usually translated *understanding*. Finally, when the newly acquired knowledge is perfected and has become fully assimilated by the student, it is called דַּעַת.'

When newly acquired knowledge is perfected and has become fully assimilated by the student, it is called דַּעַת.

It is instructive that the Torah insists that the performance of the *succah mitzvah* be accompanied by knowledge [דַּעַת] of what it represents. The Torah commands that Jews should dwell in *succos* לְמַעַן יֵדְעוּ דֹרֹתֵיכֶם, *so that your generations will know.* The key word is יֵדְעוּ, *will know,* from דַּעַת, the final step in the knowledge process. This requirement of knowledge is part of the *mitzvah* of *succah;* one has not fulfilled it unless he has borne in mind the *succah* experience of the Wilderness. The festival-agricultural-human cycle must culminate in the conviction that the lessons it teaches are not only true, but they have become basic to the one who performs and lives them. This concept is implied by דַּעַת, the final degree of knowledge that the *succah* must confer on the Jew who has gone through the process, from the birth of his religious understanding to the ingathering of his mature perceptions, faith, study, development.

The festival-agricultural-human cycle must culminate in the conviction that the lessons it teaches become basic to the one who performs and lives them.

III. The Double Role of Succos

Return of the Clouds

The connection between the Days of Awe and Succos is based on more than their calendrical proximity. Our Sages in the various Midrashim point out that Succos flows naturally from the cleansing and ennobling process of Rosh Hashanah and Yom Kippur. According to R' Avin (*Vayikra*

Rabbah 30:2) the spear-like *lulav* is an allusion to the triumphant stance of Israel which emerges victorious from the heavenly judgment of Rosh Hashanah and Yom Kippur. The commentators elaborate on the idea that only one who has cleansed himself through repentance is capable of being imbued with the message of faith and the joy of fulfillment represented by Succos. [See "Insights" for more on this topic.] It would seem that Succos belongs not only to the cycle of the Three Pilgrimage Festivals, but also to the cycle of repentance and atonement. Or, better said perhaps, that it cannot fulfill its role in the festival cycle without the intervention of the judgment days of Tishrei. Let us try to understand why.

Only one who has cleansed himself through repentance is capable of being imbued with the message of faith and the joy of fulfillment.

The booths of the Wilderness, of whichever sort they were, appeared many months before the fifteenth of Tishrei, the date of the Succos observance. Already on the seventh day of Pesach, when Israel was confronted at the Sea of Reeds by the pursuing Egyptians, God led them and protected them with the Clouds of Glory. Immediately after passing through the sea, Israel was in a desert where it required the shelter of actual *succah*-booths. Yet, unlike Pesach and Shavuos that are celebrated on the anniversary of the events they commemorate, the Torah ordains the observance of Succos nearly half a year later. According to the familiar explanation of *Tur* (see "Insights"), the Torah deliberately postponed the formal observance of Succos so that it would be clear to all that the cool, breezy booths were not being built for comfort upon the approach of the warm and sunny part of the year.

Vilna Gaon (comm. to *Shir HaShirim* 1:2) explains that the date of Succos is very closely connected to the appearance of the Clouds of Glory. According to his formulation, when Israel sinned by building the Golden Calf, it became unworthy of having the Clouds of Glory. Those manifestations of God's pleasure withdrew from the people, not to return until they had once more become deserving. Moses spent forty days in prayer that Israel not be

The date of Succos is very closely connected to the appearance of the Clouds of Glory.

destroyed for its sin of idolatry and another forty days being taught the Torah a second time. Finally on the tenth of Tishrei, the date that would later become Yom Kippur, he descended from Mount Sinai with the second Tablets, the proof that God had forgiven and renewed His convenant with Israel. On the next day, Moses convened the people and revealed to them yet another mark of God's renewed esteem — they were asked to contribute to the building of the Tabernacle, upon which God's Presence would rest among them. The contributions streamed in for the next two days until, on the fourteenth of Tishrei, the treasures were weighed and measured and handed over to the artisans who would construct the Tabernacle and its utensils. The next morning, the fifteenth of Tishrei, the construction began — and the Clouds of Glory returned. Accordingly, as *Vilna Gaon's* chronology shows, the Clouds of Glory that Israel earned by its repentance and rededication, and that accompanied it for the next forty years in the Wilderness, came back on the date that God would later proclaim as Succos.

The Clouds of Glory that Israel earned by its repentance and rededication came back on the date that God would later proclaim as Succos.

The shelter of faith [צְלָּא דִּמְהֵימְנוּתָא] implies that the person that reposes under it is himself lofty. Unlike steel armor, those clouds in the Wilderness did not accept everyone automatically. Their presence was indicative that those they sheltered were elevated above ordinary concerns or dangers. Sin banished the clouds, repentance brought them back. Only the spiritually worthy could retain them.

In this sense, Succos belongs to both the festivals and the Days of Awe. Had sin never intervened in the history of the nation or the individual, life would be a progression from Pesach to Shavuos to Succos, from birth to mission to fulfillment. But sin *does* intervene.

Repentance was one of the prerequisites to creation; the universe could not be created unless man were to have the ability to gain atonement.

Nevertheless, all is not lost. The Sages teach that repentance was one of the prerequisites to creation; the universe could not be created unless man were to have the ability to gain atonement — otherwise the world could not endure (*Nedarim* 39b). As man is about to fail, Rosh Hashanah and Yom Kippur and

the Ten Days of Atonement arrive. He is accused. He repents. God judges — and forgives. Then the Jew emerges from his trial cleansed and vindicated — his status symbolized by his *lulav* and other species held aloft like a spear of triumph — and walks to his *succah*, his awaiting Clouds of Glory. This is one reason why it is preferable to begin the construction of the *succah* immediately after Yom Kippur is over; only because of the atonement proferred by one is the other's highest manifestation made possible.

Aaron and Succos

The Clouds of Glory remained with our ancestors in the Wilderness because of the merit of Aaron.

Our Sages tell us that the Clouds of Glory remained with our ancestors in the Wilderness because of the merit of Aaron (*Taanis* 9a). He was the one who epitomized peace among people; he was the quintessential אוֹהֵב שָׁלוֹם וְרוֹדֵף שָׁלוֹם, *lover of peace and pursuer of peace* (*Avos* 1:12). Not content to be like most people who praise harmonious personal relationships but do little to advance their cause, Aaron would strive to bring peace and love back to squabbling families and contentious friends (see *Avos d'R' Nassan* 12:3). In the literature of Kabbalah, Aaron symbolizes the *sefirah*-emanation of הוֹד, *Glory*. *Hod* has two characteristics, both exemplified by Aaron: a willingness to accept circumstances imposed by God rather than to contest them, and a personal initiative to grow and accomplish in the service of God.

There are times when the most "glorious" course a person can take is silent acceptance of God's will.

There are times when the most "glorious" course a person can take is silent acceptance of God's will, a trait Aaron demonstrated when he reacted to the sudden death of his two oldest sons with silent acceptance (*Leviticus* 10:3). At the same time Aaron was not a passive person. *Vayikra Rabbah* (26:6) teaches that Aaron exemplified fear of God and because he developed this virtue he earned the privileges and obligations of the priesthood as a legacy for his descendants. We find further that Aaron was the pioneer in deciding major questions of Halachah based on applying halachic logic to the matter at hand (see *Rashi* to *Leviticus* 10:19). As *Harav Gedaliah Schorr (Ohr Gedalyahu* p. 76)

explains, *R' Tzadok HaKohen* articulates the general rule that the chapter has special significance. Accordingly, the fact that the Oral Law's principle of logical application is stated first in connection with Aaron is proof that Aaron was the first person to demonstrate this utilization of the Oral Law. A person's distinction in knowledge and development of the Oral Law is the greatest possible indication of his strenuous dedication to personal growth. Only the profound Torah scholar knows the extent of the mental and physical exertion and agony without which one can never aspire to the sublime gift of God's Own wisdom *(Megillah* 6a).

A person's distinction in the Oral Law is the greatest possible indication of his strenuous dedication to personal growth.

The personal humility evident in the *Hod*-Glory of Aaron's personality is essential to peace. Arrogant, self-assertive people are always prone to dispute. Why should a "superior" person make accommodations and concessions to placate his "inferior"? If his personal status is uppermost in his mind, why should he assign equal importance to the wishes of others? If he is convinced of his own infallibility — or, which is just as bad, too proud to admit a mistake — how can he say, "I'm sorry, you were right"? Aaron's task of fostering harmony among Israel required him to convince people to ignore their own egos in the interest of the common good. Only thus could the entire nation be blanketed by God's shelter. As we pray in the daily evening service וּפְרוֹשׂ עָלֵינוּ סֻכַּת שְׁלוֹמֶךְ, *and spread over us the shelter of Your peace.* God's own *succah,* the one represented by the Clouds of Glory, requires peace; strife drives it away.

Aaron's task of fostering harmony among Israel required him to convince people to ignore their own egos in the interest of the common good.

Another role of Aaron, that of *Kohen Gadol* in the Tabernacle, also contributes to the common harmony, because a truly repentant nation cannot be riven by personal bickering. People who have gone through the cleansing experience of sincerely acknowledging their worthlessness in God's presence cannot immediately indulge in the petty selfishness that gives birth to animosity. Especially according to the view cited above that the Clouds of Glory commemorated on Succos are those that

returned as a result of Israel's repentance and the atonement that was expressed by the command to begin construction of the Tabernacle, the connection between Aaron and Succos is even more vivid. The clouds could return as a result of repentance and they rested upon Israel only on the day when the Tabernacle, Aaron's domain, began to be built *(Sfas Emes)*.

The clouds rested upon Israel only on the day when the Tabernacle, Aaron's domain, began to be built.

Triumphant Unity

The aspect of peace is related to the Four Species of Succos. The Midrash likens the Four Species to various major organs of the human body. The myrtle leaf is shaped like an eye and the *esrog* like a heart. As the Sages have taught, these two organs can unite in a perverted partnership of sin. The eye sees and the heart lusts, with the result that the person's better instincts are inundated by the power of his temptations. The willow leaf is shaped like a mouth, the organ of speech, which is the tool of Torah, prayer, and encouragement, but which is so often corrupted into a weapon that tears away at man's spiritual fiber. The straight, tall *lulav* resembles man's spinal column, the organ through which all the brain's impulses are conveyed to the rest of the body. By combining these species in the performance of a *mitzvah*, we symbolize our repentance and desire for atonement. Every sin finds atonement when man takes a tool he once used for evil and converts it to good. One who had squandered funds on gluttony and debauchery must use his wealth to support worthy causes. One whose barbed mouth had inflicted pain on defenseless victims must learn to use the divine gift of speech for holy and helpful ends. The taking of the Four Species, which symbolize major organs, represents this resolve to utilize the body and its emotional and intellectual drive for the good — and thereby, the *mitzvah* is an instrument of atonement.

By combining these species in the performance of a mitzvah, we symbolize our repentance and desire for atonement.

There is another organism in addition to the individual human body: the national organism of Israel with its many kinds of people. The Four Species symbolize them all. The *esrog* is a desirable

food containing both טַעַם וְרֵיחַ, *taste and pleasant aroma;* it symbolizes righteous people who possess both Torah and good deeds. The *lulav,* the branch of a date palm, is odorless but it produces nourishing food; it symbolizes the scholar who possesses Torah knowledge but is deficient in good deeds. The fragrant, tasteless myrtle leaf represents common people who possess good deeds, but lack Torah scholarship. Finally, the odorless, tasteless willow leaf symbolizes someone who lacks both Torah and good deeds. The nation is often — too often — divided, but God wishes it to be a *community* of Israel. When all segments of Israel come together in the service of the common goal of national dedication to His will, then *everyone* belongs, from the august *esrog* to the lowly willow. And when every shade and manner of Jew joins with every other in pursuit of that good, then God accepts their common repentance.

As noted above, the Midrash calls the *lulav* a triumphant symbol of Israel's vindication in the judgment of Rosh Hashanah and Yom Kippur. But the *lulav* has no efficacy when it stands alone. Only when the Four Species are held together — symbolizing peace and harmony — has the commandment been performed properly. Only when man is at peace within himself and at peace with his fellows can he rejoice in his personal and national festival of completion. This is why the Four Species were chosen to symbolize Israel's victory over the internal and external enemies that condemn and attack it *(Shem MiShmuel).*

Universal Concern

In this quest for peace, Israel does not limit itself to its own national interests. The *Mussaf* offerings of Succos include seventy bulls that are sacrificed to bring Heavenly blessing upon the seventy nations. The Jewish mission to the nations was expressed in our earliest history in the name of the Patriarch Abraham, whose name is Scripturally described as an acronym of אַב הֲמוֹן גּוֹיִם, [spiritual] *father of the multitude of nations (Genesis 17:5).* The chosenness

of Israel lies in its sole responsibility to carry out all the commandments of the Torah. Thereby it is to serve as an example of Godly service and be a leader to the other nations. When they submit to Israel's leadership, they, too, will experience the blessings prophesied for Messianic times; as we say in the prayers of Rosh Hashanah and Yom Kippur: וְיֵעָשׂוּ כֻלָּם אֲגֻדָה אֶחָת לַעֲשׂוֹת רְצוֹנְךָ בְּלֵבָב שָׁלֵם, *may they* [the nations] *form a single band to do Your will with a perfect heart.*

When they submit to Israel's leadership, they, too, will experience the blessings prophesied for Messianic times.

This explains why the seventy offerings of Succos are divided as follows: thirteen are brought on the first day, twelve on the second, eleven on the third and so on until the last of the seven days of Succos when only seven are brought. This alludes to the diminishing status of the nations as history winds down to the End of Days and the Messianic era. It is a mistake to regard this as a derogation of the nations, however, just as it is no derogation to say that the Levites are subservient to the *Kohanim* or that human passions should be subservient to the intellect. Organs, people, and nations have their respective roles, each at its proper level in the hierarchy of creation. Freedom and anarchy are not synonymous. Even free men have responsibilities they have no right to shirk.

The seventy offerings of Succos display Jewish concern for all humanity.

The seventy offerings of Succos display Jewish concern for all humanity. The Jewish national title *Yeshurun* [יְשׁוּרוּן, from the word יָשָׁר, *upright* or *just*] means "those who make others upright." It expresses the national mission to bring the message of justice to the world at large. Were it to refer only to Israel's *own* status as an upright nation, the word would have been *Yesharim* [יְשָׁרִים, *upright ones*].

This, too, is an aspect of the peace based on concern for others and harmonious unity exemplified and fostered by Aaron *(Sfas Emes).*

IV. The Leviathan and Fulfillment

עָתִיד הַקָּדוֹשׁ בָּרוּךְ הוּא לַעֲשׂוֹת סְעוּדָה לַצַּדִּיקִים
מִבְּשָׂרוֹ שֶׁל לִוְיָתָן.

The Holy One, Blessed is He, will make a
feast for the righteous from the flesh of the
Leviathan (Bava Basra 75a).

עָתִיד הַקָּדוֹשׁ בָּרוּךְ הוּא לַעֲשׂוֹת סֻכָּה לַצַּדִּיקִים
מֵעוֹרוֹ שֶׁל לִוְיָתָן.

The Holy One Blessed is He will make a
succah for the righteous from the hide of
the Leviathan (ibid.).

The Feast's
Significance

The Leviathan, mentioned frequently in Scripture, Talmud and Midrashim, is described as a gigantic fish of mind-boggling dimensions and capabilities. The commentators differ on whether these descriptions are meant literally and, if not, what they are meant to allegorize. As is obvious from the above citations and many others, the Leviathan is of particular relevance to the World to Come and Messianic times, when mankind will have achieved the purpose of its creation and God will present the long-awaited, well-earned reward to the righteous. Although the Talmudic sources do not indicate that this will take place on Succos in preference to any

Only the prayers of
the succah mention
the Leviathan.

other time, only the prayers of the *succah* mention the Leviathan. This may be for no other reason than the simple fact that the Sages refer to a *succah* made of the Leviathan's hide. It may well be, however, that the reference has a stronger relation to the uniqueness of Succos itself. Succos represents the culmination and perfection not only of the festival cycle, but of man himself, as elaborated upon earlier. This being so, the Leviathan's role as an ultimate reward destined for the righteous is particularly relevant to Succos.

It is beyond the scope of this essay to discuss and explain all the Rabbinic literature on the Leviathan,

but a brief introductory discussion may be enlightening and beneficial. It will follow the similar commentaries of *Rashba* and *Maharal*, both of whom interpret the Leviathan allegorically, maintaining that all references to it refer to spiritual concepts that the Sages chose to disguise in tales of a monster fish.

The term "eating" can be understood in two ways.

The term "eating" can be understood in two ways. Obviously, it can refer to the physical consumption of food. The better the ingredients and the more tastefully they are mixed, prepared, and spiced, the better the dish and the more delicious and tempting it will be. Naturally, food must be nutritious, and a food that is not only delicious but nourishing is ideal. In the second sense, eating refers to a person taking in something that he desires and that helps him achieve personal betterment. A person "eats up" information, he "devours" compliments, he is "ravenous" for the friendship of important people. Sometimes the appetite is beneficial, sometimes harmful — like a craving for various kinds of food — but in all such figurative uses, it refers to someone's desire to improve himself by absorbing something that he lacks and wants.

When the Sages speak of the future "feast" awaiting the righteous, they do not speak of a sumptuous repast filled with epicurean delicacies.

When the Sages speak of the future "feast" awaiting the righteous, they do not speak of a sumptuous repast filled with epicurean delicacies — that much is obvious to anyone with any feeling for the context of the Rabbinic descriptions of future bliss! The righteous of all generations have aspired to spiritual growth. Their reward can only be the greatest possible enhancement of their Torah knowledge, personal sanctity, and closeness to God. To people with highly developed spiritual appetites, such is a feast of the highest order. Therefore, *Rashba* and *Maharal* insist, the feast of the Leviathan can only mean a spiritual repast.

In this sense, the Torah promises וְאָכַלְתָּ אֶת כָּל הָעַמִּים, *And you shall devour all the nations* (Deuteronomy 7:16). Israel was not given the blessing of cannibalism. The verse refers to the *virtues* of the respective nations. Some are generous, some are scholarly, some are resourceful. As Israel

makes its way among the nations, it has the task of absorbing all their good traits until it perfects itself to an ever increasing degree.

There are, however, foods that can enhance a person's ability to elevate himself. Since human beings require physical nourishment in order to function properly, food and drink gives them the strength and serenity to engage in spiritual pursuits.

Hunger and depression are the enemies of spiritual enhancement, for they interfere with concentration and peace of mind. Isaac's request for a repast before he could confer a blessing (*Genesis* 27:4) and Elisha's request for music so that he could prophesy (*II Kings* 3:15) are examples of the need to satisfy human needs so that one's spiritual capacities can come to fruition.

Related, though different, is the Torah's command that people are to eat the flesh of sacrifices. They are described as guests eating at God's table, as it were (*Kiddushim* 52b), yet the eating of the *Kohanim* is a factor in the atonement the offering provides for its owner (*Pesachim* 59b). In this case, a human being absorbs into himself a sacred food and his act of eating achieves a sacred goal.

On yet a higher level was the *manna*. It was a food of heavenly origin and nature. R' Akiva called it the food of angels; R' Yishmael says it was absorbed entirely into the body without waste (*Yoma* 75a). We cannot imagine what it was, but it was a major factor in raising an entire nation to supernatural heights.

הָעוֹלָם הַבָּא אֵין בּוֹ אֲכִילָה וּשְׁתִיָּה רַק צַדִּיקִים יוֹשְׁבִים וְעַטְרוֹתֵיהֶם בְּרָאשֵׁיהֶם וְנֶהֱנִים מִזִּיו הַשְּׁכִינָה.

In the World to Come there is neither eating nor drinking — rather the righteous sit with their crowns on their heads and enjoy the splendor of the Shechinah [the Divine Presence] (Berachos 17a).

The World to Come refers to the time and conditions when the righteous have achieved *total* perfection in proportion to their efforts and achievement in life. In that completely spiritual

world, there is no longer an opportunity for the performance of *mitzvos* or any other form of spiritual improvement (see *Avos* 4:17). Then, the righteous enjoy the reward they have earned through their striving on earth.

But there is a transitionary stage — when the Messiah has come and the righteous have achieved as much spiritual perfection as unaided *human* efforts make possible, but before they have entered the World to Come. Then, God will provide them with a supreme gift: the lofty spiritual qualities the Sages call the Leviathan. There are varying interpretations of what they are. Whatever the Leviathan represents, these qualities are so exalted, so sublime, so extraordinary that God could not allow them to multiply and blanket the earth until the last stage before perfection was at hand. If man had been exposed to such qualities early in his history and if such holy traits had been permitted to proliferate from the beginning of time, the battle between good and evil would have been won before it even began. The course of good would have been so obvious that man would have been left with no room for the operation of his free will.

If such holy traits had been permitted to proliferate from the beginning of time, the battle between good and evil would have been won before it even began.

But when the final moments of This Wordly existence will have arrived, the battle will be over. The righteous will have triumphed. Only one thing will they lack. They will hunger after the virtues represented by the Leviathan — desire them, crave them like someone who has been denied food for ever so long. How true. From the beginning of time, the righteous will have been denied the feast of the Leviathan's spiritual delicacies. That will be their final reward: The feast of sanctity and elevation.

Achievement and Honor

Achievement abd Honor The difference between achievement and the honor that accrues to the achiever is like the difference between flesh and hide. An animal's flesh is part of its essence while its hide is a covering; important, of course, but not equal to the animal itself.

The Sages refer to a person's clothing as his "honor." Indeed, everyone is aware that different

occasions and different positions call for different clothing and different uniforms. 'Clothes *make* the man' is a concept foreign to Jewish thought, but it certainly is true that clothes *honor* the man. Similarly, the admiration and imitation — even flattery — that follow an accomplished person are the honor he has earned. They are not part of him, but they cling to him, like his clothing or an animal's hide. Clearly, the sort of honor a person gets can be an indication of the man he is. An entertainer or athlete will have a hysterical coterie; a great sage and *tzaddik* will attract serious, dedicated people who seek to study the elements of his greatness and benefit from his wisdom.

At the climax of their human accomplishment, the righteous will feast on the Leviathan. As an extra measure of reward, they will be granted an honor reflective of their stature. They will be sheltered lovingly and respectfully by a *succah* made of the sanctity that follows naturally upon so great a gift as the Leviathan.

What is it, this protective honor? We do not know. But Israel once had a form of protective honor that was surely similar. At the beginning of its national existence, Israel was ennobled and protected by עֲנָנֵי הַכָּבוֹד, *Clouds of Glory*, that testified eloquently to the stature of the Godly nation that reposed within them. Those who feast on the Leviathan will be absorbing the last, highest spiritual gift. Their *succah* will be commensurate with their achievement.

⋙ Background and Insights:

The Biblical Commands

The Festival

The Season

The Succah

Ushpizin

The Four Species

The Water-Drawing

Hallel

Hakhel

Koheles on Succos

Hoshanos and Hoshanah Rabbah

—Rabbi Meir Zlotowitz

Insights

The Biblical Commands

Leviticus 23:33-36, 39-44

וַיְדַבֵּר יהוה אֶל־מֹשֶׁה לֵּאמֹר: דַּבֵּר אֶל־בְּנֵי יִשְׂרָאֵל לֵאמֹר בַּחֲמִשָּׁה עָשָׂר
יוֹם לַחֹדֶשׁ הַשְּׁבִיעִי הַזֶּה חַג הַסֻּכּוֹת שִׁבְעַת יָמִים לַיהוה: בַּיּוֹם הָרִאשׁוֹן
מִקְרָא־קֹדֶשׁ כָּל־מְלֶאכֶת עֲבֹדָה לֹא תַעֲשׂוּ: שִׁבְעַת יָמִים תַּקְרִיבוּ אִשֶּׁה
לַיהוה בַּיּוֹם הַשְּׁמִינִי מִקְרָא־קֹדֶשׁ יִהְיֶה לָכֶם וְהִקְרַבְתֶּם אִשֶּׁה לַיהוה
עֲצֶרֶת הִוא כָּל־מְלֶאכֶת עֲבֹדָה לֹא תַעֲשׂוּ:
אַךְ בַּחֲמִשָּׁה עָשָׂר יוֹם לַחֹדֶשׁ הַשְּׁבִיעִי בְּאָסְפְּכֶם אֶת־תְּבוּאַת הָאָרֶץ תָּחֹגּוּ
אֶת־חַג־יהוה שִׁבְעַת יָמִים בַּיּוֹם הָרִאשׁוֹן שַׁבָּתוֹן וּבַיּוֹם הַשְּׁמִינִי שַׁבָּתוֹן:
וּלְקַחְתֶּם לָכֶם בַּיּוֹם הָרִאשׁוֹן פְּרִי עֵץ הָדָר כַּפֹּת תְּמָרִים וַעֲנַף עֵץ־עָבֹת
וְעַרְבֵי־נָחַל וּשְׂמַחְתֶּם לִפְנֵי יהוה אֱלֹהֵיכֶם שִׁבְעַת יָמִים: וְחַגֹּתֶם אֹתוֹ חַג
לַיהוה שִׁבְעַת יָמִים בַּשָּׁנָה חֻקַּת עוֹלָם לְדֹרֹתֵיכֶם בַּחֹדֶשׁ הַשְּׁבִיעִי תָּחֹגּוּ
אֹתוֹ: בַּסֻּכֹּת תֵּשְׁבוּ שִׁבְעַת יָמִים כָּל־הָאֶזְרָח בְּיִשְׂרָאֵל יֵשְׁבוּ בַּסֻּכֹּת: לְמַעַן
יֵדְעוּ דֹרֹתֵיכֶם כִּי בַסֻּכּוֹת הוֹשַׁבְתִּי אֶת־בְּנֵי יִשְׂרָאֵל בְּהוֹצִיאִי אוֹתָם מֵאֶרֶץ
מִצְרַיִם אֲנִי יהוה אֱלֹהֵיכֶם: וַיְדַבֵּר מֹשֶׁה אֶת־מֹעֲדֵי יהוה אֶל־בְּנֵי יִשְׂרָאֵל:

³³ HASHEM spoke to Moses, saying, ³⁴ "Speak to the children of Israel,
saying: On the fifteenth day of this seventh month is a Feast of Succah-
booths, for seven days unto HASHEM. ³⁵ On the first day there shall be a
holy convocation; any laborious work you shall not perform. ³⁶ Seven
days bring fire-offerings to HASHEM. On the eighth day there shall be a
holy convocation for you, and you shall bring a fire-offering to
HASHEM; it is a retention-day — any laborious work you shall not
perform.
³⁹ Only the fifteenth day of the seventh month, when you have
gathered in the land's grain, shall you celebrate the festival of HASHEM
for seven days; on the first day there shall be a rest-day, and on the
eighth day there shall be a rest-day.
⁴⁰ And you shall take for yourselves on the first day the fruit of a
beautiful [esrog] tree, the branches of date palms, twigs of a plaited
tree, and brook willows, and you shall rejoice before HASHEM your
God seven days. ⁴¹ You shall celebrate it as a celebration to HASHEM
seven days in the year. It is an eternal law throughout your generations;
in the seventh month you shall celebrate it.
⁴² You shall dwell in Succah-booths for seven days; all citizens in
Israel are to dwell in Succah-booths. ⁴³ So that your future generations
may know that I housed the Israelites in booths when I brought them
out from the land of Egypt; I am HASHEM your God." ⁴⁴ And Moses
declared the seasons of HASHEM to the Israelites.

חַג הַסֻּכֹּת תַּעֲשֶׂה לְךָ שִׁבְעַת יָמִים בְּאָסְפְּךָ מִגָּרְנְךָ וּמִיִּקְבֶךָ: וְשָׂמַחְתָּ בְּחַגֶּךָ
אַתָּה וּבִנְךָ וּבִתֶּךָ וְעַבְדְּךָ וַאֲמָתֶךָ וְהַלֵּוִי וְהַגֵּר וְהַיָּתוֹם וְהָאַלְמָנָה אֲשֶׁר
בִּשְׁעָרֶיךָ: שִׁבְעַת יָמִים תָּחֹג לַיהוה אֱלֹהֶיךָ בַּמָּקוֹם אֲשֶׁר־יִבְחַר יהוה כִּי
יְבָרֶכְךָ יהוה אֱלֹהֶיךָ בְּכֹל תְּבוּאָתְךָ וּבְכֹל מַעֲשֵׂה יָדֶיךָ וְהָיִיתָ אַךְ שָׂמֵחַ:
שָׁלוֹשׁ פְּעָמִים בַּשָּׁנָה יֵרָאֶה כָל־זְכוּרְךָ אֶת־פְּנֵי יהוה אֱלֹהֶיךָ בַּמָּקוֹם אֲשֶׁר
יִבְחָר בְּחַג הַמַּצּוֹת וּבְחַג הַשָּׁבֻעוֹת וּבְחַג הַסֻּכּוֹת וְלֹא יֵרָאֶה אֶת־פְּנֵי יהוה
רֵיקָם: אִישׁ כְּמַתְּנַת יָדוֹ כְּבִרְכַּת יהוה אֱלֹהֶיךָ אֲשֶׁר נָתַן־לָךְ:

13 Make yourself a Succos festival for seven days when you gather in
[the produce] from your threshing floor and your wine vat. 14 And you
are to rejoice on your festival — you with your son and your daughter,
your slave and your maidservant, the Levite, the convert, the orphan,
and the widow within your gates. 15 For seven days you are to celebrate
to HASHEM your God in the place that HASHEM will choose, for
HASHEM your God will bless you in all your crops and in all your undertakings, and you shall be nothing but joyous.

16 Three times each year all your menfolk shall appear in the presence
of HASHEM your God in the place that He will choose: On the festival
of Matzos, on the festival of Shavuos, and on the festival of Succos, and
it shall not appear empty-handed before HASHEM's Presence. 17 Each
person according to what is given him, according to the blessing of
HASHEM your God, which He has granted you.

The Festival

Actual Booths or Clouds of Glory?

◆§ "So that your future generations may know that I housed the children of Israel in
succah-booths when I brought them out from the land of Egypt" (Leviticus
23:43).

□ Rashi's commentary to the Torah follows the view of the Talmudic sage R'
Eliezer (Succah 11b) that the expression succos in the Torah refers to the
overhanging Clouds of Glory which symbolized God's Presence, and by means
of which God sheltered His People from the blazing sun in the desert.

□ Rashbam, however, follows the view (of R' Akiva ibid.) that God provided actual booths for them. He explains:

"The reason for the matter is as follows. You shall celebrate the festival of
Succos when you gather in from your threshing floor and your wine-vat [Deut.
16:13], when you gather in the crops of your land, and your houses are full of all
good things — grain, wine, and oil — so that you may remember that I housed
the children of Israel in succah-booths for forty years in the desert, where there
was neither settlement nor possessions. Accordingly, you are to give praise to
Him Who has granted you this heritage and abundant good, and be deterred
from thinking, 'My own power and the strength of my own hands have
accomplished for me with all this abundance.' ... We therefore leave our

abundantly filled homes at harvest-time and take up residence in succah-booths to commemorate that our ancestors had neither possessions in the desert nor permanent houses. It is for this reason that this festival was ordained at harvest-time — to deter man from feeling excessive pride at the sight of his abundance [but instead induce in man a sense of dependence upon God]."

□ For wealth does not safeguard life, and God alone sustains all — even those who live in frail booths. We are in possession of our wealth only by God's graciousness, and it is He alone Who affords security and protection *(Sh'lah)*.

□ The poor, too, must find security and strength in the *succah,* recalling how God housed our ancestors in *succah*-booths in the desert, feeding and providing for them till they lacked for nothing *(Rambam)*.

Both Views are the Words of the Living God

◆§ Some commentators synthesize the above interpretations of both R' Eliezer and R' Akiva: At first God housed the Jews in actual booths. Subsequently, in reward for having submitted themselves totally to God's protection, God enveloped them in His Clouds of Glory so that the redeemed generation and its descendants would realize that there is no meaningful dwelling other than one built by God *(Sefer HaToda'ah)*. [See also Overview.]

Utter Reliance

◆§ *Sfas Emes* notes that Scripture stresses the fact that *future generations may know* of God's miracle. This implies that the *mitzvah* of *succah* arouses the desire to rely on the Holy One, Blessed is He, as did our ancestors who departed from Egypt. As the prophet Jeremiah writes [*Jeremiah* 2:2]: *I remember for you the devotion of your youth … when you followed Me in the wilderness in a land not sown.*

God recalls this to every generation, thereby to instill in them that same yearning to follow after God faithfully.

Reminder of God's Power

◆§ *Tur (Orach Chaim 625)* feels that the mention of the Exodus from Egypt in connection with the *mitzvah* of *succah* implies that the *succah* also serves as a memorial to the miracles of the Exodus. "For [the Exodus] is something we saw with our own eyes and heard with our own ears and no one can contradict us." It teaches the truth of God's existence, His omniscience, and that it is in His power to perform miracles and supersede the laws of nature.

The Mitzvos Associated with Succos

◆§ Five mitzvos are uniquely associated with the festival. Three are of Biblical origin [מִדְאוֹרַיְיתָא] — specifically stated in the Torah; one is a law transmitted to Moses orally at Sinai and not specifically recorded in the Torah [הֲלָכָה לְמשֶׁה מִסִּינַי]; and one is Prophetic in origin [מִדִּבְרֵי נְבִיאִים].

□ Of Biblical origin:
- *Succah*
- *The Four Species*
- *To rejoice in the festival*

□ Transmitted to Moses at Sinai:
  • *The libation of water on the altar* [נִיסּוּךְ הַמַּיִם]

□ Of Prophetic origin
  • *The holding of the willow* [עֲרָבָה]
    on Hoshanah Rabbah

The Names of the Festival

⋖§ The Torah records several names for the *yom tov* of *Succos:*
  • חַג הָאָסִיף, *The Festival of the Ingathering* [of the crops] *(Exodus 26:16);*
  • חַג הַסֻּכֹּת, *The Festival of Succah-booths (Leviticus 23:34);*
  • חַג ה', *The Festival of HASHEM (Leviticus 23:39);*
  • הֶחָג, *The Festival (I Kings 8:2)* [i.e., the festival *par excellence,* connoting its preeminence in the cycle of the Jewish year (see below)].

□ Of the three major festivals — Pesach, Shavuos, and Succos — only the latter is designated in *Shemoneh Esrei* and *Kiddush* as זְמַן שִׂמְחָתֵנוּ, *the season of our rejoicing.* Among the several reasons offered for this designation is that only regarding Succos does the Torah specifically command us to rejoice on a festival *(Leviticus 23:40; Deut. 16:14-15).* Furthermore, the very season of the festival — harvest — is a joyous one, when one's house is filled with abundance. Another reason for this designation was the שִׂמְחַת בֵּית הַשּׁוֹאֵבָה, *Rejoicing at the House of the Water Drawing* [see p. 59], a great public ceremony that was celebrated with great joy. And finally, the festival was joyous because it so closely followed Yom Kippur, when every Jew had atoned for his sins against God.

□ Thus, all the observances of Succos are performed with joy, for the Torah mentions joy with reference to Succos more frequently than to any other festival. No explicit reference is made to joy with regard to Pesach and only one such reference is made with regard to Shavuos, but in the case of Succos, joy is mentioned three times: *And you shall rejoice before HASHEM your God (Leviticus 23); And you shall rejoice in your festival (Deut. 15); And you shall be only joyous (ibid.).*

Succos Preeminent

⋖§ *Tzror HaMor* points out that many facets of Succos indicate that it is to be regarded as the paramount of festivals. This is indicated by such special features as the abundance of sacrifices (70 bulls, 98 sheep et al.), the special water libation, four species, special processions around the altar, the stress placed on rejoicing on this holiday, the recitation of the 'complete' *Hallel* on every day of the festival. The reason for Succos' preeminence can be understood from the historical sequence commemorated by the festival. Pesach recalls Israel's degraded national origins as a nation of slaves, and its Exodus to freedom. Shavuos marks the giving of the Torah — but only a few weeks thereafter, Israel sinned by making the Golden Calf. Not until Yom Kippur was the nation forgiven and given the second Tablets of the Covenant. Thus, Succos celebrates the Jewish nation as it attains the pinnacle of human perfection and fulfills the purpose of creation.

Remembering Past Conditions

◆§ The two festivals, Pesach and Succos, imply the teaching of certain truths and moral lessons. Pesach teaches us to perpetuate the memory of the miracles that God wrougnt in Egypt; the festival of Succos reminds us of the miracles He wrought in the wilderness. The moral lesson derived from these festivals is this: during the days of his prosperity, man should remember his bad times. He will thereby be inspired to thank God repeatedly and to lead a modest and humble life. We eat, therefore, matzah and bitter herbs on Pesach in commemoration of what happened to us and we leave our houses on Succos in order to dwell in booths, like inhabitants of deserts who are deprived of comfort.

We thereby remember that this was once our condition; as we read: "*I housed the children of Israel in succah-booths*" [*Leviticus* 23:43]. Although we now dwell in elegant houses, in the best and most fertile land, this is by the kindness of God and because of His promises to our forefathers, Abraham, Isaac, and Jacob, who were perfect in their thoughts and in their conduct.

This [last] idea is likewise an important element in our religion: whatever good we have received and ever will receive from God, is due to the merits of the Patriarchs, who "*kept the way of HASHEM to do justice and judgment*" (*Gen.* 18:19). Accordingly, we join Shemini Atzeres to the festival of Succos in order to make our celebration complete, for it cannot be perfect in booths, but only in comfortable and well-built houses (*Rambam, Moreh Nevuchim* 3:43).

The Season

The First Day for the Calculation of Sins

◆§ וּלְקַחְתֶּם לָכֶם בַּיּוֹם הָרִאשׁוֹן, *And you shall take for yourselves on the first day* [*Leviticus* 23:40]. In the literal sense, *first day* refers to the first day of the festival, which is the fifteenth day of Tishrei. [But since the previous verse has already specified the date in question, why must our verse tell us it is the *first day* of the festival? (*Maharzu*)] Accordingly, the Midrash perceives the expression "*first*" day in this context to imply: רִאשׁוֹן לְחֶשְׁבּוֹן עֲוֺנוֹת, "The first day in the accounting of sins."

As the *Tur* and Midrashic commentators explain, on Yom Kippur the penitent Jew became a "*baal teshuvah*"; his slate was wiped clean of sins, so to speak, as it is written [*Leviticus* 16:30]: *For on this day atonement shall be made for you to cleanse you of all your sins.* Thus cleansed, the Jew does not remain idle. What does he do? In the several days following the Holy Day, the Jew engages in preparations for the Succos festival — building and decorating a *succah*, obtaining the Four Species, etc., and generally involving himself in *mitzvos*. Thus when the Jew stands before God on the first day of the festival with *lulav* and *esrog* in hand, God says, "Let bygones be bygones. From now on we shall begin a new account." Moses therefore forewarned them that on this "first day for the calculation of sins" they are to continue to be engaged in *mitzvos*.

☐ R' David of Talna cited the above to refute the cynics who scoff at God-fearing Jews who diligently spend much time in devotedly preparing themselves to do *mitzvos*. "The Midrashic explanation is, at first glance, difficult," the Rebbe

would say. "If the *preparations* of the Succos *mitzvos* protect the Jews from sinning, how much more so should the actual *performance* of the *mitzvah* shield people from sin? Why then is the first day of Succos — when Jews are already engaged in *performing* the actual *mitzvah* — called the "first day in the accounting of sins?"

"Thus," the Rebbe concluded, "we see that proper preparation is in certain ways loftier than the actual performance of the *mitzvah*."

□ The author of *Nesivos Chaim* homiletically explains the Midrash as follows:

"According to one Rabbinic opinion, the fruit of the Tree of Knowledge of which Adam ate was an *esrog* [see comm. to ArtScroll *Bereishis* 2:9, page 95]. It emerges, accordingly, that with this fruit the first sin began. Thus, the *mitzvah* of *esrog* [i.e. *succah* and the Four Species] evokes memories of history's first accounting of sin."

□ The author of *Tiferes Shlomo* similarly remarks that the *mitzvah* of *esrog* repairs the defect caused by Adam's sin of the Tree of Knowledge.

Joy to the Upright

⇜§ וּלְיִשְׁרֵי לֵב שִׂמְחָה, *And for the upright of heart [there is] joy [Psalms* 97:11]. In addition to the simple meaning of this passage it alludes also to the sequence of Rosh Hashanah, Yom Kippur, and Succos. Because the Jews become "upright of heart" by virtue of their sincere repentance on the High Holy Days, they deserve to achieve joy during Succos *(Chidushei HaRim)*.

Atonement for Exile

⇜§ Another reason that Succos follows Yom Kippur is found in the Midrash: If one is decreed exile on Yom Kippur, then his leaving his home to find shelter in his *succah* will be considered as atonement for that decree.

Symbol of Confidence

⇜§ Rosh Hashanah and Yom Kippur are days of atonement, and their mood is one of awe and anguish. Once Yom Kippur has passed and we are assured of atonement, we leave our houses and dwell on the open field in a gesture symbolizing our confidence in God's forgiveness and protection *(Tzror HaMor)*.

Joy Following Affliction

⇜§ R' S. R. Hirsch perceives the celebration of Succos to be a natural outcome of the successful attainment of the spiritual goal of Yom Kippur. By abstaining from food — an absolute necessity for our survival — on Yom Kippur, we demonstrate our realization that our sinfulness makes us undeserving of further life. Because we do so, we earn God's mercy and forgiveness, and a renewal of our right to live. To symbolize this renewal, God commands that on the first day of Succos we are to "take for ourselves" [וּלְקַחְתֶּם לָכֶם] the Four Species that represent the good fruits of His creation and rejoice with them. From the affliction of Yom Kippur we advance to the joy of Succos.

Channeled Rejoicing

⇜§ *Make yourself a Succos festival for seven days when you gather in [the produce]*

from your threshing floor and your wine-vat; and you shall rejoice on your festival (Deut. 16:13-14).

When one gathers in his produce and fills his home with abundance he is naturally filled with joy. God desired to accord Israel merit and He therefore *commanded* them to rejoice in this season. Accordingly, their natural rejoicing is raised to a level of שִׂמְחָה שֶׁל מִצְוָה, *rejoicing in fulfillment of a commandment (Sefer HaChinuch).*

Tishrei Rather than Nissan

⊷§ Although it was Nissan — the month of spring — when God removed us from Egypt and housed us in the *succah*-booths, He commanded us to observe the festival of Succos in Tishrei, during autumn. Why was the celebration not mandated during Nissan?

Tur explains that Hashem wanted the *mitzvah* to be done in such a way that it would be readily apparent to all that the booths were being put up for the sake of the *mitzvah* and not for personal convenience. Given the weather conditions in *Eretz Yisrael,* this is possible only in the fall. In *Eretz Yisrael,* the warm and dry season, which begins in Nissan, is a time when it is common for people to leave their homes and live in cool huts outdoors. On the other hand, when Tishrei comes, the summer is over and the rainy season is imminent. Then, naturally, people will leave their huts and move back indoors. Consequently, when the Jew leaves his home in favor of his *succah* in Tishrei, it is readily apparent that he does so only to serve God, and not in response to the onset of summer.

□ Moreover, we celebrate the *mitzvah* of *succah* after the ingathering of the harvest in *Eretz Yisrael.* Then, when homes are filled with the plentiful blessings of the soil, one tends to turn to his house and make the necessary repairs — waterproof the roof, strengthen the foundation, etc. — so that the oncoming rains will harm neither him nor his possessions.

Specifically at this time, therefore, when there is danger that one might place all his trust upon his material possessions, is one commanded to forsake the security of his home and dwell in a temporary *succah.* Thereby one demonstrates that he puts his trust not in his own strength, but that he seeks protection under the shadow of the Divine Presence — in HASHEM, Who is the Source of all blessings and protection *(Menoras Hamaor).* [See Overview.]

□ According to the Chassidic writings, Passover was ordained at the onset of the summer months, and Succos at the onset of the winter months in order to sanctify all beginnings to the Holy One, Blessed is He.

Commemoration of Boundless Joy

⊷§ The question is often asked: Why do we have a festival commemorating the *succah*-booths in the desert, while there is no festival commemorating the other miracles performed for our ancestors in the desert — such as the daily provision of the manna and water?

However, in the case of the manna we find that in Chazeroth and DiZahav, the Jews expressed severe dissatisfaction with the manna, referring to it derogatorily as "unsubstantial bread" [see *Numbers* 11:6, 21:5].

In the case of the water, too, we find that they complained, as it is said [*Exodus* 15:24]: *And the people murmured against Moses, saying, "What shall we drink?"*

However, in the case of the Clouds of Glory, symbolized by Succos, they never complained, but rejoiced boundlessly. Therefore, we commemorate this with the festival of Succos which is called זְמַן שִׂמְחָתֵנוּ, *the time of our rejoicing.* This recalls the Talmudic dictum [*Shabbos* 130]: Whatever *mitzvah* the Jews accepted with joy they still fulfill with joy *(Sifsei Tzaddik).*

◆§ Another answer to the above is offered in *Bnei Yisas'char:*

The manna as well as the water well were essential to Israel's survival in the desert, and they could not have endured without them; therefore, God had no choice but to give these to them, as it were. The *succah*-booths on the other hand, while beneficial, were not crucial to their very existence. Consequently, God's provision of these miraculous *succah*-booths demonstrates His compassionate concern for even the less urgent needs of His nation. Therefore the commemoration of this is celebrated for all generations.

Therefore, it is written [*Leviticus* 23:43]: *So that future generations may know that I housed the Israelites in succah-booths ... I am HASHEM.* — The housing in *succah*-booths was performed by God in His aspect of *"HASHEM,"* the Name which designates Him as the Divine Dispenser of Mercy.

◆§ The days of Succos are also festive because they coincide with the days of the consecration of the altar during the First Temple.

◆§ According to the calculations of Vilna Gaon, the protective Clouds of Glory [עַנְנֵי הַכָּבוֹד] were taken away from Israel. On the first day of Succos, they were returned — another reason for the joy of the festival.

The 70 Oxen — Atonement for the 70 Nations

◆§ During Temple times, in addition to the regular daily sacrifices, the wine libation and the water libations, *mussaf* [additional] sacrifices were offered each day of Succos. As prescribed in *Numbers* 29, a different number of oxen was offered each day — thirteen on the first day, twelve on the second, with the total decreasing by one on each successive day. The total number of oxen offered throughout the festival came to seventy, corresponding to the seventy nations who descended from Noah and who were the ancestors of all the nations of the world. The Temple in Jerusalem was perceived as 'a house of prayer for all the peoples' and these seventy oxen were sacrificed in atonement for these nations and in prayer for their well-being and peace (see *Rashi* to *Numbers* 29).

☐ "Woe to the idolaters," moaned the Talmudic Sage R' Yochanan in *Succah* 55b, "for they had a loss [by the destruction of the Temple] and they do not know what they have lost. When the Temple was in existence, the altar atoned for them, but now that it is no longer in existence who shall atone for them?"

☐ The Midrash similarly expounds the verse in *Psalms* 109:4: *In return for my love they hate me, and I am prayer.* — Notwithstanding Israel's love as manifested by their praying and sacrificing the seventy oxen during Succos as intercession on behalf of the seventy nations, the gentile nations hate them, instead of being grateful.

The Two-Day Yom Tov in the Diaspora

◆§ Every *Yom Tov* day is celebrated outside of *Eretz Yisrael* for two days. This is an outgrowth of the fact that, according to Torah law, the fixing of Rosh Chodesh was done by the *beis din* upon acceptance of the testimony of witnesses who sighted the new moon. One knew when a *Yom Tov* in a particular month was to be celebrated if he knew which day had been designated as Rosh Chodesh. To ensure that the public was informed, messengers were dispatched to the rest of the land as far as they could travel from Rosh Chodesh till the holiday that fell in that month. Ancient modes of transportation did not allow them to get very far. In Tishrei, since they could not travel on Rosh Hashanah, Yom Kippur, or on the Sabbath, they would generally have only ten days of travel before Succos. As a result, although the exact day of *Yom Tov* was known in *Eretz Yisrael,* the Diaspora would not know the exact day until the *Yom Tov* had already passed.

☐ Because Rosh Chodesh can only be the thirtieth or the thirty-first day from the previous Rosh Chodesh, the question of which day to observe as *Yom Tov* was limited to two days. For example, if the thirtieth day after Rosh Chodesh Adar was a Tuesday, the choice of Rosh Chodesh Nissan was limited to that day, Tuesday, or the next day, Wednesday. Accordingly, Jews in very distant lands knew that the first day of Pesach (the fifteenth day of Nissan) would be either Tuesday or Wednesday — but the margin of error could not be greater than that. Consequently, they would be forced to observe two days as the beginning of Pesach, while the Jews of *Eretz Yisrael* and the nearby Diaspora who knew which day was Pesach would celebrate only one day. By the time the next Rosh Chodesh arrived, even the people in the Diaspora would have had time to learn when the last Rosh Chodesh had been, so that the doubt never grew beyond two days.

☐ R' Saadiah Gaon *(Teshuvos HaGeonim)* ascribes the obligation to celebrate two days of *Yom Tov* to a הֲלָכָה לְמשֶׁה מִסִּינַי, *oral tradition given to Moses by God on Mount Sinai.* R' Hai Gaon *(ibid.),* disagreeing with R' Saadiah, traces this practice back to an ordinance promulgated by the early prophets (גְּזֵירָה מִימוֹת נְבִיאִים רִאשׁוֹנִים), perhaps even by Joshua when he entered *Eretz Yisrael.* As a result of Roman persecution in *Eretz Yisrael,* R' Hillel HaNassi (who lived in the fourth century C.E.) feared that the institution of *semichah* would pass into oblivion. [*Semichah* was the rabbinical ordination that began with Moses and continued from teacher to student.] *Semichah* was a prerequisite for the *beis din* charged with pronouncing Rosh Chodesh; without it, the months could not be consecrated and the Jewish calendar would have lost its halachic basis. Because R' Hillel and his court *were* properly ordained, they were competent to formulate and promulgate a calendar that would remain binding even after *semichah* ceased to exist (as, in fact, it did). In the year 4118 (358 C.E.) they instituted the calendar that remains in use to this day (quoted by R' Avraham ben Chiya HaNassi in *Sefer Halbur* 3:7; *Zemach David* 4118; cf. *Rambam, Kiddush HaChodesh* 5:3).[1]

---

1. R' Yitzchak HaYisraeli *(Yesod Olam* 4:5) gives the date as 4260. But this must be a copyist's or typographical error. Elsewhere *(op. cit.* 4:9) he says that the calendar was adopted about 300 years after the destruction of the Temple, which means roughly 4130 — very close to the date (4118) given by R' Hai Gaon.

□ Once R' Hillel's calendar was adopted, it seemed logical that the Diaspora communities would begin observing a single *Yom Tov* day as in *Eretz Yisrael,* since all Jews observed the same calendar without resorting to the decisions of .the court.

The *beis din* of *Eretz Yisrael,* however, admonished the Diaspora 'to safeguard the custom of your fathers, (i.e., celebrate two days of *Yom Tov*) lest the government enact legislation forbidding Jewish observance' and the exact dates of the holy days would become widely unknown (*Beitzah* 4b). Though this reasoning applies to *Eretz Yisrael* as well, the Sages specifically limited their decree to the preservation of the status quo, but they did not wish to add new restrictions.

The Succah

Symbolism of סכה

⋖§ The Chida perceived the Hebrew letters סכה, *succah,* to allude to laws of construction of a *succah:*

ס—Scrupulous people build a *succah* enclosed by walls on all sides, like the completely enclosed letter **ס.**

כ—Some construct only three walls, like the letter **כ** which is also permissible.

ה—It is also permissible to construct one of two walls and a third partial, unattached wall, like the letter **ה.**

Composition of the S'chach

⋖§ From the verse, "*Make yourself a Succos festival for seven days when you gather in* [the produce] *from your threshing floor and of the wine-vat*" (*Deut.* 16:13), the Talmud learns the nature of halachically valid *s'chach* [*succah*-covering]: "the leavings of the threshing floor and of the wine-vat" (פְּסוֹלֶת גּוֹרֶן וְיֶקֶב). That is, like these "leavings," *s'chach* must be something which (a) grows from the earth (גְּדוּלוֹ מִן הָאָרֶץ), but (b) is no longer attached to the earth (תָּלוּשׁ), and (c) is not susceptible to ritual contamination (אֵינוֹ מְקַבֵּל טוּמְאָה). A material that lacks any of these three qualifications is invalid as *s'chach.* Thus, animal skins, the branches of a still-growing tree, utensils, metals, and food — these and their like and their corollaries are all invalid, since each of them lacks [at least] one of the above three qualifications. And this is why the people who had returned from exile in Babylonia were told (*Nechemiah* 8:15): "*Go out to the mountain and bring olive leaves and leaves of the wild olive and leaves of the myrtle and leaves of the palm and leaves of thick trees, to make succos*" (*Succah* 12a) [see R' Zevin, *The Festivals in Halachah;* see also R' Kitov, *Sefer HaToda'ah, The Book of Our Heritage*].

An 'Easy' Mitzvah

⋖§ The Talmud [*Avodah Zarah* 3a] records that in the World to Come, when the Holy One, Blessed is He, castigates the gentile nations for not accepting the Torah, they will reply, "Offer us the Torah anew and we will obey it."

To test them, God will say, "I have an easy *mitzvah* called *succah*, go and perform it." (The Talmud explains that it is termed 'easy' because it is inexpensive to perform.)

Immediately, every gentile will go and make a *succah* on his roof, but God will cause the sun to blaze on them and each of them will kick over his *succah* and go away [by kicking contemptuously, they will prove how insincere is their commitment to Torah].

'Dwell' as You Ordinarily Live

⋖§ *"You shall dwell in succah-booths for seven days" (Levit. 23:42)." You shall "dwell"* implies: in the same manner that you ordinarily live in your home [תֵּשְׁבוּ כְּעֵין תָּדוּרוּ]. Accordingly, the Rabbis ruled that all the seven days of Succos one should make his *succah* his permanent abode, and his house his temporary abode. In what manner? — If one has beautiful vessels and beautiful divans he should bring them up into the *succah;* he should eat and drink and pass his leisure in the *succah;* he should also engage in deep study in the *succah (Succah 29a).*

Exemptions Due to "Distress"

⋖§ "If one is distressed [(in the *succah)* due to such conditions as rain or cold], he is exempt from the *mitzvah*" [מִצְטַעֵר פָּטוּר מִן הַסּוּכָּה] *(Succah 26a)].* Such an exemption is unique to *succah;* it appears nowhere else. The reason is, as mentioned above, that one should dwell in his *succah* as if it were his permanent home: "...'Dwell' [in your *succah*] *as you ordinarily live* [in your home]". That is, if one would not stay in his home because of distress, he need not stay in his *succah* under similar uncomfortable circumstances.

▢ *Chidushei HaRim* explained that a מִצְטַעֵר, *distressed person,* is exempt from *succah* because a distressed person loses composure and presence of mind and the *mitzvah* of *succah* must be performed with full awareness of its symbolic lesson — for the Torah specifically commands [*Leviticus* 23:43]: לְמַעַן יֵדְעוּ דֹרֹתֵיכֶם, *"So that your future generations may know."* This teaches that the *succah* must impart knowledge, something that is possible only when one is not preoccupied with thoughts of his personal discomfort.

⋖§ According to the Rebbe of Kotzk, the exemption is based on the concept that the innermost implication of *succah* is בִּיטוּל, *self-effacement,* demonstrated when man humbles himself, leaves his home and moves into a *succah*. But one who is conscious of his personal distress is exempt from the obligation since he has not yet reached the level of true self-abasement.

Hospitality Overrides Distress

⋖§ The Gaon, R' Chaim Ozer Grodzenski of Vilna, was a frail man whose poor health made it impossible for him to eat in the *succah* in cold weather. Once he had a guest who, being in good health, went out to eat in the *succah* on a cold day. To the visitor's surprise, Reb Chaim Ozer, bundled in heavy clothing, came out with his food to join him in the *succah*.

In reply to the guest's insistence that the rabbi should not sit in the cold, Reb Chaim Ozer said, "One who is exempt by reason of 'distress' is released only

from the obligation of *succah* — not from other *mitzvos*. Here there is a *mitzvah* of hospitality to guests, and from that I am not exempt." Thus, notwithstanding the cold, Reb Chaim Ozer ate in the *succah* to fulfill the obligation of hospitality rather than let his guest eat there alone [see R' Moshe Sternbuch, *Moadim Uzemanim* §88].

Needy Guests

⋘ In a similar vein, the Chofetz Chaim makes a halachic ruling based on a host's responsibility to his guests. In the event it rains on the first night of Succos, it is highly preferable to wait until midnight before eating in the hope that the rain will stop (see Halachah section). However, the Chofetz Chaim rules, if someone has invited a poor person to eat with him — and presumably his guest has not eaten all day and is extremely hungry — the host should serve the meal immediately, even in the rain. Furthermore, to delay the poor man's meal may well be a violation of the Scriptural injunction not to delay payment of vows to the poor. [See *Mishnah Berurah, Shaar HaTziyun* 639:67.]

All Encompassing Mitzvah

⋘ "I love the *mitzvah* of *succah*" declared the Ba'al Shem Tov "for a man can enter it with his whole body — even with the mud adhering to the soles of his boots!"

Succah and Eretz Yisrael

⋘ The Vilna Gaon observes that there are two *mitzvos* that the Jew observes by entering with his entire being — dwelling in a *succah* and in *Eretz Yisrael*. An allusion to this thought is found in *Psalms* 76:3: וַיְהִי בְשָׁלֵם סֻכּוֹ וּמְעוֹנָתוֹ בְצִיּוֹן, *In Shalem* [i.e. Jerusalem, but literally *whole, complete*] *is his succah, and his dwelling place in Zion*. The Vilna Gaon explained the passage this way: "Man is whole when he is in His *succah*; and likewise when his dwelling place is in Zion."

The Sanctity of the Succah

⋘ "It was the custom of my mentor, R' Moshe Cordovero of sainted memory, not to speak in the *succah* throughout the festival except in matters of Torah, for the sanctity of the *succah* is very great. Witness that the very wood of the *succah* assumes sanctity and may not be put to any other use throughout all seven days of the festival ... Accordingly, when one enters a *succah* he is enveloped in the atmosphere of holiness; and how holy it is indeed! It is therefore proper for one to avoid lightheadedness and frivolity but scrupulously to fulfill the mandate: *Rejoice with trepidation* [*Psalms* 2:1 (i.e., temper joy with a reverence of the Holy One, Blessed is He)]" (R' Eliyahu deVidas, *Reishis Chochmah* chapt. 14).

⋘ When the Chassidic Rebbe, R' Mordechai of Lechovitz of sainted memory, would enter his *succah* on the first night of the festival, he would fall to the ground of the *succah*, kiss it and sigh: "How dare a flesh-and-blood body tread upon such a beloved *mitzvah* as *succah*!"

□ Similarly, it is the commendable practice of spiritually exalted people to kiss the *succah* upon entering and upon leaving to demonstrate love for the *mitzvah* (*Ba'er Heitev* §677 citing *Sh'lah*).

A Stolen Succah

◄§ Rabbinic exegesis elicits from the command חַג הַסֻּכֹּת תַּעֲשֶׂה לְךָ, *Make yourself a Succos festival*, the *succah* must be *yours* [תַּעֲשֶׂה לְךָ-מִשֶּׁלְּךָ, *for yourself — from that which is yours*] thus disqualifying a stolen *succah* [see *Succah* 9a] ...

□ In *The Festivals in Halachah*, R' Zevin writes: It is difficult to construct a case of a *"succah acquired by robbery"* (סֻכָּה גְזוּלָה). If one man attacks another, forcibly ejects him from his *succah,* and dwells in it, this is not a case of a stolen *succah;* for the halachah is that only movable objects (chattels) can be considered stolen — i.e., can be illegally transferred from one man's possession to another's — but a *succah* is classified as real estate (קַרְקַע), and never considered stolen; one who occupies it illegally is not considered to "possess" it, but simply is obligated to return it to the rightful owner. This puts the property not in the category of "stolen," but "borrowed."

If on the other hand, one steals *s'chach* or boards and builds a *succah* with them, then the Rabbinic decree called *takkanas marish* applies. As the mishnah in Tractate *Gittin* tells us, this is an exception to the usual law — that when movables are stolen the thief must return the items themselves and not simply pay for them. Since the prospect of dismantling one's house in order to return a stolen beam would tend to discourage the thief from repenting, the Sages decreed that "If one steals a beam *(marish)* and builds it into a house, he has no obligation other than to pay for the beam, because of *takkanas hashavim,* the decree for the benefit of penitents." Hence, even though the items taken for the *succah* were movables, again the obligation incurred has the status of a debt rather than the return of the stolen objects, so that here, too, the *succah* is not classified as "stolen" (see *Succah* 31a).

Thus, the only possible case of a stolen *succah* is one that was built on a wagon or a boat. In this case the *succah* is not considered real estate, since it is not attached to the ground. And since no dismantling is involved, the principle of *takkanas hashavim* does not apply. This is the case constructed by *Rashi*. But *Tosafos* suggests a different possibility. If Reuven builds a *succah* in Shimon's courtyard and Shimon comes and attacks Reuven, ejecting him from the *succah* and dwelling in it himself — this, says *Tosafos*, would be classified as a stolen *succah*. The rule that real estate cannot be "stolen" would not apply here, because the ground to which the *succah* is attached does not belong to Reuven.

The Future Succah for the Righteous

◄§ "In the Time to Come the Holy One, Blessed is He, will make a banquet for the righteous from the flesh of Leviathan ... the rest of Leviathan will be distributed and sold in the markets of Jerusalem.

" . . . Furthermore, in the Time to Come the Holy One, Blessed is He, will make a *succah* for the righteous from the skin of Leviathan . . . The rest of Leviathan will be spread by the Holy One, Blessed is He, upon the walls of Jerusalem and its radiance will shine from one end of the world to the other" (*Bava Basra* 75a). [On Leviathan, see also pp. 34 and 118.]

◄§ R' Levi Yitzchak of Berditchev was always sure to invite guests to his *succah* table, especially very simple people.

When asked about this, he replied: "In the Messianic future when the

righteous will repose in the *succah* made of the skin of Leviathan, I will want to join their banquet. But I will certainly be stopped and told, 'Who are you, simpleton, pushing to sit among the righteous?'

"I will be able to justify myself, 'In my *succah*, too, I welcomed simple people ...' "

Ushpizin

Exalted Holy Guests

◄§ The *Zohar* teaches that for dwelling faithfully in their *succos*, the people of Israel merit the privilege of welcoming the *Shechinah* [God's Presence] and the seven "faithful shepherds" who descend from their heavenly abode in *Gan Eden* and enter these *succos* as exalted guests. There they observe how their descendants fulfill the *mitzvah* of *succah* dwelling under God's protection.

These seven "faithful shepherds" of Israel are: Abraham, Isaac, Jacob, Joseph, Moses, Aaron and King David. All seven are guests in every *succah* throughout the seven days of ther festival, but on each day one of them leads the others.

For example, on the first day Abraham leads the other six, and that day is referred to as the *"Ushpizin* of Abraham." On the second day Isaac leads the others, the day being referred to as the "Ushpizin of Isaac." And so on until Hoshanah Rabbah when King David is the leader.

☐ According to R' Isaac Luria, the *Arizal*, Joseph follows Moses and Aaron, the sequence being: Abraham, Isaac, Jacob, Moses, Aaron, Joseph and David. However, many liturgies follow the chronological sequence of their lives, according to which Joseph precedes Moses and Aaron. [See p. 98.]

☐ In the literature of Kabbalah they are known as the אוּשְׁפִּיזִין עִלָּאִין קַדִּישִׁין, *Exalted Holy Guests*. The following is a citation from the *Zohar* [*Emor* 103a] referred to above:

> When a man sits in the *succah* of the shadow of faith, the *Shechinah* spreads its 'wings' over him from above, ... and Abraham and five righteous ones and David with them make their abode with him. ... A man should rejoice each day of the festival with these guests who abide with him.
>
> ... Accordingly, when Rav Hamnuna the Elder would enter the *succah* he used to stand inside the door and say, "Let us invite the guests and prepare a table." And he used to stand up and greet them, saying *"In booths you shall dwell* seven days. Sit, most exalted guests, sit; sit, guests of faith, sit." He would then raise hands in joy and say, "Happy is our portion; happy is the portion of Israel ..."
>
> One must also gladden the poor, because the portion of these guests whom he invites must go to the poor. For if a man sits in the shadow of faith [i.e. the *succah* under God's protection] and invites those guests and does not give them their portion, they all hold aloof from him ...
>
> Rav Elazar said, The Torah does not demand more of a man than he can perform, as it is written [*Deut.* 16:17] *Each person according to the gift of*

his hand [i.e., commensurate with his means]. One should not say, "I will first satisfy myself with food and drink, and what is left I shall give to the poor," rather the *first* of everything must be for one's guests. If one gladdens his guests and satisfies them, God rejoices over him. Abraham, Isaac, Jacob and the other righteous shower him with propitious verses ... "Happy is the man who attains to all of this!"

◆§ Thus, following the *Zohar,* it is proper to invite poor "guests from below" to one's *succah* table, to correspond to the "guests from above." If this is impossible, one should at least provide meals, or money for meals, so that the poor can joyously observe the festival in their own *succah.*

Spirit, Not Stomach

◆§ After describing how each person, according to his or her own taste, should find means to make a festival enjoyable, Rambam *(Hil. Yom Tov* 6:18) writes: While eating and drinking himself, one is obliged to feed the stranger, orphan, and widow, along with the other unfortunate poor. But one who locks his courtyard doors and eats and drinks with his wife and children, but does not give food and drink to the poor and embittered — this is not the joy of a *mitzvah,* but joy of his stomach. Of such people it is said, *Their offerings are like the bread of mourners for themselves, whoever eats them will be contaminated for their food is for selfishness (Hosea 9:4).* Such celebration is a disgrace for them as it is said, *I shall fling filth in their faces, the filth of their festival offerings (Malachi 2:3).*

Clarity of Faith

◆§ The Rebbe of Kotzk used to say: "Some people maintain that they *see* the *Ushpizin* guests in their *succah.* I say, however, that I *believe* that the *Ushpizin* guests come to my *succah.* Faith is clearer and more certain than seeing."

The Four Species

The Biblical Command [Leviticus 23:40-41]

וּלְקַחְתֶּם לָכֶם בַּיּוֹם הָרִאשׁוֹן פְּרִי עֵץ הָדָר כַּפֹּת תְּמָרִים וַעֲנַף עֵץ־עָבֹת וְעַרְבֵי־נַחַל וּשְׂמַחְתֶּם לִפְנֵי יהוה אֱלֹהֵיכֶם שִׁבְעַת יָמִים: וְחַגֹּתֶם אֹתוֹ חַג לַיהוה שִׁבְעַת יָמִים בַּשָּׁנָה חֻקַּת עוֹלָם לְדֹרֹתֵיכֶם בַּחֹדֶשׁ הַשְּׁבִיעִי תָּחֹגּוּ אֹתוֹ:

And you shall take for yourselves on the first day the fruit of a beautiful [esrog] tree, the branches of date palms, twigs of a plaited tree, and brook willows, and you shall rejoice before HASHEM your God seven days. You shall celebrate it as a celebration to HASHEM seven days in the year. It is an eternal law throughout your generations; in the seventh month you shall celebrate it.

Fruits of Joy

◆§ These Four Species naturally cause man joy by virtue of their beauty. God therefore commanded that we take them during the festival of our joy *(Sefer HaChinuch).*

Symbolic Expression of Joy

◄§ Rambam (Moreh Nevuchim 3:43) writes: I believe that the Four Species are a symbolical expression of our rejoicing over the Israelites having emerged from the wilderness, 'not a place of seed, figs, vines, or pomegranates, and without water to drink' (Numbers 20:5), to a country full of fruit-trees and rivers.

In order to remember this we take the most pleasant fruit of the land, the best-smelling branches, the most beautiful leaves, and also the best of herbs, or the willows of the brook. These four species also have these three virtues: First, they were plentiful in those days in *Eretz Yisrael*, so that every one could easily get them. Secondly, they have a pleasant appearance; some of them — the *esrog* and the myrtle — are also excellent as regards their aroma, the branches of the palm-tree and the willow having neither good nor bad smell. Thirdly, they keep fresh and green for seven days, which is not the case with peaches, pomegranates, asparagus, and the like.

Symbol of Triumph

◄§ R' Avin explained the *mitzvah* of the Four Species with a parable: Two people came to a judge to adjudicate their dispute. When they leave the courtroom, how can we know which one was victorious? If one of them raises his spear in triumph we all know he was victorious. So it is with Israel and the nations of the world. Each accuses the other on Rosh Hashanah and we do not know who won the dispute in the Heavenly Court. But when the Jews go out on Succos with *lulavim* and *esrogim* in their hands, this demonstrates Israel's victory (*Midrash Vayikra Rabbah* 30:2). [See Overview.]

Adorn Yourself in Mitzvos

◄§ One must strive for beauty [הִדּוּר מִצְוָה] in the performance of *mitzvos*. This is derived in the Talmud [*Shabbos* 133b] from the verse [*Exodus* 15:2]: זֶה אֵלִי וְאַנְוֵהוּ, *This is my God and I will adorn Him*, which is interpreted to teach: "Adorn yourself before Him in the fulfillment of *mitzvos*. Make a beautiful *succah* for Him, a beautiful *lulav*, a beautiful *shofar*, beautiful *tzitzis* and a beautiful Torah Scroll, and write it with fine ink, a fine quill and a skilled scribe, and wrap it about with beautiful silks."

◄§ Even if a person spends profuse sums on *mitzvos* — beyond what is required — he suffers no loss. In the words of the Sages [*Bava Kamma* 9b]: "Until one third — the expense is his; from here on — it is God's." That is, if someone chooses to enhance his performance of a *mitzvah* by spending more to beautify it, he is reimbursed providentially from Above for whatever he spends in excess of one third of the normal cost of the *mitzvah*.

Pure Kavanah

◄§ The initials of the word אֶתְרֹג represent the verse אַל תְּבוֹאֵנִי רֶגֶל גַּאֲוָה, *Bring me not to the point of arrogance* [*Psalms* 36:12], the implication being that the *esrog* figuratively pleads with its owner that he not become arrogant by virtue of his owning a beautiful, costly, *esrog*. Instead let him perform the *mitzvah* totally for the Sake of Heaven (*Baal Shem Tov*).

Without Reward

▪§ Once in a year of drought no *esrogim* were available. A Jew who had acquired an *esrog* approached the Vilna Gaon with a proposition: He would give his *esrog* to the Gaon on condition that the Gaon give him the heavenly reward that would be earned from the performance of the *mitzvah*. The Gaon replied that it was worth transferring such benefits in order to perform the *mitzvah* of *esrog* properly. When the arrangement was concluded and the *esrog* transferred into the Gaon's hand, a great joy shone from his radiant face and he exclaimed, "How great will the *mitzvah* of *esrog* be for me this year; I will be fulfilling it totally for the Sake of Heaven with absolutely no thought of reward!"

Representative of the Human Body

▪§ The Rabbis in the Midrash compare the Four Species with parts of the human body to which they are similar in shape:

The *lulav* represents the spine;
The *esrog* — the heart;
The *myrtle* — the eyes;
The *willow* — the lips.

By bringing together the plants that symbolize these four organs, man unites all his organs in the service of God, and the sins he did with his limbs are atoned for through the performance of this *mitzvah* with the proper devotion.

▪§ Therefore the Torah stresses specifically that the *esrog* be beautiful (*Leviticus* 23:40), because it symbolizes the heart which represents the seat of the emotions and is the source of all actions. If a person's emotions and desires are refined and brought to their highest potential, the other organs will follow suit (*R' Naftali of Ropshitz, Zera Kodesh*).

▪§ *Anaf Yosef* preserves a similar Midrashic thought (taken from R' Elazar HaKalir's liturgy for *shacharis* of the first day of Succos) on this theme:

"Why the *esrog*? — It is similar to the heart and atones for the heart's evil thoughts.

"Why the myrtle? It is similar to the eyes, and atones for the evil sights which the eyes seeks; as it is said: '*And you shall stray after your hearts and after your eyes.*'

"Why the willow? It is similar to the lips, and atones for the expressions of the lips.

"Why the *lulav*? As this *lulav* has only one heart, so does Israel have only one heart — for their Father in Heaven."

Symbolic of the Jews

▪§ Moreover the Four Species represents Israel.

Just as the *esrog* has taste as well as fragrance, so the Jews have among them those who possess learning as well as good deeds;

As the *lulav* has taste but not fragrance, so the Jews have among them those who possess learning but not good deeds;

As the myrtle has fragrance but not taste, so the Jews have among them those who possess good deeds but not learning;

As the willow has neither fragrance nor taste, so the Jews have among them those who possess neither good deeds nor learning.

What does the Holy One, Blessed is He, do to them? ... He says, "Let them all be tied together in one band, and they will atone one for another" *(Midrash Vayikra Rabbah 30)*.

Three Plus One

◈§ Although all the Four Species are mentioned in the same Scriptural passage, the practice is to bind together the latter three species — *lulav*, willows, and myrtle branches — leaving the *esrog* unbound, but held close to the others.

The Talmud [*Succah* 34b] explains that this arrangement is implied in the wording of the verse itself, which reads [*Lev.* 23:40]: *And you shall take for yourselves on the first day the fruit of a beautiful [esrog] tree, the branches of a date palms **and** twigs of a plaited tree **and** brook willows.* Only the latter three species are connected by the conjunctive ו, *and,* implying that the verse contains two groupings: a) the *esrog;* b) the three remaining species. However, all four species are essential to the fulfillment of the *mitzvah*.

☐ Though many kabbalistic explanations have been advanced for this arrangement, it remains one of the sublime mysteries of the Torah *(Likutei Mahariach)*.

The Four in Unison

◈§ "The *esrog* must be held near the other species while waving. The kabbalistic secret was revealed to me in a dream once on the first night of Succos when a devout Ashkenazi by the name of Reb Yitzchak was a guest in my home.

"In my dream, I saw that my guest was writing the Divine Name י־ה־ו and separated the fourth letter ה from the other three. When I asked him to explain why he wrote the Name in this way he replied, 'Such is the custom in our place.' I then protested to him and rewrote the Name correctly. I remained bewildered at the dream and did not understand it.

"The next morning, during the waving of the *lulav*, I saw that R' Yitzchak did not wave the *esrog* together with the other three species. At that moment the implication of the dream became clear to me; I related it to R' Yitzchak and he retracted" (comm. of R' Menachem Recanati [13th cent.] to *Emor).*

Seven Days in the Temple

◈§ When the Temple stood, the Four Species were taken on all seven days of Succos in the Temple, but only on the first day outside of the Temple area. This is derived from the simple meaning of the Scriptural verse [*Lev.* 23:40], which says that we are to take the Four Species *on the first day,* but that we are to rejoice with them *before HASHEM* [i.e. in the Temple] for all seven days. After the Destruction, when the obligation to rejoice in the Temple could no longer be performed, Rabban Yochanan ben Zakkai instituted that the *lulav* be taken in the provinces seven days in remembrance of the Temple *(Mishnah Succah 3:13)*.

◈§ Nowadays, however, the Four Species are taken all seven days of the Festival with full Rabbinic force, and the benediction recited throughout contains the formula "... Who has sanctified us with His commandments and commanded us," i.e. through the Divinely sanctioned Rabbinic ordinances.

Taking of One's Own

◦§ In commanding us regarding the Four Species, the Torah [*Leviticus* 23:40] states: *And you shall take for yourselves.* — 'For yourselves,' that is: of your own property. This excludes that which is borrowed or stolen. It is based upon this exegesis that the Sages concluded that one does not fulfill his obligation on the first day of the festival by using his friend's *lulav* unless the latter gave it to him as a gift.

◦§ It once happened that Rabban Gamliel, R' Yehoshua, R' Elazar ben Azariah and R' Akiva were traveling on a ship and only Rabban Gamliel had a *lulav* which he had bought for a thousand zuz. Rabban Gamliel fulfilled the *mitzvah,* and in turn, the species were presented to the others as a gift so that each could fulfill it properly ... "For what purpose does it mention that Rabban Gamliel bought it for one thousand *zuz?* — In order to let you know how precious they considered the opportunity of fulfilling a *mitzvah*" (*Succah* 41b).

Religious Ecstasy

◦§ It was the custom of R' Levi Yitzchak of Berditchev to remain awake the entire first night of Succos, anxiously awaiting daylight and the time for waving the *lulav.* When the prescribed time finally arrived, he would rush to perform the *mitzvah.* Once, Reb Levi Yitzchak eagerly reached out for his *esrog* which was in its box in a glass-doored cabinet. In his spiritual ecstasy he put his hand right through the glass, shattering it and cutting his hand in the process. But the Berditchever uttered the blessing and waved the Four Species with blood-stained hands, remaining totally oblivious to the pain.

Allusions

◦§ The kabbalistic masters observe that the three *hadasim* [willow branches] allude to the three Patriarchs; the two *aravos* [myrtle branches] to Moses and Aaron; the *lulav* to Joseph, and the *esrog* to David, King of Israel (*Vayikra Rabbah* 30:10).

◦§ "We accordingly bind three *hadasim* so we will recall thereby the chain of ancestry, and the holiness of Abraham, Isaac and Jacob, who were unified unwaveringly in their devotion to the Creator of the world, may His Name be Blessed. They always focused upward, and we, their descendants, emulate them by 'grasping the deeds of our forefathers in our hands' and totally unifying our hearts in the service of God" (*Seder HaYom*).

Na'anu'im / The Waving of the Species

◦§ As soon as one picks up the Four Species, he has fulfilled the obligation — this is the *mitzvah* on the Scriptural level. But in the words of *Rambam,* "The proper way of performing this *mitzvah* [מִצְוָה כְּהִלְכָתָהּ] is to pick up the *lulav* ... and move it out and back, upwards and downwards, and to shake the *lulav* three times in every direction" (*Hil. Lulav* 7:10). These "shakings" or "wavings" [נַעֲנוּעִים] are a *mitzvah* handed down by tradition. *Beis Shammai* and *Beis Hillel* debated how the shakings were to be co-ordinated with the verses of the *Hallel,* the cycle of psalms of praise recited on the festival (*Succah* 37b).

The meaning of these *na'anu'im* (shakings) is given in the Talmud (*ibid.*) as follows: "One waves them back and forth to Him Who is the Master of the four

directions; up and down, to Him Who is the Master of heaven and earth. Thus, the Four Species allude to God's creation of all existence, and testify that there is naught besides Him."

The Talmud also states: "One waves them back and forth to restrain harmful winds; up and down to restrain harmful dews." Since Succos is the time of judgment for water and rain for the entire year, the nature of the Four Species symbolizes our prayers for water: the esrog tree requires more water than others; palm trees grow best in valleys that have abundant water; myrtles and willows grow near water. In waving the Four Species in all six directions, we therefore symbolically say to God: Just as these Four Species cannot exist without water, so can the world not exist without water. And when You give us water, let no harmful winds or dew negate Your blessing.

The na'anu'im are made once when the mitzvah of holding the Four Species is performed, and during Hallel, at the places indicated in the Mishnah (Succah 37b) and Shulchan Aruch; see The Laws, p. 84.

Concerning the order of the na'anu'im, there are two popular customs: Eastwards, southwards, westwards, northwards, upwards, downwards; or southwards, northwards, eastwards, upwards, downwards, westwards (see Shulchan Aruch O.C. 651:10 with Ba'er Heitev).

◆§ [On the wording of the benedictions, see Ritual section page 114. The Laws of the Four Species are summarized on pages 82-89.]

Disposing of the Lulav

◆§ It is the custom of many to put away the lulav after Succos where it will not be disturbed, and to burn it together with the chametz erev Pesach (Minhagim).

The Water-Drawing Festivities

The Libation of Water

◆§ Apart from the daily and festival sacrifices offered in the Temple during Succos — most of which were accompanied by an offering of fine flour mixed with oil, and a libation of wine — the height of the season's joy was expressed through and during a libation of water.

Among the many reasons offered for this ceremony is that on Succos [which is the beginning of the rainy season in Eretz Yisrael (Meiri)] judgment is passed in regard to the rainfall (Mishnah Rosh Hashanah 1:2). The Gemara (ibid. 16) notes that the libation of water was performed only on Succos in order to invoke God's blessing on the year's rainfall in this time of judgment. "Pour out water before Me on the Festival," God is quoted as saying, as it were, "in order that your rains for the year may be blessed."

☐ As explained in the Yad Avraham commentary to ArtScroll Mishnah Succah 4:9, this special water libation was performed only during the seven days of Succos. All other libations in the Temple were of wine poured on the altar, but during the seven days of Succos water was poured simultaneously with the wine libation in conjunction with the daily burnt offering. This water pouring was

performed only in the morning, after the offering of the daily morning meal offering (Yoma 26b).

☐ This water libation is not mentioned specifically in the Torah. It was commanded to Moses orally on Sinai [הֲלָכָה לְמשֶׁה מִסִּינַי] (Succah 44a), and has the force of Scriptural law.

It is, however, alluded to in the Torah. As R' Yehudah ben Besaira noted, in the section (Numbers 29) describing the mussaf sacrifices of Succos the Torah inserts superfluous letters that spell the word מַיִם, water. In v. 19, describing the mussaf of the second day, the Torah uses the word וְנִסְכֵּיהֶם, their libation (rather than וְנִסְכָּהּ, its libation — the expression used for all the other days). Thus, there is an extra ם. For the sixth day the Torah uses וּנְסָכֶיהָ, lit. her libation (v. 31), providing an extra י. And in v. 33, describing the seventh, the Torah uses the word כְּמִשְׁפָּטָם rather than the word כַּמִּשְׁפָּט which appears on all the other days — again, an extra ם. The three extra letters spell מַיִם, water, an allusion to the Succos water-libation (Taanis 2b).

·☐ The libation of water was a ceremony to which great importance was attached. As recorded in the Mishnah (Succah ch. 4), a golden pitcher holding three lugim was filled by a Kohen with water from the Shiloach and brought into the Temple through the Water Gate, while the shofar was sounded. The water was then poured simultaneously with a wine libation into bowls atop the altar, one bowl for water and the other for wine. The water and wine mingled as they flowed through tubes under the bowls, leading to an underground passage to the Deep [תְּהוֹם]. According to another opinion, they flowed to an enclosed space beneath the altar. [According to this latter opinion, "once in seventy years the young Kohanim would climb down into this place and gather the solidified wine ..."]

Pelted with Esrogim

◆§ As noted above, the water libation is a הֲלָכָה לְמשֶׁה מִסִּינַי, oral tradition transmitted to Moses at Sinai. Accordingly, the Sadducees, who denied the validity of the oral tradition, refused to perform the libation properly. Not only that, they would seek to influence the Kohanim to pour the water on the ground instead of into the bowls. The Mishnah records that the people would ask the Kohen who performed the water libation to keep his hands high as he poured so that all could see that he was pouring it into the bowl, "for once someone [i.e. the Kohen who was a Sadducee] poured it over his feet [instead of into the proper bowl, thus invalidating the ceremony], and all the people pelted him with their esrogim."

☐ As related by Josephus Flavius (Antiquities 13:13, 5), the Hasmonean king Alexander Yannai, who was indeed a Sadducee, was pelted with esrogim while engaged in the sacrificial service. [Apparently Josephus was not familiar with the exact circumstances of this event.] The tragic sequel to this occurrence (as related by Josephus) was that Alexander's soldiers massacred six thousand of the congregants in the Temple (cf. Yossipon ch. 33).

The Festivities of the Beis HaSho'evah

◆§ The festivities associated with the drawing of the water for the libation on Succos

were the highpoint of the festival. These festivities, as Rashi explains, were in fulfillment of the verse in *Isaiah* [12:3] וּשְׁאַבְתֶּם מַיִם בְּשָׂשׂוֹן, *and you shall draw forth water with gladness.*

The Name

◄§ The name given to these festivities was שִׂמְחַת בֵּית הַשּׁוֹאֵבָה, *Simchas Beis HaSho'evah,* familiarly translated "The Rejoicing of the Place of the Water Drawing."

□ There is a difference of opinion among the Amoraim as to whether the word in the *mishnah* is *sho'evah* ("drawing") or *chashuvah* ("important"). Why *chashuvah?* "It is an important *mitzvah,* and dates from the Six Days of Creation" (for it was then that the *shisin* — the canals under the altar through which the libation drained to the Deep — were created). And why *sho'evah?* According to the Babylonian Talmud, this term refers to the *she'ivah* (drawing up) of the water, as hinted by the verse וּשְׁאַבְתֶּם מַיִם בְּשָׂשׂוֹן, *And you shall draw forth water with gladness.* In the *Yerushalmi* we find a different interpretation of the term: "Because from there they drew the spirit of prophecy" שֶׁמִּשָּׁם שׁוֹאֲבִים רוּחַ הַקֹּדֶשׁ). It is told that the prophet Yonah ben Amitai was one of those who made the pilgrimage on the Festivals; when he joined the rejoicing of *Beis HaSho'evah* the spirit of prophecy descended on him; this teaches us that the spirit of prophecy rests only on a joyous heart, as Scripture teaches: *"And it came to pass, when the musician played, that the hand of God was upon him* וְהָיָה כְּנַגֵּן הַמְנַגֵּן; וַתְּהִי עָלָיו יַד ה'; II *Kings* 3:15]." *(Tos. Succah* 50b; for additional information, see R' S. Y. Zevin, *HaMoadim Behalachah* citing *Yerushalmi Succah* 5:1.)

□ In his commentary to the Mishnah, Rambam comments tersely that בֵּית הַשּׁוֹאֵבָה [lit. *the place of water drawing*] was the name given the place that was prepared for the rejoicing, apparently because the water drawing ceremony took place there. Thus שִׂמְחַת בֵּית הַשּׁוֹאֵבָה is rendered the *Rejoicing* [which was carried out] *in the Place of Water Drawing.* This is consistent with the view ascribed to Rambam that the rejoicing which took place in the Temple was in honor of Succos, and was not integrally connected with the water drawing ceremonies. Therefore, this particular rejoicing was identified according to the *area* where it took place, rather than with the ceremony. R' Y.F. Perla *(Sefer HaMitzvos, R' Saadiah Gaon* 5:3) points out that for this reason it is called שִׂמְחַת בֵּית הַשּׁוֹאֵבָה, the Rejoicing of the 'Place' of Water Drawing, rather than merely שִׂמְחַת הַשּׁוֹאֵבָה, the Rejoicing of the Water Drawing *(ibid.).*

Preparation is Primary

◄§ *Imrei Emes* asks: The essence of the *mitzvah* is the *libation* of the water; why, then, did the Sages place such emphasis on celebrating the *drawing* of the water? We learn from this that the preparation is sometimes greater than the *mitzvah* itself [because the effort and enthusiasm associated with the preparation instills a profound influence on a person].

The Rejoicing during Temple Times

◄§ So intense were the festivities associated with the water drawing that the Sages in

the Mishnah are quoted as saying: "Whoever did not see the rejoicing of the *Beis HaSho'evah,* never saw rejoicing in his lifetime."

☐ This is how Rambam in *Hilchas Lulav* describes the festivities:

"Although it is a *mitzvah* to rejoice on all festivals, there was a day of special rejoicing in the Temple during the festival of Succos, in accordance with the verse, *And you shall rejoice before HASHEM, your God, seven days (Lev. 23:40).* What was their procedure? On the eve of the first day of the festival, an upper section was prepared in the Temple for women and a lower section for men to ensure that the sexes did not mix. Rejoicing began at the termination of the first day of the festival; on each day of *Chol Hamoed* it began after the regular 'tamid' afternoon sacrifice had been offered, and went on for the rest of the day and all of the following night.

"What form did this rejoicing take? Fifes were sounded; they played harps, lyres, and cymbals; whoever could play a musical instrument did so, and whoever could sing, sang. Others would stamp their feet, slap their thighs, clap their hands, leap, or dance, each one to the best of his ability, while they recited songs and hymns of praise. However, this rejoicing did not override the Sabbath or the first day of the festival.

☐ "It is a *mitzvah* to make this rejoicing as great as possible. But participation in it was not open to anyone who wished to participate. Only the great scholars in Israel, heads of yeshivos, members of the Sanhedrin, elders, and men distinguished for their piety and good deeds — only these danced and clapped, made music, and rejoiced in the Temple during the festival of Succos. All others — men and women — came to watch and listen" *(ibid.).*

The "Great Improvement"

◆§ Rambam's reference to a specially constructed upper section for women to separate the sexes is mentioned in the Talmud, *Succah* 51b, where it is called תִּיקוּן גָּדוֹל, *A great improvement.*

The Mishnah there reads: "At the conclusion of the first festival day of Succos they would descend to the Court of the Women [in the Temple] where they had made a great improvement."

The *Gemara* explains: "What was the 'great improvement'? R' Elazar replied: As we have learned ... originally the women used to sit within the Court of the Women while the men were outside, but as this caused levity, it was instituted that the women should sit outside and the men within. As this, however, still led to levity, it was instituted that the women should sit above [on a gallery constructed for them] and the men below."

☐ The *mechitzah* or dividing wall currently separating the men and the women in synagogues is based on this separation of men and women in the Temple. The practice of building upper galleries in the large synagogues derives from the "great improvement" enacted in the Temple.

☐ Rambam *(Lulav 8:12)* writes that the great improvement was actually made *before* Succos. According to this, it is as if the mishnah had said, "At the conclusion of the first festival day of Succos they descended to the Women's Court where they **had** made a great improvement." *Aruch LaNer* (51b)

Shoshanim L'David, and *Mishneh Lechem* explain that the erection of a balcony in the Women's Court on the Intermediate Days would be a desecration of the festival.

The Mishnah continues ...

❧ "There were golden candelabra there, each one with four golden beakers at the top; four ladders were placed at each candelabrum; there were four youths from among the young *Kohanim,* and in their hands, pitchers of oil containing one hundred and twenty *lugim* [*Tiferes Yisrael:* thirty *lugim* to each youth], which they emptied into each of the beakers. From worn-out trousers of the priestly garments and from their girdles, they would tear [strips of cloth for wicks] and with these they would kindle [the candelabra]. And there was not a single courtyard in Jerusalem that did not shine with the light of *Beis HaSho'evah.*" A *baraisa* adds: [So bright was the glow of the candelabra that] "a woman would sit and sort wheat by the light of *Beis HaSho'evah.*"

[In praising the physical prowess of these young *Kohanim,* each of whom carried thirty *lugim* up a fifty-cubit ladder, the *Gemara* states that they were superior in strength to the son of Marta daughter of Baitus. He was a *Kohen* who could carry two sides of a huge ox and walk with them in a slow, dignified manner up the ramp of the altar to deposit them on the altar.]

☐ We read further in the Mishnah: "Men of piety and zeal (חֲסִידִים וְאַנְשֵׁי מַעֲשֶׂה) with fiery torches in their hands would dance in front [of the assemblage] reciting words of song and praise. And the Levites with harps (כִּנּוֹרוֹת), lutes (נְבָלִים), cymbals (מְצַלְתַּיִים), trumpets (חֲצֹצְרוֹת) and countless musical instruments [stood] on the fifteen steps that descend from the Courtyard of the Israelites to the Women's Court, corresponding to the fifteen Songs of Ascent [the fifteen Psalms beginning *Shir HaMaalos* (Psalms 120-134)], where Levites were stationed with musical instruments, singing songs of praise.

"Two *Kohanim* stood at the Upper Gate that descends from the Court of the Israelites to the Women's Court, with two trumpets in their hands. When the crier called out, they sounded a *tekiah,* a *teruah,* and a *tekiah* (Rashi: 'This was a signal to go and fill [the flask] with water for the libation from the Shiloach.' [When] they reached the tenth step, they sounded a *tekiah,* a *teruah, and a tekiah.* Whey they reached the Court they sounded a *tekiah,* a *teruah,* and a *tekiah.* They would continue sounding the trumpets until they reached the gate leading out [to the] east.

"When they reached the gate leading out to the east, they turned to the west and said, 'Our forefathers, who were in this place [with] their backs toward the Sanctuary and their faces toward the east, bowed eastward toward the sun. But as for us — our eyes are toward *YAH.*' R' Yehudah says: They repeated and said, 'We are for *YAH* and toward *YAH* are our eyes.' "

The Sages Rejoice

❧ It was said of the Talmudic sage R' Simeon b. Gamliel that, "when he rejoiced at the *Simchas Beis HaSho'evah* he used to juggle eight lighted torches and they did not touch one another ...

"Levi used to juggle in the presence of Rabbi Yehudah HaNassi with eight knives, Samuel before King Shapur with eight glasses of wine, and Abaye before

Rabbah with eight eggs, or as some say, with four eggs. It was taught: R' Yehoshua ben Chananiah stated, When we used to rejoice at the place of the water drawing, our eyes saw no sleep. How was this? At the first hour there was the daily morning sacrifice, after which we were occupied with prayer, then with the additional sacrifice, then to the house of study, then the eating and drinking, then the afternoon prayer, then the daily evening sacrifice, and finally the Rejoicing at the Place of the Water Drawing [all night]" *(Succah 53a).*

Rejoicing out of Sheer Love of God

⏤§ Rejoicing in the performance of a *mitzvah* and in love for God Who had ordained the *mitzvah* is a great act of Divine service. One who refrains from such
· rejoicing deserves punishment as it is written, *Because you did not serve HASHEM your God with gladness, and with goodness of heart (Deut.* 28:47). Whoever is arrogant and is concerned with his own dignity on such occasions, is a sinner as well as a fool ... However, one who humbles himself on such occasions, is indeed great and deserves honor, since he serves HASHEM out of sheer love ... Greatness and honor involve rejoicing before HASHEM as it is said *King David was leaping and dancing before HASHEM, etc. (II Samuel* 6:16) *(Rambam ibid.).*

Hallel

The Entire Hallel

⏤§ On each of the seven days of Succos and on the concluding holiday, Shemini Atzeres, the entire *Hallel (Psalms* 113-118) is recited [see *Succah* 4:1, 8)]. This is in contrast to Pesach when the entire *Hallel* is recited only on the first day (in the Diaspora on the first two days). The Talmud *(Arachin* 10a-b) explains that this distinction between Succos and Pesach is based on the difference between their respective *mussaf* offerings *(Numbers* 28:19-25; 29:13-34). During Pesach the *mussaf* offerings consist of the same number of oxen, rams, sheep, and goats for each day. On Succos, although the numbers of rams, sheep, and goats are the same every day, the amount of oxen is diminished by one on each successive day. Rashi *(Taanis* 28b, s.v. יחיד) and Tosafos (loc. cit., s.v. ויום) explain that this changing number of offerings indicates that Succos should be considered a set of one-day festivals, each of which requires its own recitation of *Hallel,* whereas all of Pesach should be regarded as a single festival spread out over a seven-day period, for which a single full *Hallel* at the beginning of the festival is sufficient.

[Although the entire *Hallel* is not recited on the last six days of Pesach, an abridged version which omits the first eleven verses of Psalms 115 and 116 is recited on these days. The same verses are omitted on Rosh Chodesh. This abridged form is popularly known as 'half *Hallel.'*]

☐ [The more familiar interpretation of why only 'half' *Hallel* is said on the intermediate and final day(s) of Pesach is that the Egyptians drowned on the seventh day of Pesach and it would be inappropriate to offer praise to God thereon. As the Talmud [*Megillah* 10b] records, the angels wished to utter songs of praise to God upon the drowning of the Egyptians, but He rebuked them saying: "My handiwork [the Egyptians] are drowning in the sea and you utter praise!" Accordingly, so as not to make the Intermediate Days of Pesach appear more

important than the final day(s), we recite only 'half' *Hallel* throughout the Intermediate Days of Pesach as well *(Turei Zahav, Orach Chaim* 490:3; see *Beis Yosef* there).]

Hakhel / Assemblage

The Biblical Command [*Deut.* 31:10-13]

וַיְצַו מֹשֶׁה אוֹתָם לֵאמֹר מִקֵּץ שֶׁבַע שָׁנִים בְּמֹעֵד שְׁנַת הַשְּׁמִטָּה בְּחַג הַסֻּכּוֹת: בְּבוֹא כָל־יִשְׂרָאֵל לֵרָאוֹת אֶת־פְּנֵי יהוה אֱלֹהֶיךָ בַּמָּקוֹם אֲשֶׁר יִבְחָר תִּקְרָא אֶת־הַתּוֹרָה הַזֹּאת נֶגֶד כָּל־יִשְׂרָאֵל בְּאָזְנֵיהֶם: הַקְהֵל אֶת־הָעָם הָאֲנָשִׁים וְהַנָּשִׁים וְהַטַּף וְגֵרְךָ אֲשֶׁר בִּשְׁעָרֶיךָ לְמַעַן יִשְׁמְעוּ וּלְמַעַן יִלְמְדוּ וְיָרְאוּ אֶת־ יהוה אֱלֹהֵיכֶם וְשָׁמְרוּ לַעֲשׂוֹת אֶת־כָּל־דִּבְרֵי הַתּוֹרָה הַזֹּאת: וּבְנֵיהֶם אֲשֶׁר לֹא־יָדְעוּ יִשְׁמְעוּ וְלָמְדוּ לְיִרְאָה אֶת־יהוה אֱלֹהֵיכֶם כָּל־הַיָּמִים אֲשֶׁר אַתֶּם חַיִּים עַל־הָאֲדָמָה אֲשֶׁר אַתֶּם עֹבְרִים אֶת־הַיַּרְדֵּן שָׁמָּה לְרִשְׁתָּהּ:

[10] *Moses then instructed them saying: At the end of each seven years, at the ordained time of the Shemittah year, at the festival of Succos,* [11] *when all Israel comes to appear before HASHEM your God in the place which He shall choose, you shall read this Torah in the presence of all Israel in their hearing.* [12] *Assemble the people — the men, women, little children and the proselytes within your gates — that they may hear and that they may learn and revere HASHEM, your God, and observantly perform all the words of this Torah.* [13] *Their children, too, who have not known, will listen and learn to revere HASHEM, your God, all the days you live on the land that you are about to cross the Jordan to occupy.*

□ Thus, as Rambam codifies the law in *Mishneh Torah, Chagigah* 3:1-17:

"It is a positive commandment to assemble all Israelites, men, women, and children after the close of every *Shemittah* year when they go up to make the pilgrimage, and in their hearing to read chapters of the Torah that make them zealous in the *mitzvos* and encourage them in the true religion ...

"When do they read? At the end of the first holiday of the Succos Festival, which begins the Intermediate Days of the festival in the eighth year. It is the king who reads in their hearing ... He may read sitting, but if he reads standing it is deemed praiseworthy. Where does he read? From the beginning of *Deuteronomy* to the end of the section שְׁמַע יִשְׂרָאֵל, *Hear O Israel* ... (*Deut.* 6:4), and he skips to וְהָיָה אִם שָׁמֹעַ, *And it shall come to pass if you shall diligently listen* ... (*Deut.* 1:13), then skips to עַשֵּׂר תְּעַשֵּׂר, *You shall surely tithe* ... (*Deut.* 14:22ff.), reading from *You shall surely tithe* continuing until the end of the Blessings and the Curses (*Deut.* 27:15-28:69) as far as מִלְּבַד הַבְּרִית אֲשֶׁר כָּרַת אִתָּם בְּחֹרֵב, *aside from the covenant that He made with them in Choreb,* then he stops."

"How does he read? They would sound trumpets throughout Jerusalem to assemble the people. They would bring a high wooden platform and erect it in the center of the Women's Court. The king would ascend and sit on it so that

they could hear his reading. All Jews who went up for the festival would gather around him; the attendant of the community would take a Torah Scroll and give it to the head of the community, and the head of the community would give it to the deputy (סְגָן), and the deputy to the High Priest and the High Priest to the king, in order to honor him through the service of many men. The king receives it standing, but if he wishes he may sit. He opens and looks in it; then recites a blessing as do all who read the Torah in the synagogue. He reads the chapters we have cited until he concludes. Then he rolls up the Scroll and recites a blessing after it as do those who bless in synagogues, and then he added seven benedictions …

"If the day of Assembly fell on the Sabbath, it is postponed until after the Sabbath because of the trumpet blowing and the supplications, which do not override the Sabbath."

Children, too

◄§ *"Assemble the people — the men, women and little children ..."*

The men came to learn; the women came to hear. But why must the little children come? — In order to grant reward to those that bring them *(Chagigah 3a)*.

☐ Actually, Arizal maintained, the Torah had no need to *command* parents to bring their children; we may assume that parents would certainly bring their children with them in any event — otherwise, where would they leave them? However, if parents had brought their children not in obedience to God's command, but only for lack of a convenient alternative, they would not have earned a reward for doing so. In order to make the presence of the children a *mitzvah* — meritorious act — and one for which the parents are entitled to a reward — the Torah specifies that they are to be brought. This was the intent of the Sages' remark: "To grant reward to those who bring the children." — The Torah's command that parents bring the children was given only to give the parents reward for what they would do in any event.

☐ By bringing their children to hear the king read the Torah, parents earn great merit, because they signify their dedication to God's word, not only for themselves but for their precious children. Thereby they assure the future strength of Torah in Jewry. Such a great assemblage makes a lasting impression even on children who are too young to study the Torah, but who will never forget the spectacle of the entire nation gathered to hear its king read the Torah *(R' Hirsch)*.

Koheles on Succos

The Futility of Material Possessions

◄§ King Solomon's Book of *Koheles* [Ecclesiastes] is read on the *Shabbos* of *Chol HaMoed* Succos [or on Shemini Atzeres if it occurs on *Shabbos*]. The most familiar reason why this Book is read on Succos is that it describes the futility of worldly striving and extols the virtue of fear of God and His *mitzvos*. This theme

is especially appropriate to Succos, for the *succah* symbolizes the futility of material possessions and encourages man to live frugally under God's protection (*Magen Avraham;* see *Sefer HaManhig*).

□ According to *Abudraham, Koheles* is read on Succos because it was at the *Hakhel* assembly that King Solomon preached the exhortation contained in that Book.

□ *Darkei Moshe* records that the association of *Koheles* and Succos might be based on the passage in that Book [11:2]: *Distribute portions to seven or to eight.* According to the Midrash, the verse alludes to the seven day Succos festival followed by Shemini Atzeres, the eighth festival day. [A full commentary and Overview to *Koheles* are available in the ArtScroll Series.]

Hoshanos and Hoshana Rabbah

Hakafah-circuits

◆§ On each day of Succos, a Torah Scroll is brought to the *bimah* [the table from which the Torah is read]. There it is held by one of the congregants while the rest of the congregation, each person with his Four Species in hand, circles the *bimah* and recites the *Hoshana* liturgy of the day. On the first six days of Succos, one *hakafah*-circuit is made, and on the seventh day, Hoshana Rabbah, seven *hakafos* are made.

Though this custom is not mentioned in the Talmud it is found in the tenth century *siddurim* of R' Amram and R' Saadiah Gaon and, indeed, it may very well have been practiced even in Talmudic times. The liturgy said by Ashkenazic communities during the *hakafos* was composed by *R' Elazar HaKalir,* one of the earliest *paytanim.*

Origin of the Hakafah-circuits

◆§ The Mishnah (*Succah* 4:5) describes the encircling of the altar with *aravah* [willow] branches in the Holy Temple:

"How was the *mitzvah* of the willow [performed]? There was a place below Jerusalem called Motza. They descended there, gathered from there large willow branches, and came and stood them up against the sides of the altar, with their tops drooping over the top of the altar.

"They blew [on the trumpet] a *tekiah,* a *teruah,* and a *tekiah.* Each day they would circle the altar one time and say, אָנָּא ה' הוֹשִׁיעָה נָּא, *Please HASHEM bring salvation now;* אָנָּא ה' הַצְלִיחָה נָא, *please HASHEM bring success now!'* R' Yehudah says: [They would say] אֲנִי וָהוֹ הוֹשִׁיעָה נָּא,*ANI VAHO* [two mystical Names of God], *bring salvation now!'* But on that day [i.e., Hoshana Rabbah] they circled the altar seven times.

"When they left what did they say? 'Beauty is yours, O altar! Beauty is yours, O altar!' R' Eliezer says: [They said,] 'To YAH [an abbreviated form of the Ineffable Name] and to you, O altar! To YAH and to you, O altar!' "

□ This part of the Temple service was conveyed to Moses at Sinai [הֲלָכָה לְמֹשֶׁה מִסִּינַי] and, though it is not specified in Scripture, it has the status of Torah law.

Throughout the era of the First Temple it was limited to the Temple Courtyard. When the Second Temple was built, the *aravah* services were broadened. The prophets Chaggai, Zechariah, and Malachi, who were members of the Great Assembly, instituted the custom that on Hoshana Rabbah, Jews could take part in the *aravah* service wherever they were, even outside the Temple *(Succah 44a)*.

After the Temple was destroyed, the practice of circuits and the *aravah* service came to an end — for a while. But the people of Israel did not forget. Just as the prophets extended the *aravah* service throughout the Land in happier times, so the collective soul of Israel would not remain stifled by the tragedy of exile. We do not know precisely when, but perhaps in Talmudic times or during the time of the *geonim* who headed the great academies of Babylon after the end of the Talmudic era, the people instituted a זֵכֶר לְמִקְדָּשׁ, *a reminder of the Temple.*

Holy Arks were opened and Torah Scrolls were withdrawn and taken to the *bimah.* Around them, congregations with *lulav* and *esrog* in hand made their circuits and prayed for God's help.

□ Vilna Gaon *(Orach Chaim* 660:1) explains that when the Temple stood, its altar was the focus of a nation seeking God's help and His blessing of prosperity. The · Temple is gone but the focus remains. At the table where the Torah is read stands a man holding a Torah Scroll — and as R' Chiya, a first generation *Amora,* teaches *(Yalkut Tehillim* 703) — the scene represents the altar. The *bimah,* the table from which the Torah is read, represents the altar's extension into every realm of life and every corner of the universe. In the person of the man holding the Torah, the existence of Israel is embodied, and around him walk his fellow Jews, *lulav*-bundle in hand, saying הוֹשַׁעְנָא, [*Hoshana*] *Please save!,* just as their ancestors did in the sacred precincts of old.

□ R' Yisrael Meir HaKohen, better known as the *Chofetz Chaim,* enlarges upon a theme suggested by Vilna Gaon and explains that the connection between the altar in the Holy Temple and the *bimah* in the synagogue is based on a Talmudical exegesis regarding the Covenant Between the Parts:

When God promised Abraham that he would be given the Land of Canaan as an inheritance, Abraham said, *'My Lord HASHEM/ELOHIM, whereby shall I know that I am to inherit it?' (Genesis* 15:8). [Now it is incongruous with Abraham's image as the Prime Believer — who allowed himself to be thrown into the fiery furnace of Kasdim and who unquestioningly followed God's call to leave his father's house — that he be so lacking in faith as to incredulously request a definite sign and reassurance that God would keep His promise.

The Talmud *(Megillah* 31b) explains Abraham's question: Abraham said before the Holy One, Blessed is He, 'Master of the world, perhaps, Heaven forbid, Israel will sin before You, and You will do to them as You have done to the generation of the Flood or the generation of the Dispersion!' When God responded that He would not do so, Abraham asked, 'Master of the world, whereby shall I know [what to teach my children regarding how they may atone for their sins *(Rashi)*]?

God replied, *'Bring Me three heifers ...' (Genesis* 15:9) [i.e., the altar sacrifices will atone for their sins *(Rashi)*].

Once again Abraham asked, 'Master of the world, this is fine for the era of the Holy Temple. But in the period after the Destruction of the Temple, what will become of them?'

'I have already set forth [the Torah passages relating to] the order of the

sacrifices,' replied God. 'Wherever they read them, I shall consider them as having actually brought the sacrifices before Me, and I shall forgive their sins.'

Thus, concludes the Chofetz Chaim, if the reading of the Torah passage takes the place of the actual sacrifices, then the *bimah* upon which the Torah is read signifies the Temple altar *(Mishnah Berurah 660:1)*.

Once each day, seven times on the seventh day

◄§ R' Chiya further taught *(Yalkut Tehillim 703)* that the *hakafah*-circuits of Succos correspond to the encirclement of Jericho by Joshua and the Israelite army as described in the sixth chapter of *Joshua: And HASHEM said to Joshua, 'See I have given you Jericho ... and you shall go around the city ... encircle the city once. Thus shall you do for six days ... On the seventh day you shall go around the city seven times' ... And he [Joshua] caused the Ark of HASHEM to go around the city, encircling one time ... So they did for six days ... on the seventh day ... they went around the city in this manner seven times ... and the wall sank into its place ...*

☐ The connection between Jericho and Hoshana Rabbah is explained by R' Bachya (in *Kad HaKemach*): On this seventh day of Succos, Israel completed its decreasing order of seventy sacrifices that served to invoke God's protection on the gentile nations, and also invoked the greatest benefit they could gain — that they be shorn of their illusory power and become subservient to the nation that represents God's will on earth. So the circuits of the altar and of the *bimah* are both evocative of Jericho, not merely in commemoration of an ancient event, but of the continuing goal of human history: that evil disappear and mankind recognize the purpose for which it was created.

First it was Jericho. Then it was all seventy nations. Now it is primarily Edom, the embodiment of evil, descendant of Esau and Amalek, initiator of the current, final exile that has plunged man into nearly twenty centuries of darkness.

The Hoshana Prayers

◄§ The prayers recited during the *hakafah*-circuits are called *Hoshanos* because their constant refrain — reminiscent of the one used in the Temple — is הוֹשַׁעְנָא [*Hoshana*], *please save*. The prayers used in the Ashkenazic rite were composed by the medieval *paytan*, R' Elazar HaKalir. Each contains twenty-two verses, the initial letters of which form an alphabetical acrostic, following the order of the *Aleph Beis*. Although each prayer has its own theme, the primary theme of all is the plea — repeated after each verse — 'Hoshana!'

☐ Both spiritual and material prosperity form the themes of the *Hoshanos*. The first three of the seven prayers of the Hoshana Rabbah circuits are requests for: the return of the *Shechinah* [Divine Presence] to the Land of Israel; restoration of Jerusalem and the Holy Temple; and redemption of the Israelite nation from exile. The next three are pleas for the material goods we need to devote our time to a spiritual life: sustenance in general; rainfall and abundant crops; and protection of our crops from destructive forces. The seventh and final *hakafah* is accompanied by a prayer that we be successful in emulating the achievements of our forebears, our spiritual models, and that we be released from our exile in the merit of their deeds.

☐ After the seven circuits, more prayers are recited, most of them for abundant rainfall — for on Succos the world is judged with regard to the coming year's rainfall — and culminating with a soulful plea for the coming of Elijah, the herald who will proclaim the arrival of the Messiah.

Time of Judgment

◄§ 'At four junctures of the year the world is judged: On Pesach for the grain; on Shavuos for the fruit of the tree; on Rosh Hashanah all who walk the earth pass before Him ...; and on Succos for the water' (Mishnah, Rosh Hashanah 1:2).

☐ Succos in general and its seventh day, Hoshanah Rabbah, in particular, are periods of judgment in two ways: one specific and the other general.

Despite the awesome nature of the Ten Days of Repentance from Rosh Hashanah to Yom Kippur, not all is decided during this period of general judgment. Once the overall decisions have been made for humanity as a whole and for each individual in particular, God determines what will be done with regard to particular needs. On Pesach He judges man with regard to the grain crops, on Shavuos with regard to the fruit crops, and on Succos with regard to the water supply (Rosh Hashanah 16a). The decision regarding water is not rendered until the end of Succos; for this reason, certain specific mitzvos of Succos revolve around water: in the Temple, water libations were offered at the altar; the mitzvah of the Four Species is performed with plants that depend on abundant water for their existence; and the willow, which assumes the spotlight on the climatic day of the water-judgment, Hoshana Rabbah, is identified by the Torah (Leviticus 23:40) as a plant that grows alongside streams.

Hoshana Rabbah—Akin to Yom Kippur

◄§ But Hoshana Rabbah has a significance broader than the universal need for water. The Zohar (Tzav 31b) describes it as a judgment day akin to Yom Kippur itself, for on Hoshana Rabbah the parchments containing the Yom Kippur decrees are made final. Consequently, Hoshana Rabbah assumes special importance as a day of prayer and repentance. On Rosh Hashanah all people were judged. The righteous were given a favorable judgment, those found wanting — but not totally evil — were given until Yom Kippur to repent. If they failed to do so, the verdict against them was written and sealed, but not yet "delivered." That is not done until Hoshana Rabbah, a day when Jews assemble in prayer, dedication, and supplication. The joy of Succos reaches its climax not in revelry but in devotion. In His mercy God finds ample reason to tear up the parchment bearing harsher sentences, as it were, and replace them with brighter tidings (see Overview to ArtScroll Hoshanos, pp. xxi-xxiii).

◄§ Other customs which have arisen owing to the day's status as a time of Divine judgment are cited in the halachic literature.

☐ It is customary to remain awake and spend the entire night of Hoshana Rabbah reading from the Torah and Psalms. The particular order to be followed is printed in special tikunim for this purpose (Magen Avraham 664).

☐ Extra lights are lit in the synagogue (Shulchan Aruch 664:1). The psalms added to the Yom Tov morning services are recited on Hoshana Rabbah as well, except

for the *Nishmas* prayer which is omitted. At that point, the service reverts to that of a *Chol HaMoed* day. When the Torah Scroll is removed from the Ark, the liturgy reverts to that of *Yom Tov (Rama)*. Sabbath garments are worn by the congregants, and the *chazzan* wears the white *kittel* worn on Yom Kippur. [It is customary to recite many sections of the liturgy with the melody reserved for Rosh Hashanah and Yom Kippur.] During the *mussaf* prayer, the full *Kedushah*, usually reserved for the Sabbath and *Yom Tov*, is recited in place of the abridged form used on the other days of *Chol HaMoed* and Rosh Chodesh *(Mishnah Berurah)*.

☐ Even forms of labor permitted during *Chol HaMoed* are abstained from until the morning services have ended *(Rama)*. Some people do not even handle money at this time *(Levush)*.

The Aravah Ceremony Today

◄§ The practice of taking willow twigs on Hoshana Rabbah was instituted in remembrance of the Temple observance. In the words of Rambam *(Hil. Lulav 7:22)*: "Since this willow twig is not specifically mentioned in the Torah, we do not take it all seven days in commemoration of the Temple ceremonies. Only on the seventh day alone do we take it in present times."

☐ Though one willow twig suffices for this *mitzvah* the widely accepted custom is to take five twigs. This is based on the procedure set forth by Arizal *(Mishnah Berurah 664:16)*.

☐ There is a difference of opinion as to how this *mitzvah* is accomplished. Rashi holds that the willow twig is held and waved. This has its counterpart in the Temple ceremony, in which, according to Rashi *(Succah 43b s.v. והביאום)*, the willow branches were also waved [probably for the same reason as the waving of the *lulav;* see above]. Rambam rules that the twigs should be beaten on the ground, a utensil, or a piece of furniture two or three times. This, too, is based on the Temple procedure, where palm fronds were beaten on the earth *(Mishnah, Succah 4:6)*. R' Yosef Karo *(Orach Chaim 664:4)* rules that beating the twig is sufficient, but Rama *(ibid.)* adds that the (Ashkenazic) custom is to do both — waving and beating. Many follow the custom of Arizal and beat the *aravah* on the ground [and not on a utensil or furniture] exactly five times.

☐ An interesting interpretation of the practice of beating the *aravah*-bundle is given in a responsum ხ, R' Zemach Gaon *(Teshuvos HaGeonim Shaarei Teshuvah, 340)*. The leaves of the willow are shaped like the lips and these twigs have the purpose of atoning for the sins of the lips. We beat them on the earth to symbolize our resolution that from now on we will not sin with our lips again, but rather we will *'put his mouth to the dust ...' (Lamentations 3:29)*.

R' Zemach cites a second interpretation in the name of the ancients. During the preceding holidays — Rosh Hashanah and Yom Kippur — Satan incites God's Attributes of Judgment against Israel. But now, after we have accumulated many *mitzvos*, we are confident that no one's lips, not even Satan's, can harm us. So we beat the symbolic lips — the willow — to the earth.

☐ *Orchos Chaim (664:1)* points out the significance of a custom being instituted זֵכֶר לַמִּקְדָּשׁ, *in remembrance of the Temple*, to be performed on Hoshanah

Rabbah, the twenty-first day of Tishrei. For it was on this day that the Prophet Haggai (2:9) received the prophecy culminating in: *Greater shall be the glory of this latter* [i.e., Second] *Temple than that of the First ... and in this place shall I establish peace ...*

Excerpts from the Hoshana liturgy

◆§ הוֹשַׁעְנָא כְּלִילַת יוֹפִי — *Please save* [the city that is] *perfectly beautiful.*

Strangely, Scripture refers to two cities with the appellation כְּלִילַת יוֹפִי, *perfectly beautiful*: Jerusalem *(Lamentations 2:15)* and Tyre *(Ezekiel 27:3)*. But there is a difference. When speaking of Jerusalem the verse reads: *The city of which* **they** *said, 'Perfectly beautiful!'* That is, others described the city in this manner. Of Tyre, however, the prophet states: *Tyre,* **you** *have said, 'I am perfectly beautiful!'* These are words of boasting and self-praise, others did not see her in this light. This is the meaning of the folk saying: [Believe] not what her mother says of her, but what her neighbors say of her *(Midrash Tehillim 48:3).*

◆§ כָּל שִׂיחַ תַּדְשֵׁא וְתוֹשִׁיעַ — *All trees, let sprout and save.*

R' Naftali of Ropshitz explains this verse homiletically: The word שִׂיחַ, *trees*, may also be translated *speech* or *conversation*. Sometimes an extremely righteous person is able to exercise his influence in heaven by merely mentioning what is lacking. In his merit, the void will be filled even before he exerts his energies and offers prayers for Divine interception. For example, when asked the health of an ill person, one often replies, 'He is in need of a cure!' We pray that these few words be sufficient to effect that cure. Thus: *All conversation, let sprout — and thereby bring salvation.*

◆§ שַׁעֲרֵי שָׁמַיִם פְּתַח — *Open the gates of heaven.*

In his kabbalistic work *Pri Etz Chaim*, R' Yitzchak Luria, the famed Arizal, explains that the divergent liturgies which have arisen among the Jews are based upon the different life's purpose of the twelve tribes of Israel. Since each tribe's specific spiritual task in this world differed from all the others, the prayer services of each were necessarily different. When the nation was driven from its land and the tribes became intermingled, portions of the various tribal prayers were adapted by others until many forms of the liturgy became prevalent. The prophet Ezekiel (48:31-34) speaks of twelve gateways corresponding to the twelve tribes. Arizal teaches that the gateways alluded to are the portals by which our prayers enter heaven. But since each of the tribes used its own liturgy which complemented its life's work, twelve gateways were needed. It is these gates that we ask God to open, that our prayers may enter *(Iyun Tefillah).*

☐ [For a full treatment of the *Hoshanos* liturgy, see *Hoshanos, ArtScroll* edition. The festivals of Shemini Atzeres and Simchas Torah will אי"ה be treated in a separate forthcoming volume in the ArtScroll Festivals Series.]

❧ Observance /
Selected Laws and Customs

The Days before Succos

The Sabbath

The Succah

The Four Species

—Rabbi Hersh Goldwurm

✍ Selected Laws and Customs

compiled by Rabbi Hersh Goldwurm

This digest cannot cover all eventualities and should be regarded merely as a guide to enable the reader to familiarize himself with the complex laws of the *mitzvos* central to the Yom Tov. It should not be taken as a substitute for the source texts, but as a learning and familiarizing tool. For halachic questions, one should consult the *Shulchan Aruch* and its commentaries and/or a halachic authority.

The laws and customs have been culled, in the main, from the most widely accepted authorities: the *Shulchan Aruch Orach Chaim* [here abbreviated O.C.]; *Mishnah Berurah* [M.B.]; and R' Ephraim Zalman Margulies' classic work, *Matteh Ephraim*, on the laws and customs of the period from Rosh Chodesh Elul through Succos.

When a particular *halachah* is in dispute, we generally follow the ruling of *Mishnah Berurah*. On occasion, however (usually when *Mishnah Berurah* does not give a definitive ruling), we cite more than one opinion.

✍ The Days before Succos

1. One should begin to build the *succah*, if possible, on *Motza'ei Yom Kippur* (the evening following Yom Kippur), in order to go from one *mitzvah* to the next (*Rama O.C.* 624:5), and complete its construction on the next day (*M.B.* 624:19; *Rama* 625:1).

2. One should begin *Shacharis* early on the morning after Yom Kippur (*Magen Avraham* 624:7), so as not give Satan the pretext to denounce Israel by saying that the people shirk their duties as soon as Yom Kippur is over (*Shelah* cited in *Machatzis HaShekel*).

3. The days between Yom Kippur and Succos are festive, because they are the anniversary of the fourteen-day dedication of the Holy Temple by King Solomon (see *I Kings* 8:2, 65; *II Chronicles* 5:3, *Moed Kattan* 9a), which began on the eighth day of Tishrei. We commemorate this by assigning quasi-festival status to these days. *Tachanun* is omitted, as is the prayer אָב הָרַחֲמִים, *Father of Compassion*, before Mussaf. Also, one may not fast on a *yahrzeit* (*Matteh Ephraim* 624:2; cf. *Rama* in O.C. 284:7).

4. On the *Minchah* of the Sabbath afternoon before Succos, צִדְקָתְךָ, *Your Righteousness*, is not said (*Rama O.C.* 624:5 *Magen Avraham*); nor are *Pirkei Avos* or בָּרְכִי נַפְשִׁי, *Bless HASHEM, O my soul* (*M.B.* 624:18).

5. Some congregations do not say לַמְנַצֵּחַ, *For the Conductor*, (between *Ashrei* and *U'va*

L'Zion) on *Erev Succos*. However, all agree that אֵל אֶרֶךְ אַפַּיִם, *O God slow to anger*, (before the reading of the Torah) is said (*M.B.* 624:18).

✍ The Eve of Yom Tov

6. The eve of Succos is a propitious time for distributing charity (*Matteh Ephraim* 625:21, *Sha'arei Teshuvah* to O.C. 625). One should invite those unable to have their own Yom Tov meal (*Matteh Ephraim* 625:21). *Rambam* (*Hil. Yom Tov* 6:18) rules: "When one eats and drinks [on Yom Tov] he is obligated to feed the proselyte, orphan, widow, as well as other unfortunate poor people. However if one locks the gates of his courtyard and eats and drinks . . . but does not feed and give drink to the poor and embittered, this is not a rejoicing of *mitzvah*, rather it is a rejoicing of his own stomach . . . Such a rejoicing is a disgrace to them . . ."

7. On the afternoon preceding the first day of Succos, one may not eat a meal after about three o'clock (standard time) so that he will be able to eat at night in the *succah* with a good appetite (authorities cited by *M.B.* 639:27).

[More precisely, the day (from morning until night) is divided into twelve equal parts called שְׁעוֹת זְמַנִיּוֹת, or proportional hours. The prohibition against eating begins with the onset of the tenth hour. *Rama* rules that this prohibition begins from noon. *Matteh Ephraim* (625:7) rules that it is preferable to

Selected Laws and Customs   [74]

follow *Rama*, but if one did not eat before noon he may do so until mid-afternoon, the tenth hour.]

8. A 'meal' is defined as anything such as bread or cake, that is made from the five types of grain (wheat, rye, barley, oats, and spelt). Snacks of fruit, vegetables, meat, etc. are permitted in small amounts, but one should not 'fill his stomach' with them (*O.C.* 639:3 with *M.B.*; *O.C.* 471:1 with *M.B.* §3).

9. If one did not cut his hair before Rosh Hashanah, and his hair is long, he is obligated to have a haircut in honor of *Yom Tov*. Although one may cut hair all day, it is preferable to do so before noon (*Matteh Ephraim* 625:11).

Similarly one should cut his finger nails and toe nails on the eve of *Yom Tov*, if necessary (*Matteh Ephraim* 625:13). However, it is preferable that the fingernails and toenails not be cut on the same day (*M.B.* 260 §6).

10. It is a *mitzvah* to bathe in warm water on Erev Yom Tov, and one should also immerse himself in a *mikveh* in honor of the *Yom Tov* (*Matteh Ephraim* 625:14).

11. Even if everyone will eat in the *succah*, one should cover the tables in the house, as one does for the Sabbath (*Matteh Ephraim* 625:31).

12. The *Yom Tov* candles should be lit in the *succah* (*Matteh Ephraim* 625:33). [One may bring the candles into the house because of lack of space, but some of the candles should be left in the *succah*. If more than one woman lit candles in the *succah*, each should leave at least one of her candles there (see *M.B.* 263:48).]

THE SABBATH

13. If *Yom Tov* falls on the Sabbath several additions are made to the liturgy of the *Shemoneh Esrei* and *Kiddush*. Some of them are essential and, if omitted, the *Amidah* must be repeated, while others are not. In the passage beginning וַתִּתֶּן לָנוּ, *and You gave us*, the word בְּאַהֲבָה *with love*, is added after the mention of the Sabbath and *Yom Tov*. This addition is not essential, and the prayer need not be repeated if it has been omitted (*Matteh Ephraim* 582:16). Also, if one erred and added בְּאַהֲבָה on a weekday he need not repeat the phrase. The same applies if יִשְׂמְחוּ is omitted from *Mussaf* or וַיְכֻלּוּ from *Kiddush*.

14. A different group of additions, essential in nature, consists of the inclusion of the Sabbath wherever the *Yom Tov* is mentioned (except in יַעֲלֶה וְיָבֹא where our custom omits the mention of the Sabbath). Thus we say וַתִּתֶּן לָנוּ . . . אֶת יוֹם הַשַּׁבָּת הַזֶּה וְאֶת יוֹם הַסֻּכּוֹת הַזֶּה and . . . מְקַדֵּשׁ הַשַּׁבָּת and זְמַן שִׂמְחָתֵנוּ בָּרוּךְ אַתָּה ה' . . . וְיִשְׂרָאֵל וְהַזְּמַנִּים. If *both* of these additions were omitted — so that the Sabbath was not mentioned at all — then that blessing (beginning with אַתָּה בְחַרְתָּנוּ) must be repeated. Thus if one has not yet finished the *Shemoneh Esrei* [or *Kiddush*], he returns to the beginning of that blessing, and continues from there. If he has already concluded it he must start again from the beginning of *Shemoneh Esrei* [or *Kiddush*]. The 'conclusion of *Shemoneh Esrei*' in this regard is defined as the recitation of the verse יִהְיוּ לְרָצוֹן . . . וְגוֹאֲלִי just before עוֹשֶׂה . . . שָׁלוֹם.

15. There are cases, however, regarding both *Shemoneh Esrei* and *Kiddush*, where it is not clear whether or not the blessing must be repeated. If one mentioned the Sabbath at the beginning of the blessing [i.e., in וַתִּתֶּן לָנוּ], but failed to do so in the concluding formula [i.e., . . . בָּרוּךְ אַתָּה ה'], it is questionable whether the blessing has to be repeated (see *M.B.* 487:7, *Be'ur Halachah* there). *Mishnah Berurah* does not give a clear ruling on these questions (although he implies his preference for some of the views). In the absence of a ruling from a competent halachic authority, one should not repeat *Shemoneh Esrei* in this case, since the general rule is that סָפֵק בְּרָכוֹת לְהָקֵל, *when there is doubt whether a blessing should be repeated, we rule leniently*, in order to avoid the possibility of reciting a blessing that is not required.

16. Conversely, if one mentioned the Yom Tov in וַתִּתֶּן לָנוּ but concluded the blessing with a mention only of the Sabbath, there is controversy over whether the blessing must be repeated. According to *Magen Avraham* (*O.C.* 487:2), in this case one should not repeat the blessing. However, many authorities differ (*Pri Chadash, Be'ur Halachah*, et al.; see *Hagahas R' Akiva Eiger*).

If the omission occurred in the concluding formula, one can correct it by immediately saying only the words הַשַּׁבָּת וְיִשְׂרָאֵל וְהַזְּמַנִּים. This correction is valid only if it was begun before enough time to say the words שָׁלוֹם עָלֶיךָ רַבִּי has elapsed from when the erroneously phrased formula was concluded.

17. If, however, the blessing has not yet been completed, there are cases where the error can be corrected and the above halachic problem avoided. If one omitted the Sabbath in וַתִּתֶּן לָנוּ, he simply goes back to וַתִּתֶּן לָנוּ and continues from there. If he has said the three words בָּרוּךְ אַתָּה ה׳ of the concluding formula, he should add the words לַמְּדֵנִי חֻקֶּיךָ. [By doing so he has recited the verse בָּרוּךְ אַתָּה ה׳ לַמְּדֵנִי חֻקֶּיךָ, *Blessed are you* HASHEM, *teach me Your statutes* (*Psalms* 119:12); thus no wrong or needless blessing has been recited.] Then he can go back to וַתִּתֶּן לָנוּ and correct his omission. However, if he has recited more than three words of the blessing [i.e., . . . בָּרוּךְ אַתָּה ה׳ מְקַדֵּשׁ], he must finish the blessing.

◄§ The End of Sabbath

18. When the second day of *Yom Tov* follows the Sabbath, it is necessary to recite a prayer differentiating between the greater sanctity of the Sabbath and the lesser sanctity of the Festival. In the *Amidah*, this prayer — וַתּוֹדִיעֵנוּ — is recited in the fourth benediction. The rules outlined for אַתָּה חוֹנַנְתָּנוּ (see below §20) apply here as well (*Be'ur Halachah* to O.C. 294:1). If the Sabbath has already ended and one wishes to do work permitted on the Festival, but he has not said וַתּוֹדִיעֵנוּ, he must say the following formula: בָּרוּךְ הַמַּבְדִּיל בֵּין קֹדֶשׁ לְקֹדֶשׁ, *Blessed is He Who separates between holy and holy* (*M.B.* 299:36).

19. One should not begin to eat a meal in the three-hour period preceding the Sabbath (*O.C.* 249:2). If the second day of Yom Tov occurred on Friday and one began the festival meal within the three-hour period, he should have a smaller meal than usual, so that he will have an appetite to eat the Sabbath meal in the evening (*Matteh Ephraim* 601:5).

SABBATH, HAVDALAH, THE SECOND NIGHT

◄§ The End of Yom Tov

20. In the first weekday *Maariv* prayer following the first two day Festival, a special prayer אַתָּה חוֹנַנְתָּנוּ, *You have favored us*, is inserted in the fourth benediction of *Shemoneh Esrei*. The function of this prayer is to declare the distinction between the higher holiness of the Festivals and the more mundane nature of Chol HaMoed [Intermediate Days]. If one forgets to insert this prayer he may not repeat the benediction, nor should he insert this prayer in the benediction שְׁמַע קוֹלֵנוּ. Rather he should rely on the *Havdalah* which will be recited over wine after *Maariv* (*O.C.* 294:1; *M.B.* §6).

Even after the *Yom Tov* has ended, it is prohibited to do any forbidden work before reciting אַתָּה חוֹנַנְתָּנוּ or *Havdalah*. Therefore, if one has not yet recited either, one should be very careful not to do any work even after dark. Since women generally do not recite *Maariv*, they should be careful not do any work before hearing *Havdalah*. However, by saying the words: בָּרוּךְ הַמַּבְדִּיל בֵּין קֹדֶשׁ לְחוֹל, *Blessed is He Who separates between holy and secular*, one becomes permitted to do work (*O.C.* 299:10; see *Sha'ar HaTziyun* §51).

◄§ Preparing for the Second Day

21. It is forbidden to cook on the first day of Yom Tov for the second day, or to make any kind of preparations on one day for the other (*O.C.* 503:1 with *M.B.*). Even in the twilight period between the two days [בֵּין הַשְּׁמָשׁוֹת] it is forbidden to make any preparations for the night; one must wait until it is definitely night (*Pri Megadim* cited in *Be'ur Halachah* to 503:1).

22. It is customary not to begin *Maariv* until it is definitely night because most families assume that they are permitted to prepare the evening meal upon commencement of the service (*Matteh Ephraim* 599:2).

23. One may light candles at the end of the afternoon of the first day (except on the Sabbath) if their light is needed at the time they are lit, even though their main use will be at night (*Matteh Ephraim* 598:8). However, the Festival candles, which are lit with the recitation of a blessing, should be lit only after it is definitely night (preface of *Prishah* to *Yoreh Deah*; see *Eleph LaMatteh* 625:51 and *K'tzei HaMatteh* there). [The candles may only be lit from an existing fire, such as a gas pilot light; in no case may a match or cigarette lighter be struck on the Festival.]

24. Likewise it should be noted that Chol HaMoed too has restrictions on the types of labor which may be performed. However, as already noted these laws are not within the purview of this digest.

THE SUCCAH

Many of the laws discussed below deal with the measurements of the *succah* and the Four Species, and are expressed in terms of טְפָחִים, *fists*. Contemporary *poskim* (halachic authorities) do not agree on the translation of the Mishnaic measurements into present-day terminology. For the convenience of the reader, we present three of the most prevalent views for the equivalent of the fist. *Chazon Ish*, as presented by R' Yisrael Yaakov Kanievsky (the Steipler) in *Shiurin shel Torah*, maintains that the fist measures 3.8 inches. However, in cases of Scriptural law (דְאוֹרַיְתָא) one must follow the more stringent view, as the case may be (see *Shiurin shel Torah*, p. 67). R' Moshe Feinstein *(Igros Moshe)* reckons the fist at 3.54 inches, and in the opinion of R' Avraham Chaim No'eh *(Shiurei Torah)* it measures 3.2 inches.

25. The laws regarding the minimum number of the walls — in the event one will not have four full walls — are complicated, so it is advisable to make four sturdy walls (*Rama* in O.C. 630:5).

The walls may be of any material (O.C. but must be sturdy enough to withstand an ordinary wind (O.C. 630:10). If one uses cloth for the walls, it must be tied down securely so that it does not flap in the wind; otherwise the *succah* does not qualify for the *mitzvah*. If possible, however, one should not use a cloth *succah* at all, because of the apprehension that one of the flaps may become detached (and not be noticed) thus disqualifying the *succah* (O.C. 630:10). In the case of canvas *succos* manufactured especially for this purpose nowadays, this apprehension is probably non-existent. [This writer has not found the problem discussed in contemporary halachic literature. In view of the widespread custom to use canvas *succos*, we must assume that the *rabbanim* distinguish between a specially manufactured canvas *succah*, which is designed for sturdiness, and one erected on a make-shift basis.]

26. The minimum height of the walls must be ten *tefachim* (fists), totalling approximately forty inches.

27. The area enclosed by the walls must be at least 7 *tefachim* (fists; approx. 23-28 inches) wide and 7 *tefachim* long (O.C. 634:1). If the *succah* is narrower than this minimum it is not qualified for the *mitzvah* even if the total area is equal to or greater than 7x7 *tefachim*; for example, if the dimensions are 5x10 *tefachim* (*Acharonim* cited in M.B. 630:1). If a cove adjoins the *succah*, one may not eat in it unless the cove has the minimum dimensions on its own (*M.B.* 634:1).

28. The material of the *succah* walls may be borrowed, but not stolen. Therefore, one may not use a *succah* against the owner's

wishes. When the owner is not present, one may enter and use his *succah* on the assumption that he is willing to lend his property for the performance of a *mitzvah*. When the owner is present one may not use the *succah* without his explicit permission, since the owner may regard this as an intrusion on his privacy. Moreover if one entered a *succah* under such circumstances he may not recite the blessing for the *succah*. Even if the owner is not present when one enters the *succah* but may soon arrive, one may not use the *succah* without prior permission from the owner or his wife (O.C. 637:3 with M.B.).

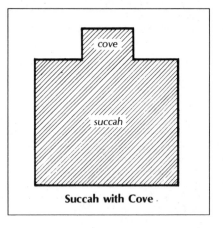

Succah with Cove

29. One may not erect his *succah* on someone else's property without permission. Thus one may not erect a *succah* on public property (e.g., streets, parks) unless he is granted explicit permission by the appropriate authorities (*Rama* in O.C 637:3). If one has done so without obtaining such permission, *post facto* (בְּדִיעֲבַד), he is considered to have discharged his duty and may even recite the *berachah* (*Acharonim* in M.B. 637:10 and *Be'ur Halachah* there).

30. The covering of the *succah*, or as it is more commonly known, the *s'chach*, must be composed of materials which: a) grew from the earth; b) have been detached from the earth; and c) are not susceptible to *tumah* [contamination] (*O.C.* 629:1-2). Thus metals and leather, growing trees, and foodstuffs, are excluded respectively for the above three reasons. Cloth and thread (or the prepared raw material they are made of) are also excluded, as are discarded parts of materials or furniture, for they are now, or had been, susceptible to *tumah* (*O.C.* 629:1-2,4).

31. Mats made of reeds are not qualified for *s'chach* if they are manufactured to be used as cots (or for some other use). If the intent of the manufacture is unknown, a competent *rav* should be consulted. However, if this type of mat is generally manufactured to be used as a cot, it is not qualified even if the individual manufacturer made it expressly for use as *s'chach* (*O.C.* 629:6 with *M.B.* §17).

32. Bundles of reeds containing more than twenty-five pieces do not qualify while they are still bundled. However, one may place the entire bundle upon the *succah* and open it afterward, in which case the individual reeds qualify (*O.C.* 629:15,17).

33. One should not use *s'chach* materials that emit an unpleasant odor or whose leaves drop off continually (*O.C.* 629:14).

34. Boards or beams measuring more than four fists in width (approx. 12-16 inches) may not be used even if they are stood on edge, because such wide boards are similar to the roof of a house. Some authorities maintain that since nowadays even boards less than four fists wide are used as roofing materials, these boards should not be used for *s'chach* (*O.C.* 629:18 with *M.B.* §49). Some maintain that even narrow slats should not be used because they can be placed so tightly together as to be rainproof (*M.B.* loc. cit.).

35. Ideally (לְכַתְּחִילָה), one should not support the *s'chach* upon something susceptible to *tumah*. Thus one should not place the *s'chach* on metal poles. However, it is permissible to support the *s'chach* on the walls of the *succah* although they are made of materials not fit for *s'chach* (e.g., a stone or metal wall; *O.C.* 629:7 with *M.B.* 22). However, some prohibit even this (see *Ran* cited in *Magen Avraham* 629:9). Therefore some people place

a wooden slat upon the walls and support the *s'chach* upon the slat (see *R' Tzvi Pesach Frank, Mikra'e Kodesh* p. 92).

36. The *s'chach* must be spread over the *succah* so that it covers most of the open space and the "shade is greater than the sun" (*O.C.* 631:1).

37. The *s'chach* should be porous enough to enable one to see the stars at night (*O.C.* 631:3), but it is sufficient if the stars can be sighted from even one spot in the *succah* (*M.B.* 631 §3). Moreover, in general one may assume that stars can be sighted even when the *s'chach* is thick, for it is virtually impossible for *s'chach* not to have some openings (*M.B.* §5).

⊷ᔰ Disqualified S'chach in the Succah

38. *S'chach* not qualified for use in a *succah* may be used in small amounts without disqualifying the *succah* as a whole. If this *s'chach* does not cover an area three fists wide (or long; approximately 9-12 inches) one may even eat or sleep directly underneath it (see *M.B.* 632:3).

39. If invalid *s'chach* measuring four *tefachim* (approximately 12-16 inches), or an empty air space measuring three *tefachim* wide (9-12 inches) runs across the full length (or width) of the *succah*, it is possible that the entire *succah* (even those parts covered with *kosher s'chach*) may be disqualified. A competent authority should be consulted. The details of this law are too complicated to be discussed here (see *O.C.* 632:1).

40. If the invalid *s'chach* is placed immediately adjacent to the walls of the *succah* it does not disqualify the *succah* as long as its width does not equal four cubits (approx. 72 in.). Thus one may open a skylight in the roof of his home, cover the open area with *s'chach* and have a kosher *succah*, provided that not more than one side of the skylight is four cubits removed from the walls. In such cases, the unfit *s'chach* or the ceiling adjacent to the skylight is considered as if it were part of an overhanging wall [דּוֹפֶן עֲקוּמָה, *a bent wall*]. However one may not eat under the area not covered by *s'chach* (and that area is not included in the computation determining whe-ther the *succah* contains the minimum necessary area as outlined in §27). This distinction does not apply to air spaces; even a three-fist air space may (under certain condi-

tions) disqualify the *succah*, whether it occurs in the middle of the *succah* or along the walls (O.C. 632:1-2).

41. Even if *succah* decorations are made from materials not qualified to be *s'chach*, they do not disqualify the *succah*, provided they are hung within four *tefachim* (appr. 12-16 inches) of the *s'chach*. One may even eat beneath them (O.C. 627:4). If they are hung four fists or more below the *s'chach*, they are judged as invalid *s'chach*. Therefore *Rama* rules that one should not hang any decorations four *tefachim* below the *s'chach* (ibid.). Lighting fixtures are treated as decorations. However, if suspending them within four *tefachim* of the *s'chach* will create a fire hazard, they may and should be suspended more than four *tefachim* below the *s'chach* (see M.B. 627:15).

42. If any opening in the *s'chach* is long enough to admit the head and most of the body of a person lengthwise (see *Aruch HaShulchan* 632:5) one may not eat beneath that space, although the *succah* as a whole is kosher. The same is true if even a small air space runs uninterruptedly across the entire *succah* (O.C. 632:2). [Therefore when the *succah* is covered with bamboo poles or slats placed parallel to each other, one should place some poles at right angles to the rest of the *s'chach*, so as to break up the long spaces usually created by this type of *s'chach*.]

43. A *succah* may not be erected under a tree or the overhang of a house (O.C. 626:1). If a branch covers part of a *succah* a competent authority should be consulted, since the subject is complex.

◄§ Removable Roofs

44. One may construct a portable roof for the *succah* to enable him to cover the *succah* when it rains. Indeed some urge that such a device be constructed (*Matteh Ephraim* 625:29).

45. Many authorities maintain that *s'chach* placed upon the *succah* while the portable roof is in place is disqualifed. Their opinion should be followed (M.B. 626:18). Therefore, if this had been done, the *s'chach* should be picked up and placed on the *succah* again, piece by piece, after the roof has been removed. [It is not necessary to remove all the *s'chach* before replacing it.]

◄§ Miscellaneous Laws of S'chach

46. One should first erect the walls and then place the *s'chach* upon them (*Rama* O.C. 635:1). If the procedure was reversed, the *s'chach* is disqualified according to some and each piece must be removed and placed on the *succah* again after the walls have been completed (M.B. 635:10).

47. A *succah* may be left to stand from year to year with its *s'chach*. However one must cover at least a small part of the *succah* with *s'chach* within thirty days before the festival to demonstrate that this hut has been thatched over to serve as a *succah* (O.C. 636:1 with M.B. 7). One may comply with this requirement by covering an area running the entire length or width of the *succah* (ibid.). However a *succah* erected expressly for this year's festival may be covered with *s'chach* any time of the year, and the thirty-day limitation does not apply (ibid.).

◄§ Living in the Succah

48. The essence of the *mitzvah* of *succah* is to establish one's residence in the *succah* for the duration of the festival. The Torah commands us to *'dwell' in succos for seven days* (*Lev.* 23:42), meaning that any activity normally done in one's home should be done in the *succah*. Thus, one should eat, drink, sleep, and pass one's time (מְטַיֵּל) in the *succah* (O.C. 639:1). If he wishes to converse with his friend he should do so in the *succah*. However, in deference to the great sanctity of the *succah* one should refrain as much as possible from idle talk while in it and devote his time to Torah and matters of sanctity (M.B. 639:2).

49. One should treat the *succah* with the greatest respect and endeavor to adorn it as much as possible. One's finest table utensils should be used in the *succah*. Pots and pans should never be brought into the *succah* and dirty plates should be removed immediately after eating, but drinking utensils may be left there (O.C. 639:1; M.B. §4-6).

◄§ Eating in the Succah

50. Although in general one should establish the *succah* as his dwelling for the duration of the festival, the obligation of the *mitzvah* is the most stringent and is spelled out in the greatest detail in regard to eating and sleeping — the most characteristic components of 'dwelling.'

51. Snacks may be eaten outside the *succah*. As formulated in *Shulchan Aruch* (*O.C.* 639:2), even large quantities of beverages are in the category of a snack. However, since some authorities are more stringent in this regard and rule that one should not drink beverages in a formal setting (e.g., in a group) or in great quantity (דֶּרֶךְ קֶבַע) outside of the *succah*, it is preferable to follow this view, if possible. However the *succah*-blessing should not be recited when drinking beverages (*M.B.* 639:13). Moreover, some hold that in regard to wine, the law is even more stringent and the even a *revi'is* (3-6 fl. oz.) may not be drunk outside the *succah* (*Be'ur Halachah O.C.* 639:2).

The same difference of opinion applies to fruits, vegetables, meat, and fish. *Shulchan Aruch* (ibid.) rules that they may be eaten outside the *succah* in any quantity. Some authorities, however, rule that a *meal* of meat, fish, or cheese should not be eaten outside the *succah* (*M.B.* 639:15). Some are stringent even regarding a meal of fruit, but *Mishnah Berurah* (*Sha'ar HaTziyun* 38) leans to the lenient view in the case of fruits (or vegetables).

As stated above in regard to beverages, no *succah*-blessing should be recited for these foods.

52. Bread and cake up to the volume of an egg may be eaten outside the *succah*; but an amount greater than this must be eaten in the *succah*. In regard to the recitation of a blessing, it must definitely be recited even over the above quantity of bread. In regard to cake the halachah is not clear.

If enough cake is eaten to constitute a meal there is no question that it requires a *succah* and the *succah* blessing should be recited. Thus if one has coffee and cake for breakfast, he must eat in the *succah* and recite the blessing over it (*M.B.* 639:16). If the cake is slightly more than the volume of an egg, there are conflicting views (although bread would surely require a *succah* in this instance), and one should eat it in the *succah* but not recite the *berachah*. However, there is a widespread custom to recite a *berachah* even in this instance. Therefore one should spend some time in the *succah* after eating so that the *berachah* will apply not only to the eating but also to the time in the *succah* (see §48, 57) which is surely a *mitzvah*. However when one makes *Kiddush* after *Mussaf* on the Sabbath or *Yom Tov*, and eats cake, this is definitely considered a meal, and a *berachah* must be recited (*M.B.* 639:16).

53. The above articulates only the parameters for the *obligation* to eat in the *succah*. However, one who is stringent with himself and abstains from drinking even water outside the *succah* is to be commended (*O.C.* 639:2).

Sleeping in the Succah

54. With regard to sleep, the law is more stringent. It is forbidden even to nap outside of the *succah* (*O.C.* 639:2). However, nowadays most people do not sleep in the *succah* and their behaviour is condoned by *Rama* (ibid.) based on the premise that it is too cold to sleep comfortably in the outdoors in the northern latitudes, and because of other contributing factors. Nevertheless many of those who are punctilious in the performance of the *mitzvos* observe even this facet of dwelling in the *succah* (ibid.).

Exemptions from the Mitzvah

55. One to whom any facet of 'dwelling' in the *succah* causes physical distress is exempt from performing that activity in the *succah*. Therefore if a significant amount of rain penetrates the *succah* one may leave and eat his entire meal in the house. The amount of rain that exempts one from his *succah* obligation is an amount sufficient to spoil a food that is very susceptible to water spoilage (*O.C.* 639:5). Similarly, if one is ill, even slightly, he is exempted from the performance of this *mitzvah* and may eat (and sleep) outside the *succah* (*O.C.* 640:3). Other examples of this exemption are one who is distressed by the wind, flies, foul smells, or is afraid of being robbed (*O.C.* 640:4). However, one must not erect his *succah* in a place where he can anticipate hindrances to his performance of the *mitzvah* (ibid.).

Someone who must travel on the Intermediate Days and will not have access to a *succah* should ask a competent *rav* as to how to conduct himself.

The Blessing

56. Just as one is required to recite a benediction before the performance of most *mitzvos*, so must he say the blessing לֵישֵׁב בַּסֻּכָּה, *to dwell in the succah*, before fulfilling this particular *mitzvah*. However, one recites it only if he will perform a function requiring him to be present in the *succah*. Thus, if one enters the *succah* to eat, he recites the blessing only if the food is of sufficient quantity and

quality to obligate him to consume it in the *succah* (see §51-52; see also *M.B.* end of 639:16).

57. If one enters the *succah* to spend time there, the blessing is required (see *M.B.* 639:46), but the custom is to defer the recitation of the blessing until the beginning of the meal (*O.C.* 639:8). It is better, though, to eat something requiring the *berachah* (see §51-52) immediately upon entering the *succah* (*M.B.* 639:46).

58. If one leaves the *succah* temporarily in the middle of a meal with the intent to return immediately, the blessing need not be recited when the meal is resumed (*M.B.* 639:47).

59. If one remained in the *succah* from one meal to the next, the blessing need not be recited before the second meal. According to most opinions, one need not recite the blessing even if he left temporarily (as above) between meals, but this opinion is not held by all. However if one left the *succah* to attend the synagogue or to attend to business or other matters, all agree that a new blessing must be recited upon his return (ibid.).

60. If one leaves his *succah* during his meal to visit his friend's *succah*, he need not recite the blessing again; the blessing he recited in his own *succah* suffices (*M.B.* 639:48).

61. If one had begun to eat and only later realized that he had forgotten to remove the covering from the *succah*, he must recite the blessing again before resuming the meal. If this happened on the first two nights of the festival he is obligated to eat another *kezayis* of bread after the covering was removed (see §65). He should not, however, recite the *Kiddush* and the *shehecheyanu* blessing again (*M.B.* 639:48).

62. On the Intermediate Days of the festival the blessing is recited after the *hamotzi* and before one eats the bread. On the first (two) night(s) of the festival, or on the Sabbath, when *Kiddush* is said, the blessing follows *Kiddush* and is said before drinking the wine (*O.C.* 643:3; see §65). On the Sabbath and *Yom Tov* mornings, some recite the blessing immediately after *Kiddush*, whereas others defer it until after *hamotzi* (*M.B.* 643:9).

63. Women are exempt from the *mitzvah* of *succah* (*O.C.* 640:1), but they may perform it if they wish and recite the blessing (*M.B.* 640:1).

64. A male child who does not need the constant supervision of his mother is obligated in this *mitzvah* under Rabbinic law (מִדְּרַבָּנָן), so as to train him in the performance of *mitzvos* (*O.C.* 640:2).

✎§ The First Night of the Festival

65. The first night (and in the Diaspora the first two nights) differs from the rest of the festival in regard to the *mitzvah* of *succah*. On this night one is obligated to eat bread of at least the volume of an olive (*kezayis*) in the *succah*. One cannot discharge this *mitzvah* with cake (see *Sha'arei Teshuvah* to *O.C.* 639:3 *Mishnah Berurah* there §21; and at length in *Mikra'e Kodesh* pp. 133-5). This obligatory *kezayis* should be consumed within a time span not exceeding כְּדֵי אֲכִילַת פְּרָס (*M.B.* 639:22; see *Shiurei Torah* 3:15 about the length of the duration of אֲכִילַת פְּרָס; according to divergent opinions, this time span ranges from four to nine minutes). An olive's volume of bread is the smallest amount upon which one may recite the blessing for the *mitzvah* of *succah*, even on the first night. Various estimates are given for the volume of an olive (*kezayis*), but *Shulchan Aruch* (*O.C.* 486) rules that it equals half an egg. Since the *mitzvah* of eating this volume on the first night is of Scriptural origin (דְּאוֹרַיְיתָא), this ruling should be followed (see *M.B.* 486:1). Moreover some hold that the average egg nowadays equals only approximately *half* the volume of the eggs referred to by the Sages, so that it is necessary to eat the equivalent of an average egg (see *Tzlach* toward end of *Pesachim*, *Sha'arei Teshuvah* and *M.B.* to *O.C.* 486; *Chazon Ish O.C.* ch. 17; *Shiurin shel Torah*). However according to many *poskim* one does not fulfill the *mitzvah* (nor can one recite the blessing) unless he eats slightly more than the volume of an egg. All agree that it is preferable to eat this amount in order to ensure that one has fulfilled the *mitzvah* (*M.B.* 639:22). During other meals of Succos all agree that one must eat a quantity slightly greater than the volume of an egg (see *O.C.* 639:2; see above §52).

66. Since there is an obligation to eat in the *succah* on the first night of the *Yom Tov*, one should not begin the meal, or even recite *Kiddush* before it is halachically night (*Rama O.C.* 639:3 with *Magen Avraham*). If one ate during the twilight period [בֵּין הַשְּׁמָשׁוֹת], he should eat at least an olive's volume of bread again after nightfall, but not repeat the blessing (*M.B.* 25). In the Diaspora,

one should follow this practice on the second night as well.

67. The first night differs also in regard to the stringency of the obligation. On the rest of the festival one need not eat in the *succah* when heavy rain penetrates the *s'chach* or one feels some other form of distress through eating in the *succah* in any way (see above §55), but on the first night this does not pertain. One must eat (the minimum amount) in the *succah* even when it is raining (*Rama* in *O.C.* 639:5). However, many authorities dispute this ruling. Therefore no blessing should be recited in such an instance. Moreover one should wait for an hour or two for the rain to stop, so that he can perform the *mitzvah* properly according to all opinions. If it is not possible to wait so long (e.g., there are guests, little children, etc.) or the rain has not stopped even after this wait, one should make *Kiddush* and eat the minimum amount required to be eaten in the *succah* (but without reciting the *succah* blessing) and then he may finish the meal indoors. If the rain stops later he should again go into the *succah*, recite the blessing and eat the minimum requirement. This should be done even when one has already recited the *Bircas HaMazon* after the meal, in which case he must wash his hands again with the appropriate blessing (M.B. 639:35-36 with *Sha'ar HaTziyun* §67).

68. In the Diaspora the above applies to the second night as well, with one difference: If it rains on the second night, one may recite the *Kiddush* in the house and eat the

meal without waiting for the rain to stop, and then go to the *succah* and eat the minimum there. If possible, however, one should wait a reasonable time for the rain to stop, even on the second night (*M.B.* 639:36).

69. In the *Kiddush* of the first night the blessing over the *mitzvah* of *succah* follows the blessing of *Kiddush*. *Shehecheyanu* is recited last. On the second night some reverse this sequence, placing *shehecheyanu* immediately after *Kiddush*. Others maintain the same order as on the first day (*O.C.* 643:1 and 661 with M.B. and *Sha'ar HaTziyun*).

70. One should make sure to eat the minimum requirement before midnight (*Rama* 639:3). However if he had been detained until midnight, he may still recite the blessing on the *succah* just as he does at any time during the rest of the festival (*M.B.* 439:26).

71. When one eats the first *kezayis* on the first night, he should concentrate on the reason given by the Torah for this *mitzvah*: *So that your generations shall know that I settled the Children of Israel in succos when I took them out of Egypt* (*Lev.* 23:43). This is in addition to the mental intent common to all *mitzvos* that the act is being done because it has been bidden by God. On Succos one should meditate on the status of the *succah* as a commemoration of the Exodus from Egypt, and that God surrounded Israel at that time with Heavenly Clouds (עֲנָנֵי הַכָּבוֹד) to protect them from the elements (*M.B.* 625:1).

THE FOUR SPECIES

72. The Torah (*Lev.* 23:40) commands us to *take on the first day of the Succos festival, the Four Species.* As identified by the oral tradition handed down to the Sages, they are an *esrog* (citron), a *lulav* (branch of a date palm), three myrtle twigs (*hadassim*), and two willow twigs (*aravos*). The specifications for each of these species will be described later at length. Here only the general laws applying to the Four Species as a unit will be discussed.

73. The essence of the *mitzvah* is *taking* these species in one's hands, as indicated by the phraseology used by the Torah in the above cited verse (*And you shall take for yourselves ...*). The well-known rite of 'waving' the Four Species to the points of the compass and to 'heave' them up and down, although a Rabbinical *mitzvah*, is not

essential to the fulfillment of the Scriptural obligation.

74. The Scriptural *mitzvah* of taking the Four Species was not the same in all places. A seven day observance of 'taking' is mandated for the Temple, whereas outside it only on the first day of Succos were the species taken. However after the destruction of the Temple, the Sages decreed that, in commemoration of the Temple observance, the species be taken everywhere for seven days (*O.C.* 658:1 with *M.B.*).

75. A very important provision of the *mitzvah* on the first (or the first two days; see *M.B.* 658:23 and *O.C.* 649:5) day of the festival is that the species must belong to the person performing the *mitzvah*. However, one may

ask a friend to give him the Four Species as a gift, on the condition that he will return then (O.C. 658:3-4). Nevertheless, if someone gives the species to a friend on the condition that they will be his only for the duration of the mitzvah, after which they will automatically revert to their original owner, it is considered a loan, since the acquisition is terminated after a certain time has elapsed (O.C. 658:3). One should not give the species to a minor on such a condition because, as a minor, he is not legally empowered to transfer ownership back to the original owner; thus the species will remain in the minor's possession. Nor will the child be deprived of his ownership for not having fulfilled the conditions, because such conditions are not legally binding on a minor (O.C. 658:6).

76. On the Intermediate Days, when the mitzvah is performed only in commemoration of the Temple, one may borrow the species from his colleague without acquiring ownership (ibid. and O.C. 649:5).

77. As with every mitzvah, a blessing (עַל נְטִילַת לוּלָב) is recited before 'taking' the species. The procedure common to all mitzvos is that one holds the object used for the mitzvah in his hand and recites the blessing prior to the performance. For example, one jholds the Four Species before reciting the blessing. This presents a difficulty in regard to the Four Species, for once one has 'taken' them in his hand, the mitzvah has been fulfilled and it is too late to recite the blessing.

The most widely practiced solution to this problem is based on the rule that the species must be held in the direction in which they grew. Accordingly, if the esrog is held facing down (with the pitam toward the ground) the mitzvah is not fulfilled although one has 'taken' the species in hand (O.C. 651:5). Only after the berachah has been recited is the esrog inverted so that the pitam (see diagram further) faces up. Another method is to hold only the lulav (which has the myrtles and willows attached to it). After the blessing the esrog is picked up (ibid.).

78. Since the Four Species is a mitzvah dependent on time, women are exempt from it, but they have taken this mitzvah upon themselves as an obligation. Thus they may recite the blessing (O.C. 17:2; cf. O.C. 589:6).

79. On the first day that one performs the mitzvah, an additional shehecheyanu blessing is recited immediately following the blessing over the mitzvah, and before the performance of the mitzvah (O.C. 651:5).

80. Three of the species — the lulav, myrtle twigs and willows — should be tied together (O.C. 651:1). It is customary to tie them with lulav fronds. The lulav is held with its 'backbone' facing the person. The three myrtle twigs should be on the right and the two willows on the left as one faces the lulav (M.B. 651:12; Shelah cited in Magen Avraham 651:8; M.B. 650:8). Some people arrange the willows and myrtle twigs in different ways and some even add to the number of myrtle twigs in accordance with the kabbalistic teachings of Arizal and his disciples. The above is the custom most widely practiced.

81. The myrtles should be placed so that their tops are higher than the willows, but both should be attached to the lower end of the lulav, so that when one grasps the lulav he holds the myrtles and willows as well (Rama O.C. 651:1). Moreover, at least a tefach (fist; approx. 3-4 inches) of the lulav's 'backbone' should be visible above the tips of the myrtle and willow twigs (O.C. 650:2).

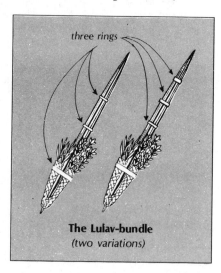

three rings

The Lulav-bundle
(two variations)

82. The lulav should be tied in three places with palm fronds. Some consider the attachment of the myrtles and willows to the lulav as one of the places and tie the lulav in only two more places, while others maintain that the three ties are in addition to the attachment. At least one tefach (fist; approx. 3-4 in.) from the top of the backbone should be left untied so that its leaves rustle when the lulav is shaken (M.B. 651:14).

83. The *esrog* should be held in the left hand and the *lulav* in the right (O.C. 651:2). If one reversed this order he should 'take' the species again (without reciting the blessing), because according to some the reversal invalidates the performance (M.B. 651:19).

84. A lefthanded person should hold the *lulav* in his left hand and the *esrog* in his right, but someone who is ambidextrous should hold the *lulav* in his right (*Rama* 651:3). There are differences of opinion how the *hadassim* and *aravos* should be arranged on the *lulav* of a lefthanded person (see *Reishis Bikurim*).

85. There are two views as to how the Four Species should be picked up when one is ready to perform the *mitzvah*. According to a widely held view one first takes the *lulav* in the right hand, and takes the *esrog* (upside down) in his left (*Dagul Mer'vavah* and *Sha'arei Teshuvah* to O.C. 651:3). Others reverse the procedure: First the *esrog* is picked up (upside down) in the left hand, and only then is the *lulav* taken. When putting away the species this procedure is reversed; the *lulav* is put away first and then the *esrog* (*Magen Avraham* 651:8; see *Dagul Mervavah* and *Sha'arei Teshuvah* for divergent views).

86. If the *esrog* and *lulav* were held in one hand during the performance of the *mitzvah* the 'taking' is invalid according to some authorities and the *mitzvah* should be performed again (without a blessing; M.B. 651:15).

87. Nothing should cover the hand or be in it while one performs the *mitzvah*, so that there will be no barrier (חֲצִיצָה) between the hand and the species (see O.C. 651:7). The custom is to remove even the straps of the *tefillin* (for those who wear *tefillin* on the Intermediate Days) and rings from one's fingers, to avoid even this partial interposition (*Rama* O.C. 651:7). Some authorities are stringent in this matter and rule that if this is not done the species should be taken again, without recital of the *berachah* (M.B. 651:36).

◄§ Waving the Species

88. Although the *mitzvah* is accomplished by merely holding the species in one's hands, one should follow this with the ritual of waving (נַעֲנוּעִים). The procedure which is most widely practiced is to wave the species by stretching one's arms while holding the species away from his body and shaking them, and then bringing them back close to the chest and

shaking them again (M.B. 651:37). This motion is repeated three times to each of the four points of the compass, and upward and downward (a total of 36 to and fro movements). Enough force should be used during each movement to rustle the *lulav* leaves slightly (*Rama* in O.C. 651:9). The hands should be held close together so that the *esrog* will remain close to the *lulav* (O.C. 651:11).

89. There are varying customs regarding the sequence of these movements. The following is the mode practiced in Ashkenazic communities. One begins by waving the species to the east (the direction directly ahead of him), then he turns clockwise toward the other three directions, and finally move the species up and down. Thus the sequence is east, south, west, north, up and down (see *Shulchan Aruch* O.C. 651:10). However, *Arizal* (see *Ba'er Heitev* and *Sha'arei Teshuvah* 651:20) teaches that the sequence should be south, north, east, upward, downward, and west. Communities following the Chassidic custom of prayer (commonly known as *Nusach Sfard*) and many Sephardic Jews follow *Arizal's* practice.

The species are pointed horizontally in the direction toward which they are being waved (*Rama* in O.C. 651:9). However, it is preferable that the tips of the species not be lower than the stems, even during the downward motion (ibid. M.B. §45). According to *Arizal* the species should be kept upright throughout the waving, with only the arms extended in the appropriate directions (cited by *Kaf HaChaim* 651:47,99 and *Siddur Baal HaTanya*).

Some remain facing eastward and merely point the species to the indicated directions in accordance with *Maharil's* custom (M.B. 651:37), while others conduct themselves as indicated by *Arizal* and turn in the direction of the waving (*Kaf HaChaim* 651:96).

90. The species should also be held during the recital of *Hallel* and *Hoshanos* (see O.C. 660:2). During certain verses of *Hallel*, the species should be waved again in the manner described above. The custom recorded by *Rama* (O.C. 651:8) is to wave during each of the four times the verse הודו is repeated, each of the the two times the verse אָנָּא ה' הושיעה נָא is said, and finally, the two times the verse הודו is repeated (again) toward the end of the *Hallel* (a total of eight times). This custom is practiced in the communities using the Ashkenazic rite of prayer.

91. The most widely accepted custom is to recite the word הודו during or after the first movement (i.e., the complete set of three back-and-forth motions toward the east or

south) then to recite the word לְךָ; the word כִּי is recited during or after the next movement; and so on for the remaining four words of this verse. For the verse אָנָּא, which contains only four words, the procedure is as follows: The words אָנָּא ה' are said in conjunction with the first two movements: הוֹשִׁיעָה in conjunction with the next two movements; and נָא in conjunction with the last two movements (M.B. 651:37).

92. The *mitzvah* of taking the species may be fulfilled only during daytime, i.e., after sunrise (O.C. 652:1). Therefore one should be careful when praying with an early *minyan* to delay the 'taking' of the species as much as possible. However if one performed this *mitzvah* before sunrise but after dawn (i.e., seventy-two minutes before sunrise), he has, *post facto* (בְּדִיעֲבַד), discharged his obligation (M.B. 652:3).

93. One who must leave his home early may 'take' the 'species' before sunrise, providing it is after dawn (O.C. 652:1).

94. According to the view expressed in Shulchan Aruch (O.C. 644:1), one should perform the *mitzvah* of taking the species after the *Shacharis* prayer — immediately before *Hallel*. However, many conduct themselves in accordance with *Arizal* who teaches that it is highly desirable to perform the *mitzvah* in the *succah*. Since it is not practical to go home to one's *succah* between *Shacharis* and *Hallel*, they perform the *mitzvah* before *Shacharis* (M.B. 652:4, Shelah). In many communities it is customary to have a *succah* near the synagogue, to enable people to perform the *mitzvah* in the *succah* at its most desirable time — before *Hallel*.

95. It is prohibited to eat before performance of the *mitzvah* (O.C. 652:2), but one may have a snack if this is absolutely necessary. If the species are not available in the morning, however, one should not defer his meal until past noon, for it is forbidden to fast on the Festival or the Intermediate Days (M.B. 652:7). Many people desist even from drinking before the performance of the *mitzvah* (see *Da'as Torah* to O.C. 652:2; *Arba'as Haminim HaShalem* p. 25-6).

GENERAL RULES OF THE FOUR SPECIES

◆§ General Disqualifications

Although the *halachos* vary for each of the Four Species, there are nevertheless general rules that apply across the board, and that are the basis for most of the other laws. A description of these general *halachos* will permit a better understanding of the laws which flow from them.

a) לָכֶם – *Possession*. The command to *take* the Four Species is expressed as (*Lev.* 23:40) *You shall take* לָכֶם, *for yourselves* . . . The expression *for yourselves* means that one must own the Four Species before he can use them to perform the *mitzvah* (see *Sifra* there, *Gem. Succah* 41b). Thus, one cannot discharge his obligation with a set of borrowed species (see §75).

b) גָּזוּל – *Stolen*. If any of the species had been stolen they are disqualified (see *Succah* 29b). This disqualification is not unique to the Four Species; rather it derives from the general rule that disqualifies מִצְוָה הַבָּאָה בַּעֲבֵירָה, *the performance of any mitzvah through a transgression*. This invalidation applies even in some instances where the species have become the property of the thief by the time he performs the *mitzvah* (see M.B. 649:32).

c) הָדָר – *Beauty*. Esthetic beauty is a precondition for the validity of all of the Four Species. One example of this is the disqualification of a withered *lulav* (see Succah 29b). The *mitzvah* of the Four Species differs in this respect from other *mitzvos* where — although it is commendable to beautify objects used for *mitzvos* — it is not essential to the point where an object is disqualified if it is not beautiful.

d) שָׁלֵם – *Completeness*. The species must be whole, as they were in their natural state. A common example is the disqualification of an *esrog* whose rind with some of the underlying flesh has been peeled off.

e) שִׁיעוּר – *Minimum dimensions*. Each of the species must have certain minimum dimensions. Thus the *lulav* may not measure less than four fists in its length, et al.

◆§ General Disqualification on the Intermediate Days

The mitzvah of taking the Four Species on the Intermediate Days is Rabbinic; (see §74) accordingly the Sages did not apply some of the Scriptural disqualifications that are in effect on the first day. According to the view accepted by *Rama*, all the above disqualifications apply also after the first day, (and in the Diaspora after the first two days) except a. (Possession) and d. (Completeness). Thus one may perform the mitzvah with borrowed species, and one may use an esrog which is not whole (O.C. 649:6).

All the other disqualifications, and also species that do not have the required physical characteristics are invalid throughout Succos. Examples of this are *hadassim* whose leaves do not grow from the stem in threefold clusters (מְשֻׁלָּשׁ), and *aravos* whose leaves have substantial serrations (*O.C.* 649:6 with *M.B.* 46).

৯§ The Lulav

96. The leaves of the *lulav* should point upward in the general direction of its 'backbone' and be bunched closely together; if they sag and are only slightly separated, the *lulav* is kosher. Ideally (לְכַתְּחִילָה), however, such a *lulav* should not be used. But if the leaves sag downward so much that they do not point at all in the general direction of the *lulav's* backbone, it is invalid (*O.C.* 645:1,2).

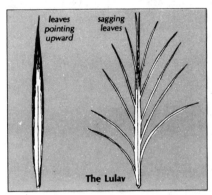

The Lulav

leaves pointing upward

sagging leaves

97. *Lulav* leaves usually grow 'doubled over' lengthwise. If most of the leaves grew singly or were split lengthwise (along most of the length of the leaf; *M.B.* 645:11) the *lulav* is invalid (*O.C.* 645:3). *Ritva* ponders whether a *lulav* whose leaves *grew* singly is invalid for the entire duration of the festival or if it may be used on the Intermediate Days (*M.B.* 645:13; see General Rules of the Four Species).

98. The middle-leaf, extending uppermost from the *lulav's* backbone, enjoys a special status. If this leaf is split until the point where it meets the backbone, the *lulav* is invalid even if the rest of the leaves are intact (*Rama* in *O.C.* 645:3). If there are two middle leaves, both have this status and if either one is split the *lulav* is invalid (*M.B.* 645:15). *Vilna Gaon* invalidates the *lulav* even if only most of the middle leaf is split. Similarly, if the middle leaf grew singly (i.e., it was not doubled over as in §97) the *lulav* is invalid (*Rama O.C.* 645:3). Furthermore, *Rama* (there) cautions that ideally one should look for a *lulav* that is not split at all. Thus if one has a choice of two *lulavim*, one split slightly and the other not at all, he should prefer the latter *lulav*. However,

if someone's own *lulav* is not split for most of its length, he need not go so far as to use someone else's unsplit *lulav* (*M.B.* 645:17-8). Moreover, in *Turei Zahav's* view, as long as the split does not measure a fist (טֶפַח), one need not even attempt to look for another *lulav*, but *Chaye Adam* maintains that ideally one should seek a *lulav* whose middle leaf is entirely intact (*M.B.* 645:19).

99. If the middle leaf was so split that the two parts are separated by a space and they seem like two separate leaves, the *lulav* is invalid even if the length of the split is not enough to invalidate it *per se* (*O.C.* and *Rama* 645:7). One should be very careful in regard to this (*M.B.* 645:32). The same is true if the middle leaf is intact but most of the other leaves are split in the manner described above (*Be'ur Halachah* to *O.C.* 645:7).

100. The disqualifications arising out of a split middle leaf are in effect only on the first day of the festival (in the Diaspora, the first two days). On the Intermediate Days they do not apply (*M.B.* 645:17).

101. A *lulav* is invalid if it has dried out to two point where its leaves have lost their green color and are now whitish (*O.C.* 645:5).

102. If most of the points of the leaves growing out of the tip of the *lulav's* backbone were broken or snipped off (i.e., the tips of the middle double leaf and those of the two double leaves to either side of it) the *lulav* is invalid (*O.C.* 645:6; see *Be'ur Halachah* there). *Rama* (loc. cit.) rules that even if only the middle leaf was mutilated in this manner one should not use this *lulav*. This invalidation is in effect for the entire festival (see *M.B.* 645:27). *Rama* adds that in the latter case if one has no other *lulav* he may use it and even recite the blessing over it (ibid.). However, this ruling is complicated by a controversy among the *Acharonim* if even a slight (מַשֶׁהוּ) mutilation along the length of these leaves invalidates the *lulav*, or if it is disqualified only if most of the leaf is missing (*M.B.* 645:26). Based on this, *Mishnah Berurah* (§30) rules that *Rama's* lenient ruling be relied upon only in the case of a slight mutilation. However, if most of the middle leaf is missing one should not recite the blessing. Similarly if the mutilation occurred on most of the upper leaves (the first case) the

blessing should not be recited (*M.B.* 645:30).

103. The *lulav* may not be crooked. If it is curved like a sickle to the sides or forward (i.e., when the *lulav* is held with its backbone toward the person, it curves away from him) it is invalid. However if it curves backward (i.e., toward the person) it is valid, for this is a normal curvature (*O.C.* 645:8).

104. If the backbone [שִׁדְרָה] of the *lulav* is straight for most of its length and is bent (hooklike) at its top, it is invalid (*O.C.* 645:9) even if it is bent backward (*M.B.* 645:38). However, if only the tops of the leaves were bent, the *lulav* is kosher (*O.C.* 645:9); indeed many prefer such a *lulav* because its leaves will be unlikely to split (see *Tur* 645 citing *Rosh; Sha'arei Teshuvah* to *O.C.* 645:9; *M.B.* §40). But if the leaves were doubled over it is invalid (*M.B.* 645:40).

105. All invalidations listed above are in effect for the whole duration of the festival except that concerning split leaves (see §97-100), which applies only on the first (two) day(s) of the festival (*Magen Avraham* 645:6).

106. The minimum length for the *lulav's* backbone is four fists (*Rama* in *O.C.* 650:1). According to *Chazon Ish* this equals approx. 16 inches (40 centimeters) while according to *Shiurei Torah* approx. 13 inches (32 centimeters) suffices. If the *lulav's* backbone is slightly shorter than four fists it is kosher *post facto* if it meets the minimum dimensions accepted by the most lenient view in *Shulchan Aruch O.C.* 650:1 (see there), but a *lulav* shorter than that is invalid for the entire duration of the festival (*M.B.* 650:8). The backbone of the *lulav* should jut out one fist above the myrtle and willow twigs (*O.C.* 650:2).

◆§ The Myrtle Twigs (Hadassim)

107. The myrtle twigs must have three leaves growing out of each level of the twig. This is called a threefold myrtle הֲדַס (מְשֻׁלָּשׁ). If only two leaves grow at each level it is invalid (*O.C.* 646:3 see *Be'ur Halachah* there).

108. Ideally the leaves along the entire required length (3 fists) of the myrtle twigs should be threefold. Nevertheless if only most of this length (slightly more than 1½ fists) was threefold, it is kosher (*O.C.* 646:5) even if the threefold leaves are not situated at the upper segment of the twig (*Rama* there). If the threefold leaves are not found in one continuous stretch there is a question whether it is kosher (*Be'ur Halachah* to 646:5). [Thus, according to *Chazon Ish* the total minimum

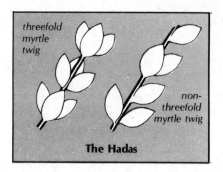

threefold myrtle twig

non-threefold myrtle twig

The Hadas

length of the myrtle is slightly less than 12 inches (30 cm.) and 'most of its length' is 6 inches. According to the dimensions given in *Shiurei Torah* the total length of the myrtle is slightly less than 10 inches (25 cm.) and 'most of its length' would be 5 inches.]

109. If most of the leaves (within the top 3 fists) fell off it is invalid. But if only a minority fell off it is valid (*O.C.* 646:2,4) providing that there are two remaining leaves in each threefold set (*M.B.* 646:17,18). In the latter case, however, the myrtle twigs should be used only in cases of emergency (ibid.). One should be very careful when inserting the twigs into the palm frond receptable which is used to attach them to the *lulav* not to invalidate the twigs by tearing off the leaves (see *Magen Avraham* 647:1).

110. If all of the leaves in a twig have dried up it is invalid, but if they are merely wilted it may be used. The definition of 'dry' is that the leaf has lost its green color and has become whitish (*O.C.* 646:6-7).

111. However, if the threefold set of leaves at the top of the twig are still fresh, it is kosher although all the others are dry (*O.C.* 646:8 with *M.B.* §21). If the top leaves are not fresh but wilted and the rest are dry there is questionable whether the twig is kosher (*O.C.* 646:9); therefore one should be stringent on the first day of the festival, but one may use it on the second [even in the Diaspora] (*M.B.* 646:27). But if all of the other leaves (or at least most of them) were fresh, then the wilted leaves at the top do not disqualify the twig (see *O.C.* 646:6).

112. If the top set of leaves dried up, the twig is invalid according to *Bach* even if the rest of the leaves are fresh. This is disputed by many authorities and one may rely on their view (see *M.B.* 646:34 and *Be'ur Halachah*). However, if one removes the dry top leaves, the twig is valid even according to *Bach* (ibid., see below §19).

113. If the top of the twig was broken off there is a question as to its validity (*O.C.*

646:10). Therefore one should not use it if he can get another twig (*Rama*).

114. The above is true only in reference to the stem of the twig itself. If only the top leaves are ripped [or even if they fell off entirely] it is valid (ibid.).

115. The small branches sometimes growing out of the stems of the twig should be removed before *Yom Tov* (*M.B.* 646:33; *Sha'ar HaTziun* §36).

116. All the disqualifications of the myrtle twigs apply for the entire duration of the festival (*Be'ur Halachah* to 646:1). Where no kosher twig is available, a competent *rav* should be consulted (see *M.B.* 649:53).

117. Three myrtle twigs, each three *tefachim* (fists) long, are required for the performance of the *mitzvah* (*O.C.* 651:1). However if only one kosher twig is available one may discharge his obligation with it (*Rama*) and recite the blessing (*M.B.* 651:6).

◈§ The Willow Twigs (Aravos)

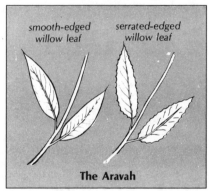

smooth-edged willow leaf

serrated-edged willow leaf

The Aravah

118. Many species are similar to the twigs mandated by the Torah. The prime means of identifying the proper twigs are the leaves. They should be elongated with smooth edges and the stems should be red. However green-stemmed willows are also kosher since they tend to turn red if exposed to the sun. Only those with whitish stems are invalid (*M.B.* 647:2). The sub-species whose leaves are slightly serrated, but otherwise resemble the species described above, is also kosher (*O.C.* 647:1), although some people prefer to use twigs whose leaves have no readily discernible serration. One should be careful when buying willow twigs, for many times the people selling them are not knowledgeable (*M.B.* 647:6).

119. If most of the leaves on a twig fell off or dried up it is invalid (*O.C.* 647:2 with

M.B.). Dryness is defined as a total loss of the green color (*Sha'ar HaTziyun* 647:6). If the leaves are merely wilted the twig is kosher (*O.C.* 647:2). However, there is a difference of opinion among the *Acharonim* whether twigs that had lost less than the majority of their leaves should be used initially (לְכַתְּחִילָה). *Mishnah Berurah* (647:11) advises conformance with the stringent ruling since willow twigs are easy to attain. One should be very careful in regard to tearing off the leaves, because this often happens when the *lulav* is handled or when the twigs are inserted into the palm frond receptacle attaching them to the *lulav* (*M.B.* 647:8).

120. If the twig's tip was broken off it is invalid (*O.C.* 647:2 with *M.B.* §12). However, if only the tip of the topmost leaf is missing [or the entire leaf was torn off] it is kosher (*M.B.* 647:10).

121. If most of the leaves of a twig are split or partly detached from the stem one should not use it (*M.B.* 647:9).

122. All disqualifications of the willow twigs are in effect for the entire duration of the festival (see *M.B.* 647:10; but cf. *M.B.* 649:48). If kosher willows are not available, a competent *rav* should be consulted.

Two willow twigs, each measuring three *tefachim* (fists), are required for the fulfillment of the *mitzvah* (651:1).

◈§ The Esrog

123. The laws concerning the validity of the *esrog* are complicated and numerous, and an exhaustive digest would be beyond the scope of this book. We will limit ourselves to a discussion of the most common problems. Any condition out of the ordinary should be shown to a competent *rav*.

124. Even a rudimentary understanding of the laws of *esrog* is predicated upon an acquaintance with the *esrog's* parts and the terms used to refer to them. The *esrog* is topped by a woodlike protuberance which is called the *pitam* (פִּיטָם). This protuberance is crowned with a flowerlike top — the *shoshanta* (שׁוֹשַׁנְתָּא). The upper part of the *esrog*, from the point where the *esrog* begins to become narrow, is called the *chotam* (חוֹטָם), nose. At the broad bottom of the *esrog* is the stem, actually the remainder of the twig by which it was attached to the tree — the *ukatz* (עוּקָץ).

125. The *esrog* must be whole. If even the minutest part is missing it is invalid for the first (two) day(s). It is however valid for the Intermediate Days. If only the thin yellow rind (but not the underlying flesh) was partially

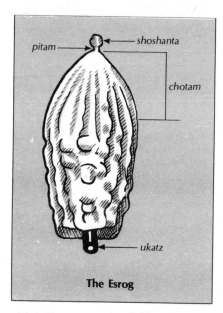

pitam — — shoshanta

chotam

ukatz

The Esrog

peeled off, and the underlying rind retained the *esrog* color it is valid (*O.C.* 648:6). An expert should be consulted in such an instance since it is very difficult to ascertain whether only the rind was peeled off or if even some of the underlying flesh is missing.

126. If the *shoshanta* is missing, the *esrog* is kosher, but if one has a choice of two *esrogim* equal in all other respects, he should choose the *esrog* whose *shoshanta* is intact. If, however, the *esrog* with the missing *shoshanta* was superior (in beauty or *kashrus*) it should be first choice (*Rama O.C.* 648:7 with *M.B.* 31). The above refers to an instance where only the *shoshanta* was missing and the *pitam* under it is fully intact. But if part of the *pitam* is missing, although the *esrog* is kosher, another *esrog* would be preferred, regardless of the former's superiority in other respects (ibid.). According to one view, one should not recite the blessing over such an *esrog* on the first (two) day(s) of the festival, but can on the Intermediate Days (*Bikkurei Yaakov* 648:23; cf. *Daas Torah*).

127. If the entire *pitam*, including the part that was embedded in the tip of the *esrog*, is missing, thus leaving a cavity, it is invalid. It is valid, however, if the part of the *pitam* jutting out above the tip of the *esrog* was broken off (*Rama O.C.* 648:7). Some authorities rule that the *esrog* remains kosher only if part of the *pitam* remains above the tip of the *esrog*; but if it is broken off flush with the top of the *esrog*, it is invalid (*M.B.* 30). If this happened, a competent *rav* should be consulted.

128. A missing *pitam* disqualifies the *esrog* only if it was broken off. If the *esrog* grew without a *pitam*, as do many strains of this fruit, it is kosher (*Rama* 648:7) and should not be judged as inferior (*M.B.* 648:32).

129. Although the disqualification caused by missing portions (חָסֵר) of an *esrog* does not apply on the Intermediate Days (see §125 and General Rules of the Four Species), some authorities feel that a (totally) missing *pitam* carries with it the additional disqualification of lacking beauty (הָדָר) and is therefore invalid even on the Intermediate Days. Thus one should endeavor to perform the *mitzvah* with an *esrog* which retains its *pitam*, at least partially, even on the Intermediate Days.

If none is available one can fulfill his obligation with an *esrog* lacking the *pitam* (even where a cavity was caused by the break). It is however questionable whether a *berachah* may be recited in such a case (*M.B.* 649:36).

130. If the entire *ukatz* (stem) was missing, leaving a small cavity at the bottom of the *esrog*, it is invalid on the first (two) day(s) (*O.C.* 648:8) but kosher on the Intermediate Days. But if enough of the *ukatz* remained so that there is no cavity, it is kosher even on the first day (*Rama O.C.* 648:8 with *M.B.*).

131. A hairline puncture in the *esrog* may be a disqualification and an authority should be consulted, for the laws governing punctures are complex (see *O.C.* 648:2-3). However where a hole was made by the thorns on the tree while the *esrog* was growing and a scab covers the hole it is valid (*Rama O.C.* 648:2 with *M.B.*).

132. A blister-like growth called *chazazis* (חֲזָזִית), caused by rot and the like (see *Be'ur Halachah* to *O.C.* 648:13), may invalidate an *esrog* if it is noticeably higher than the rest of the *esrog* so that it can be felt (*O.C.* 648:13), and is of a different color than the rest of the *esrog* (see *Pri Megadim* in *Eshel Avraham* 648:19; *Sha'ar HaTziyun* 648:56). *Pri Megadim* seems to hold that a *chazazis* disqualifies only if it is of a color which, in itself, would disqualify the *esrog* (see §217). *R' Meir Arik* (*Minchas Pittim O.C.* 648:13) disputes this and maintains that a *chazazis* disqualifies whenever its color differs from the general coloring of that particular *esrog*.

133. Certain discolorations of the *esrog's* rind may disqualify it under the conditions outlined below. Black and white are disqualifying colors (*O.C.* 648:16); red discoloration may disqualify the *esrog*, depending on

the intensity of the color (see *Be'ur Halachah* to O.C. 648:16). An authority should be consulted.

134. Discolorations and *chazazis* disqualify an *esrog* in any of the following ways:

(a) If it occurs on the *chotam* (the upper part of the *esrog* which slopes toward the tip) it disqualifies even if it covers only a most minute area (O.C. 648:12). However it must be easily visible to the naked eye. A discoloration that can be seen only upon close inspection is, from a halachic viewpoint, considered non-existent (*M.B.* 648:46).

(b) If it occupies most of the surface area of the *esrog*.

(c) If two or more discolorations or *chazazis* cover even less than half of the surface of the *esrog*. In this instance the *esrog* is disqualified only if the major part of the *esrog's* circumference is covered by the discolorations or blisters plus the space between them. If they are all on one side of the *esrog* it is kosher (O.C. 648:10 with *M.B.*). However if there were more than three spots it is doubtful if it is kosher even in such an instance (*Be'ur Halachah* there s.v. שבולם). There is controversy concerning discolorations dispersed in more than one spot: According to one view, in this case, too, disqualification will apply only where the discoloration was of the specific colors listed in §133. Others, however, hold that any spotted *esrog* (מְנוּמָר) is disqualified even if the discoloration is of other colors (*M.B.* 648:55).

135. The disqualifications arising out of discolorations and *chazazis* apply even on the Intermediate Days (*Rama* 649:5).

136. Some discolorations, specifically black dots, are very common and many are disqualifications. In cases of doubt a *rav* should be consulted. However if these spots are merely specks of dirt adhering to the surface of the *esrog* they do not constitute a disqualification.

137. The minimum size for an *esrog* is the volume of an egg (כְּבֵיצָה). According to many *poskim* (*Noda BiYehudah, Chazon Ish;* cf. *Teshuvos Chasam Sofer Orach Chaim 181)* the volume should be that of two medium eggs. An *esrog* weighing approximately 3.53 oz. is definitely the equivalent of two eggs. [This above figure has been arrived at using the following figures. *Shiurin shel Torah* (p. 4 and 65) fixes the weight of the water displaced by a *kebeitzah* at 100 grams or 3.53 oz. av. Since an *esrog* weighs less than its equivalent volume of water, an *esrog* weighing less than this may also be kosher. Another way of approximating is to bear in mind that adding approximately 1/5 to the circumference of an egg will double its volume (*Shiurin shel Torah*, p. 66).]

138. Some authorities (*Teshuvos Beis Yitzchok, Yoreh Deah* §135) maintain that it is not sufficient that the total volume of the *esrog* be equal to that of an egg, but hold that the *esrog* must also have an egg's overall dimensions. Thus an *esrog* which is narrower than an egg but makes up for the volume in its length is invalid. However many *poskim* (*Teshuvos, Maharsham* 2:129; *Chazon Ish* cited in *Shiurin shel Torah* p. 66) dispute this (see R' E. Weissfish, *Arbaas HaMinim HaShalem* p. 263-4).

139. Most *Poskim* invalidate an *esrog* grown on an *esrog* twig that was grafted onto another tree species or vice versa. They rule that even if such an *esrog* is the only one available it should be taken without reciting the blessing (*M.B.* 648:65, *Da'as Torah* there, *Sha'arei Teshuvah* 649:7, *Arbaas HaMinim HaShalem*).

❧ Disqualified Species

140. If some of a person's Four Species are invalid, and no kosher set is available in the entire town, he should 'take' what he has without a blessing. Even if some of the species are missing entirely, one should take whatever species he has, but without a blessing (O.C. 649:6). However, under no circumstances should one substitute another species, e.g., willows similar to the prescribed one, or stolen species for the missing one (*M.B.* 649:53). Regarding the very complex question of what is defined as stolen in this regard see O.C. 649:1 with *M.B.*

141. If the disqualification was because of dryness, a blessing may be recited if no valid specimens of this species are available in the entire town (*M.B.* 649:58).

142. The second day of *Yom Tov* in the Diaspora is, generally speaking, accorded the same stringency as is the first day, and the disqualifications in effect on the first day are in effect on the second. Nevertheless, if one does not have a completely kosher set of the Four Species, he may 'take' species that are disqualified only on the first day but acceptable during the Intermediate Days. In such an instance, however, one should not recite the blessing (O.C. 649:6). On the first day this may be done only if there is no valid specimen to be obtained in the entire town, whereas on the second day it is sufficient that a valid specimen is available only with great exertion (*M.B.* 649:50). The above holds true only for disqualifications not in effect on the Intermediate Days, e.g., if it is difficult to obtain an *esrog* that will be one's own, he may borrow an *esrog* and 'take' it without a blessing.

✒ Observance /
Prayers and Ritual

Kindling Yom Tov Lights

Ushpizin

Kiddush

Bircas HaMazon / Grace after Meals

The Four Species

Kiddusha Rabba

Farewell to the Succah

— Rabbi Avie Gold

On each *Yom Tov* night of Succos two blessings are recited. Preferably the lights should be kindled in the Succah, even if some will later be brought into the home (see *Laws* §12). When Succos coincides with the Sabbath, light the candles, then cover the eyes and recite the blessings. Uncover the eyes and gaze briefly at the candles. When Succos falls on a weekday, some follow the above procedure, while others recite the blessings before lighting the candles. When Succos coincides with the Sabbath, the words in brackets are added.

[It is forbidden to create a new flame — for example, by striking a match — on *Yom Tov*. Therefore, on the second night the candles must be lit from a flame that has been burning from before *Yom Tov*.]

בָּרוּךְ אַתָּה יהוה אֱלֹהֵינוּ מֶלֶךְ הָעוֹלָם, אֲשֶׁר קִדְּשָׁנוּ בְּמִצְוֹתָיו, וְצִוָּנוּ לְהַדְלִיק נֵר* שֶׁל [שַׁבָּת וְשֶׁל] יוֹם טוֹב.*

בָּרוּךְ אַתָּה יהוה אֱלֹהֵינוּ מֶלֶךְ הָעוֹלָם, שֶׁהֶחֱיָנוּ* וְקִיְּמָנוּ וְהִגִּיעָנוּ לַזְּמַן הַזֶּה.

It is customary to recite the following prayer after the kindling.
The words in brackets are included as they apply.

יְהִי רָצוֹן* לְפָנֶיךָ, יהוה אֱלֹהַי וֵאלֹהֵי אֲבוֹתַי, שֶׁתְּחוֹנֵן אוֹתִי [וְאֶת אִישִׁי, וְאֶת בָּנַי, וְאֶת בְּנוֹתַי, וְאֶת אָבִי, וְאֶת אִמִּי] וְאֶת כָּל קְרוֹבַי; וְתִתֵּן לָנוּ וּלְכָל יִשְׂרָאֵל חַיִּים טוֹבִים וַאֲרוּכִים; וְתִזְכְּרֵנוּ בְּזִכְרוֹן טוֹבָה וּבְרָכָה; וְתִפְקְדֵנוּ בִּפְקֻדַּת יְשׁוּעָה וְרַחֲמִים; וּתְבָרְכֵנוּ בְּרָכוֹת גְּדוֹלוֹת; וְתַשְׁלִים בָּתֵּינוּ; וְתַשְׁכֵּן שְׁכִינָתְךָ בֵּינֵינוּ. וְזַכֵּנִי לְגַדֵּל בָּנִים וּבְנֵי בָנִים חֲכָמִים וּנְבוֹנִים, אוֹהֲבֵי יהוה, יִרְאֵי אֱלֹהִים, אַנְשֵׁי אֱמֶת, זֶרַע קֹדֶשׁ, בַּיהוה דְּבֵקִים, וּמְאִירִים אֶת הָעוֹלָם בַּתּוֹרָה וּבְמַעֲשִׂים טוֹבִים, וּבְכָל מְלֶאכֶת עֲבוֹדַת הַבּוֹרֵא. אָנָּא שְׁמַע אֶת תְּחִנָּתִי בָּעֵת הַזֹּאת, בִּזְכוּת שָׂרָה וְרִבְקָה וְרָחֵל וְלֵאָה אִמּוֹתֵינוּ, וְהָאֵר נֵרֵנוּ שֶׁלֹּא יִכְבֶּה לְעוֹלָם וָעֶד, וְהָאֵר פָּנֶיךָ וְנִוָּשֵׁעָה. אָמֵן.

Since women generally look after household matters, the *mitzvah* of kindling the lights has devolved upon the mistress of the house (*Rambam*). Nevertheless, a man living alone is required to kindle the lights and recite the proper blessing. Similarly, if a woman is too ill to light, her husband should light the candles and recite the blessing (*Magen Avraham*).

There should be some light in every room where it will be needed—and indeed this is a

halachic requirement—nevertheless, the blessing is recited upon the flames that are kindled in the dining room (*Mishnah Berurah*). The lights honor the Sabbath and Festival by brightening and dignifying the festive meal (*Rashi*).

נֵר — *The light.* Prevalent custom calls for at least two candles. According to *Eliyah Rabbah*, they symbolize man and wife. Nevertheless, since one can fulfill the *mitzvah* with a single candle [indeed, *Mishnah Berurah* advises one with extremely limited means to purchase one good

❊{ KINDLING LIGHTS }❊

On each *Yom Tov* night of Succos two blessings are recited. Preferably the lights should be kindled in the Succah, even if some will later be brought into the home (see *Laws* §12). When Succos coincides with the Sabbath, light the candles, then cover the eyes and recite the blessings. Uncover the eyes and gaze briefly at the candles. When Succos falls on a weekday, some follow the above procedure, while others recite the blessings before lighting the candles. When Succos coincides with the Sabbath, the words in brackets are added.

[It is forbidden to create a new flame — for example, by striking a match — on *Yom Tov*. Therefore, on the second night the candles must be lit from a flame that has been burning from before *Yom Tov*.]

בָּרוּךְ *Blessed are You, HASHEM, our God, King of the universe, Who has sanctified us with His commandments, and has commanded us to kindle the light* of [the Sabbath and of] the Festival.**

בָּרוּךְ *Blessed are You, HASHEM, our God, King of the universe, Who has kept us alive,* sustained us, and brought us to this season.*

It is customary to recite the following prayer after the kindling.
The words in brackets are included as they apply.

יְהִי רָצוֹן *May it be Your will,* HASHEM, my God and God of my forefathers, that You show favor to me [my husband, my sons, my daughters, my father, my mother] and all my relatives; and that You grant us and all Israel a good and long life; that You remember us with a beneficent memory and blessing; that You consider us with a consideration of salvation and compassion; that You bless us with great blessings; that You make our households complete; that You cause Your Presence to dwell among us. Privilege me to raise children and grandchildren who are wise and understanding, who love HASHEM and fear God, people of truth, holy offspring, attached to HASHEM, who illuminate the world with Torah and good deeds and with every labor in the service of the Creator. Please, hear my supplication at this time, in the merit of Sarah, Rebecca, Rachel, and Leah, our mothers, and cause our light to illuminate that it be not extinguished forever, and let Your countenance shine so that we are saved. Amen.*

---

candle rather than two inferior ones] the blessing is couched in the singular form, נֵר, *light*, and not נֵרוֹת, *lights*.

שֶׁל [שַׁבָּת וְשֶׁל] יוֹם טוֹב — *Of [the Sabbath and of] the Festival.* The Sabbath is mentioned first, following the Talmudic rule that a more frequently performed *mitzvah* takes precedence over a less frequent one.

שֶׁהֶחֱיָנוּ — *Who has kept us alive.* Some authorities rule that women should not recite the שֶׁהֶחֱיָנוּ blessing at this point, but instead should listen to the blessing during *Kiddush*, as does the rest

of the family. However, it is a virtually universal custom that women do recite the blessing when kindling the lights.

❊§ יְהִי רָצוֹן — *May it be Your will.* It is customary to recite this prayer after the kindling. Because of the Talmudic declaration, 'One who is scrupulous in the kindling of lights will be blessed with children who are Torah scholars' (*Shabbos* 23b), the prayer stresses the supplication that the children of the home grow up learned and righteous.

Upon entering the *succah* we invite the *Ushpizin*-guests [see commentary] to join us, and we offer prayers that our fulfillment of the *mitzvah* of *succah* be found worthy of Divine favor. Customs vary regarding these prayers. Some recite the full text, others omit various paragraphs. [The first paragraph is said only by those who follow the *Sefirah* order of the *Ushpizin*-guests (see below).]

עוּלוּ אוּשְׁפִּיזִין עִלָּאִין קַדִּישִׁין, עוּלוּ אֲבָהָן עִלָּאִין קַדִּישִׁין, לְמֵיתַב בְּצֵלָּא דִמְהֵימְנוּתָא עִלָּאָה בְּצֵלָא דְקֻדְשָׁא בְּרִיךְ הוּא. לְעוּל אַבְרָהָם רְחִימָא, וְעִמֵּיהּ יִצְחָק עֲקִידְתָּא, וְעִמֵּיהּ יַעֲקֹב שְׁלֵמְתָא, וְעִמֵּיהּ מֹשֶׁה רַעֲיָא מְהֵימְנָא, וְעִמֵּיהּ אַהֲרֹן כַּהֲנָא קַדִּישָׁא, וְעִמֵּיהּ יוֹסֵף צַדִּיקָא, וְעִמֵּיהּ דָּוִד מַלְכָּא מְשִׁיחָא. בְּסֻכּוֹת תֵּשְׁבוּ, תִּיבוּ אוּשְׁפִּיזִין עִלָּאִין תִּיבוּ, תִּיבוּ אוּשְׁפִּיזֵי מְהֵימְנוּתָא תִּיבוּ.

הֲרֵינִי מוּכָן וּמְזֻמָּן לְקַיֵּם מִצְוַת סֻכָּה כַּאֲשֶׁר צִוַּנִי הַבּוֹרֵא יִתְבָּרַךְ שְׁמוֹ: בַּסֻּכֹּת תֵּשְׁבוּ שִׁבְעַת יָמִים, כָּל הָאֶזְרָח בְּיִשְׂרָאֵל יֵשְׁבוּ בַּסֻּכֹּת. לְמַעַן יֵדְעוּ* דֹרֹתֵיכֶם, כִּי בַסֻּכּוֹת הוֹשַׁבְתִּי אֶת בְּנֵי יִשְׂרָאֵל, בְּהוֹצִיאִי אוֹתָם מֵאֶרֶץ מִצְרָיִם.¹

תִּיבוּ תִּיבוּ אוּשְׁפִּיזִין עִילָּאִין, תִּיבוּ תִּיבוּ אוּשְׁפִּיזִין קַדִּישִׁין, תִּיבוּ תִּיבוּ אוּשְׁפִּיזִין דִמְהֵימְנוּתָא, תִּיבוּ בְּצֵלָּא דְקֻדְשָׁא בְּרִיךְ הוּא. זַכָּאָה חוּלְקָנָא, וְזַכָּאָה חוּלְקְהוֹן דְּיִשְׂרָאֵל, דִּכְתִיב: כִּי חֵלֶק יהוה עַמּוֹ, יַעֲקֹב חֶבֶל נַחֲלָתוֹ.*² לְשֵׁם יִחוּד* קֻדְשָׁא בְּרִיךְ הוּא וּשְׁכִינְתֵּהּ, לְיַחֲדָא שֵׁם י"ה בְּו"ה בְּיִחוּדָא שְׁלִים עַל יְדֵי הַהוּא טָמִיר וְנֶעְלָם, בְּשֵׁם כָּל יִשְׂרָאֵל. וִיהִי נֹעַם אֲדֹנָי אֱלֹהֵינוּ עָלֵינוּ, וּמַעֲשֵׂה יָדֵינוּ כּוֹנְנָה עָלֵינוּ,* וּמַעֲשֵׂה יָדֵינוּ כּוֹנְנֵהוּ.³

It is customary to invite and welcome seven exalted אוּשְׁפִּיזִין [*Ushpizin*], *guests*, to join us when we enter the *succah*. No ordinary guests, the *Ushpizin* are Abraham, Isaac, Jacob, Moses, Aaron, Joseph and David. Each day of Succos another of these guests leads the others into the *succah*.

This custom is based on a passage of *Zohar*: When a man sits in the *succah*, 'the shade of faithfulness' [צֵלָא דִמְהֵימְנוּתָא], the *Shechinah* spreads Its wings over him from above and ... Abraham, five other righteous ones, and King David make their dwelling with him ... Thus, a person should rejoice with shining countenance each and every day [of the festival] together with these guests who take lodging with him ... Upon entering the *succah*, Rav Hamnuna Sava would rejoice and, standing inside the doorway, say, 'Let us invite the guests and prepare the table.' Then he would remain on his feet and bless [them], saying '*In succos you shall dwell. Be seated, exalted guests, be seated; be seated guests of faithfulness, be seated.*' He would then raise his hands in joy

and say, 'Worthy is our portion, worthy is the portion of Israel, as it is written (*Deuteronomy* 32:9): *For HASHEM's portion is His people.*' Then he would sit down (*Zohar, Emor* 103b).

However, the blessings to be gained by inviting the exalted *Ushpizin* to join us must be activated by our own conduct, by the acts of kindness and charity that we ourselves perform.

Indeed, the passage cited above goes on to say that the portions of food one would normally serve the honored *Ushpizin* should be distributed among the poor, preferably as guests in one's own *succah*. Moreover, "if one scrupulously serves and gladdens his guests, then God Himself rejoices with him. Abraham blesses the host, '*You shall be granted delight with HASHEM*' (*Isaiah* 58:14); Isaac proclaims, '*Mighty in the land will his offspring be*' (*Psalms* 112:2); Jacob says, '*Then shall your light burst forth just like the dawn*' (*Isaiah* 58:8); the other righteous ones [Moses, Aaron and Joseph] say, '*HASHEM will forever lead you, and He will satisfy you*' (ibid. 58:11); King David proclaims, '*Any weapons that are honed against you shall not succeed*' (ibid. 54:17) ... Praises to the portion of the person worthy of all this; praises to the portions

⌘{ USHPIZIN }⌘

Upon entering the *succah* we invite the *Ushpizin*-guests [see commentary] to join us, and we offer prayers that our fulfillment of the *mitzvah* of *succah* be found worthy of Divine favor. Customs vary regarding these prayers. Some recite the full text, others omit various paragraphs. [The first paragraph is said only by those who follow the *Sefirah* order of the *Ushpizin*-guests (see below).]

עוּלוּ Enter, exalted holy guests, enter, exalted holy Patriarchs, to be seated in the shade of exalted faithfulness in the shade of the Holy One, Blessed is He. Enter, Abraham the beloved one, Moses the faithful shepherd, Aaron the holy Kohen, Joseph the righteous one, and David the anointed king. In succos you shall dwell, be seated, exalted guests, be seated; be seated, guests of faithfulness, be seated.

הֲרֵינִי Behold, I am prepared and ready to perform the commandment of succah as the Creator, Blessed is His Name, commanded me: In succos shall you dwell for seven days; every citizen in Israel shall dwell in succos; in order that your generations may know* that I caused the Children of Israel to dwell in succos when I brought them forth from the land of Egypt.[1]

Be seated, be seated, exalted guests; be seated, be seated, holy guests; be seated, be seated, guests of faithfulness; be seated in the shade of the Holy One, Blessed is He. Worthy is our portion, worthy is the portion of Israel, as it is written: For HASHEM's portion is His people, Jacob the lot of His heritage.*[2] For the sake of the unification* of the Holy One, Blessed is He, and His Presence, to unify the Name Yud-Kei with Vav-Kei in perfect unity through Him Who is hidden and inscrutable — [I pray] in the name of all Israel.

May the pleasantness of my Lord, our God, be upon us — may He establish our handiwork for us;* our handiwork may He establish.[3]

---

(1) *Leviticus* 23:42-43. (2) *Deuteronomy* 32:9. (3) *Psalms* 90:17.

of the righteous in this world and in the World to Come. About them is written, *'Regarding your nation — all of them are righteous' "* (ibid. 60:21; *Zohar, Emor* 104a).

Customs regarding the invitation and the associated prayers differ. Some recite the full text presented above, others include some paragraphs and omit others. Additionally, some repeat the invitations and prayers before each meal, while others recite them only once each day. A third difference, regarding the order of the *Ushpizin*, is discussed below.

לְמַעַן יֵדְעוּ . . . בְּסֻכֹּת תֵּשְׁבוּ — *In succos shall you dwell . . . in order that your generations may know . . .* The Torah specifies that the *mitzvah* of *succah* is to serve as a reminder *'that I caused the Children of Israel to dwell in succos when I brought them forth from the land of Egypt.'* Unlike the overwhelming majority of *mitzvos*, knowledge of this reason is necessary to the proper fulfillment of the *mitzvah* of *succah* — *'in order that your generations may know.'* Two other *mitzvos* in which the reason for the

mitzvah is an integral part of its fulfillment are *tzitzis* and *tefillin.* Due to this unusual relationship between performance and understanding, the author of the halachic code *Tur* — in addition to listing the halachic requirements — departs from his usual style of simply describing the form of the *mitzvah* and adds an interpretation of the verses along with the proper כַּוָּנוֹת, *intentions,* upon which one should concentrate while performing these three *mitzvos* (*Bach* 625). Thus, upon entering the *succah* we declare the reason for our doing so.

תֵּיבוּ . . . נַחֲלָתוּ — *Be seated . . . His heritage.* This passage is almost a direct quote from the words of Rav Hamnuna cited by *Zohar* [see above, prefatory note to *Ushpizin*].

לְשֵׁם יִחוּד — *For the sake of the unification.* This kabbalistic formulation is similar to the one customarily recited before many *mitzvos.*

וּמַעֲשֵׂה יָדֵינוּ כּוֹנְנָה עָלֵינוּ — *May He establish our handiwork for us* [lit. *upon us*]. In any material

יְהִי רָצוֹן מִלְּפָנֶיךָ, יהוה אֱלֹהַי וֵאלֹהֵי אֲבוֹתַי, שֶׁתַּשְׁרֶה שְׁכִינָתְךָ בֵּינֵינוּ,
וְתִפְרוֹשׂ עָלֵינוּ סֻכַּת שְׁלוֹמֶךָ — בִּזְכוּת מִצְוַת סֻכָּה שֶׁאָנוּ
מְקַיְּמִין* — לְיַחֲדָא שְׁמָא דְקֻדְשָׁא בְּרִיךְ הוּא וּשְׁכִינְתֵּהּ, בִּדְחִילוּ וּרְחִימוּ,
לְיַחֲדָא שֵׁם י"ה בְּו"ה בְּיִחוּדָא שְׁלִים, בְּשֵׁם כָּל יִשְׂרָאֵל, וּלְהַקִּיף אוֹתָנוּ
מִזִּיו כְּבוֹדְךָ הַקָּדוֹשׁ וְהַטָּהוֹר, נָטוּי עַל רָאשֵׁינוּ מִלְמַעְלָה כְּנֶשֶׁר יָעִיר קִנּוֹ;*[1]
וּמִשָּׁם יַשְׁפִּיעַ שֶׁפַע הַחַיִּים לְעַבְדְּךָ (Hebrew name) בֶּן (mother's Hebrew name)
אֲמָתֶךָ.* וּבִזְכוּת צֵאתִי מִבֵּיתִי הַחוּצָה — וְדֶרֶךְ מִצְוֹתֶיךָ אָרוּצָה[2] — יֵחָשֵׁב
לִי בְּזֹאת כְּאִלּוּ הִרְחַקְתִּי נְדוֹד.[3] וְהֶרֶב כַּבְּסֵנִי מֵעֲוֹנִי, וּמֵחַטָּאתִי טַהֲרֵנִי.*[4]
וּמֵאוּשְׁפִּיזִין עִילָאִין, אוּשְׁפִּיזִין דִּמְהֵימְנוּתָא, תִּהְיֶינָה אָזְנֶיךָ קַשֻּׁבוֹת רַב
בְּרָכוֹת. (וְלָרְעֵבִים גַּם צְמֵאִים תֵּן לַחְמָם וּמֵימָם הַנֶּאֱמָנִים.) וְתִתֶּן לִי זְכוּת
לָשֶׁבֶת וְלַחֲסוֹת בְּסֵתֶר צֵל כְּנָפֶיךָ — בְּעֵת פְּטִירָתִי מִן הָעוֹלָם — וְלַחֲסוֹת
מִזֶּרֶם וּמִמָּטָר,* כִּי תַמְטִיר עַל רְשָׁעִים פַּחִים.[6] וּתְהֵא חֲשׁוּבָה מִצְוַת סֻכָּה
זוּ שֶׁאֲנִי מְקַיֵּם כְּאִלּוּ קִיַּמְתִּיהָ בְּכָל פְּרָטֶיהָ וְדִקְדוּקֶיהָ וּתְנָאֶיהָ וְכָל מִצְוֹת
הַתְּלוּיִם בָּהּ. וְתֵיטִיב לָנוּ הַחֲתִימָה. וּתְזַכֵּנוּ לֵישֵׁב יָמִים רַבִּים עַל הָאֲדָמָה,
אַדְמַת קֹדֶשׁ, בַּעֲבוֹדָתְךָ וּבְיִרְאָתֶךָ. בָּרוּךְ יהוה לְעוֹלָם, אָמֵן וְאָמֵן.[7]

---

activity, a craftsman shapes his creation, but remains dependent on it, in a sense. For example, architects and builders can erect a structure, but it rests on the earth, not on them, and *they* must depend on *it* for shelter. In the spiritual world, the opposite is true. One's performance of a *mitzvah* has as much spiritual content as he puts into it. We pray now that our deeds be worthy of God's pleasure and that He 'establish' them *upon us*, i.e., on the basis of our own spiritual handiwork (*Malbim*).

וְתִפְרוֹשׂ עָלֵינוּ סֻכַּת שְׁלוֹמֶךָ — בִּזְכוּת מִצְוַת סֻכָּה שֶׁאָנוּ מְקַיְּמִין — *That You spread over us the succah of Your peace — in the merit of the mitzvah of succah that we are fulfilling.* In His dealings with mankind, God treats every person מִדָּה כְּנֶגֶד מִדָּה, *measure for measure* (*Sotah* 8b). This attribute may be understood in light of *R' Yisrael Baal Shem Tov's* explanation of the verse, ה' צִלְּךָ, HASHEM is *your shade*, i.e., shelter (*Psalms* 121:5). The words ה' צִלְּךָ may also be translated HASHEM is *your shadow*. When you jump, your shadow jumps; when you stand still, you shadow does too. And when you perform a *mitzvah*, then God — as your shadow — also performs that *mitzvah* (cited in *Kedushas Levi, Exodus* 15:1). Having performed the *mitzvah* of erecting and dwelling in the *succah*, we ask that God spread over us His *succah* of peace.

כְּנֶשֶׁר יָעִיר קִנּוֹ — *Like an eagle arousing its brood* [lit., *its nest*]. This phrase is taken from *Deuteronomy* 32:11. *Rashi* there explains that the eagle takes pity on its young. If, upon returning to its nest, the parent bird finds the eaglets asleep, it will first flit from branch to branch, beating its wings and shaking the

foliage until the gentle sounds awaken the young ones so that they do not become startled when their parent enters the nest.

In like manner, we pray that God spread the aura of His honor over our heads — not in a way that will overwhelm us with the sudden manifestation of His full splendor and glory, but with a merciful gradual approach that enables us to bear His honor.

לְעַבְדְּךָ (...) בֶּן (...) אֲמָתֶךָ — *Your servant (...) son of (...) Your handmaid.* One who prays for a person's welfare — whether himself or someone else (*Sefer Chassidim* 237) — should mention the person's name and that of his mother (*Shabbos* 66b as explained by *Rashi*).

וּבִזְכוּת צֵאתִי מִבֵּיתִי ... כְּאִלּוּ הִרְחַקְתִּי נְדוֹד ... וּמֵחַטָּאתִי טַהֲרֵנִי — *And in the merit of my leaving my house ... as if I have wandered afar ... and from my sin purify me.* On Rosh Hashanah God sits in judgment over all of creation and on Yom Kippur the verdict is sealed. But perhaps Israel was not found worthy and was fated to exile! — In return for the Jewish 'exile' of leaving their homes and dwelling in the *succah*, God considers it as if they had been exiled all the way to Babylon (*Pesikta deRav Kahana* 29).

וְלַחֲסוֹת מִזֶּרֶם וּמִמָּטָר ... — *To take refuge from the stream [of fire] and the [fiery] rain ...* The prophet (*Isaiah* 4:6) describes the protective cloud which will be spread over the righteous in Messianic times: *It will be a succah ... to give refuge ... from the stream and the rain.* Stream refers to a stream of fire (*Daniel* 7:10) that will engulf the wicked (see *Jeremiah* 23:19). Rain refers to fiery coals that will rain upon them (see

יְהִי רָצוֹן May it be Your will, HASHEM, my God and the God of my forefathers, that You cause Your Presence to reside among us; that You spread over us the succah of Your peace — in the merit of the mitzvah of succah that we are fulfilling* — to unify the Name of the Holy One, Blessed is He, and His Presence, in fear and love, to unify the Name Yud-Kei with Vav-Kei in perfect unity, in the name of all Israel; and to surround us with the aura of Your honor, holy and pure, spread over our heads from above like an eagle arousing its brood;*[1] and from there cause an abundant outpouring of life for Your servant (Hebrew name) son of (mother's Hebrew name) Your handmaid.* And in the merit of my leaving my house to go out — and I will enthusiastically pursue the path of Your commandments[2] — may this be reckoned for me as if I have wandered afar.[3] Cleanse me thoroughly from my iniquity, and from my sin purify me.*[4] From the exalted guests, the guests of faithfulness, may Your ears hear abundant blessings. (To the hungry and thirsty, may You give their food and their unfailing supply of water.) May You endow me with the privilege to dwell and take refuge in the sheltering protection of Your wings — at the time of my departure from the world — to take refuge from the stream [of fire] and the [fiery] rain,*[5] when You rain coals upon the wicked.[6] May this mitzvah of succah that I perform be reckoned as if I had fulfilled it in all its details, implications and specifications, as well as all the mitzvos dependent on it. May You seal [the Book of Life] for our benefit,* and allow us the opportunity to dwell many days upon the land, the Holy Land, in Your service and in Your reverence. Blessed is HASHEM forever, Amen and Amen.[7]

---

(1) *Deuteronomy* 32:11. (2) Cf. *Psalms* 119:32. (3) Cf. 55:8.
(4) 51:4. (5) Cf. *Isaiah* 4:6. (6) Cf. *Psalms* 11:6. (7) 89:53.

Psalms 11:6) in retribution for their evil (*Rashi*). In the merit of sitting in the *succah* today, may we, in time to come, be found worthy of dwelling under the protective cloud-*succah*.

וְתֵיטִיב לָנוּ הַחֲתִימָה — *May You seal [the Book of Life] for our benefit [lit., may You make beneficial for us the seal].* Succos in general and its seventh day, Hoshana Rabbah, in particular, are periods of judgment in two ways: one specific and the other general. During the ten Days of Awe overall decisions have been made for humanity as a whole and for each individual in particular. Later God determines what will be done with regard to *particular* needs. On Pesach He judges man with regard to the grain crops, on Shavuos with regard to fruit crops, and on Succos with regard to the water supply [the climactic day of the water judgment coming on Hoshana Rabbah] (ibid. 16a).

But Hoshana Rabbah has a significance broader than the universal need for water. *Zohar* (*Tzav* 31b) describes it as a judgment day akin to Yom Kippur itself. On this day the judgment of Yom Kippur is sealed finally, and 'the parchments containing the decrees are given to angels to deliver.' On Rosh Hashanah all people were judged. The righteous were given a favorable judgment, those found wanting — but not totally evil — were given until Yom Kippur to repent. If they failed to do so, the verdict against them was written and sealed, but is not delivered until Hoshana Rabbah, when Jews assemble in prayer, dedication and supplication. The joy of Succos reaches its climax not in dissolute behavior, but in devotion. Then, God in His mercy finds ample reason to tear up the parchment bearing harsh sentences, as it were, and replace them with brighter tidings.

Thus for as long as we sit in the *succah* we still pray to be sealed in the Book of Life for goodness.

◆§ The Order of the Ushpizin

Days	Sefirah-emanations		Ushpizin
1st	חֶסֶד,	Lovingkindness	Abraham
2nd	גְּבוּרָה,	Power	Isaac
3rd	תִּפְאֶרֶת,	Splendor	Jacob
4th	נֶצַח,	Eternality	Moses
5th	הוֹד,	Glory	Aaron
6th	יְסוֹד,	Foundation	Joseph
7th	מַלְכוּת,	Kingship	David

רבּוֹן כָּל הָעוֹלָמִים, יְהִי רָצוֹן מִלְּפָנֶיךָ שֶׁיְּהֵא חָשׁוּב לְפָנֶיךָ מִצְוַת יְשִׁיבַת סֻכָּה זוֹ, כְּאִילוּ קִיַּמְתִּיהָ בְּכָל פְּרָטֶיהָ וְדִקְדּוּקֶיהָ וְתַרְיַ״ג מִצְוֹת הַתְּלוּיִים בָּהּ, וּכְאִילוּ כִּוַּנְתִּי בְּכָל הַכַּוָּנוֹת שֶׁכִּוְּנוּ בָהּ אַנְשֵׁי כְנֶסֶת הַגְּדוֹלָה.

There are two traditions regarding the order of the *Ushpizin* (see commentary).

CHRONOLOGICAL ORDER	SEFIRAH ORDER

CHRONOLOGICAL ORDER

אֲזַמֵּן לִסְעָדָתִי אֻשְׁפִּיזִין – Each day עִלָּאִין: אַבְרָהָם יִצְחָק יַעֲקֹב יוֹסֵף מֹשֶׁה אַהֲרֹן וְדָוִד.

בְּמָטוּ מִנָּךְ אַבְרָהָם – On the first day אֻשְׁפִּיזִי עִלָּאִי, דְּיֵתְבוּ עִמִּי וְעִמָּךְ כָּל אֻשְׁפִּיזֵי עִלָּאֵי, יִצְחָק יַעֲקֹב יוֹסֵף מֹשֶׁה אַהֲרֹן וְדָוִד.

בְּמָטוּ מִנָּךְ יִצְחָק – On the second day אֻשְׁפִּיזִי עִלָּאִי, דְּיֵתְבוּ עִמִּי וְעִמָּךְ כָּל אֻשְׁפִּיזֵי עִלָּאֵי, אַבְרָהָם יַעֲקֹב יוֹסֵף מֹשֶׁה אַהֲרֹן וְדָוִד.

בְּמָטוּ מִנָּךְ יַעֲקֹב – On the third day אֻשְׁפִּיזִי עִלָּאִי, דְּיֵתְבוּ עִמִּי וְעִמָּךְ כָּל אֻשְׁפִּיזֵי עִלָּאֵי, אַבְרָהָם יִצְחָק יוֹסֵף מֹשֶׁה אַהֲרֹן וְדָוִד.

בְּמָטוּ מִנָּךְ יוֹסֵף – On the fourth day אֻשְׁפִּיזִי עִלָּאִי, דְּיֵתְבוּ עִמִּי וְעִמָּךְ כָּל אֻשְׁפִּיזֵי עִלָּאֵי, אַבְרָהָם יִצְחָק יַעֲקֹב מֹשֶׁה אַהֲרֹן וְדָוִד.

בְּמָטוּ מִנָּךְ מֹשֶׁה – On the fifth day אֻשְׁפִּיזִי עִלָּאִי, דְּיֵתְבוּ עִמִּי וְעִמָּךְ כָּל אֻשְׁפִּיזֵי עִלָּאֵי, אַבְרָהָם יִצְחָק יַעֲקֹב יוֹסֵף אַהֲרֹן וְדָוִד.

בְּמָטוּ מִנָּךְ אַהֲרֹן – On the sixth day אֻשְׁפִּיזִי עִלָּאִי, דְּיֵתְבוּ עִמִּי וְעִמָּךְ כָּל אֻשְׁפִּיזֵי עִלָּאֵי, אַבְרָהָם יִצְחָק יַעֲקֹב יוֹסֵף מֹשֶׁה וְדָוִד.

בְּמָטוּ מִנָּךְ דָּוִד – On Hoshana Rabbah אֻשְׁפִּיזִי עִלָּאִי, דְּיֵתְבוּ עִמִּי וְעִמָּךְ כָּל אֻשְׁפִּיזֵי עִלָּאֵי, אַבְרָהָם יִצְחָק יַעֲקֹב יוֹסֵף מֹשֶׁה וְאַהֲרֹן.

SEFIRAH ORDER

אֲזַמֵּן לִסְעָדָתִי אֻשְׁפִּיזִין – Each day עִלָּאִין: אַבְרָהָם יִצְחָק יַעֲקֹב מֹשֶׁה אַהֲרֹן יוֹסֵף וְדָוִד.

בְּמָטוּ מִנָּךְ אַבְרָהָם – On the first day אֻשְׁפִּיזִי עִלָּאִי, דְּיֵתְבוּ עִמִּי וְעִמָּךְ כָּל אֻשְׁפִּיזֵי עִלָּאֵי, יִצְחָק יַעֲקֹב מֹשֶׁה אַהֲרֹן יוֹסֵף וְדָוִד.

בְּמָטוּ מִנָּךְ יִצְחָק – On the second day אֻשְׁפִּיזִי עִלָּאִי, דְּיֵתְבוּ עִמִּי וְעִמָּךְ כָּל אֻשְׁפִּיזֵי עִלָּאֵי, אַבְרָהָם יַעֲקֹב מֹשֶׁה אַהֲרֹן יוֹסֵף וְדָוִד.

בְּמָטוּ מִנָּךְ יַעֲקֹב – On the third day אֻשְׁפִּיזִי עִלָּאִי, דְּיֵתְבוּ עִמִּי וְעִמָּךְ כָּל אֻשְׁפִּיזֵי עִלָּאֵי, אַבְרָהָם יִצְחָק מֹשֶׁה אַהֲרֹן יוֹסֵף וְדָוִד.

בְּמָטוּ מִנָּךְ מֹשֶׁה – On the fourth day אֻשְׁפִּיזִי עִלָּאִי, דְּיֵתְבוּ עִמִּי וְעִמָּךְ כָּל אֻשְׁפִּיזֵי עִלָּאֵי, אַבְרָהָם יִצְחָק יַעֲקֹב אַהֲרֹן יוֹסֵף וְדָוִד.

בְּמָטוּ מִנָּךְ אַהֲרֹן – On the fifth day אֻשְׁפִּיזִי עִלָּאִי, דְּיֵתְבוּ עִמִּי וְעִמָּךְ כָּל אֻשְׁפִּיזֵי עִלָּאֵי, אַבְרָהָם יִצְחָק יַעֲקֹב מֹשֶׁה יוֹסֵף וְדָוִד.

בְּמָטוּ מִנָּךְ יוֹסֵף – On the sixth day אֻשְׁפִּיזִי עִלָּאִי, דְּיֵתְבוּ עִמִּי וְעִמָּךְ כָּל אֻשְׁפִּיזֵי עִלָּאֵי, אַבְרָהָם יִצְחָק יַעֲקֹב מֹשֶׁה אַהֲרֹן וְדָוִד.

בְּמָטוּ מִנָּךְ דָּוִד – On Hoshana Rabbah אֻשְׁפִּיזִי עִלָּאִי, דְּיֵתְבוּ עִמִּי וְעִמָּךְ כָּל אֻשְׁפִּיזֵי עִלָּאֵי, אַבְרָהָם יִצְחָק יַעֲקֹב מֹשֶׁה אַהֲרֹן וְיוֹסֵף.

In naming the *Ushpizin*-guests, the *Zohar* (cited above) lists, 'Abraham, five other righteous ones, and King David.' A second passage in *Zohar* adds Isaac and Jacob. Although the remaining three *Ushpizin* are not identified, they are universally recognized as Joseph, Moses and Aaron, and they are assigned the fourth,

fifth and sixth days of Succos. But the order in which the days are assigned is a matter of controversy which has given rise to two distinct orderings. Most *machzorim* of *Nusach Ashkenaz* follow a chronological order according to when the respective *Ushpizin* lived, i.e., Joseph on the fourth day, Moses on the fifth, and

רִבּוֹן Master of all the worlds, may it be Your will that this mitzvah of dwelling in the succah be reckoned before You as if I had fulfilled it in all its details and implications, as well as the six hundred thirteen mitzvos that are dependent upon it; and as if I had concentrated upon all the intentions which the Men of the Great Assembly concentrated upon regarding it.

There are two traditions regarding the order of the *Ushpizin* (see commentary).

SEFIRAH ORDER	CHRONOLOGICAL ORDER
Each day: *I invite to my meal the exalted guests: Abraham, Isaac, Jacob, Moses, Aaron, Joseph and David.*	Each day: *I invite to my meal the exalted guests: Abraham, Isaac, Jacob, Joseph, Moses, Aaron and David.*
On the first day: *May it please you, Abraham, my exalted guest, that all the other exalted guests dwell here with me and with you — Isaac, Jacob, Moses, Aaron, Joseph and David.*	On the first day: *May it please you, Abraham, my exalted guest, that all the other exalted guests dwell here with me and with you — Isaac, Jacob, Joseph, Moses, Aaron and David.*
On the second day: *May it please you, Isaac, my exalted guest, that all the other exalted guests dwell here with me and with you — Abraham, Jacob, Moses, Aaron, Joseph and David.*	On the second day: *May it please you, Isaac, my exalted guest, that all the other exalted guests dwell here with me and with you — Abraham, Jacob, Joseph, Moses, Aaron and David.*
On the third day: *May it please you, Jacob, my exalted guest, that all the other exalted guests dwell here with me and with you — Abraham, Isaac, Moses, Aaron, Joseph and David.*	On the third day: *May it please you, Jacob, my exalted guest, that all the other exalted guests dwell here with me and with you — Abraham, Isaac, Joseph, Moses, Aaron and David.*
On the fourth day: *May it please you, Moses, my exalted guest, that all the other exalted guests dwell here with me and with you — Abraham, Isaac, Jacob, Aaron, Joseph and David.*	On the fourth day: *May it please you, Joseph, my exalted guests, that all the other exalted guests dwell here with me and with you — Abraham, Isaac, Jacob, Moses, Aaron and David.*
On the fifth day: *May it please you, Aaron, my exalted guest, that all the other exalted guests dwell here with me and with you — Abraham, Isaac, Jacob, Moses, Joseph, and David.*	On the fifth day: *May it please you, Moses, my exalted guest, that all the other exalted guests dwell here with me and with you — Abraham, Isaac, Jacob, Joseph, Aaron and David.*
On the sixth day: *May it please you, Joseph, my exalted guest, that all the other exalted guests dwell here with me and with you — Abraham, Isaac, Jacob, Moses, Aaron, and David.*	On the sixth day: *May it please you, Aaron, my exalted guest, that all the other exalted guests dwell here with me and with you — Abraham, Isaac, Jacob, Joseph, Moses and David.*
On Hoshana Rabbah: *May it please you, David, my exalted guest, that all the other exalted guests dwell here with me and with you — Abraham, Isaac, Jacob, Moses, Aaron and Joseph.*	On Hoshana Rabbah: *May it please you, David, my exalted guest, that all the other exalted guests dwell here with me and with you — Abraham, Isaac, Jacob, Joseph, Moses and Aaron.*

Aaron on the sixth. [Although Aaron was three years older than Moses, Moses takes precedence for he was the prophet and leader.] However, according to the kabbalistic tradition of R' Yitzchak Luria (known as *Arizal*), Joseph

appears after Moses and Aaron even though he predated them by several generations.

Arizal's view is based on the kabbalistic concepts of *Sefiros*, generally translated *emanations*. This concept teaches that man can have

On Friday night, some recite the following before *Kiddush*.
Each of the first four stanzas is recited three times.

שָׁלוֹם עֲלֵיכֶם, מַלְאֲכֵי הַשָּׁרֵת, מַלְאֲכֵי עֶלְיוֹן, מִמֶּלֶךְ מַלְכֵי
הַמְּלָכִים הַקָּדוֹשׁ בָּרוּךְ הוּא.

בּוֹאֲכֶם לְשָׁלוֹם, מַלְאֲכֵי הַשָּׁלוֹם, מַלְאֲכֵי עֶלְיוֹן, מִמֶּלֶךְ מַלְכֵי
הַמְּלָכִים הַקָּדוֹשׁ בָּרוּךְ הוּא.

בָּרְכוּנִי לְשָׁלוֹם, מַלְאֲכֵי הַשָּׁלוֹם, מַלְאֲכֵי עֶלְיוֹן, מִמֶּלֶךְ מַלְכֵי
הַמְּלָכִים הַקָּדוֹשׁ בָּרוּךְ הוּא.

צֵאתְכֶם לְשָׁלוֹם, מַלְאֲכֵי הַשָּׁלוֹם, מַלְאֲכֵי עֶלְיוֹן, מִמֶּלֶךְ מַלְכֵי
הַמְּלָכִים הַקָּדוֹשׁ בָּרוּךְ הוּא.

כִּי מַלְאָכָיו יְצַוֶּה לָּךְ, לִשְׁמָרְךָ בְּכָל דְּרָכֶיךָ.[1]
יהוה יִשְׁמָר צֵאתְךָ וּבוֹאֶךָ, מֵעַתָּה וְעַד עוֹלָם.[2]

(משלי לא:י-לא)

אֵשֶׁת חַיִל מִי יִמְצָא, וְרָחֹק מִפְּנִינִים מִכְרָהּ.
בָּטַח בָּהּ לֵב בַּעְלָהּ, וְשָׁלָל לֹא יֶחְסָר.
גְּמָלַתְהוּ טוֹב וְלֹא רָע, כֹּל יְמֵי חַיֶּיהָ.
דָּרְשָׁה צֶמֶר וּפִשְׁתִּים, וַתַּעַשׂ בְּחֵפֶץ כַּפֶּיהָ.
הָיְתָה כָּאֳנִיּוֹת סוֹחֵר, מִמֶּרְחָק תָּבִיא לַחְמָהּ.
וַתָּקָם בְּעוֹד לַיְלָה, וַתִּתֵּן טֶרֶף לְבֵיתָהּ, וְחֹק לְנַעֲרֹתֶיהָ.
זָמְמָה שָׂדֶה וַתִּקָּחֵהוּ, מִפְּרִי כַפֶּיהָ נָטְעָה כָּרֶם.
חָגְרָה בְעוֹז מָתְנֶיהָ, וַתְּאַמֵּץ זְרוֹעֹתֶיהָ.
טָעֲמָה כִּי טוֹב סַחְרָהּ, לֹא יִכְבֶּה בַלַּיְלָה נֵרָהּ.
יָדֶיהָ שִׁלְּחָה בַכִּישׁוֹר, וְכַפֶּיהָ תָּמְכוּ פָלֶךְ.
כַּפָּהּ פָּרְשָׂה לֶעָנִי, וְיָדֶיהָ שִׁלְּחָה לָאֶבְיוֹן.
לֹא תִירָא לְבֵיתָהּ מִשָּׁלֶג, כִּי כָל בֵּיתָהּ לָבֻשׁ שָׁנִים.
מַרְבַדִּים עָשְׂתָה לָּהּ, שֵׁשׁ וְאַרְגָּמָן לְבוּשָׁהּ.
נוֹדָע בַּשְּׁעָרִים בַּעְלָהּ, בְּשִׁבְתּוֹ עִם זִקְנֵי אָרֶץ.
סָדִין עָשְׂתָה וַתִּמְכֹּר, וַחֲגוֹר נָתְנָה לַכְּנַעֲנִי.
עוֹז וְהָדָר לְבוּשָׁהּ, וַתִּשְׂחַק לְיוֹם אַחֲרוֹן.
פִּיהָ פָּתְחָה בְחָכְמָה, וְתוֹרַת חֶסֶד עַל לְשׁוֹנָהּ.
צוֹפִיָּה הֲלִיכוֹת בֵּיתָהּ, וְלֶחֶם עַצְלוּת לֹא תֹאכֵל.
קָמוּ בָנֶיהָ וַיְאַשְּׁרוּהָ, בַּעְלָהּ וַיְהַלְלָהּ.
רַבּוֹת בָּנוֹת עָשׂוּ חָיִל, וְאַתְּ עָלִית עַל כֻּלָּנָה.
שֶׁקֶר הַחֵן וְהֶבֶל הַיֹּפִי, אִשָּׁה יִרְאַת יהוה הִיא תִתְהַלָּל.
תְּנוּ לָהּ מִפְּרִי יָדֶיהָ, וִיהַלְלוּהָ בַשְּׁעָרִים מַעֲשֶׂיהָ.

no perception of God, for His true Being is
beyond human intelligence. All we can know
are His 'manifestations,' the various ways in
which He seems to behave toward us, i.e., mercy,
power, judgment, etc. Even these can come to

us only through intermediaries, known as
Sefirah-emanations, for we can never perceive
God's essence. Each day of Succos is related to
one of seven *Sefirah*-emanations, which in turn
is represented by one of the seven *Ushpizin*-

On Friday night, some recite the following before *Kiddush.*
Each of the first four stanzas is recited three times.

שָׁלוֹם עֲלֵיכֶם *Peace upon you, O ministering angels, angels of the Exalted One — from the King Who reigns over kings, the Holy One, Blessed is He.*

בּוֹאֲכֶם לְשָׁלוֹם *May your coming be for peace, O angels of peace, angels of the Exalted One — from the King Who reigns over kings, the Holy One, Blessed is He.*

בָּרְכוּנִי לְשָׁלוֹם *Bless me for peace, O angels of peace, angels of the Exalted One — from the King Who reigns over kings, the Holy One, Blessed is He.*

צֵאתְכֶם לְשָׁלוֹם *May your departure be to peace, O angels of peace, angels of the Exalted One — from the King Who reigns over kings, the Holy One, Blessed is He.*

He will charge His angels for you, to protect you in all your ways.[1]
May HASHEM protect your going and returning, from this time and forever.[2]

(Proverbs 31:10-31)

אֵשֶׁת חַיִל *An accomplished woman, who can find? —*
Far beyond pearls is her value.
ב *Her husband's heart relies on her and he shall lack no fortune.*
ג *She repays his good, but never his harm, all the days of her life.*
ד *She seeks out wool and linen, and her hands work willingly.*
ה *She is like a merchant's ships, from afar she brings her sustenance.*
ו *She arises while it is yet nighttime,*
and gives food to her household and a ration to her maidens.
ז *She envisions a field and buys it,*
from the fruit of her handiwork she plants a vineyard.
ח *With strength she girds her loins, and invigorates her arms.*
ט *She discerns that her enterprise is good —*
so her lamp is not snuffed out by night.
י *Her hands she stretches out to the distaff, and her palms support the spindle.*
כ *She spreads out her palm to the poor, and extends her hands to the destitute.*
ל *She fears not snow for her household,*
for her entire household is clothed with scarlet wool.
מ *Luxurious bedspreads she made herself, linen and purple wool are her clothing.*
נ *Distinctive in the councils is her husband,*
when he sits with the elders of the land.
ס *She makes a cloak to sell, and delivers a belt to the peddler.*
ע *Strength and majesty are her raiment, she joyfully awaits the last day.*
פ *She opens her mouth with wisdom, and a lesson of kindness is on her tongue.*
צ *She anticipates the ways of her household,*
and partakes not of the bread of laziness.
ק *Her children arise and praise her, her husband, and he lauds her:*
ר *'Many daughters have amassed achievement, but you surpassed them all.'*
ש *False is grace and vain is beauty,*
a God-fearing woman — she should be praised.
ת *Give her the fruits of her hand*
and let her be praised in the gates by her very own deeds.

(1) *Psalms* 91:11. (2) 121:8.

guests (see chart above). Consequently, Moses and Aaron, who personify the fourth and fifth *Sefiros* of נצח, *Eternality,* and הוד, *Glory,* are the *Ushpizin* on the fourth and fifth days. The righteous Joseph, who represents יְסוֹד, *Foundation —* צַדִּיק יְסוֹד עוֹלָם, *the righteous one is the foundation of the world* (Proverbs 10:25) — is the guest on the sixth day of the festival.

When the Festival falls on Friday night, begin here:

(Recite silently – וַיְהִי עֶרֶב* וַיְהִי בֹקֶר)

יוֹם הַשִּׁשִּׁי. וַיְכֻלּוּ* הַשָּׁמַיִם וְהָאָרֶץ* וְכָל צְבָאָם. וַיְכַל אֱלֹהִים
בַּיּוֹם הַשְּׁבִיעִי מְלַאכְתּוֹ אֲשֶׁר עָשָׂה, וַיִּשְׁבֹּת בַּיּוֹם
הַשְּׁבִיעִי מִכָּל מְלַאכְתּוֹ אֲשֶׁר עָשָׂה. וַיְבָרֶךְ אֱלֹהִים אֶת יוֹם הַשְּׁבִיעִי
וַיְקַדֵּשׁ אֹתוֹ, כִּי בוֹ שָׁבַת מִכָּל מְלַאכְתּוֹ אֲשֶׁר בָּרָא אֱלֹהִים לַעֲשׂוֹת.¹

On all nights other than Friday begin here (on Friday night include all words in brackets):

סַבְרִי מָרָנָן וְרַבָּנָן וְרַבּוֹתַי:

בָּרוּךְ אַתָּה יהוה אֱלֹהֵינוּ מֶלֶךְ הָעוֹלָם, בּוֹרֵא* פְּרִי הַגָּפֶן.

(All present respond– אָמֵן.)

בָּרוּךְ אַתָּה יהוה אֱלֹהֵינוּ מֶלֶךְ הָעוֹלָם, אֲשֶׁר בָּחַר בָּנוּ מִכָּל
עָם,* וְרוֹמְמָנוּ מִכָּל לָשׁוֹן, וְקִדְּשָׁנוּ בְּמִצְוֹתָיו. וַתִּתֶּן לָנוּ
יהוה אֱלֹהֵינוּ בְּאַהֲבָה [שַׁבָּתוֹת לִמְנוּחָה וּ]מוֹעֲדִים לְשִׂמְחָה חַגִּים
וּזְמַנִּים לְשָׂשׂוֹן, אֶת יוֹם [הַשַּׁבָּת הַזֶּה וְאֶת יוֹם] חַג הַסֻּכּוֹת הַזֶּה, זְמַן
שִׂמְחָתֵנוּ [בְּאַהֲבָה] מִקְרָא קֹדֶשׁ, זֵכֶר לִיצִיאַת מִצְרָיִם. כִּי בָנוּ
בָחַרְתָּ וְאוֹתָנוּ קִדַּשְׁתָּ מִכָּל הָעַמִּים, [וְשַׁבָּת] וּמוֹעֲדֵי קָדְשֶׁךָ
[בְּאַהֲבָה וּבְרָצוֹן] בְּשִׂמְחָה וּבְשָׂשׂוֹן הִנְחַלְתָּנוּ. בָּרוּךְ אַתָּה יהוה,
מְקַדֵּשׁ [הַשַּׁבָּת וְ]יִשְׂרָאֵל וְהַזְּמַנִּים.   (All present respond– אָמֵן.)

ON SATURDAY NIGHT CONTINUE BELOW. ON ALL OTHER NIGHTS CONTINUE ON NEXT PAGE.

On Saturday night, add the following two *Havdalah*· blessings. Two candles with flames
touching each other should be held before the person reciting the *Havdalah*.
After the first blessing, hold the fingers up to the flames to see the reflected light.

[It is forbidden to create a new flame — for example, by striking a match — on *Yom Tov*.
Therefore, the *Havdalah* candle must be lit from a flame that has been burning from before the
Sabbath. It is likewise forbidden to extinguish the flame.]

בָּרוּךְ אַתָּה יהוה אֱלֹהֵינוּ מֶלֶךְ הָעוֹלָם, בּוֹרֵא מְאוֹרֵי הָאֵשׁ.

(All present respond– אָמֵן.)

⌇§ Kiddush

Every Sabbath and *Yom Tov* is ushered in by
Kiddush, a declaration of the day's sanctity.
Even though we have already proclaimed the
holiness of the day in our evening prayers, its
proper celebration belongs in the home (tonight,
of course, home is in the *succah*), where we
usually pursue our weekday activities. As we
begin our festive meal, therefore, we dedicate
ourselves to the special message of the day.

וַיְהִי עֶרֶב — *And there was evening.* When Yom

Tov falls on the Sabbath, we preface the
Kiddush with the same verses that we recite
every Friday night, and which describe the
Sabbath of the week of creation, to remind us
of the profound purpose of the Sabbath.

וַיְכֻלּוּ — *Were finished.* The Midrash interprets
וַיְכֻלּוּ and וַיְכַל homiletically as *longing*, as we
find כָּלְתָה נַפְשִׁי, *my soul longed* (Psalms 84:3).
Heaven and earth, and God Himself, long for
the coming of the Sabbath, because it infuses
all of creation with holiness (*Tzror HaMor*).

וַיְכֻלּוּ הַשָּׁמַיִם וְהָאָרֶץ — *Thus the heavens and the*

When the Festival falls on Friday night, begin here:
(Recite silently— And there was evening* and there was morning)

יוֹם הַשִּׁשִּׁי *The sixth day. Thus the heavens and the earth were finished,* and all their array. On the seventh day God completed His work which He had done, and He abstained on the seventh day from all His work which He had done. God blessed the seventh day and hallowed it, because on it He abstained from all His work which God created to make.*[1]

On all nights other than Friday begin here (on Friday night include all words in brackets):
By your leave, my masters, rabbis and teachers:

בָּרוּךְ *Blessed are You, HASHEM, our God, King of the universe, Who creates* the fruit of the vine.* (All present respond— *Amen.*)

בָּרוּךְ *Blessed are You, HASHEM, our God, King of the universe, Who has chosen us from every people,* exalted us above every tongue, and sanctified us with His commandments. And You gave us, HASHEM, our God, with love [Sabbaths for rest], appointed festivals for gladness, festivals and times for joy, [this day of Sabbath and] Succos, the time of our gladness [with love], a holy convocation, a memorial of the Exodus from Egypt. For You have chosen us and You have sanctified us above all the peoples, [and the Sabbath] and Your holy festivals [in love and in favor] in gladness and in joy have You granted us as a heritage. Blessed are You, HASHEM, Who sanctifies [the Sabbath and] Israel and the seasons.* (All present respond— *Amen.*)

ON SATURDAY NIGHT CONTINUE BELOW. ON ALL OTHER NIGHTS CONTINUE ON NEXT PAGE.

On Saturday night, add the following two Havdalah* blessings. Two candles with flames touching each other should be held before the person reciting the Havdalah.
After the first blessing, hold the fingers up to the flames to see the reflected light.

[It is forbidden to create a new flame — for example, by striking a match — on Yom Tov. Therefore, the Havdalah candle must be lit from a flame that has been burning from before the Sabbath. It is likewise forbidden to extinguish the flame.]

בָּרוּךְ *Blessed are You, HASHEM, our God, King of the universe, Who creates the illumination of the fire.* (All present respond— *Amen.*)

(1) *Genesis* 1:31-2:3.

---

earth were finished. The verse uses the passive form *were finished* rather than the active *and HASHEM finished.* This implies that, despite the magnitude of the task, God expended only minimum effort in the creation of the universe (*Tzror HaMor*).

בָּרוּךְ אַתָּה ... בּוֹרֵא — *Blessed are You ... Who creates.* The blessing begins by addressing God directly in second person — אַתָּה, *You* — it then reverts to third person, בּוֹרֵא, *(He) Who creates.* This is also true of all blessings. They begin by addressing God in second person because prayer is so exalted that it enables mortal man to turn directly to God, so to speak. Then the blessings change to third person because the balance of

the blessing speaks of His outward manifestations as He guides and controls the universe. Of that aspect of God, we have no direct understanding — only an imperfect perception of outward appearances (*Michtav MeEliyahu*).

אֲשֶׁר בָּחַר בָּנוּ מִכָּל עָם ... — *Who has chosen us from every people* ... The wording of *Kiddush* is reminiscent of the Festival *Shemoneh Esrei.*

◆§ Havdalah

If the second day of Succos falls on Sunday, we must mark the end of the Sabbath with הַבְדָּלָה, *Havdalah,* the ceremony by which we separate the Sabbath with its greater holiness from the rest of the week.

If, for whatever the reason, one does not recite *Kiddush* in a *succah*, the first of the following blessings is omitted. On the second night, some reverse the order of these two blessings.

בָּרוּךְ אַתָּה יהוה אֱלֹהֵינוּ מֶלֶךְ הָעוֹלָם, אֲשֶׁר קִדְּשָׁנוּ בְּמִצְוֹתָיו וְצִוָּנוּ לֵישֵׁב בַּסֻּכָּה.*

(אָמֵן.‏ —All present respond)

בָּרוּךְ אַתָּה יהוה אֱלֹהֵינוּ מֶלֶךְ הָעוֹלָם, שֶׁהֶחֱיָנוּ* וְקִיְּמָנוּ וְהִגִּיעָנוּ לַזְּמַן הַזֶּה.

(אָמֵן.‏ —All present respond)

‏ברכת המזון‏ ﷽

תהלים קכו

שִׁיר הַמַּעֲלוֹת, בְּשׁוּב יהוה אֶת שִׁיבַת צִיּוֹן, הָיִינוּ כְּחֹלְמִים. אָז יִמָּלֵא שְׂחוֹק פִּינוּ וּלְשׁוֹנֵנוּ רִנָּה, אָז יֹאמְרוּ בַגּוֹיִם, הִגְדִּיל יהוה לַעֲשׂוֹת עִם אֵלֶּה. הִגְדִּיל יהוה לַעֲשׂוֹת עִמָּנוּ, הָיִינוּ שְׂמֵחִים. שׁוּבָה יהוה אֶת שְׁבִיתֵנוּ, כַּאֲפִיקִים בַּנֶּגֶב. הַזֹּרְעִים בְּדִמְעָה בְּרִנָּה יִקְצֹרוּ. הָלוֹךְ יֵלֵךְ וּבָכֹה נֹשֵׂא מֶשֶׁךְ הַזָּרַע, בֹּא יָבֹא בְרִנָּה, נֹשֵׂא אֲלֻמֹּתָיו.

הִנְנִי מוּכָן וּמְזוּמָּן לְקַיֵּם מִצְוַת עֲשֵׂה שֶׁל בִּרְכַּת הַמָּזוֹן, שֶׁנֶּאֱמַר: וְאָכַלְתָּ וְשָׂבָעְתָּ, וּבֵרַכְתָּ אֶת יהוה אֱלֹהֶיךָ, עַל הָאָרֶץ הַטֹּבָה אֲשֶׁר נָתַן לָךְ.[1]

We are permitted certain activities on *Yom Tov*, such as baking or cooking, that are forbidden on the Sabbath; therefore it is necessary to declare the Sabbath as ended. For this purpose, we pronounce the blessing, 'Who creates the illumination of the fire,' and also the blessing of *Havdalah*, which distinguishes between the greater holiness of Sabbath and the lesser holiness of *Yom Tov*. This latter blessing alludes to seven distinctions: the distinction between the sacred and the profane, between light and darkness, between Israel and the nations, between the Sabbath and weekdays, between the holiness of Sabbath and that of *Yom Tov* and *Chol HaMoed* (the Intermediate Days of the *Yom Tov*), and — within the Jewish people — between *Kohanim* and Levites, and between Levites and Israelites.

◄§ Succah Blessing

לֵישֵׁב בַּסֻּכָּה — *To dwell in the succah*. Blessings recited before the performance of a *mitzvah* take one of two forms. The more common form uses the word עַל, *upon* or *concerning*, to precede the name of the *mitzvah*, e.g., עַל אֲכִילַת מַצָּה, *concerning the eating of matzah*. The second form uses an infinitive clause, preceded by the prefix ל, e.g., לֵישֵׁב בַּסֻּכָּה, *to dwell in the succah*. Generally speaking, the former version is used when a short period is required for the performance of the *mitzvah*, e.g., the *mitzvah* of matzah is fulfilled as soon as the required amount is eaten. When the *mitzvah* consists of an activity performed over an extended time period, e.g., the *mitzvah* of succah lasts for seven full days, the infinitive form is used (*Mateh Moshe*).

בָּרוּךְ Blessed are You, HASHEM, our God, King of the universe, Who distinguishes between the sacred and secular, between light and darkness, between Israel and the peoples, between the seventh day and the six days of labor. Between sanctity of the Sabbaths and the sanctity of the holidays You have distinguished, and the seventh day, from among the six days of labor You have sanctified. You have distinguished and You have sanctified Your people Israel with Your holiness. Blessed are You, HASHEM, Who distinguishes between holiness and holiness.

(All present respond— *Amen.*)

If, for whatever the reason, one does not recite *Kiddush* in a *succah*, the first of the following blessings is omitted. On the second night, some reverse the order of these two blessings.

בָּרוּךְ Blessed are You, HASHEM, our God, King of the universe, Who has sanctified us with His commandments and has commanded us to dwell in the succah.* (All present respond— *Amen.*)

בָּרוּךְ Blessed are You, HASHEM, our God, King of the universe, Who has kept us alive,* sustained us, and brought us to this season. (All present respond— *Amen.*)

⊰ GRACE AFTER MEALS ⊱

Psalm 126

שִׁיר הַמַּעֲלוֹת A song of ascents. When HASHEM will return the captivity of Zion, we will be like dreamers. Then our mouth will be filled with laughter and our tongue with glad song. Then they will declare among the nations, 'HASHEM has done greatly with these.' HASHEM has done greatly with us, we were gladdened. O HASHEM — return our captivity like springs in the desert. Those who tearfully sow will reap in glad song. He who bears the measure of seeds walks along weeping, but will return in exultation, a bearer of his sheaves.

הִנְנִי Behold! I am prepared and ready to perform the commandment of Grace after Meals, as it is said: 'And you shall eat and you shall be satisfied and you shall bless HASHEM, your God, for the good land which He gave you.'[1]

---

(1) *Deuteronomy* 8:10.

⊰§ Shehecheyanu

שֶׁהֶחֱיָנוּ — *Who has kept us alive.* This blessing is called בִּרְכַּת הַזְּמַן, *the blessing of the time,* or simply זְמַן, *time.* It is recited: on the festivals; over fruits of a new season, provided they ripen at recurring intervals and are not always available; upon *mitzvos* that are performed at seasonal interval such as *succah, lulav,* and others connected with the annual festivals; upon seeing a friend whom one has not seen for a significant interval; upon purchasing a new garment of significance; and upon benefiting from a significant event [see *Orach Chaim* 225].

This blessing is technically in the category of בִּרְכוֹת הוֹדָאָה, *blessings of thanksgiving.* It expresses our gratitude to God for having granted us the life and sustenance to celebrate another festive season.

⊰ בִּרְכַּת הַמָּזוֹן / GRACE AFTER MEALS ⊱

For commentary see the *ArtScroll Bircas HaMazon* or *The Complete ArtScroll Siddur.*

If three or more males, aged thirteen or older, participate in a meal, a leader is appointed to formally invite the others to join him in the recitation of *Bircas HaMazon*. This invitation is called *zimun*.

Leader – רַבּוֹתַי מִיר וֶועלֶען בֶּענְטְשֶׁען. or – רַבּוֹתַי נְבָרֵךְ.

Others – יְהִי שֵׁם יהוה מְבֹרָךְ מֵעַתָּה וְעַד עוֹלָם.[1]

If ten men join in the *zimun* the words in parentheses are added.

Leader – יְהִי שֵׁם יהוה מְבֹרָךְ מֵעַתָּה וְעַד עוֹלָם.[1]

בִּרְשׁוּת מָרָנָן וְרַבָּנָן וְרַבּוֹתַי, נְבָרֵךְ (אֱלֹהֵינוּ) שֶׁאָכַלְנוּ מִשֶּׁלּוֹ.

Others° – בָּרוּךְ (אֱלֹהֵינוּ) שֶׁאָכַלְנוּ

°Those who have not eaten respond:

מִשֶּׁלּוֹ וּבְטוּבוֹ חָיִינוּ.   בָּרוּךְ (אֱלֹהֵינוּ) וּמְבֹרָךְ שְׁמוֹ תָּמִיד לְעוֹלָם וָעֶד.

Leader – בָּרוּךְ (אֱלֹהֵינוּ) שֶׁאָכַלְנוּ מִשֶּׁלּוֹ וּבְטוּבוֹ חָיִינוּ.

בָּרוּךְ הוּא וּבָרוּךְ שְׁמוֹ.

The *zimun* leader should recite *Bircas HaMazon* (or, at least, the conclusion of each blessing) aloud thus allowing the others to respond *Amen* to his blessings. Otherwise it is forbidden to interrupt *Bircas HaMazon* for any response other than those permitted during the *Shema*.

ברכת הזן

בָּרוּךְ אַתָּה יהוה אֱלֹהֵינוּ מֶלֶךְ הָעוֹלָם, הַזָּן אֶת הָעוֹלָם כֻּלּוֹ, בְּטוּבוֹ, בְּחֵן בְּחֶסֶד וּבְרַחֲמִים, הוּא נֹתֵן לֶחֶם לְכָל בָּשָׂר, כִּי לְעוֹלָם חַסְדּוֹ.[2] וּבְטוּבוֹ הַגָּדוֹל, תָּמִיד לֹא חָסַר לָנוּ, וְאַל יֶחְסַר לָנוּ מָזוֹן לְעוֹלָם וָעֶד. בַּעֲבוּר שְׁמוֹ הַגָּדוֹל, כִּי הוּא אֵל זָן וּמְפַרְנֵס לַכֹּל, וּמֵטִיב לַכֹּל, וּמֵכִין מָזוֹן לְכָל בְּרִיּוֹתָיו אֲשֶׁר בָּרָא. כָּאָמוּר: פּוֹתֵחַ אֶת יָדֶךָ, וּמַשְׂבִּיעַ לְכָל חַי רָצוֹן.[3] ❖ בָּרוּךְ אַתָּה יהוה, הַזָּן אֶת הַכֹּל. (Others – אָמֵן.)

ברכת הארץ

נוֹדֶה לְךָ יהוה אֱלֹהֵינוּ, עַל שֶׁהִנְחַלְתָּ לַאֲבוֹתֵינוּ אֶרֶץ חֶמְדָּה טוֹבָה וּרְחָבָה. וְעַל שֶׁהוֹצֵאתָנוּ יהוה אֱלֹהֵינוּ מֵאֶרֶץ מִצְרַיִם, וּפְדִיתָנוּ מִבֵּית עֲבָדִים, וְעַל בְּרִיתְךָ שֶׁחָתַמְתָּ בִּבְשָׂרֵנוּ, וְעַל תּוֹרָתְךָ שֶׁלִּמַּדְתָּנוּ, וְעַל חֻקֶּיךָ שֶׁהוֹדַעְתָּנוּ, וְעַל חַיִּים חֵן וָחֶסֶד שֶׁחוֹנַנְתָּנוּ, וְעַל אֲכִילַת מָזוֹן שָׁאַתָּה זָן וּמְפַרְנֵס אוֹתָנוּ תָּמִיד, בְּכָל יוֹם וּבְכָל עֵת וּבְכָל שָׁעָה.

וְעַל הַכֹּל יהוה אֱלֹהֵינוּ אֲנַחְנוּ מוֹדִים לָךְ, וּמְבָרְכִים אוֹתָךְ, יִתְבָּרַךְ שִׁמְךָ בְּפִי כָּל חַי תָּמִיד לְעוֹלָם וָעֶד. כַּכָּתוּב, וְאָכַלְתָּ וְשָׂבָעְתָּ, וּבֵרַכְתָּ אֶת יהוה אֱלֹהֶיךָ, עַל הָאָרֶץ הַטֹּבָה אֲשֶׁר נָתַן לָךְ.[4] ❖ בָּרוּךְ אַתָּה יהוה, עַל הָאָרֶץ וְעַל הַמָּזוֹן. (Others – אָמֵן.)

בנין ירושלים

רַחֵם נָא יהוה אֱלֹהֵינוּ עַל יִשְׂרָאֵל עַמֶּךָ, וְעַל יְרוּשָׁלַיִם עִירֶךָ, וְעַל צִיּוֹן מִשְׁכַּן כְּבוֹדֶךָ, וְעַל מַלְכוּת בֵּית דָּוִד מְשִׁיחֶךָ, וְעַל הַבַּיִת הַגָּדוֹל וְהַקָּדוֹשׁ שֶׁנִּקְרָא שִׁמְךָ עָלָיו. אֱלֹהֵינוּ אָבִינוּ רְעֵנוּ זוּנֵנוּ פַּרְנְסֵנוּ

ZIMUN/INVITATION

If three or more males, aged thirteen or older, participate in a meal, a leader is appointed to formally invite the others to join him in the recitation of Grace after Meals. This invitation is called *zimun*.

Leader — *Gentlemen, let us bless.*

Others — *Blessed be the Name of HASHEM from this time and forever!*[1]

If ten men join in the *zimun* the words in brackets are added.

Leader— *Blessed be the Name of HASHEM from this time and forever!*[1]
With the permission of the distinguished people present,
let us bless [our God,] He of Whose we have eaten.

Others°— *Blessed is [our God,] He of Whose*
we have eaten and through
Whose goodness we live.

°Those who have not eaten respond:
Blessed is He [our God] and blessed
is His Name continuously forever.

Leader— *Blessed is [our God,] He of Whose we have eaten and through Whose*
goodness we live.
Blessed is He and Blessed is His Name.

The *zimun* leader should recite Grace after Meals (or, at least, the conclusion of each blessing) aloud thus allowing the others to respond *Amen* to his blessings. Otherwise it is forbidden to interrupt Grace after Meals for any response other than those permitted during the *Shema*.

FIRST BLESSING: FOR THE NOURISHMENT

בָּרוּךְ *Blessed are You, HASHEM, our God, King of the universe, Who nourishes the entire world, in His goodness — with grace, with kindness, and with mercy. He gives nourishment to all flesh, for His kindness is eternal.*[2] *And through His great goodness, we have never lacked, and may we never lack, nourishment, for all eternity. For the sake of His great Name, because He is God Who nourishes and sustains all, and benefits all, and He prepares food for all of His creatures which He has created. As it is said: 'You open Your hand, and satisfy the desire of every living thing.'*[3] Leader— *Blessed are You, HASHEM, Who nourishes all.* (Others— *Amen.*)

SECOND BLESSING: FOR THE LAND

נוֹדֶה *We thank You, HASHEM, our God, because You have given to our forefathers as a heritage a desirable, good and spacious land; because You removed us, HASHEM, our God, from the land of Egypt and You redeemed us from the house of bondage; for Your covenant which You sealed in our flesh; for Your Torah which You taught us and for Your statutes which You made known to us; for life, grace, and lovingkindness which You granted us; and for the provision of food with which You nourish and sustain us constantly, in every day, in every season, and in every hour.*

וְעַל הַכּל *For all, HASHEM, our God, we thank You and bless You. May Your Name be blessed by the mouth of all the living, continuously for all eternity. As it is written: 'And you shall eat and you shall be satisfied and you shall bless HASHEM, your God, for the good land which He gave you.'*[4] Leader— *Blessed are You, HASHEM, for the land and for the nourishment.* (Others— *Amen.*)

THIRD BLESSING: FOR JERUSALEM

רַחֵם *Have mercy, please, HASHEM, our God, on Israel Your people; on Jerusalem, Your city, on Zion, the resting place of Your Glory; on the monarchy of the house of David, Your anointed; and on the great and holy House upon which Your Name is called. Our God, our Father — tend us, nourish us, sustain us,*

(1) *Psalms* 113:2. (2) 136:25. (3) 145:16. (4) *Deuteronomy* 8:10.

וְכַלְכְּלֵנוּ וְהַרְוִיחֵנוּ, וְהַרְוַח לָנוּ יהוה אֱלֹהֵינוּ מְהֵרָה מִכָּל צָרוֹתֵינוּ. וְנָא אַל תַּצְרִיכֵנוּ יהוה אֱלֹהֵינוּ, לֹא לִידֵי מַתְּנַת בָּשָׂר וָדָם, וְלֹא לִידֵי הַלְוָאָתָם, כִּי אִם לְיָדְךָ הַמְּלֵאָה הַפְּתוּחָה הַקְּדוֹשָׁה וְהָרְחָבָה, שֶׁלֹּא נֵבוֹשׁ וְלֹא נִכָּלֵם לְעוֹלָם וָעֶד.

On the Sabbath add the following. [If forgotten, see box below.]

רְצֵה וְהַחֲלִיצֵנוּ יהוה אֱלֹהֵינוּ בְּמִצְוֹתֶיךָ, וּבְמִצְוַת יוֹם הַשְּׁבִיעִי הַשַּׁבָּת הַגָּדוֹל וְהַקָּדוֹשׁ הַזֶּה, כִּי יוֹם זֶה גָּדוֹל וְקָדוֹשׁ הוּא לְפָנֶיךָ, לִשְׁבָּת בּוֹ וְלָנוּחַ בּוֹ בְּאַהֲבָה כְּמִצְוַת רְצוֹנֶךָ, וּבִרְצוֹנְךָ הָנִיחַ לָנוּ יהוה אֱלֹהֵינוּ, שֶׁלֹּא תְהֵא צָרָה וְיָגוֹן וַאֲנָחָה בְּיוֹם מְנוּחָתֵנוּ, וְהַרְאֵנוּ יהוה אֱלֹהֵינוּ בְּנֶחָמַת צִיּוֹן עִירֶךָ, וּבְבִנְיַן יְרוּשָׁלַיִם עִיר קָדְשֶׁךָ, כִּי אַתָּה הוּא בַּעַל הַיְשׁוּעוֹת וּבַעַל הַנֶּחָמוֹת.

אֱלֹהֵינוּ וֵאלֹהֵי אֲבוֹתֵינוּ, יַעֲלֶה, וְיָבֹא, וְיַגִּיעַ, וְיֵרָאֶה, וְיֵרָצֶה, וְיִשָּׁמַע, וְיִפָּקֵד, וְיִזָּכֵר זִכְרוֹנֵנוּ וּפִקְדוֹנֵנוּ, וְזִכְרוֹן אֲבוֹתֵינוּ, וְזִכְרוֹן מָשִׁיחַ בֶּן דָּוִד עַבְדֶּךָ, וְזִכְרוֹן יְרוּשָׁלַיִם עִיר קָדְשֶׁךָ, וְזִכְרוֹן כָּל עַמְּךָ בֵּית יִשְׂרָאֵל לְפָנֶיךָ, לִפְלֵיטָה לְטוֹבָה לְחֵן וּלְחֶסֶד וּלְרַחֲמִים, לְחַיִּים (טוֹבִים) וּלְשָׁלוֹם בְּיוֹם

On Shemini Atzeres and Simchas Torah: On Succos:

שְׁמִינִי עֲצֶרֶת הַחַג הַזֶּה.   חַג הַסֻּכּוֹת הַזֶּה.

זָכְרֵנוּ יהוה אֱלֹהֵינוּ בּוֹ לְטוֹבָה, וּפָקְדֵנוּ בוֹ לִבְרָכָה, וְהוֹשִׁיעֵנוּ בוֹ לְחַיִּים טוֹבִים. וּבִדְבַר יְשׁוּעָה וְרַחֲמִים, חוּס וְחָנֵּנוּ וְרַחֵם עָלֵינוּ וְהוֹשִׁיעֵנוּ, כִּי אֵלֶיךָ עֵינֵינוּ, כִּי אֵל חַנּוּן וְרַחוּם אָתָּה.[1]

✧ **וּבְנֵה** יְרוּשָׁלַיִם עִיר הַקֹּדֶשׁ בִּמְהֵרָה בְיָמֵינוּ. בָּרוּךְ אַתָּה יהוה, בּוֹנֵה בְרַחֲמָיו יְרוּשָׁלָיִם. אָמֵן.   (אָמֵן. – Others)

[When required, the compensatory blessing is recited here.]

◆§ If One Omitted רְצֵה or יַעֲלֶה וְיָבֹא

If one omitted יַעֲלֶה וְיָבֹא on Succos (and/or רְצֵה on Succos that falls on the Sabbath):

(a) If he realizes his omission after having recited the word בּוֹנֵה, Who rebuilds, of the next paragraph, but has not yet begun the following blessing, he completes the blessing until אָמֵן, and then makes up for the omission by reciting the appropriate Compensatory Blessing (facing page).

(b) If he realizes his omission after reciting the words בָּרוּךְ אַתָּה ה', Blessed are You, HASHEM, but had not yet said the word בּוֹנֵה, Who rebuilds, he concludes with the phrase, לַמְּדֵנִי חֻקֶּיךָ, teach me Your statutes; then recites the omitted paragraph and continues from there. [This ruling is based on the fact that בָּרוּךְ אַתָּה ה' לַמְּדֵנִי חֻקֶּיךָ, Blessed are You, HASHEM; teach me Your statutes, is a verse in Psalms (119:12) and not a blessing. Only if one has recited the next blessing of Bircas HaMazon is it forbidden to go back to a previous blessing, but if one has merely inserted a verse from Psalms, he is still in the middle of the prayer and may go back to correct an omission.]

(c) If he realizes his omission after having recited the first six words of the fourth blessing, he may still switch immediately into the compensatory blessing since the words בָּרוּךְ אַתָּה ... הָעוֹלָם are identical in both blessings.

(d) If he realizes his omission after having recited the word הָאֵל, the Almighty, of the fourth blessing, it is too late for the compensatory blessing to be recited. In that case, at the first two meals of Shabbos and Yom Tov (but not Chol HaMoed), Bircas HaMazon must be repeated in its entirety; at the third meal, nothing need be done.

support us, relieve us; HASHEM, our God, grant us speedy relief from all our troubles. Please, make us not needful — HASHEM, our God — of the gifts of human hands nor of their loans, but only of Your Hand that is full, open, holy, and generous, that we not feel inner shame nor be humiliated for ever and ever.

On the Sabbath add the following. [If forgotten, see box below.]

רְצֵה May it please You, HASHEM, our God — give us rest through Your commandments and through the commandment of the seventh day, this great and holy Sabbath. For this day is great and holy before You to rest on it and be content on it in love, as ordained by Your will. May it be Your will, HASHEM, our God, that there be no distress, grief, or lament on this day of our contentment. And show us, HASHEM, our God, the consolation of Zion, Your city, and the rebuilding of Jerusalem, City of Your holiness, for You are the Master of salvations and Master of consolations.

אֱלֹהֵינוּ Our God and God of our forefathers, may there rise, come, reach, be noted, be favored, be heard, be considered, and be remembered — the remembrance and consideration of ourselves; the remembrance of our forefathers; the remembrance of Messiah, son of David, Your servant; the remembrance of Jerusalem, the City of Your Holiness; the remembrance of Your entire people the Family of Israel — before You for deliverance, for goodness, for grace, for kindness, and for compassion, for (good) life, and for peace on this Day of the

On Succos:	On Shemini Atzeres and Simchas Torah:
Succos Festival.	*Shemini Atzeres Festival.*

Remember us on it, HASHEM, our God, for goodness; consider us on it for blessing; and help us on it for good life. In the matter of salvation and compassion, pity, be gracious and compassionate with us and help us, for our eyes are turned to You, because You are God, gracious and compassionate.[1]

❖ **וּבְנֵה** Rebuild Jerusalem, the Holy City, soon in our days. Blessed are You, HASHEM, Who rebuilds Jerusalem in His mercy. Amen.

(Others— Amen.)

[When required, the compensatory blessing is recited here.]

(1) Cf. Nechemiah 9:31.

⛬ Compensatory Blessings (see facing page)

If יַעֲלֶה וְיָבֹא was omitted on any day other than the Sabbath.

בָּרוּךְ אַתָּה יהוה אֱלֹהֵינוּ מֶלֶךְ הָעוֹלָם, אֲשֶׁר נָתַן יָמִים טוֹבִים לְעַמּוֹ יִשְׂרָאֵל לְשָׂשׂוֹן וּלְשִׂמְחָה, אֶת יוֹם [חַג הַסֻּכּוֹת/שְׁמִינִי עֲצֶרֶת הַחַג] הַזֶּה. בָּרוּךְ אַתָּה יהוה, מְקַדֵּשׁ יִשְׂרָאֵל וְהַזְּמַנִּים.

Blessed are You, HASHEM, our God, King of the universe, Who gave festivals to His people Israel for happiness and gladness, this day of the [Succos/Shemini Atzeres] Festival. Blessed are You, HASHEM, Who sanctifies Israel and the seasons.

If רְצֵה and יַעֲלֶה וְיָבֹא were omitted on Succos that falls on the Sabbath:

בָּרוּךְ אַתָּה יהוה אֱלֹהֵינוּ מֶלֶךְ הָעוֹלָם, אֲשֶׁר נָתַן שַׁבָּתוֹת לִמְנוּחָה לְעַמּוֹ יִשְׂרָאֵל בְּאַהֲבָה, לְאוֹת וְלִבְרִית, וְיָמִים טוֹבִים לְשָׂשׂוֹן וּלְשִׂמְחָה, אֶת יוֹם [חַג הַסֻּכּוֹת/שְׁמִינִי עֲצֶרֶת הַחַג] הַזֶּה. בָּרוּךְ אַתָּה יהוה, מְקַדֵּשׁ הַשַּׁבָּת וְיִשְׂרָאֵל וְהַזְּמַנִּים.

Blessed are You, HASHEM, our God, King of the universe, Who gave Sabbaths for contentment to His people Israel with love as a sign and as a covenant, and festivals for happiness and gladness, this day of the [Succos/Shemini Atzeres] Festival. Blessed are You, HASHEM, Who sanctifies the Sabbath, Israel, and the seasons.

If יַעֲלֶה וְיָבֹא was recited, but רְצֵה was omitted on the Sabbath:

בָּרוּךְ אַתָּה יהוה אֱלֹהֵינוּ מֶלֶךְ הָעוֹלָם, אֲשֶׁר נָתַן שַׁבָּתוֹת לִמְנוּחָה לְעַמּוֹ יִשְׂרָאֵל בְּאַהֲבָה, לְאוֹת וְלִבְרִית. בָּרוּךְ אַתָּה יהוה, מְקַדֵּשׁ הַשַּׁבָּת.

Blessed are You, HASHEM, our God, King of the universe, Who gave Sabbaths for contentment to His people Israel with love, as a sign and as a covenant. Blessed are You, HASHEM, Who sanctifies the Sabbath.

בָּרוּךְ אַתָּה יהוה אֱלֹהֵינוּ מֶלֶךְ הָעוֹלָם, הָאֵל אָבִינוּ מַלְכֵּנוּ אַדִּירֵנוּ
בּוֹרְאֵנוּ גּוֹאֲלֵנוּ יוֹצְרֵנוּ קְדוֹשֵׁנוּ קְדוֹשׁ יַעֲקֹב, רוֹעֵנוּ רוֹעֵה
יִשְׂרָאֵל, הַמֶּלֶךְ הַטּוֹב וְהַמֵּטִיב לַכֹּל, שֶׁבְּכָל יוֹם וָיוֹם הוּא הֵטִיב, הוּא
מֵטִיב, הוּא יֵיטִיב לָנוּ. הוּא גְמָלָנוּ הוּא גוֹמְלֵנוּ הוּא יִגְמְלֵנוּ לָעַד, לְחֵן
וּלְחֶסֶד וּלְרַחֲמִים וּלְרֶוַח הַצָּלָה וְהַצְלָחָה, בְּרָכָה וִישׁוּעָה נֶחָמָה פַּרְנָסָה
וְכַלְכָּלָה ❖ וְרַחֲמִים וְחַיִּים וְשָׁלוֹם וְכָל טוֹב, וּמִכָּל טוּב לְעוֹלָם אַל
יְחַסְּרֵנוּ. (Others— אָמֵן.)

הָרַחֲמָן הוּא יִמְלוֹךְ עָלֵינוּ לְעוֹלָם וָעֶד. הָרַחֲמָן הוּא יִתְבָּרַךְ בַּשָּׁמַיִם
וּבָאָרֶץ. הָרַחֲמָן הוּא יִשְׁתַּבַּח לְדוֹר דּוֹרִים, וְיִתְפָּאַר בָּנוּ לָעַד
וּלְנֵצַח נְצָחִים, וְיִתְהַדַּר בָּנוּ לָעַד וּלְעוֹלְמֵי עוֹלָמִים. הָרַחֲמָן הוּא
יְפַרְנְסֵנוּ בְּכָבוֹד. הָרַחֲמָן הוּא יִשְׁבּוֹר עֻלֵנוּ מֵעַל צַוָּארֵנוּ, וְהוּא יוֹלִיכֵנוּ
קוֹמְמִיּוּת לְאַרְצֵנוּ. הָרַחֲמָן הוּא יִשְׁלַח לָנוּ בְּרָכָה מְרֻבָּה בַּבַּיִת הַזֶּה,
וְעַל שֻׁלְחָן זֶה שֶׁאָכַלְנוּ עָלָיו. הָרַחֲמָן הוּא יִשְׁלַח לָנוּ אֶת אֵלִיָּהוּ הַנָּבִיא
זָכוּר לַטּוֹב, וִיבַשֶּׂר לָנוּ בְּשׂוֹרוֹת טוֹבוֹת יְשׁוּעוֹת וְנֶחָמוֹת.

The Talmud (*Berachos* 46a) gives a rather lengthy text of the blessing that a guest inserts here for
the host. It is quoted with minor variations in *Shulchan Aruch* (*Orach Chaim* 201) and many
authorities are at a loss to explain why the prescribed text has fallen into disuse in favor of the
briefer version commonly used. The text found in *Shulchan Aruch* is:

יְהִי רָצוֹן שֶׁלֹּא יֵבוֹשׁ וְלֹא יִכָּלֵם בַּעַל הַבַּיִת הַזֶּה, לֹא בָּעוֹלָם הַזֶּה וְלֹא
בָּעוֹלָם הַבָּא, וְיַצְלִיחַ בְּכָל נְכָסָיו, וְיִהְיוּ נְכָסָיו מֻצְלָחִים
וּקְרוֹבִים לָעִיר, וְאַל יִשְׁלוֹט שָׂטָן בְּמַעֲשֵׂה יָדָיו, וְאַל יִזְדַּקֵּק לְפָנָיו שׁוּם דְּבַר
חֵטְא וְהִרְהוּר עָוֹן, מֵעַתָּה וְעַד עוֹלָם.

Guests recite the following (children at their parents' table include the words in parentheses):	Those eating at their own table recite (including the words in parentheses that apply):
הָרַחֲמָן הוּא יְבָרֵךְ אֶת (אָבִי מוֹרִי) בַּעַל הַבַּיִת הַזֶּה, וְאֶת (אִמִּי מוֹרָתִי) בַּעֲלַת הַבַּיִת הַזֶּה, אוֹתָם וְאֶת בֵּיתָם וְאֶת זַרְעָם וְאֶת כָּל אֲשֶׁר לָהֶם.	הָרַחֲמָן הוּא יְבָרֵךְ אוֹתִי (וְאֶת אִשְׁתִּי / בַּעֲלִי וְאֶת זַרְעִי) וְאֶת כָּל אֲשֶׁר לִי.

אוֹתָנוּ וְאֶת כָּל אֲשֶׁר לָנוּ, כְּמוֹ שֶׁנִּתְבָּרְכוּ אֲבוֹתֵינוּ אַבְרָהָם יִצְחָק וְיַעֲקֹב
בַּכֹּל מִכֹּל כֹּל,[1] כֵּן יְבָרֵךְ אוֹתָנוּ כֻּלָּנוּ יַחַד בִּבְרָכָה שְׁלֵמָה, וְנֹאמַר, אָמֵן.

בַּמָּרוֹם יְלַמְּדוּ עֲלֵיהֶם וְעָלֵינוּ זְכוּת, שֶׁתְּהֵא לְמִשְׁמֶרֶת שָׁלוֹם. וְנִשָּׂא
בְרָכָה מֵאֵת יהוה, וּצְדָקָה מֵאֱלֹהֵי יִשְׁעֵנוּ, וְנִמְצָא חֵן וְשֵׂכֶל
טוֹב בְּעֵינֵי אֱלֹהִים וְאָדָם.[2]

On the Sabbath add:

הָרַחֲמָן הוּא יַנְחִילֵנוּ יוֹם שֶׁכֻּלּוֹ שַׁבָּת וּמְנוּחָה לְחַיֵּי הָעוֹלָמִים.

FOURTH BLESSING: GOD'S GOODNESS

בָּרוּךְ *Blessed are You, HASHEM, our God, King of the Universe, the Almighty, our Father, our King, our Sovereign, our Creator, our Redeemer, our Maker, our Holy One, Holy One of Jacob, our Shepherd, the Shepherd of Israel, the King Who is good and Who does good for all. For every single day He did good, He does good, and He will do good to us. He was bountiful with us, He is bountiful with us, and He will forever be bountiful with us — with grace and with kindness and with mercy, with relief, salvation, success, blessing, help, consolation, sustenance, support,* Leader— *mercy, life, peace, and all good; and of all good things may He never deprive us.* (Others— *Amen.*)

הָרַחֲמָן *The compassionate One! May He reign over us forever. The compassionate One! May He be blessed in heaven and on earth. The compassionate One! May He be praised throughout all generations, may He be glorified through us forever to the ultimate ends, and be honored through us forever and for all eternity. The compassionate One! May He sustain us in honor. The compassionate One! May He break the yoke of oppression from our necks and guide us erect to our Land. The compassionate One! May He send us abundant blessing to this house and upon this table at which we have eaten. The compassionate One! May He send us Elijah, the Prophet — he is remembered for good — to proclaim to us good tidings, salvations, and consolations.*

The Talmud (*Berachos* 46a) gives a rather lengthy text of the blessing that a guest inserts here for the host. It is quoted with minor variations in *Shulchan Aruch* (*Orach Chaim* 201) and many authorities are at a loss to explain why the prescribed text has fallen into disuse in favor of the briefer version commonly used. The text found in *Shulchan Aruch* is:

יְהִי רָצוֹן *May it be God's will that this host not be shamed nor humiliated in This World or in the World to Come. May he be successful in all his dealings. May his dealings be successful and conveniently close at hand. May no evil impediment reign over his handiwork, and may no semblance of sin or iniquitous thought attach itself to him from this time and forever.*

Those eating at their own table recite (including the words in parentheses that apply):	Guests recite the following (children at their parents' table include the words in parentheses):
The compassionate One! May He bless me (my wife/husband and my children) and all that is mine.	*The compassionate One! May He bless (my father, my teacher) the master of this house, and (my mother, my teacher) lady of this house, them, their house, their family, and all that is theirs.*

Ours and all that is ours — just as our forefathers Abraham, Isaac, and Jacob were blessed in everything, from everything, with everything.[1] *So may He bless us all together with a perfect blessing. And let us say: Amen!*

בַּמָּרוֹם *On high, may merit be pleaded upon them and upon us, for a safeguard of peace. May we receive a blessing from HASHEM and just kindness from the God of our salvation, and find favor and good understanding in the eyes of God and man.*[2]

On the Sabbath add:
The compassionate One! May He cause us to inherit the day which will be completely a Sabbath and rest day for eternal life.

(1) Cf. *Genesis* 24:1; 27:33; 33:11. (2) Cf. *Proverbs* 3:4.

הָרַחֲמָן הוּא יַנְחִילֵנוּ יוֹם שֶׁכֻּלּוֹ טוֹב.

The following paragraph is not recited on Shemini Atzeres and Simchas Torah:

הָרַחֲמָן הוּא יָקִים לָנוּ אֶת סֻכַּת דָּוִד הַנֹּפֶלֶת.[1]

הָרַחֲמָן הוּא יְזַכֵּנוּ לִימוֹת הַמָּשִׁיחַ וּלְחַיֵּי הָעוֹלָם הַבָּא. מִגְדּוֹל יְשׁוּעוֹת מַלְכּוֹ וְעֹשֶׂה חֶסֶד לִמְשִׁיחוֹ לְדָוִד וּלְזַרְעוֹ עַד עוֹלָם.[2] עֹשֶׂה שָׁלוֹם בִּמְרוֹמָיו, הוּא יַעֲשֶׂה שָׁלוֹם עָלֵינוּ וְעַל כָּל יִשְׂרָאֵל. וְאִמְרוּ, אָמֵן.

יְראוּ אֶת יהוה קְדֹשָׁיו, כִּי אֵין מַחְסוֹר לִירֵאָיו. כְּפִירִים רָשׁוּ וְרָעֵבוּ, וְדֹרְשֵׁי יהוה לֹא יַחְסְרוּ כָל טוֹב.[3] הוֹדוּ לַיהוה כִּי טוֹב, כִּי לְעוֹלָם חַסְדּוֹ.[4] פּוֹתֵחַ אֶת יָדֶךָ, וּמַשְׂבִּיעַ לְכָל חַי רָצוֹן.[5] בָּרוּךְ הַגֶּבֶר אֲשֶׁר יִבְטַח בַּיהוה, וְהָיָה יהוה מִבְטַחוֹ.[6] נַעַר הָיִיתִי גַּם זָקַנְתִּי, וְלֹא רָאִיתִי צַדִּיק נֶעֱזָב, וְזַרְעוֹ מְבַקֶּשׁ לָחֶם.[7] יהוה עֹז לְעַמּוֹ יִתֵּן, יהוה יְבָרֵךְ אֶת עַמּוֹ בַשָּׁלוֹם.[8]

מֵעֵין שָׁלֹשׁ

The following blessing is recited after partaking of (a) grain products (other than bread or matzah) made from wheat, barley, rye, oats, or spelt; (b) grape wine or grape juice; (c) grapes, figs, pomegranates, olives, or dates. (If foods from two or three of these groups were consumed, then the insertions for each group are connected with the conjunctive ו, thus וְעַל. The order of insertion in such a case is grain, wine, fruit.)

בָּרוּךְ אַתָּה יהוה אֱלֹהֵינוּ מֶלֶךְ הָעוֹלָם,

After fruits:	*After wine:*	*After grain products:*
עַל הָעֵץ	עַל הַגֶּפֶן	עַל הַמִּחְיָה
וְעַל פְּרִי הָעֵץ,	וְעַל פְּרִי הַגֶּפֶן,	וְעַל הַכַּלְכָּלָה,

וְעַל תְּנוּבַת הַשָּׂדֶה, וְעַל אֶרֶץ חֶמְדָּה טוֹבָה וּרְחָבָה, שֶׁרָצִיתָ וְהִנְחַלְתָּ לַאֲבוֹתֵינוּ, לֶאֱכֹל מִפִּרְיָהּ וְלִשְׂבּוֹעַ מִטּוּבָהּ. רַחֵם נָא יהוה אֱלֹהֵינוּ עַל יִשְׂרָאֵל עַמֶּךָ, וְעַל יְרוּשָׁלַיִם עִירֶךָ, וְעַל צִיּוֹן מִשְׁכַּן כְּבוֹדֶךָ, וְעַל מִזְבְּחֶךָ וְעַל הֵיכָלֶךָ. וּבְנֵה יְרוּשָׁלַיִם עִיר הַקֹּדֶשׁ בִּמְהֵרָה בְיָמֵינוּ, וְהַעֲלֵנוּ לְתוֹכָהּ, וְשַׂמְּחֵנוּ בְּבִנְיָנָהּ, וְנֹאכַל מִפִּרְיָהּ, וְנִשְׂבַּע מִטּוּבָהּ, וּנְבָרֶכְךָ עָלֶיהָ בִּקְדֻשָּׁה וּבְטָהֳרָה. [On the Sabbath – וּרְצֵה וְהַחֲלִיצֵנוּ בְּיוֹם הַשַּׁבָּת הַזֶּה.] וְשַׂמְּחֵנוּ בְּיוֹם

On Shemini Atzeres/Simchas Torah: | *On Succos:*
שְׁמִינִי עֲצֶרֶת הַחַג הַזֶּה. | חַג הַסֻּכּוֹת הַזֶּה.

כִּי אַתָּה יהוה טוֹב וּמֵטִיב לַכֹּל, וְנוֹדֶה לְּךָ עַל הָאָרֶץ וְעַל

After fruit:	*After wine:*	*After grain products*
הַפֵּרוֹת.°	פְּרִי הַגָּפֶן.	הַמִּחְיָה (וְעַל הַכַּלְכָּלָה).

בָּרוּךְ אַתָּה יהוה, עַל הָאָרֶץ וְעַל

הַפֵּרוֹת.°	פְּרִי הַגָּפֶן.	הַמִּחְיָה (וְעַל הַכַּלְכָּלָה).

°*If the fruit grew in Eretz Yisrael, substitute* פֵּירוֹתֶיהָ *for* הַפֵּרוֹת.

After eating or drinking any food for which neither Bircas HaMazon nor the Three-Faceted Blessing applies, such as fruits other than the above, vegetables or beverages other than wine, recite:

בָּרוּךְ אַתָּה יהוה אֱלֹהֵינוּ מֶלֶךְ הָעוֹלָם, בּוֹרֵא נְפָשׁוֹת רַבּוֹת וְחֶסְרוֹנָן, עַל כָּל מַה שֶּׁבָּרָא(תָ) לְהַחֲיוֹת בָּהֶם נֶפֶשׁ כָּל חָי. בָּרוּךְ חֵי הָעוֹלָמִים.

הָרַחֲמָן *The compassionate One! May He cause us to inherit the day which is completely good.*

The following paragraph is *not* recited on *Shemini Atzeres* and *Simchas Torah:*

הָרַחֲמָן *The compassionate One! May He erect for us David's fallen booth.[1]*

הָרַחֲמָן *The compassionate One! May He make us worthy of the days of Messiah and the life of the World to Come. He Who is a tower of salvations to His king and does kindness for His anointed, to David and to his descendants forever.[2] He Who makes peace in His heights, may He make peace upon us and upon all Israel. Now respond: Amen!*

יְראוּ *Fear HASHEM, you — His holy ones — for there is no deprivation for His reverent ones. Young lions may want and hunger, but those who seek HASHEM will not lack any good.[3] Give thanks to God for He is good; His kindness endures forever.[4] You open Your hand and satisfy the desire of every living thing.[5] Blessed is the man who trusts in HASHEM, then HASHEM will be his security.[6] I was a youth and also have aged, and I have not seen a righteous man forsaken, with his children begging for bread.[7] HASHEM will give might to His people; HASHEM will bless His people with peace.[8]*

THE THREE-FACETED BLESSING

The following blessing is recited after partaking of (a) grain products (other than bread or matzah) made from wheat, barley, rye, oats or spelt; (b) grape wine or grape juice; (c) grapes, figs, pomegranates, olives, or dates. (If foods from two or three of these groups were consumed, then the insertions for each group are connected with the conjunctive וְ, thus וְעַל. The order of insertion in such a case is grain, wine, fruit.)

בָּרוּךְ *Blessed are You, HASHEM, our God, King of the universe, for the*

After grain products:	After wine:	After fruits:
nourishment and the sustenance,	*vine and the fruit of the vine,*	*tree and the fruit of the tree,*

and for the produce of the field; for the desirable, good and spacious Land that You were pleased to give our forefathers as a heritage, to eat of its fruit and to be satisfied with its goodness. Have mercy, please, HASHEM, our God, on Israel, Your people; on Jerusalem, Your city; and on Zion, the resting place of Your glory; upon Your altar, and upon Your Temple. Rebuild Jerusalem, the city of holiness, speedily in our days. Bring us up into it and gladden us in its rebuilding and let us eat from its fruit and be satisfied with its goodness and bless You upon it in holiness and purity. [On the Sabbath — And be pleased to let us rest on this Sabbath day.] And gladden us on this day of the [Succos/Shemini Atzeres] festival. For You, HASHEM, are good and do good to all and we thank You for the land and for the

After grain products:	After wine:	After fruit:
nourishment (and sustenance).	*fruit of the vine.*	*fruit.°*

Blessed are You, HASHEM, for the land and for the

After grain products:	After wine:	After fruit:
nourishment (and sustenance).	*fruit of the vine.*	*fruit.°*

° If the fruit grew in Eretz Yisrael, *substitute 'its fruit.'*

After eating or drinking any food for which neither *Bircas HaMazon* nor the Three-Faceted Blessing applies, such as fruits other than the above, vegetables or beverages other than wine, recite:

בָּרוּךְ *Blessed are You, HASHEM, our God, King of the universe, Who creates numerous living things with their deficiencies; for all that You have created with which to maintain the life of every being. Blessed is He, the life of the worlds.*

---

(1) Cf. *Amos* 9:11. (2) *Psalms* 18:51. (3) 34:10-11. (4) 136:1 et al. (5) 145:16. (6) *Jeremiah* 17:7. (7) *Psalms* 37:25. (8) 29:11.

Many recite the following declaration of intent before taking the Four Species:

יְהִי רָצוֹן* מִלְּפָנֶיךָ, יהוה אֱלֹהַי וֵאלֹהֵי אֲבוֹתַי, בִּפְרִי עֵץ הָדָר,* וְכַפּוֹת תְּמָרִים,* וַעֲנַף עֵץ עָבוֹת,* וְעַרְבֵי נָחַל,* אוֹתִיּוֹת¹ שִׁמְךָ הַמְּיֻחָד* תְּקָרֵב אֶחָד אֶל אֶחָד, וְהָיוּ לַאֲחָדִים בְּיָדִי, וְלֵידַע אֵיךְ שִׁמְךָ נִקְרָא עָלַי, וְיִירְאוּ מִגֶּשֶׁת אֵלַי. וּבְנַעֲנוּעַי אוֹתָם תַּשְׁפִּיעַ שֶׁפַע בְּרָכוֹת מִדַּעַת עֶלְיוֹן לִנְוֵה אַפִּרְיוֹן, לִמְכוֹן בֵּית אֱלֹהֵינוּ. וּתְהֵא חֲשׁוּבָה לְפָנֶיךָ מִצְוַת אַרְבָּעָה מִינִים אֵלּוּ, כְּאִלּוּ קִיַּמְתִּיהָ בְּכָל פְּרָטוֹתֶיהָ וְשָׁרָשֶׁיהָ וְתַרְיַ״ג מִצְוֹת הַתְּלוּיִם בָּהּ. כִּי כַוָּנָתִי לְיַחֵד שֵׁם י״ה בּו״ה בְּיִחוּדָא שְׁלִים, בְּשֵׁם כָּל יִשְׂרָאֵל. אָמֵן. בָּרוּךְ יהוה לְעוֹלָם, אָמֵן, וְאָמֵן.²

The Four Species — *lulav, haddasim, aravos, esrog* — are taken in hand every day of Succos — through *Hoshana Rabbah* — except on the Sabbath. The *lulav*-bundle is picked up with the right hand, then the *esrog* (with the *pitam* facing down) with the left. After the blessings are recited, the *esrog* is turned over and the Four Species are waved in the six directions.

בָּרוּךְ אַתָּה יהוה אֱלֹהֵינוּ מֶלֶךְ הָעוֹלָם, אֲשֶׁר קִדְּשָׁנוּ בְּמִצְוֹתָיו, וְצִוָּנוּ עַל נְטִילַת* לוּלָב.*

The following blessing is added only on the first day that the Four Species are taken.

בָּרוּךְ אַתָּה יהוה אֱלֹהֵינוּ מֶלֶךְ הָעוֹלָם, שֶׁהֶחֱיָנוּ וְקִיְּמָנוּ וְהִגִּיעָנוּ לַזְּמַן הַזֶּה.

נְטִילַת לוּלָב / THE FOUR SPECIES

The Torah commands the taking of the Four Species and concludes: *You shall be joyous before* HASHEM ... (*Leviticus* 23:40). The Midrash explains the connection between this *mitzvah* and joyousness:

In earlier days if a litigant's claim before the royal court was decided in his favor, he would receive a spear from the king. When he left the palace holding the king's spear aloft all knew that he had been victorious in his suit. Similarly, during the Days of Awe, the Jewish people were on trial before the Heavenly Court. On Succos, 'the season of joy,' we celebrate our happiness that God has accepted our repentance — a confidence symbolized by the *lulav* held aloft.

יְהִי רָצוֹן — *May it be Your will.* This prayer, as well as many others that are heavy with kabbalistic impications, was introduced by the seventeenth-century master of kabbalah, R' Nassan of Hanover, and first appeared in his *Sha'arei Tzion* (Prague, 5422/1662).

בִּפְרִי עֵץ הָדָר — *Through the fruit of the esrog* [lit. *beautiful*] *tree.* The Torah does not specify the *esrog* by name, but uses this descriptive phrase. *Targum* renders הָדָר, *beautiful,* as אֶתְרוֹגִין, *es-rogim.*

From the Torah's use of the word פְּרִי, *fruit* (in the singular), rather than פֵּרוֹת, *fruits,* the Tal-

mud (*Succah* 34b) derives that only a single *esrog* is taken.

וְכַפּוֹת תְּמָרִים — *Date-palm branches,* i.e., *the lulav.* Although this term appears in *Leviticus* 23:40 in the plural form, branches, the Talmud understands the verse to indicate that only a single *lulav* be used. In the Torah, the word for branches is spelled כַּפֹּת with the letter ו omitted. Since the Torah is written without vowelpoints, it is possible to read the words as כַּפַּת תְּמָרִים, a 'branch' of date-palms (*Succah* 34b as explained by *Rashi*). Generally, a word written in the plural form is taken to mean exactly two; if more were required, the Torah should have specified how many (see below). In our case, however, the use of the deficient spelling implies that the word is to be understood in the singular.

In the Scriptural verse, the terms for *esrog* and *lulav* are not connected by the conjunctive ו, *and.* However, conjunctions do connect the terms for *lulav, haddasim* (myrtle), and *aravos* (willow). From this it is derived that the species are to be held in two groups: the *esrog* by itself; and a bundle containing the *lulav, haddasim* and *aravos* (*Succah* 24b).

וַעֲנַף עֵץ עָבוֹת — *Twigs of the myrtle tree,* i.e., *haddasim.* Literally, עֵץ עָבוֹת means a *thick* or *plaited* tree. The Talmud (*Succah* 32b) under-stands this to refer to a species whose leaf

Many recite the following declaration of intent before taking the Four Species:

יְהִי רָצוֹן *May it be Your will,* HASHEM, my God and the God of my fore-fathers, that through the fruit of the esrog tree,* date-palm branches,* twigs of the myrtle tree,* and brook willows,¹* the letters of Your unified Name* may become close to one another, that they may become united in my hand; and to make known that Your Name is called upon me, that [evil forces] may be fearful of approaching me. And when I wave them, may an abundant outpouring of blessings flow from the wisdom of the Most High to the abode of the tabernacle, to the prepared place of the House of our God. And may the mitzvah of these Four Species be reckoned before You as if I had fulfilled it with all its particulars, roots, and the six hundred thirteen mitzvos dependent on it. For my intention* is to unify the Name of the Holy One, Blessed is He, and His Presence, in awe and in love, to unify the Name Yud-Kei with Vav-Kei in perfect unity, in the name of all Israel; Amen. Blessed is HASHEM forever, Amen and Amen.²*

The Four Species — *lulav, haddasim, aravos, esrog* — are taken in hand every day of Succos — through *Hoshana Rabbah* — except on the Sabbath. The *lulav*-bundle is picked up with the right hand, then the *esrog* (with the *pitam* facing down) with the left. After the blessings are recited, the *esrog* is turned over and the Four Species are waved in the six directions.

בָּרוּךְ *Blessed are You, HASHEM, our God, King of the universe, Who has sanctified us with His commandments and has commanded us concerning the taking* of a palm branch.**

The following blessing is added only on the first day that the Four Species are taken.

בָּרוּךְ *Blessed are You, HASHEM, our God, King of the universe, Who has kept us alive, sustained us, and brought us to this season.*

---

(1) Cf. *Leviticus* 23:40. (2) *Psalms* 89:53.

---

coverage is thick, completely covering the twig, and whose leaves overlap each other, as if braided — and identify it as the הֲדַס, *myrtle*.

The fact that the Torah does not call the myrtle tree by name, but instead gives a three-word description, is taken to imply that three myrtle twigs should be included in the *lulav*-bundle (*Succah* 34b).

וְעַרְבֵי נָחַל — *And brook willows*. The unspecied plural is taken as meaning two, the least amount to which the plural form may be applied. If more than two were needed the number would have been given (*Succah* 34b).

Tosafos writes that although the verse implies three myrtle twigs and two willows, these numbers are given only as minimums. A larger number of either species may be taken. *Rambam* (*Lulav* 7:7), on the other hand, maintains that it is forbidden to take more or less than two willows, one *lulav* and one *esrog*. One may, however, adorn his *lulav*-bundle with additional myrtle twigs.

אוֹתִיוֹת שִׁמְךָ הַמְיֻחָד — *The letters of Your unified Name*. Kabbalah teaches that each of the Four Species is identified with another of the letters of the Four-Letter Name of God. Rabbi Michael Ber Weissmandl (in *Toras Chemed*) adduces a complex series of calculations to prove that the *aravos, lulav, haddasim*, and *esrog* correspond, in that order, with the four letters of the Name.

כַּוָּנָתִי — *My intention*. Even one who has spent much time and money on perfect species should not taint the performance of his *mitzvah* by boasting about his acquisition. Rather, his intention in fulfilling the *mitzvah* should be above personal considerations. It is not coincidental that the initials of the verse (*Psalms* 36:12): אַל תְּבוֹאֵנִי רֶגֶל גַּאֲוָה, *Bring me not [to] the foot of arrogance*, form the word אֶתְרֹג (*Baal Shem Tov*).

עַל נְטִילַת — *Concerning the taking*. In stating the *mitzvah* of *lulav*, the Torah uses the expression וּלְקַחְתֶּם, *and you shall take*, from the root לקח. Rabbinic literature, however, uses the word נְטִילָה, from the root נטל, almost exclusively when the Four Species are mentioned. Various reasons are given regarding the substitution of the Rabbinical form נְטִילָה for the Scriptural form לְקִיחָה in the blessing over the *lulav*-bundle. *Eliyah Rabbah* understands that the change is based on the desire to avoid a running together of the double ל in the two words עַל לְקִיחַת. Use of נְטִילַת prevents this corrupt pronunciation.

Some recite the *Ushpizin* prayers (p. 94) each time they enter the *succah* for a meal.

ON THE SABBATH BEGIN HERE.

Many omit some or all of these verses and begin with עַל כֵּן.

אִם תָּשִׁיב* מִשַּׁבָּת רַגְלֶךָ, עֲשׂוֹת חֲפָצֶךָ בְּיוֹם קָדְשִׁי, וְקָרָאתָ לַשַּׁבָּת עֹנֶג, לִקְדוֹשׁ יהוה מְכֻבָּד, וְכִבַּדְתּוֹ מֵעֲשׂוֹת דְּרָכֶיךָ, מִמְּצוֹא חֶפְצְךָ וְדַבֵּר דָּבָר. אָז תִּתְעַנַּג עַל יהוה, וְהִרְכַּבְתִּיךָ עַל בָּמֳתֵי אָרֶץ, וְהַאֲכַלְתִּיךָ נַחֲלַת יַעֲקֹב אָבִיךָ,* כִּי פִּי יהוה דִּבֵּר.¹

וְשָׁמְרוּ בְנֵי יִשְׂרָאֵל אֶת הַשַּׁבָּת, לַעֲשׂוֹת אֶת הַשַּׁבָּת לְדֹרֹתָם בְּרִית עוֹלָם. בֵּינִי וּבֵין בְּנֵי יִשְׂרָאֵל אוֹת הִיא לְעֹלָם, כִּי שֵׁשֶׁת יָמִים עָשָׂה יהוה אֶת הַשָּׁמַיִם וְאֶת הָאָרֶץ, וּבַיּוֹם הַשְּׁבִיעִי שָׁבַת וַיִּנָּפַשׁ.²

זָכוֹר* אֶת יוֹם הַשַּׁבָּת לְקַדְּשׁוֹ. שֵׁשֶׁת יָמִים תַּעֲבֹד וְעָשִׂיתָ כָּל מְלַאכְתֶּךָ. וְיוֹם הַשְּׁבִיעִי שַׁבָּת לַיהוה אֱלֹהֶיךָ, לֹא תַעֲשֶׂה כָל מְלָאכָה, אַתָּה וּבִנְךָ וּבִתֶּךָ עַבְדְּךָ וַאֲמָתְךָ וּבְהֶמְתֶּךָ, וְגֵרְךָ אֲשֶׁר בִּשְׁעָרֶיךָ. כִּי שֵׁשֶׁת יָמִים עָשָׂה יהוה אֶת הַשָּׁמַיִם וְאֶת הָאָרֶץ אֶת הַיָּם וְאֶת כָּל אֲשֶׁר בָּם, וַיָּנַח בַּיּוֹם הַשְּׁבִיעִי —

עַל כֵּן בֵּרַךְ יהוה אֶת יוֹם הַשַּׁבָּת וַיְקַדְּשֵׁהוּ.³

(אֵלֶּה מוֹעֲדֵי יהוה מִקְרָאֵי קֹדֶשׁ אֲשֶׁר תִּקְרְאוּ אֹתָם בְּמוֹעֲדָם.⁴)
וַיְדַבֵּר מֹשֶׁה* אֶת מֹעֲדֵי יהוה, אֶל בְּנֵי יִשְׂרָאֵל.⁵

סָבְרִי מָרָנָן וְרַבָּנָן וְרַבּוֹתַי:

בָּרוּךְ אַתָּה יהוה אֱלֹהֵינוּ מֶלֶךְ הָעוֹלָם, בּוֹרֵא פְּרִי הַגָּפֶן.

(אָמֵן – All present.)

If, for whatever reason, one does not recite *Kiddush* in a *succah*, the following blessing is omitted.

בָּרוּךְ אַתָּה יהוה אֱלֹהֵינוּ מֶלֶךְ הָעוֹלָם, אֲשֶׁר קִדְּשָׁנוּ בְּמִצְוֹתָיו וְצִוָּנוּ לֵישֵׁב בַּסֻּכָּה.

(אָמֵן – All present.)

עַל הַמִּחְיָה appears on page 112; בִּרְכַּת הַמָּזוֹן, on page 104.

Some recite the *Ushpizin* prayers (p. 94) each time they enter the *succah* for a meal.

ON THE SABBATH BEGIN HERE.
Many omit some or all of these verses and begin with *'therefore* HASHEM *blessed.'*

אִם תָּשִׁיב *If you restrain,* because of the Sabbath, your feet, refrain from accomplishing your own needs on My holy day; if you proclaim the Sabbath 'a delight,' the holy one of* HASHEM, *'honored one,' and you honor it by not doing your own ways, from seeking your needs or discussing the forbidden. Then you shall be granted pleasure with* HASHEM *and I shall mount you astride the heights of the world, and provide you the heritage of your forefather Jacob* — for the mouth of* HASHEM *has spoken.*[1]

וְשָׁמְרוּ *And the Children of Israel observed the Sabbath, to make the Sabbath for their generations an eternal covenant. Between Me and the Children of Israel it is a sign forever, that in six days did* HASHEM *make the heaven and the earth, and on the seventh day He rested and was refreshed.*[2]

זָכוֹר *Always remember* the Sabbath day to hallow it. For six days you may labor and do all your work. But the seventh day is the Sabbath for* HASHEM, *Your God; you may do no work — you, your son and your daughter, your slave and your maidservant, your animal, and the stranger who is in your gates. For in six days did* HASHEM *make the heaven and the earth, the sea and all that is in them and He rested on the seventh day;*

therefore HASHEM *blessed the Sabbath day and sanctified it.*[3]

(These are the appointed festivals of HASHEM, *holy convocations, which you are to proclaim in their appointed times.*[4]*)*
And Moses declared* HASHEM's *appointed festivals to the Children of Israel.*[5]

By your leave, my masters and teachers:

בָּרוּךְ *Blessed are You,* HASHEM, *our God, King of the universe, Who creates the fruit of the vine.* (All present – *Amen.*)

If, for whatever reason, one does not recite *Kiddush* in a *succah,* the following blessing is omitted.

בָּרוּךְ *Blessed are You,* HASHEM, *our God, King of the universe, Who has sanctified us with His commandments and has commanded us to dwell in the Succah.* (All present – *Amen.*)

The blessing after cake and wine appears on page 112; Grace after Meals, on page 104.

During the afternoon of Shemini Atzeres, before leaving the *succah* for the last time,
it is customary to recite the following prayers:

יְהִי רָצוֹן מִלְּפָנֶיךָ, יהוה אֱלֹהֵינוּ וֵאלֹהֵי אֲבוֹתֵינוּ, כְּשֵׁם שֶׁקִּיַּמְתִּי וְיָשַׁבְתִּי בְּסֻכָּה זוֹ, כֵּן אֶזְכֶּה לְשָׁנָה הַבָּאָה לֵישֵׁב בְּסֻכַּת עוֹרוֹ שֶׁל לִוְיָתָן.*

לְשָׁנָה הַבָּאָה בִּירוּשָׁלָיִם.*

Some add:

רִבּוֹנָא דְעָלְמָא, יְהֵא רַעֲוָה מִן קֳדָמָךְ שֶׁאוֹתָן מַלְאָכִים הַקְּדוֹשִׁים הַשַּׁיָּכִים לְמִצְוַת סֻכָּה, וּלְמִצְוַת אַרְבָּעָה מִינִים – לוּלָב וְאֶתְרוֹג, הֲדַס וַעֲרָבָה – הַנּוֹהֲגִים בְּחַג הַסֻּכּוֹת, הֵם יִתְלַוּוּ עִמָּנוּ בְּצֵאתֵנוּ מִן הַסֻּכָּה וְיִכָּנְסוּ עִמָּנוּ לְבָתֵּינוּ לְחַיִּים וּלְשָׁלוֹם. וְלִהְיוֹת תָּמִיד עָלֵינוּ שְׁמִירָה עֶלְיוֹנָה מִמְּעוֹן קָדְשֶׁךָ, וּלְהַצִּילֵנוּ מִכָּל חֵטְא וְעָוֹן, וּמִכָּל פְּגָעִים רָעִים, וּמִכָּל שָׁעוֹת רָעוֹת הַמִּתְרַגְּשׁוֹת לָבֹא לָעוֹלָם. וְתַעֲרֶה עָלֵינוּ רוּחַ מִמָּרוֹם; וְחַדֵּשׁ כִּלְיוֹתֵינוּ לְעָבְדָךְ בֶּאֱמֶת, בְּאַהֲבָה וּבְיִרְאָה; וְנַתְמִיד מְאֹד בְּלִמּוּד תּוֹרָתְךָ הַקְּדוֹשָׁה, לִלְמוֹד וּלְלַמֵּד. וּזְכוּת אַרְבָּעָה מִינִים וּמִצְוַת סֻכָּה תַּעֲמָד לָנוּ, שֶׁתַּאֲרִיךְ אַפְּךָ עַד שׁוּבֵנוּ אֵלֶיךָ בִּתְשׁוּבָה שְׁלֵמָה לְפָנֶיךָ; וּנְתַקֵּן כָּל אֲשֶׁר פָּגַמְנוּ; וְנִזְכֶּה לִשְׁתֵּי שֻׁלְחָנוֹת, בְּלִי צַעַר וְיָגוֹן – אֲנִי וּבְנֵי בֵיתִי וְיוֹצְאֵי חֲלָצַי – וְנִהְיֶה כֻּלָּנוּ שְׁקֵטִים וּשְׁלֵוִים, דְּשֵׁנִים וְרַעֲנַנִים, וְעוֹבְדֵי יהוה בֶּאֱמֶת לַאֲמִתּוֹ כִּרְצוֹנְךָ הַטּוֹב, בִּכְלַל כָּל בְּנֵי יִשְׂרָאֵל; אָמֵן. יִהְיוּ לְרָצוֹן אִמְרֵי פִי, וְהֶגְיוֹן לִבִּי לְפָנֶיךָ, יהוה צוּרִי וְגוֹאֲלִי.¹

‰ FAREWELL TO THE SUCCAH ‰

בְּסֻכַּת עוֹרוֹ שֶׁל לִוְיָתָן – *In the succah of the skin of Leviathan.* According to the Aggadah of the Talmud and Midrash, the לִוְיָתָן, *Leviathan*, is a giant fish created on the fifth day of Creation and who rules all the creatures of the sea.

Originally, two were created, a male and a female, as with all other species. However, God saw that if these two fish were allowed to mate and multiply, they would destroy the entire world by dint of their great strength and numbers, for the Leviathan is so enormous that all the waters that flow from the Jordan river into the sea can scarcely quench its thirst. God, therefore, killed the female and preserved it in brine, to be eaten by the righteous at the banquet prepared for them in the Time to Come. Additionally, the Leviathan is very beautiful. Its fins are so radiant that they outshine the sun. Its eyes are so bright that they sometimes illuminate the entire sea (*Bava Basra* 74b).

Another huge beast whose flesh will be served

to the righteous in the World to Come is the בְּהֵמוֹת, *Behemoth*, created on the sixth day of the creation of the world. The Behemoth is a gigantic ox, and, like the Leviathan, possesses enormous strength. It, too, was created male and female, and, like the Leviathan, had to be prevented from multiplying, lest the world be destroyed. God therefore neutered the male and eliminated the female's desire to propagate (*Bava Basra* 74b).

When the Messiah comes, God will summon the angels to enter into battle against the Leviathan, for the amusement of the righteous. But the Leviathan will cast one glance upon them, and the angels will run in fear and dismay from the field of battle. They will return to attack him with swords, spears and stones, but to no avail, since steel is like straw against his scales (*Bava Basra* 74b). Disheartened, the angels will give up the battle, and God will signal to the Leviathan and the Behemoth to fight one another. The result will be that the Leviathan will slaughter the Behemoth with a cut from his very sharp fins. Simultaneously the Behemoth will kill

During the afternoon of Shemini Atzeres, before leaving the *succah* for the last time,
it is customary to recite the following prayers:

יְהִי רָצוֹן   *May it be Your will, HASHEM, our God and the God of our*
forefathers, that just as I have fulfilled [the mitzvah] and
dwelled in this succah, so may I merit in the coming year to dwell in the
succah of the skin of Leviathan.*

Next year in Jerusalem.*

Some add:

רִבּוֹנָא   *Master of the universe, may it be Your will that the holy angels*
connected with the mitzvah of succah and the mitzvah of the Four
Species — lulav, esrog, hadas, aravah — that are performed during the Festival
of Succos, accompany us when we leave the succah, and may they enter our
homes with us in life and in peace. May there always be upon us a heavenly
protection from Your holy abode, to save us from all sin and iniquity, from evil
occurrences, from malevolent periods that are stirring to come upon the world.
Arouse upon us a spirit from above; rejuvenate our inner source of counsel that
we may serve You in truth, in love and in awe; that we may be diligent in the
study of Your holy Torah, to study and to teach. May the merit of the Four
Species and the mitzvah of succah stand by us, that You act with forbearance
until we have returned to You in full repentance before You; may we rectify all
that we have destroyed; may we merit both tables, with neither pain nor grief
— myself, my household and my offspring — may we all dwell placid and
serene, vigorous and fresh, serving HASHEM in utmost truthfulness according to
Your benevolent will, among all the Children of Israel; Amen. May the
expression of my mouth and the thoughts of my heart find favor before You,
HASHEM, my Rock and my Redeemer.[1]

---

(1) *Psalms* 19:15.

---

the Leviathan with a blow from his horns
(*Leviticus Rabbah* 13:3).

From the beautiful skin of the Leviathan, God
will construct canopies to shelter the righteous
from the sun (*Bava Basra* 75a). These canopies
are referred to in our prayer as סֻכַּת עוֹרוֹ שֶׁל לִוְיָתָן,
the succah of the skin of Leviathan. Under these
canopies they will eat the meat of the Leviathan
and the Behemoth, amid great joy and merriment
(ibid. 74b). Although the Talmud does not
specify this banquet as a reward for fulfillment of
the *mitzvah* of dwelling in the *succah*, an
introduction in *Pesikta d'R' Eliezer* reads: R' Levi
taught that God will seat all who fulfill the
mitzvah of *succah* in This World in a *succah* of
the skin of the Leviathan in the World to Come.

[The above is but a very brief synopsis of the
Aggadah on Leviathan, Behemoth, and the
banquet. See ArtScroll *Akdamus*, pp. 127-139,
for a fuller account.]

לְשָׁנָה הַבָּאָה בִּירוּשָׁלַיִם — *Next year in Jerusalem.*
This terse prayer is usually taken as an ex-

pression of faith and hope that during the next
year the Messiah will arrive to redeem Israel from
its exile and lead the nation back to the Holy
Land, to a rebuilt Temple in Jerusalem. When
viewed in this light, however, it seems to conflict
with one of the Thirteen Articles of Faith
formulated by *Rambam*. For the twelfth of those
articles states: 'I believe with perfect faith in the
advent of the Messiah, and even though he may
tarry, nevertheless, I hope, *each day*, for his
arrival.' Why, then, do we pray for his arrival
during the coming year and not during the
present one? R' Yoel of Satmar offers the
following solution. If accented on its first syllable, the word בָּאָה means *had come*, in the past
tense. If accented on the second syllable, בָּאָה
means *is coming*, in the present tense (see *Rashi*
to Genesis 29:7,9). Based upon these two possible
meanings, we may retranslate our prayer: *The*
year that **has come** [הַבָּאָה in the present tense]
in Jerusalem, i.e., may we be in Jerusalem even
during the current year, for Messiah can come at
any moment.

❧ Torah Study

Mishnayos Succah

— by Rabbi Yisroel Gornish
abridged from the ArtScroll Mishnah Series

Koheles / Ecclesiastes

— by Rabbi Meir Zlotowitz
abridged from the ArtScroll Tanach Series

It is customary to study the *mishnah* of Tractate Succah during Succos.

פרק ראשון

[א] סֻכָּה שֶׁהִיא גְבוֹהָה לְמַעְלָה מֵעֶשְׂרִים אַמָּה פְּסוּלָה. רַבִּי יְהוּדָה מַכְשִׁיר. וְשֶׁאֵינָהּ גְּבוֹהָה עֲשָׂרָה טְפָחִים, וְשֶׁאֵין לָהּ שְׁלֹשָׁה דְפָנוֹת, וְשֶׁחַמָּתָהּ מְרֻבָּה מִצִּלָּתָהּ, פְּסוּלָה. סֻכָּה יְשָׁנָה – בֵּית שַׁמַּאי פּוֹסְלִין, וּבֵית הִלֵּל מַכְשִׁירִין. וְאֵיזוֹ הִיא סֻכָּה יְשָׁנָה? כָּל-שֶׁעֲשָׂאָהּ קֹדֶם לֶחָג שְׁלֹשִׁים יוֹם. אֲבָל אִם עֲשָׂאָהּ לְשֵׁם חַג, אֲפִילוּ מִתְּחִלַּת הַשָּׁנָה, כְּשֵׁרָה.

[ב] הָעוֹשֶׂה סֻכָּתוֹ תַּחַת הָאִילָן, כְּאִלּוּ עֲשָׂאָהּ בְּתוֹךְ הַבַּיִת. סֻכָּה עַל-גַּבֵּי סֻכָּה הָעֶלְיוֹנָה כְּשֵׁרָה, וְהַתַּחְתּוֹנָה פְּסוּלָה. רַבִּי יְהוּדָה אוֹמֵר: אִם אֵין דִּיּוּרִין בָּעֶלְיוֹנָה, הַתַּחְתּוֹנָה כְּשֵׁרָה.

YAD AVRAHAM / יד אברהם

[A full treatment of these and all relevant mishnayos may be found in the ArtScroll Mishnah with the *Yad Avraham* commentary by Rabbi Yisroel P. Gornish, from which the following commentary has been adapted.]

◆§ Tractate Succah

This tractate discusses the specific laws of the festival of Succos. [General laws of *Yom Tov*, such as those pertain to labor and food preparation, are detailed in tractate *Beitzah*.] It deals with three broad subject areas: the *succah* as a dwelling, the Four Species, and the Temple ritual and festivities.

CHAPTER ONE

A *succah* is the temporary dwelling which a Jew establishes as his domicile during the festival of Succos. It has two components: its סְכָךְ, *covering*, from which it takes its name (*Rashi* 2a), and its walls. Each of these has specific laws regarding composition, dimensions, and acceptable materials, as well as various other details.

Many of the *succah's* measurements are expressed in terms of cubits, handbreadths and so on. The codifiers disagree on the conversion of these measurements into meters and inches. The three most accepted views are the following:

	טפח – **Handbreadth**	אמה – **Cubit**
Chazon Ish	3.8 in./9.6 cm.	22.7 in./57.66 cm.
Igros Moshe	3.54 in./9.1 cm.	21.25 in./53.98 cm.
R' A. C. No'eh	3.2 in./8 cm.	18.9 in./48 cm.

1. סֻכָּה שֶׁהִיא גְבוֹהָה לְמַעְלָה מֵעֶשְׂרִים אַמָּה — *A succah that is more than twenty cubits high*, i.e., the *interior* height of the *succah*. The thickness of the s'chach is not included in this measurement.

פְּסוּלָה — *Is invalid*. This is because the word *succos* refers to buildings of a temporary nature, implying that one must settle in a דִּירַת עֲרַאי, *temporary dwelling*, one for which flimsy walls suffice. Walls taller than twenty cubits must be built with a firmness which would make them permanent; walls of less than twenty cubits, however, can be built in a temporary manner (*Gem.* 2a).

If the s'chach is *exactly* twenty cubits above

its floor, the *succah* is valid; the mishnah invalidates only a *succah* whose s'chach begins more than twenty cubits above the floor.

רַבִּי יְהוּדָה מַכְשִׁיר — *R' Yehudah validates it*. He holds that the *succah* must be able to serve as a permanent structure (*Gem.* 7b). The halachah, however, follows the first *Tanna* (*Orach Chaim* 613:1).

וְשֶׁאֵינָהּ גְּבוֹהָה עֲשָׂרָה טְפָחִים — *And [a succah] that is not ten handbreadths high*. The interior, from floor to s'chach, is less than ten handbreadths high. This is invalid because it is a דִּירָה סְרוּחָה, *unpleasant dwelling*, since it is too confining for decent habitation (*Gem.* 4a). The Torah requires that one 'dwell' in a *succah*.

It is customary to study the *mishnah* of Tractate Succah during Succos.

CHAPTER ONE

[1] סֻכָּה A *succah that is more than twenty cubits high is invalid. R'
Yehudah validates it. And [a succah] that is not ten handbreadths
high, or [one] that does not have three walls, or [one] whose sun[ny area]
is greater than its shade[d area], is invalid. An old succah — Beis Shammai
invalidate it and Beis Hillel validate it. And what is [considered] an 'old'
succah? Whatever one built thirty days prior to the Festival. But if one built
it specifically for the Festival, even [if he put it up] at the beginning of the
year, it is valid.*

[2] *If one builds his succah under a tree, it is as though he had built it inside
the house. [If] a succah [is built] atop another succah the upper one is
valid, and the lower one is invalid. R' Yehudah says: If there can be no tenancy
in the upper one, [only] the lower one is valid.*

YAD AVRAHAM

The Rabbis understand this to mean תֵּשְׁבוּ כְּעֵין
תָּדוּרוּ, *you are to dwell* (in the *succah*) *just as
you would inhabit* (your home). By implication,
the Sages derived that a *succah* must contain
minimal living conditions, such as a height of
ten handbreadths.

שְׁלֹשָׁה דְפָנוֹת — *Three walls.* A *succah* must have
a minimum of three walls. Two of these walls
must be at least seven handbreadths wide [the
minimum width of a *succah*], in addition to
being at least ten handbreadths high. The third
wall, however, as defined in the oral tradition
received by Moses at Sinai [הֲלָכָה לְמשֶׁה מִסִּינַי],
need not always have seven handbreadths. See
Orach Chaim 630:2,3 for details.

וְשֶׁחַמָּתָה מְרֻבָּה מִצִּלָּתָהּ — *Or [one] whose sun[ny
area] is greater than its shade[d area].* Since by
definition, a *succah* must provide shade —
s'chach=shelter — a *succah* that lets in more
sunlight than it blocks out fails to perform its
basic function.

סֻכָּה יְשָׁנָה — *An old succah,* i.e., a *succah*, erected
more than thirty days before Succos whose
s'chach was not put up expressly for the
festival. Beis Shammai require that the *s'chach*
be laid expressly for the *mitzvah*, while Beis
Hillel hold there is no such requirement. The
walls need not be constructed expressly for
Succos (*Taz* 636:1). Although the halachah
follows Beis Hillel, *Yerushalmi* teaches that it
is preferable to make some minor change in the
s'chach in honor of the Festival, such as lifting
and replacing an area of *s'chach* measuring one
square handbreadth (*Orach Chaim* 636:1).

כָּל שֶׁעֲשָׂאָהּ קֹדֶם לֶחָג שְׁלֹשִׁים יוֹם — *Whatever one
built thirty days prior to the Festival.* [Through-
out *Mishnayos*, the Festival of Succos is referred
to simply as חָג, *the Festival.*] The presumption
is that a *succah* built before the festival season
was made for the sake of shade, not the

mitzvah. Within thirty days, when people have
begun to study the laws of Succos, it is pre-
sumed to have been constructed expressly for
this *mitzvah* (*Rav*).

2. תַּחַת הָאִילָן — *Under a tree,* i.e., the tree's
branches and leaves are directly over the
s'chach of the *succah*. While a tree is still rooted
in the earth, its branches are not valid *s'chach*
(mishnah 4).

כְּאִלּוּ עֲשָׂאָהּ בְּתוֹךְ הַבַּיִת — *It is as though he had
built it inside the house.* A *succah* built under
a roof is not valid because the Torah emphasizes
that one must dwell in a [single] *succah*, not
in a double-roofed one, such as a *succah* covered
by a tree, or the *s'chach* of another *succah*
(*Gem.*). [Thus, the area covered by the branches
and leaves is invalid.]

סֻכָּה עַל גַּבֵּי סֻכָּה — *[If] a succah [is built] atop
another succah,* i.e., the *s'chach* of the lower
succah serves as the floor of the upper *succah*.

וְהַתַּחְתּוֹנָה פְּסוּלָה — *And the lower one is invalid,*
because it is under two 'roofs.' However, if the
upper *succah* is less than ten handbreadths
high, and thus not valid as a separate *succah*
(see m. 1), then the two *s'chachim* are regarded
as a single thick one, and the lower *succah* is
valid (*Orach Chaim* 628:1).

רַבִּי יְהוּדָה אוֹמֵר . . . — *R' Yehudah says . . .* that
if the *s'chach* of the lower *succah* cannot
support the weight of the upper *succah's*
occupants, it has no standing as an independent
dwelling. Consequently, its *s'chach* is not
reckoned as a separate roof. In principle, even
the anonymous *Tanna* agrees with this. The
dispute is only where the *s'chach* of the lower
succah is just strong enough to support the
utensils of the upper one with difficulty. The
first *Tanna* considers this enough to qualify the
upper *succah* as fit for tenancy [since a *succah*
need only be a temporary abode (see comm. to

[ג] פֵּרַס עָלֶיהָ סָדִין מִפְּנֵי הַחַמָּה, אוֹ תַחְתֶּיהָ מִפְּנֵי הַנְּשָׁר, אוֹ שֶׁפֵּרַס עַל־גַּבֵּי הַקִּינוֹף, פְּסוּלָה. אֲבָל, פּוֹרֵס הוּא עַל־גַּבֵּי נַקְלִיטֵי הַמִּטָּה.

[ד] הִדְלָה עָלֶיהָ אֶת־הַגֶּפֶן, וְאֶת־הַדְּלַעַת, וְאֶת־הַקִּסּוֹס, וְסִכֵּךְ עַל־גַּבָּהּ, פְּסוּלָה. וְאִם הָיָה סְכוּךְ הַרְבֵּה מֵהֶן, אוֹ שֶׁקְּצָצָן, כְּשֵׁרָה. זֶה הַכְּלָל: כָּל־שֶׁהוּא מְקַבֵּל טֻמְאָה וְאֵין גִּדּוּלוֹ מִן־הָאָרֶץ, אֵין מְסַכְּכִים בּוֹ; וְכָל־דָּבָר שֶׁאֵינוֹ מְקַבֵּל טֻמְאָה וְגִדּוּלוֹ מִן־הָאָרֶץ, מְסַכְּכִין בּוֹ.

[ה] חֲבִילֵי קַשׁ וַחֲבִילֵי עֵצִים וַחֲבִילֵי זְרָדִין, אֵין מְסַכְּכִין בָּהֶן. וְכֻלָּן שֶׁהִתִּירָן כְּשֵׁרוֹת. וְכֻלָּן כְּשֵׁרוֹת לַדְּפָנוֹת.

[ו] מְסַכְּכִין בַּנְּסָרִים; דִּבְרֵי רַבִּי יְהוּדָה. וְרַבִּי מֵאִיר אוֹסֵר. נָתַן עָלֶיהָ נֶסֶר שֶׁהוּא רָחָב אַרְבָּעָה טְפָחִים, כְּשֵׁרָה, וּבִלְבַד שֶׁלֹּא יִישַׁן תַּחְתָּיו.

יד אברהם

m. 1)]. Thus the lower *succah* is a *succah* beneath a *succah*. R' Yehudah, however, holds that a permanent structure is required (ibid.); and since the lower *s'chach* is too weak to qualify it as a 'permanent' floor, he rules the upper *succah* unfit for tenancy. Thus the lower *succah* is not a *succah* beneath a *succah* (Rav).

3. One of the categories of materials not eligible to be used as *s'chach* are things which are susceptible to receiving *tumah* (see m. 4). This category includes finished utensils, garments, and sheets, the subject of our mishnah.

מִפְּנֵי הַחַמָּה — *Because of the sun.* Although the *succah* had sufficient *s'chach* to make it valid, a sheet was draped over it to block out sunlight. Since the purpose of the sheet is for protection, it is regarded as *s'chach* — but a sheet is invalid for *s'chach* because it can become *tamei* (Rav).

מִפְּנֵי הַנְּשָׁר — *Because of the falling leaves,* i.e., to keep them from falling onto the table.

אוֹ שֶׁפֵּרַס עַל־גַּבֵּי הַקִּינוֹף — *Or if one spread it over a four-poster bed,* to create a canopy for the bed. The canopy is not close to the *s'chach* so that it cannot be regarded as invalid *s'chach* as the previous cases. Nonetheless, since the canopy is horizontal, it is regarded as a separate roof intervening between the person and the *s'chach* (Rav).

נַקְלִיטֵי הַמִּטָּה — *A two-poster bed* — one each at the head and foot of the bed, with a horizontal bar connecting the tops of the two posts. A sheet draped over this bar and sloping down on either side is not considered a tent, because the peak does not have a level width of at least one handbreadth, the minimum dimension qualifying as a 'roof.' [The slopes of the sheet are considered walls, not a roof.] Accordingly, the person in the bed is considered as dwelling solely under the *s'chach* of the *succah* (Rav).

4. . . . הִדְלָה עָלֶיהָ — *If one raised onto it . . .* i.e., he drew any of these vines over the top of a *succah.* [Gourds and ivy also grow on vines and can easily be drawn over a large area.] They are, however, not valid as *s'chach,* since they are still attached to the ground [see m. 2] (Rav).

וְסִכֵּךְ עַל־גַּבָּהּ — *And covered it with [valid] s'chach.* As long as the vines constitute the majority of the *s'chach* it is invalid (Rav).

וְאִם הָיָה סְכוּךְ הַרְבֵּה — *But if the [valid] s'chach exceeded the amount of vine, gourd, or ivy,* the *succah* is valid based on the principle of בִּטּוּל בְּרוֹב, *nullification [of the legal qualities of the minority substance] in the majority.* However, one must mix the valid and invalid *s'chach* together so that the vines are not discernible (Rav).

אוֹ שֶׁקְּצָצָן — *Or if he detached them.* If the invalid *s'chach* exceeds the valid *s'chach,* the *succah* can be made valid by cutting the attached vines, so that they are no longer rooted in the ground. He must, however, lift each vine or branch and set it down again as part of the *s'chach.* By so doing he is, in effect, putting down new, valid *s'chach.* This is to avoid the legal pitfall of תַּעֲשֶׂה וְלֹא מִן הֶעָשׂוּי, *you must make [the s'chach], but it may not come into being indirectly* (Gem.).

טֻמְאָה — *Tumah* is a legally defined state of ritual contamination which restricts the people or objects contaminated from contact with sanctified things or entry into the Temple. Our mishnah invalidates not only *s'chach* that has already become *tamei,* but any *s'chach* that *can* become *tamei.* Examples are finished utensils, clothing, food. [Raw materials, such as wood, can become *tamei* only if processed into finished utensils. Slats or bamboo, therefore, are commonly used as *s'chach.*]

וְאֵין גִּדּוּלוֹ מִן הָאָרֶץ — *Or does not grow from the ground.* This disqualifies hides even if they have

[3] *If one spread a sheet over [the s'chach] because of the sun, or beneath it because of the falling leaves, or if one spread it over a four-poster bed, it is invalid. However, one may spread it over a two-poster bed.*

[4] *If one raised onto it a grapevine, a gourd, or ivy, and covered it with s'chach, it is invalid. But if the s'chach exceeded them, or if he detached them, it is valid. This is the rule [regarding the validity of s'chach]: Whatever is susceptible to contamination or does not grow from the ground, we may not use for s'chach; but whatever is not susceptible to contamination and grows from the ground, we may use for s'chach.*

[5] *Bundles of straw, bundles of wood, or bundles of fresh cane may not be used for s'chach; but all of these are valid when they are untied. All of them are valid for the walls.*

[6] *We may cover the succah with boards; these are the words of R' Yehudah. But R' Meir forbids it. If one placed atop it a board that is four handbreadths wide, [the succah] is valid, except that one may not sleep under [the board].*

---

not yet been fashioned into leather utensils or garments. Metal, earth or clay, although they are earth, do not grow from it (*Rama O. Ch.* 629:1).

5. ... חֲבִילֵי — *Bundles ...* are tied together to facilitate transport (*Rama* 629:15). When they are meant for kindling, they are left to dry so that they will burn better.

אֵין מְסַכְּכִין בָּהֶן — *May not be used for s'chach.* If a man places his bundle on top of the *succah* to dry out in the sun for use as fuel, and he then changes his mind and decides to leave his bundle on the *succah* as *s'chach*, it would not be valid because it would fall under the category of תַּעֲשֶׂה וְלֹא מִן הֶעָשׂוּי, *you must make [the s'chach], but it may not come into being indirectly* (see m. 4). Since his original intention had not been for shade, the *s'chach* was not 'made' by him. In order to preclude such a situation, the Sages banned the use of bundles even if they were originally set down as *s'chach* (*Rav*).

וְכֻלָּן שֶׁהִתִּירָן כְּשֵׁרוֹת — *But all of these are valid when they are untied* — if he originally set them in place as *s'chach*. Since the contents of the bundle are valid *s'chach* according to Torah law, it is sufficient to untie them and thereby remove the Rabbinical objection. But if he placed them on the *succah* in order to *dry* them, and then untied them for use as *s'chach*, they remain invalid until he lifts them and sets them back in place.

וְכֻלָּן — *All of them.* All the aforementioned classifications which are not valid as *s'chach*: (a) attached to the ground; (b) not growing from the soil; (c) susceptible to *tumah*; and (d) bundles (*Rav*).

כְּשֵׁרוֹת לַדְּפָנוֹת — *Are valid for the walls.* The word סֻכָּה [*succah*] implies the סְכָךְ [*s'chach*], *covering.* Thus all limitations on acceptable materials refer to the roof, not to the walls (*Rav*).

6. ... מְסַכְּכִין בַּנְּסָרִים — *We may cover the succah with boards ...* Both R' Yehudah and R' Meir agree that a board four handbreadths wide or more is not valid. The Sages banned the use of such boards because they resemble the ceiling boards of a house, and one might see no difference between eating under the roofing of his house and that of the *succah*. When boards are less than three handbreadths wide, both agree that they are valid, since they are regarded as no more than sticks. They disagree only regarding boards between three and four handbreadths wide. R' Meir considers their width to be significant, while R' Yehudah does not. The halachah follows R' Yehudah. However, it is our custom not to use boards even if they are less than four handbreadths wide (*Orach Chaim* 629:18), except in extenuating circumstances, because one might cover the *succah* in a way that would allow no rain to penetrate (*Mishnah Berurah*).

כְּשֵׁרָה — *[The succah] is valid.* Even though a four-handbreadth board is not valid, that applies only to the area covered by the board itself, but it need not disqualify the rest of the *s'chach.* Thus, if the *succah* is large enough to retain the minimum area of seven handbreadths square even after the space from the board to the adjacent wall is subtracted from the total area of the *succah*, it is valid, except for the area directly beneath the board (*Orach Chaim* 632:1).

וּבִלְבַד שֶׁלֹּא יִישַׁן תַּחְתָּיו — *Except that one may not sleep [or eat] under [the board].*

[ז] תִּקְרָה שֶׁאֵין עָלֶיהָ מַעֲזִיבָה – רַבִּי יְהוּדָה אוֹמֵר: בֵּית שַׁמַּאי אוֹמְרִים, מְפַקְפֵּק וְנוֹטֵל אַחַת מִבֵּינְתַיִם; וּבֵית הִלֵּל אוֹמְרִים, מְפַקְפֵּק אוֹ נוֹטֵל אַחַת מִבֵּינְתַיִם. רַבִּי מֵאִיר אוֹמֵר: נוֹטֵל אַחַת מִבֵּינְתַיִם וְאֵין מְפַקְפֵּק.

[ח] הַמְקָרֶה סֻכָּתוֹ בַּשְּׁפוּדִין אוֹ בַּאֲרוּכוֹת הַמִּטָּה, אִם יֶשׁ־רֶוַח בֵּינֵיהֶן כְּמוֹתָן, כְּשֵׁרָה. הַחוֹטֵט בַּגָּדִישׁ לַעֲשׂוֹת בּוֹ סֻכָּה, אֵינָהּ סֻכָּה.

[ט] הַמְשַׁלְשֵׁל דְּפָנוֹת מִלְמַעְלָה לְמַטָּה, אִם גָּבוֹהַּ מִן־הָאָרֶץ שְׁלֹשָׁה טְפָחִים, פְּסוּלָה; מִלְמַטָּה לְמַעְלָה, אִם גָּבוֹהַּ מִן־הָאָרֶץ עֲשָׂרָה טְפָחִים, כְּשֵׁרָה. רַבִּי יוֹסֵי אוֹמֵר: כְּשֵׁם שֶׁמִּלְמַטָּה לְמַעְלָה עֲשָׂרָה טְפָחִים, כָּךְ מִלְמַעְלָה לְמַטָּה עֲשָׂרָה טְפָחִים. הִרְחִיק אֶת־הַסִּכּוּךְ מִן הַדְּפָנוֹת שְׁלֹשָׁה טְפָחִים, פְּסוּלָה.

[י] בַּיִת שֶׁנִּפְחַת וְסִכֵּךְ עַל־גַּבָּיו, אִם יֶשׁ מִן־הַכֹּתֶל לַסִּכּוּךְ אַרְבַּע אַמּוֹת, פְּסוּלָה. וְכֵן חָצֵר שֶׁהִיא מֻקֶּפֶת אַכְסַדְרָה. סֻכָּה גְדוֹלָה שֶׁהִקִּיפוּהָ

יד אברהם

7. The mishnah now turns to the problem of how to convert an existing roof made of boards into valid *s'chach*. Some authorities (*Rambam, Ran,* and others) maintain that the planks under discussion in this mishnah are less than four handbreadths wide. As part of an actual roof, these boards would be disqualified as *s'chach* for the same reason used above to bar wider boards. A further reason for disqualification is that they were put down not for *s'chach*, but for roofing. Thus a later attempt to use them for *s'chach* would render them indirectly made *s'chach*, as in mishnah 4 [תֵּעֲשֶׂה וְלֹא מִן הֶעָשׂוּי]. This mishnah discusses how to remove both of these disqualifications.

שֶׁאֵין עָלֶיהָ מַעֲזִיבָה — *That has no plaster on it.* The roofing boards have not yet been covered with plaster [or tar], substances ineligible for *s'chach* (*Rav*).

רַבִּי יְהוּדָה אוֹמֵר — *R' Yehudah says* that Beis Shammai and Beis Hillel disagree about which steps must be taken to turn the roof boards into *s'chach*, and he presents their dispute.

בֵּית שַׁמַּאי אוֹמְרִים — *Beis Shammai say.* As the Gemara (15a) understands this, Beis Shammai mean that even if one removed the nails (and lifted the boards), it is insufficient. Rather, he must replace every other board with valid *s'chach*. Having done so, he need not loosen the remaining boards. Though lifting the boards would correct the problem of indirectly made *s'chach*, it would not suffice to remove the disqualification based on the concern that someone might conclude that an ordinary roof was equally acceptable. Beis Shammai therefore require that every second plank be replaced with valid *s'chach*. This removes both disqualifications.

וּבֵית הִלֵּל אוֹמְרִים — *But Beis Hillel say* that either loosening or replacing is sufficient. Beis Hillel consider that merely *loosening* the planks removes them from the category of a 'roof,' since a permanent roof would surely have to be secured. Thus the loosened planks may be used for *s'chach* if they are less than four handbreadths wide.

רַבִּי מֵאִיר אוֹמֵר: נוֹטֵל אַחַת מִבֵּינְתַיִם וְאֵין מְפַקְפֵּק — *R' Meir says: He removes every other one but does not loosen [them].* This is identical to the position attributed by R' Yehudah to Beis Shammai. In R' Meir's opinion, this ruling was never disputed by Beis Hillel.

8. בַּשְּׁפוּדִין אוֹ בַּאֲרוּכוֹת הַמִּטָּה — *If one roofs his succah with spits or bed-boards.* Atop his succah someone laid out a framework of spits or bed-boards upon which he will pile *s'chach* (*Rashi*). Metal spits are invalid as *s'chach* because they do not grow from the ground, and bed-boards are disqualified because they are utensils (*Rav*).

אִם יֶשׁ רֶוַח בֵּינֵיהֶן כְּמוֹתָן — *If the space between them is equal to themselves.* The *s'chach*-covered space left between the spits or bed-boards is equal to the space covered by the spits or bed-boards themselves, with the result that at least half the *succah* is covered by valid *s'chach*.

הַחוֹטֵט בַּגָּדִישׁ לַעֲשׂוֹת בּוֹ סֻכָּה — *If one hollowed out a haystack to make a succah inside it.* He removed the straw from within, until he had hollowed out a space large enough for a valid *succah* (*Rav*).

אֵינָהּ סֻכָּה — *It is not a succah.* Although the top layer of hay is an acceptable material for *s'chach*, the *succah* is not valid because the hay was not emplaced originally for the purpose of

[7] *A roof that has no plaster on it — R' Yehudah says: Beis Shammai say,
one loosens them and removes every other board; but Beis Hillel say, he
[either] loosens [them] or removes every other one. R' Meir says: He removes
every other one but does not loosen [them].*

[8] *If one roofs his succah with spits or bed-boards, if the space between
them is equal to themselves, it is valid. If one hollowed out a haystack
to make a succah inside it, it is not a succah.*

[9] *If one suspends the walls from above downwards, if [they are] three
handbreadths above the ground, it is invalid; from below upwards, if it
reaches a height of ten handbreadths above the ground, it is valid. R' Yose
says: Just as from below upwards ten handbreadths [suffice], so from above
downwards ten handbreadths [suffice]. If one moved the s'chach three
handbreadths away from the walls, it is invalid.*

[10] *A house that was breached and he placed s'chach over it, if there are
four cubits from the wall to the s'chach, it is invalid. The same [applies
to] a courtyard that is surrounded by a portico. A large succah that they ringed*

YAD AVRAHAM

shade; thus it is indirectly made s'chach (Rav).

9. הַמְשַׁלְשֵׁל דְּפָנוֹת מִלְמַעְלָה לְמַטָּה — *If one
suspends the walls from above downwards.* He
wove or plaited the succah walls working his
way downwards from the s'chach (Rav).

אִם גָּבוֹהַּ מִן הָאָרֶץ שְׁלֹשָׁה טְפָחִים — *If [they are]
three handbreadths above the ground.* If the
bottom of the wall is three or more handbreadths above the ground, it is invalid. Since
the three-handbreadths gap is large enough to
permit goats to crawl into the succah, it lacks
the halachic status of a partition (Rashi).

מִלְמַטָּה לְמַעְלָה — *From below upwards,* i.e., he
builds the succah walls from, the ground up.

גָּבוֹהַּ מִן הָאָרֶץ עֲשָׂרָה טְפָחִים — *Ten handbreadths
above the ground* is the minimum height for a
partition in halachah (see m. 1). Thus, if the wall
is directly below the s'chach, it is valid, even
though there is a large gap from the top of the
wall to the s'chach. We rely on the principle
גּוּד אָסִיק, *gud asik* (lit., *pull and bring up*),
according to which the walls are seen as
stretching upwards until the s'chach. This
principle was transmitted orally to Moses on
Sinai (Gem. 6b). If, however, the wall was not
directly below the s'chach, but off to the side,
the succah is valid only if the wall is within
three handbreadths of the s'chach (Orach
Chaim 630:9).

כָּךְ מִלְמַעְלָה לְמַטָּה עֲשָׂרָה טְפָחִים — *So from above
downwards ten handbreadths [suffice].* Even
though there may be a gap greater than three
handbreadths from the ground to the bottom
of the suspended wall, R' Yose considers it valid
as long as the wall has the minimum height of
ten handbreadths. The halachah, however, does
not follow R' Yose (Rav).

הִרְחִיק אֶת הַסְּכוּךְ מִן הַדְּפָנוֹת שְׁלֹשָׁה טְפָחִים — *If
one moved the s'chach three handbreadths
away from the walls.* This refers to a horizontal

gap between the s'chach and the wall (Rav).

פְּסוּלָה — *It is invalid,* in a succah of three
walls. A gap of three handbreadths, running between
the s'chach and the wall along the entire length
of the succah, separates the s'chach from the
wall and thus disqualifies it as a succah wall.
This leaves the succah with only two walls
(Orach Chaim 632:2).

10. בַּיִת שֶׁנִּפְחַת — *A house that was breached,*
i.e., the middle of a roof collapsed, leaving a
large gap in the ceiling over which the owner
placed s'chach (Rav).

פְּסוּלָה — *It is invalid.* A four-cubit distance
between the s'chach and the wall is considered
a separation; we do not consider the s'chach to
have walls beneath it. But if the intact part of
the ceiling between the s'chach and the walls
is less than four cubits, the succah is valid. In
line with the Sinaitic principle of דּוֹפֶן עֲקוּמָה,
bent wall, we regard the intervening section of
ceiling as part of the wall which bends over to
meet the s'chach. But one may not eat or sleep
under the ceiling part (Rav; Orach Chaim
632:1).

וְכֵן חָצֵר שֶׁהִיא מֻקֶּפֶת אַכְסַדְרָה — *The same
[applies to] a courtyard that is surrounded by
a portico,* i.e., a courtyard surrounded on three
sides by houses which open into it. From each
house, a roof projects toward the courtyard,
shading some of it and leaving the rest exposed.
If one were to lay s'chach over the exposed
portion of the courtyard using the walls of the
surrounding houses as the walls of the succah,
the portico would separate the s'chach from the
house walls. If the portico is four cubits, the
succah is not valid; if less, then it is valid based
on the principle of דּוֹפֶן עֲקוּמָה, *bent wall* (Rashi;
Rav).

סֻכָּה גְדוֹלָה — *A large succah,* i.e., an area of at
least seven handbreadths square of valid s'chach

בְּדָבָר שֶׁאֵין מְסַכְּכִים בּוֹ, אִם יֶשׁ־תַּחְתָּיו אַרְבַּע אַמּוֹת, פְּסוּלָה.

[יא] הָעוֹשֶׂה סֻכָּתוֹ כְּמִין צְרִיף, אוֹ שֶׁסְּמָכָהּ לַכֹּתֶל, רַבִּי אֱלִיעֶזֶר פּוֹסֵל, מִפְּנֵי שֶׁאֵין לָהּ גַּג; וַחֲכָמִים מַכְשִׁירִין. מַחְצֶלֶת קָנִים גְּדוֹלָה, עֲשָׂאָהּ לִשְׁכִיבָה, מְקַבֶּלֶת טֻמְאָה וְאֵין מְסַכְּכִין בָּהּ; לְסִכּוּךְ, מְסַכְּכִין בָּהּ וְאֵינָהּ מְקַבֶּלֶת טֻמְאָה. רַבִּי אֱלִיעֶזֶר אוֹמֵר: אַחַת קְטַנָּה וְאַחַת גְּדוֹלָה, עֲשָׂאָהּ לִשְׁכִיבָה, מְקַבֶּלֶת טֻמְאָה וְאֵין מְסַכְּכִין בָּהּ; לְסִכּוּךְ, מְסַכְּכִין בָּהּ וְאֵינָהּ מְקַבֶּלֶת טֻמְאָה.

פֶּרֶק שֵׁנִי

[א] **הַיָּשֵׁן** תַּחַת הַמִּטָּה בַּסֻּכָּה לֹא יָצָא יְדֵי חוֹבָתוֹ. אָמַר רַבִּי יְהוּדָה: נוֹהֲגִין הָיִינוּ, שֶׁהָיִינוּ יְשֵׁנִים תַּחַת הַמִּטָּה בִּפְנֵי הַזְּקֵנִים וְלֹא אָמְרוּ לָנוּ דָבָר. אָמַר רַבִּי שִׁמְעוֹן: מַעֲשֶׂה בְּטָבִי, עַבְדּוֹ שֶׁל רַבָּן גַּמְלִיאֵל, שֶׁהָיָה יָשֵׁן תַּחַת הַמִּטָּה. וְאָמַר לָהֶן רַבָּן גַּמְלִיאֵל לַזְּקֵנִים: "רְאִיתֶם טָבִי עַבְדִּי? שֶׁהוּא תַּלְמִיד חָכָם וְיוֹדֵעַ שֶׁעֲבָדִים פְּטוּרִין מִן־הַסֻּכָּה — לְפִיכָךְ יָשֵׁן הוּא תַּחַת הַמִּטָּה." וּלְפִי דַרְכֵּנוּ לָמַדְנוּ שֶׁהַיָּשֵׁן תַּחַת הַמִּטָּה לֹא יָצָא יְדֵי חוֹבָתוֹ.

יד אברהם

was surrounded along its sides by non-valid s'chach, which lay between it and the walls (Rav).

אם יֶשׁ תַּחְתָּיו אַרְבַּע אַמּוֹת — *If there were four cubits beneath it.* If the space covered by the invalid materials is four cubits.

פְּסוּלָה — *It is invalid,* because the walls are too far from the s'chach to be regarded as part of the *succah,* and the four-cubit expanse prevents us from considering the invalid materials part of a *bent wall.* An *empty* space of three handbreadths running through the length of the *succah* invalidates the *succah* regardless of whether it is in the middle or on the side (see m. 9).

11. הָעוֹשֶׂה סֻכָּתוֹ כְּמִין צְרִיף — *If one makes his succah like a conical hut.* A conical hut has no roof and the walls meet each other on top (Rav). In this respect the roof and the walls are one [the walls being made of valid s'chach] (Rashi).

אוֹ שֶׁסְּמָכָהּ לַכֹּתֶל — *Or he leaned it against the wall.* He built a lean-to — a single wall of valid s'chach leaning against the wall of a house with a seven-handbreadth square area beneath it (Rav).

רַבִּי אֱלִיעֶזֶר פּוֹסֵל, מִפְּנֵי שֶׁאֵין לָהּ גַּג — *R' Eliezer invalidates it, since it has no roof.* In both cases one cannot distinguish between roof and wall, and a *succah* must have a discernible roof at least one handbreadth wide (Rav, Gem. 19b). The halachah follows R' Eliezer (Rav; Orach Chaim 631:10).

עֲשָׂאָהּ לִשְׁכִיבָה, מְקַבֶּלֶת טֻמְאָה — *If made to lie*

upon, *is susceptible to contamination.* Although such a mat is generally made for shade, if one designated it to recline upon, it loses its acceptability because it then becomes a utensil and thus susceptible to *tumah* [see m. 4] (Gem. 20a).

לְסִכּוּךְ, מְסַכְּכִין בָּהּ — *If for shade, we [may] use it for s'chach.* Even a small mat — which is generally made for reclining — is valid for s'chach if it was made expressly for s'chach (Gem.).

וְאֵינָהּ מְקַבֶּלֶת טֻמְאָה — *And it is not susceptible to contamination,* since he specifically intended it for shade, and not as a mat.

רַבִּי אֱלִיעֶזֶר אוֹמֵר — *R' Eliezer says:* The Gemara explains that R' Eliezer disagrees with the Sages and holds that even a large mat is generally made for reclining. Therefore, the words עֲשָׂאָהּ לִשְׁכִיבָה here imply that they are *usually* made for reclining (Rav).

לְסִכּוּךְ — *If for s'chach.* If he expressly designated it for s'chach [which is not its usual use], it never attains the status of a utensil. It is, therefore, not subject to *tumah* and is valid as s'chach. The halachah does not follow R' Eliezer (Orach Chaim 629:6).

CHAPTER TWO

Where the previous chapter discussed the laws governing the *succah* itself — its dimensions, the *s'chach,* and related matters — this chapter will discuss the act of performing the *mitzvah,* which requires one to sleep as well as to eat there. Indeed, the Torah states generally

with material that we may not use for s'chach, if there were four cubits beneath it, it is invalid.

[11] If one makes his succah like a conical hut, or he leaned it against the wall, R' Eliezer invalidates it, since it has no roof; but the Sages declare it valid. A large reed mat, if made to lie upon, is susceptible to contamination and we may not use it for s'chach; if for shade, we may use it for s'chach and it is not susceptible to contamination. R' Eliezer says: Whether [the mat is] small or large, if he made it to lie upon, it is susceptible to contamination and we may not use it as s'chach; if for s'chach, we may use it for s'chach and it is not susceptible to contamination.

CHAPTER TWO

[1] הַיָּשֵׁן One who sleeps under the bed in the succah has not fulfilled his obligation [to sleep in a succah]. R' Yehudah said: We regularly slept under the bed in the presence of the Elders and they said nothing to us. R' Shimon said: There is a case of Tavi, Rabban Gamliel's slave, who used to sleep under the bed. Rabban Gamliel said to the Elders, 'Have you observed my slave Tavi? He is a scholar and knows that [gentile] slaves are exempt from [the obligation of] succah — that is why he sleeps under the bed.' And incidentally we deduced that one who sleeps under the bed does not fulfill his obligation [to sleep in a succah].

(Lev. 23:42): In succos shall you dwell for seven days. All activities and pastimes usually taking place in the home should be done in the succah so that it becomes one's temporary abode (see Orach Chaim 639:1). However, the mishnah singles out eating and sleeping as acts requiring a succah, because these activities are, as a rule, performed in the home.

In the temperate zones of Europe and North America, the mitzvah of sleeping in the succah has become regarded as a voluntary observance reserved for only the most devout. This apparent disregard of the law is itself based on a halachah — that of מִצְטַעֵר, feeling distressed, i.e., when climatic or other conditions are so severe that one feels a significant degree of discomfort in the succah, the mitzvah does not apply. The cool evening temperatures in temperate regions make sleeping outdoors a discomfort and consequently not obligatory.

1. הַיָּשֵׁן תַּחַת הַמִּטָּה — One who sleeps under the bed. The Gemara comments that the mishnah speaks of a bed where the area beneath is ten handbreadths high so that it is considered a 'tent' by itself. Thus, the bed acts as a barrier separating him from the succah (Rav). If the space beneath it was lower than ten hand-breadths, it is considered to be part of the succah and one can discharge his obligation by sleeping there.

אָמַר רַבִּי יְהוּדָה: נוֹהֲגִין הָיִינוּ, שֶׁהָיִינוּ יְשֵׁנִים תַּחַת הַמִּטָּה בִּפְנֵי הַזְּקֵנִים — R' Yehudah said: We regularly slept under the bed in the presence of the Elders. R' Yehudah is consistent with his view (1:1) that a succah must be a permanent

structure. Accordingly, a temporary shelter, such as the area underneath a movable bed, cannot nullify the permanent shelter of the succah proper (Rav). The halachah does not follow R' Yehudah (Orach Chaim 627:1).

שֶׁהוּא תַּלְמִיד חָכָם וְיוֹדֵעַ שֶׁעֲבָדִים פְּטוּרִין מִן הַסֻּכָּה — He is a scholar and knows that [gentile] slaves are exempt from [the obligation of] succah. Non-Jews who have been purchased as slaves, must, within twelve months of their purchase, undergo circumcision, immerse in a mikveh, and accept voluntarily the mitzvos incumbent upon slaves owned by a Jew. Upon doing so, such slaves have the same obligations to observe mitzvos as Jewish women (Chagigah 4a). Since women are exempt from the mitzvah of succah because it has a fixed time (2:8), so are slaves (Rav).

לְפִיכָךְ יָשֵׁן הוּא תַּחַת הַמִּטָּה — That is why he sleeps under the bed, i.e., Tavi demonstrated his awareness of his exemption by sleeping under the bed. If so, why was Tavi in the succah at all? Probably to serve his master, and at the same time to listen to the Torah discourses of the Sages. Presumably not wishing to take up space needed by those obligated to sleep in the succah, he slept under the bed (cf. Yerushalmi here cited by Ran).

וּלְפִי דַרְכֵּנוּ לָמַדְנוּ — And incidentally we deduced. Although Rabban Gamliel mentioned Tavi's practice only in order to praise his slave, we learned a lesson (Rav). [Our practice is to derive lessons even from the casual conversation of scholars. It is axiomatic that a scholar does

[ב] הַסּוֹמֵךְ סֻכָּתוֹ בְּכַרְעֵי הַמִּטָּה, כְּשֵׁרָה. רַבִּי יְהוּדָה אוֹמֵר: אִם אֵינָהּ יְכוֹלָה לַעֲמוֹד בִּפְנֵי עַצְמָהּ, פְּסוּלָה. סֻכָּה הַמְדֻבְלֶלֶת, וְשֶׁצִּלָּתָהּ מְרֻבָּה מֵחַמָּתָהּ, כְּשֵׁרָה. הַמְעֻבָּה כְּמִין בַּיִת, אַף־עַל־פִּי שֶׁאֵין הַכּוֹכָבִים נִרְאִים מִתּוֹכָהּ, כְּשֵׁרָה.

[ג] הָעוֹשֶׂה סֻכָּתוֹ בְּרֹאשׁ הָעֲגָלָה אוֹ בְּרֹאשׁ הַסְּפִינָה כְּשֵׁרָה, וְעוֹלִין לָהּ בְּיוֹם טוֹב. בְּרֹאשׁ הָאִילָן אוֹ עַל־גַּבֵּי גָמָל כְּשֵׁרָה, וְאֵין עוֹלִין לָהּ בְּיוֹם טוֹב. שְׁתַּיִם בָּאִילָן וְאַחַת בִּידֵי אָדָם, אוֹ שְׁתַּיִם בִּידֵי אָדָם וְאַחַת בָּאִילָן, כְּשֵׁרָה, וְאֵין עוֹלִין לָהּ בְּיוֹם טוֹב. שָׁלֹשׁ בִּידֵי אָדָם וְאַחַת בָּאִילָן כְּשֵׁרָה, וְעוֹלִין לָהּ בְּיוֹם טוֹב. זֶה הַכְּלָל: כָּל־שֶׁנִּטַּל הָאִילָן וִיכוֹלָה לַעֲמוֹד בִּפְנֵי עַצְמָהּ, כְּשֵׁרָה, וְעוֹלִין לָהּ בְּיוֹם טוֹב.

[ד] הָעוֹשֶׂה סֻכָּתוֹ בֵּין הָאִילָנוֹת, וְהָאִילָנוֹת דְּפָנוֹת לָהּ, כְּשֵׁרָה. שְׁלוּחֵי מִצְוָה פְּטוּרִין מִן־הַסֻּכָּה. חוֹלִין וּמְשַׁמְּשֵׁיהֶן פְּטוּרִין מִן־הַסֻּכָּה. אוֹכְלִין וְשׁוֹתִין עֲרַאי חוּץ לַסֻּכָּה.

יד אברהם

not make statements unless they are well considered.]

2. הַסּוֹמֵךְ סֻכָּתוֹ בְּכַרְעֵי הַמִּטָּה — *If one supports his succah on the legs of a bed.* This refers to a bed with four boards around it, which extend above the mattress for at least ten more handbreadths. S'chach is placed on top of these four boards, which thus also serve as the walls of the *succah* (*Tur Orach Chaim* 630; *Bais Yosef* there).

כְּשֵׁרָה — *It is valid.* Even though when one moves the bed, he automatically moves the entire *succah* with it (*Tif. Yis.*).

רַבִּי יְהוּדָה אוֹמֵר — *R' Yehudah says* that is invalid. R' Yehudah is consistent with his view (1:1) that a *succah* must be a permanent structure; if it is movable it is invalid. The halachah does not follow R' Yehudah (*Rav*).

סֻכָּה הַמְדֻבְלֶלֶת — *A disarranged succah* [i.e. disarranged s'chach]. Some of the s'chach points upward and some points downward, with the result that חַמָּתָהּ מְרֻבָּה מִצִּלָּתָהּ, *its sunny area is greater than its shaded area.* If the s'chach were lying evenly together, there would be more shaded area than sunny area. Since the spaces between the disarranged pieces are less than three handbreadths, we regard it as though it were all together and as such it is valid (*Rav; Orach Chaim* 631:5).

וְשֶׁצִּלָּתָהּ מְרֻבָּה מֵחַמָּתָהּ — *Or one whose shade[d area] is greater than its sun[lit] area.* There are many air spaces between the pieces of s'chach, each space being less than three handbreadths, but the total shaded area is greater than the sunny area [see m.1:1] (*Tif. Yis.; Orach Chaim* 631:4).

אַף עַל פִּי שֶׁאֵין הַכּוֹכָבִים נִרְאִים מִתּוֹכָהּ, כְּשֵׁרָה — *Even though the stars cannot be seen from inside*

it, *it is valid.* However, it is preferable [לְכַתְּחִלָּה] that the s'chach be laid on so that the stars are visible through it (*Orach Chaim* 631:3).

3. כְּשֵׁרָה — *It is valid.* Both succos meet the requirement of a temporary dwelling. A *succah* on a wagon is a livable abode even though it is mobile (*Rashi*).

So long as the *succah* is sturdy enough to stand up to normal *land* winds, it is a proper temporary dwelling, even if it could not withstand the impact of the turbulent winds that are more common at sea (*Gem.* 23a; *Orach Chaim* 629:2).

בְּרֹאשׁ הָאִילָן — *[If he makes a succah] in the top of a tree* by erecting partitions and covering them with s'chach (*Rashi* to 22b; *Rav*).

כְּשֵׁרָה, וְאֵין עוֹלִין לָהּ בְּיוֹם טוֹב — *It is valid, but we may not go up into it on the festival.* It meets the halachic requirements of a *succah* but runs afoul of the Rabbinic ban on the physical use of trees or live animals on festivals, instituted to prevent the breaking off of branches on *Yom Tov* (*Beitzah* 36b). [In the case of animals the fear is that he may break off a twig for use as a riding crop while riding the animal (*Rashi; Rav*).] Thus it may be used only during the Intermediate Days of the festival (*Rashi, Rav*).

וְאַחַת בִּידֵי אָדָם — *And one [is] man-made.* A board is set into the ground to support the part of the floor that extends beyond the tree. The third wall of the *succah* is formed by that board, or something built on it, extending upward above the floor. The s'chach is laid across the top of all three walls (*Rashi; Rav*).

וְאֵין עוֹלִין לָהּ בְּיוֹם טוֹב — *But we may not go up into it on the festival.* In either case the tree is indispensable to the *succah*; without it,

[2] *If one supports his succah on the legs of a bed, it is valid. R' Yehudah*
says: If it cannot stand by itself, it is invalid. A disarranged succah, or
one whose shade[d area] is greater than its sun[lit area], is valid. If [the succah]
is thickly covered like a house, even though the stars cannot be seen from
inside it, it is valid.

[3] *If one makes his succah on top of a wagon or on the deck of a ship it*
is valid, and we may go up into it on the festival. [If he makes a succah]
in the top of a tree or on the back of a camel it is valid, but we may not
go up into it on the festival. [If] two [walls are] in a tree and one is man-made,
or two [are] man-made and one [is] in a tree, it is valid, but we may not
go up into it on the festival. [If] three [walls are] man-made and one [is] in
a tree, it is valid, and we may go up into it on the festival. This is the general
rule: Wherever the tree can be removed and [the succah] can stand by itself,
it is valid, and we may go up into it on the festival.

[4] *If one makes his succah between the trees, and the trees serve as its walls,*
it is valid. Those who are engaged in the performance of a mitzvah are
exempt from the [mitzvah of] succah. Ill people and their attendants are
exempt from the [mitzvah of] succah. We may eat and drink casually outside
the succah.

---

the *succah* floor would collapse. Therefore, to dwell in the *succah* means to use the tree, an act that is forbidden on festivals. Consequently, it may be used only on the Intermediate Days (*Rashi; Rav*).

שָׁלֹשׁ בִּידֵי אָדָם וְאַחַת בָּאִילָן כְּשֵׁרָה, וְעוֹלִין לָהּ בְּיוֹם טוֹב — *[If] three [walls are] man-made and one [is] in a tree, it is valid, and we may go up into it on the festival,* i.e., the *succah* is on the ground. Three of its walls are man-made and a tree is used as the fourth wall. Thus, even without the tree, enough remains to constitute a valid *succah* (see 1:1).

4. הָעוֹשֶׂה סֻכָּתוֹ בֵּין הָאִילָנוֹת, וְהָאִילָנוֹת דְּפָנוֹת לָהּ — *If one makes his succah between the trees, and the trees serve as its walls,* but the floor of the *succah* is on the ground (*Rashi*). [Otherwise, the mishnah would have added that he is not permitted to 'go up into the *succah*' on Yom Tov.]

כְּשֵׁרָה — *It is valid.* We do not fear that he will make some direct use of the tree on the festival.

שְׁלוּחֵי מִצְוָה — *Those who are engaged in the performance [lit. agents] of a mitzvah.* For example: someone who is traveling to study Torah or to greet his rabbi, or is occupied with redeeming Jewish captives (*Rashi; Rav*).

פְּטוּרִין מִן הַסֻּכָּה — *Are exempt from the [mitzvah of] succah.* A person who is occupied with one mitzvah is exempt from another (הָעוֹסֵק בְּמִצְוָה פָּטוּר מִן הַמִּצְוָה), if performing the second mitzvah would require him to go out of his way.

Consequently, people engaged in such a mission are obligated to sleep in a *succah* only if one is readily available. If it would be troublesome for them to build one or even look for one, they are exempt (*Rashi; Rama, Orach Chaim* 38:8).

פְּטוּרִין מִן הַסֻּכָּה — *Are exempt from the [mitzvah of] succah.* The sick person is exempt because Scripture states (*Lev.* 23:42): בַּסֻּכֹּת תֵּשְׁבוּ, *In succos you shall dwell.* This teaches תֵּשְׁבוּ כְּעֵין תָּדֻרוּ, *as you are accustomed to dwell all year long at home, so are you to dwell in a succah.* But under conditions of extreme discomfort such as illness, which would cause one to leave his normal dwelling to go to a more comfortable place, he is not required to live in a *succah* (*Rav* from *Gem.* 26a). The attendants are exempt because they are involved in the *mitvzah* of caring for the patient, and one who is involved in a *mitzvah* is exempt from another *mitzvah*. *Rama* (ibid.), however, cautions that on the first night of Succos, even those who suffer discomfort must eat at least כַּזַּיִת, *an olive's volume* of bread in the *succah*.

אוֹכְלִין וְשׁוֹתִין עֲרַאי חוּץ לַסֻּכָּה — *We may eat and drink casually outside the succah.* The *Shulchan Aruch* (*Orach Chaim* 639:2) follows the view that up to and including an egg's volume of bread is still considered a snack. More than this is considered a 'meal,' which must be eaten in the *succah*. The laws of the types and quantities of foods and drink that must be eaten in a *succah*, and the instances when the blessing לֵישֵׁב בַּסֻּכָּה, *to dwell in the succah,* must be recited, are discussed there at length.

[ה] מַעֲשֶׂה וְהֵבִיאוּ לוֹ לְרַבָּן יוֹחָנָן בֶּן־זַכַּאי לִטְעוֹם אֶת־הַתַּבְשִׁיל,
וּלְרַבָּן גַּמְלִיאֵל שְׁתֵּי כוֹתָבוֹת וּדְלִי שֶׁל מַיִם, וְאָמְרוּ: "הַעֲלוּם לַסֻּכָּה."
וּכְשֶׁנָּתְנוּ לוֹ לְרַבִּי צָדוֹק אֹכֶל פָּחוֹת מִכַּבֵּיצָה, נְטָלוֹ בְּמַפָּה וַאֲכָלוֹ חוּץ
לַסֻּכָּה, וְלֹא בֵרַךְ אַחֲרָיו.

[ו] רַבִּי אֱלִיעֶזֶר אוֹמֵר: אַרְבַּע עֶשְׂרֵה סְעוּדוֹת חַיָּב אָדָם לֶאֱכוֹל בַּסֻּכָּה,
אַחַת בַּיּוֹם וְאַחַת בַּלַּיְלָה. וַחֲכָמִים אוֹמְרִים: אֵין לַדָּבָר קִצְבָה, חוּץ
מִלֵּילֵי יוֹם טוֹב רִאשׁוֹן שֶׁל חַג בִּלְבָד. וְעוֹד אָמַר רַבִּי אֱלִיעֶזֶר: מִי שֶׁלֹּא
אָכַל לֵילֵי יוֹם טוֹב הָרִאשׁוֹן יַשְׁלִים בְּלֵילֵי יוֹם טוֹב הָאַחֲרוֹן. וַחֲכָמִים
אוֹמְרִים: אֵין לַדָּבָר תַּשְׁלוּמִין. עַל־זֶה נֶאֱמַר: "מְעֻוָּת לֹא־יוּכַל לִתְקֹן,
וְחֶסְרוֹן לֹא־יוּכַל לְהִמָּנוֹת."

[ז] מִי שֶׁהָיָה רֹאשׁוֹ וְרֻבּוֹ בַסֻּכָּה וְשֻׁלְחָנוֹ בְּתוֹךְ הַבַּיִת — בֵּית שַׁמַּאי
פּוֹסְלִין, וּבֵית הִלֵּל מַכְשִׁירִין. אָמְרוּ לָהֶן בֵּית הִלֵּל לְבֵית שַׁמַּאי:
"לֹא כָךְ הָיָה מַעֲשֶׂה, שֶׁהָלְכוּ זִקְנֵי בֵית שַׁמַּאי וְזִקְנֵי בֵית הִלֵּל לְבַקֵּר
אֶת־רַבִּי יוֹחָנָן בֶּן־הַחוֹרָנִי, וּמְצָאוּהוּ שֶׁהָיָה יוֹשֵׁב רֹאשׁוֹ וְרֻבּוֹ בַסֻּכָּה
וְשֻׁלְחָנוֹ בְּתוֹךְ הַבַּיִת, וְלֹא אָמְרוּ לוֹ דָבָר?" אָמְרוּ לָהֶן בֵּית שַׁמַּאי: "מִשָּׁם
רְאָיָה? אַף הֵם אָמְרוּ לוֹ: ,אִם כֵּן הָיִיתָ נוֹהֵג, לֹא קִיַּמְתָּ מִצְוַת סֻכָּה
מִיָּמֶיךָ'."

יד אברהם

5. וְאָמְרוּ: הַעֲלוּם לַסֻּכָּה — *And they* [i.e., both Rabban Yochanan and Rabban Gamliel] *said, 'Bring them up to the succah.'* This contradicts the previous mishnah which states that a snack may be eaten outside the *succah*. The Gemara (26a) resolves the contradiction by saying that they wished to be strict with themselves, and our mishnah teaches that a person is not regarded as haughty if he chooses to eat even fruit and water only in the *succah*. Though water in any amount may be drunk outside the *succah*, Rambam, quoted in *Orach Chaim* (639:2), states: Whoever wishes to be strict with himself and not drink even water outside the *succah* is praiseworthy.

נְטָלוֹ בְּמַפָּה — *He took it with a cloth.* [This food required washing of the hands before eating, i.e., it was either bread or 'something which is dipped in liquid' (דָּבָר שֶׁטִּבּוּלוֹ בְּמַשְׁקֶה) which required washing of the hands (at least in Talmudic times; see *Orach Chaim* 158:4).] R' Tzaddok holds that food smaller than the volume of an egg does not require washing. Had he been required to wash his hands, wrapping the food in a cloth to avoid touching it while eating would have been no substitute for washing; it is permitted only as an emergency measure when no water is to be found for a considerable distance (*Orach Chaim* 163:1). Though R' Tzaddok held that washing was not required, he held the food in a cloth for reasons of cleanliness (*Rashi*).

וַאֲכָלוֹ חוּץ לַסֻּכָּה — *And ate it outside the succah,* thus demonstrating that one who is not strict with himself on this point is not to be considered careless in performing *mitzvos* (*Ran*).

וְלֹא בֵרַךְ אַחֲרָיו — *And did not recite the benediction after it.* R' Tzaddok held the view of R' Yehudah (*Berachos* 7:2) that one is obligated to recite *Bircas HaMazon* only after a meal of at least an egg's volume of bread. [The halachah, however, follows R' Meir who rules that eating an olive's volume of bread obligates one in *Bircas HaMazon* (*Orach Chaim* 184:6).]

6. רַבִּי אֱלִיעֶזֶר אוֹמֵר: אַרְבַּע עֶשְׂרֵה סְעוּדוֹת חַיָּב אָדָם לֶאֱכוֹל בַּסֻּכָּה — *R' Eliezer says: A man is obligated to eat fourteen meals in the succah.* Just as one eats a meal in the morning and a meal in the evening in his own house, he is to do the same in the *succah* (*Gem.* 27a).

וַחֲכָמִים אוֹמְרִים: אֵין לַדָּבָר קִצְבָה — *But the Sages say: This matter has no fixed obligation.* The Sages also agree with R' Eliezer that one should dwell in the *succah* just as he dwells at home. However, just as one is not *required* to eat at home twice a day, so it is in the *succah* (*Rav*).

חוּץ מִלֵּילֵי יוֹם טוֹב רִאשׁוֹן שֶׁל חַג בִּלְבָד — *Except for the night of the first Yom Tov of the Festival only,* i.e., the first night of Succos. The *mitzvah* of dwelling in a *succah* (*Lev.* 23:24) applies to all seven days of Succos, but on the first night of

---

[5] *Once they brought Rabban Yochanan ben Zakkai some cooked food to taste, and to Rabban Gamliel [they brought] two dates and a pail of water, and they said, 'Bring them up to the succah.' But when they gave R' Tzaddok food smaller than the volume of an egg, he took it with a cloth and ate it outside the succah, and did not recite the benediction after it.*

[6] *R' Eliezer says: A man is obligated to eat fourteen meals in the succah, one each day and one each night. But the Sages say: This matter has no fixed obligation, except for the night of the first Yom Tov of the Festival only. R' Eliezer further stated: Whoever did not eat [in the succah] on the night of the first Yom Tov must compensate for it on the night of the last Yom Tov. But the Sages say: This matter has no compensation. About this matter it is said [Ecclesiastes 1:15]: A twisted thing cannot be made straight, and what is not there cannot be numbered.*

[7] *A person who had his head and most of his body inside the succah and his table inside the house — Beis Shammai invalidate [the succah], and Beis Hillel validate it. Said Beis Hillel to Beis Shammai, 'Did it not happen that the elders of Beis Shammai and the elders of Beis Hillel went to visit R' Yochanan son of the Choranite, and found him sitting with his head and most of his body inside the succah and his table within the house, and they said nothing to him?' Beis Shammai replied to them, 'Is that [your] proof? Actually they said to him, "If this is how you have [always] conducted yourself, [then] you have never in your life fulfilled the mitzvah of succah." '*

YAD AVRAHAM

Succos, a meal *must* be eaten in the *succah* מִדְּאוֹרַיְתָא, *by Torah law.*

וְעוֹד אָמַר רַבִּי אֱלִיעֶזֶר — *R' Eliezer further stated* that one who failed to eat a meal in the *succah* on the first night should add food to his regular *Shemini Atzeres* meal to compensate for the missed meal. [However, the *Shemini Atzeres* meal is not to be eaten in the *succah*, for the *mitzvah* of *succah* no longer applies, as will be discussed below (*Rashi; Rav*).] The *Gemara* explains that R' Eliezer changed his view about the requirement of fourteen meals and concurred with the Sages that there is no set number of required meals. But he compares eating in the *succah* to sacrifices. If one failed to bring the required sacrifices on the first day of *Yom Tov,* he may compensate by bringing them on the last day (*Gemara,* following *Rashi*).

וַחֲכָמִים אוֹמְרִים — *But the Sages say* that if one missed the obligatory meal on the first night there is no way to make it up.

7. מִי שֶׁהָיָה רֹאשׁוֹ וְרֻבּוֹ בַּסֻּכָּה — *A person who had his head and most of his body inside the succah.* In Talmudic times it was customary to eat lying on a couch, rather than sitting erect, and low tables were placed next to the couch. In our mishnah's case the table was not inside the *succah,* for reasons that will be discussed below.

בֵּית שַׁמַּאי פּוֹסְלִין, וּבֵית הִלֵּל מַכְשִׁירִין — *Beis*

Shammai invalidate [the succah], and Beis Hillel validate it. Beis Shammai and Beis Hillel disagree in two cases. The first is when the *succah* is large enough to contain the person, his table, and even more people, but he chose to recline near the *succah* entrance and keep his table in the house. Beis Shammai forbid this for fear that 'he may follow his table into the house.' But Beis Hillel permitted this.

The second dispute is where the *succah* is so small that it can contain no more than his head and the greater part of his body [but not even a one-handbreadth table]; Beis Shammai invalidate that *succah* and Beis Hillel validate it. Here, too, the reason is that he may follow his table (*Rambam; Rav*). The *Gemara* notes that in this case the halachah follows Beis Shammai rather than Beis Hillel. *Seder* of R' *Amram* notes that this is one of only six disputes between the two schools where the halachah follows Beis Shammai (*Tosafos 3a*).

אִם כֵּן הָיִיתָ נוֹהֵג, לֹא קִיַּמְתָּ מִצְוַת סֻכָּה מִיָּמֶיךָ — *"If this is how you have [always] conducted yourself, [then] you have never in your life fulfilled the mitzvah of succah."* Beis Shammai admonished R' Yochanan that since he kept the table outside the *succah,* he had never fulfilled the *mitzvah* properly in accordance with the regulation of the Sages, although he had satisfied the Torah requirement (*Ritva*).

[ח] נָשִׁים, וַעֲבָדִים, וּקְטַנִּים פְּטוּרִים מִן־הַסֻּכָּה. קָטָן שֶׁאֵינוֹ צָרִיךְ לְאִמּוֹ חַיָּב בַּסֻּכָּה. מַעֲשֶׂה וְיָלְדָה כַלָּתוֹ שֶׁל שַׁמַּאי הַזָּקֵן וּפִחֵת אֶת־הַמַּעֲזִיבָה וְסִכֵּךְ עַל־גַּבֵּי הַמִּטָּה בִּשְׁבִיל הַקָּטָן.

[ט] כָּל־שִׁבְעַת הַיָּמִים אָדָם עוֹשֶׂה סֻכָּתוֹ קֶבַע וּבֵיתוֹ עֲרַאי. יָרְדוּ גְשָׁמִים, מֵאֵימָתַי מֻתָּר לְפַנּוֹת? מִשֶּׁתִּסְרַח הַמִּקְפָּה. מָשְׁלוּ מָשָׁל: לְמָה הַדָּבָר דּוֹמֶה? לְעֶבֶד שֶׁבָּא לִמְזוֹג כּוֹס לְרַבּוֹ, וְשָׁפַךְ לוֹ קִיתוֹן עַל־פָּנָיו.

פרק שלישי

[א] **לוּלָב** הַגָּזוּל וְהַיָּבֵשׁ פָּסוּל. שֶׁל אֲשֵׁרָה וְשֶׁל עִיר הַנִּדַּחַת פָּסוּל. נִקְטַם רֹאשׁוֹ, נִפְרְצוּ עָלָיו, פָּסוּל. נִפְרְדוּ עָלָיו, כָּשֵׁר. רַבִּי

יד אברהם

8. נָשִׁים, וַעֲבָדִים — *Women, slaves,* i.e., non-Jewish slaves.

פְּטוּרִים מִן הַסֻּכָּה — *Are exempt from the [mitzvah of] succah.* Although we derive some laws of Succos from Pesach, in which women and slaves are obligated [in exception to the general rule exempting them from time — specific time-related *mitzvos*], this does not obligate them to eat in the *succah* (Gem. 28a).

קָטָן שֶׁאֵינוֹ צָרִיךְ לְאִמּוֹ — *A minor who does not need his mother.* The Gemara (28b) explains that this refers to a child who is not so dependent on her that he must *continually* call her. Rather, he calls once and then remains silent (Rashi).

חַיָּב בַּסֻּכָּה — *Is obligated [to dwell] in the succah.* His obligation is the Rabbinical one of חִנּוּךְ, *training,* in the performance of *mitzvos*. Circumstances determine the age of training for each particular *mitzvah* (Tosafos).

וְסִכֵּךְ עַל גַּבֵּי הַמִּטָּה בִּשְׁבִיל הַקָּטָן — *And placed s'chach above the bed for the child.* Shammai the Elder, disagreeing with the first Tanna, imposes training even upon children who still need their mothers. The Sages, on the other hand, maintain that since the mother is exempt from the *mitzvah* and the child needs the mother, there is no obligation to train him (Ran).

9. כָּל שִׁבְעַת הַיָּמִים אָדָם עוֹשֶׂה סֻכָּתוֹ קֶבַע — *All the seven days a man must make his succah [his] permanent [abode].* If he has beautiful vessels, he should bring them into the *succah*; if he has beautiful divans, he should bring them into the *succah*; he should eat, drink and spend his leisure time in the *succah*. He should also study Torah in the *succah*, but if it is difficult for him to concentrate in the *succah*, he may study outside the *succah* (Gem. 28b; Orach Chaim 639:4).

וּבֵיתוֹ עֲרַאי — *And his house [his] temporary [abode].* He should use his house only for

functional matters (e.g., cooking), whereas the *succah* should serve as his abode (Rambam).

מֵאֵימָתַי מֻתָּר לְפַנּוֹת? מִשֶּׁתִּסְרַח הַמִּקְפָּה — *When is it permissible to leave? When the porridge becomes spoiled.* מִקְפָּה is any cooked food which is neither very loose nor very thick (Rashi, Rav). The porridge need not be in the *succah*; one need only estimate the amount of time needed for it to spoil if it were in the *succah*.

מָשְׁלוּ מָשָׁל: לְמָה הַדָּבָר דּוֹמֶה — *They* [the Sages] illustrated this with a parable: To what is this comparable? [i.e., being forced out of the *succah* by rain].

וְשָׁפַךְ לוֹ קִיתוֹן עַל פָּנָיו — *And he poured the jug at his face,* as if to say that the slave is not serving him properly, and his services are no longer needed. By causing it to rain, the Almighty is telling us that He is dissatisfied with our service and so He asks us to leave (Rashi, Rav).

CHAPTER THREE

◆§ The Four Species

As the *Gemara* states, אַרְבָּעָה מִינִים שֶׁבַּלּוּלָב, מְעַכְּבִים זֶה אֶת זֶה, *the four species connected with the lulav are dependent upon one another;* i.e., the *mitzvah* cannot be performed in the absence of any one of them. The *mitzvah*, as ordained by the Torah, is actually two fold: on the first day of Succos, the obligation of taking the species applies everywhere; for the rest of the Yom Tov, the *mitzvah* applies only in the Temple. After the destruction of the Second Temple, Rabban Yochanan Ben Zakkai instituted the performance of the *mitzvah* throughout Succos everywhere (except for the Sabbath) in commemoration of the Temple ritual (m. 12).

1. לוּלָב הַגָּזוּל — *A stolen lulav.* The Four Species must be the property of the one using them; a stolen *lulav*, therefore, is invalid. This is derived from the word (Lev. 24:20) לָכֶם [lit., *for yourself*], which is expounded to mean מִשֶּׁלָּכֶם, *from*

MISHNAYOS SUCCAH *Chapter Three* / משניות סוכה **[134]**

[8] *Women, slaves, and minors are exempt from the succah. A minor who does not need his mother is obligated [to dwell] in the succah. It once happened that the daughter-in-law of Shammai the Elder gave birth and he removed the plaster [roof] and placed s'chach above the bed for the child.*

[9] *All the seven days a man must make his succah [his] permanent [abode] and his house [his] temporary [abode]. If it rained, when is it permissible to leave? When the porridge becomes spoiled. They [the Sages] illustrated this with a parable: To what is this comparable? To a slave who came to pour a cup for his master, and he poured the jug at his face.*

CHAPTER THREE

[1] **לוּלָב** *A stolen lulav or a dry one is invalid. [One] from an asherah or from a city that was led astray is invalid. If its top was broken off, [or] its leaves severed, it is invalid. If its leaves spread apart, it is valid.*

your own property. For the same reason, even a borrowed *lulav* would be invalid. Another reason is the Talmudic dictum that מִצְוָה הַבָּאָה בַּעֲבֵרָה, *a mitzvah made possible by a transgression,* is unacceptable (*Gem.* 30a). It is this principle that distinguishes a stolen *lulav* from a borrowed one. Accordingly, though a borrowed *lulav* is unacceptable only on the first day, for its user does not own it, a stolen one is invalid for the entire Succos festival.

וְהַיָּבֵשׁ — *Or a dry one.* Either the majority of its leaves or its spine has dried out (*Orach Chaim* 645:5). The reason that a dry *lulav* is rendered invalid is because of the requirement that the Four Species possess הָדָר, *beauty* [*Lev.* 24:40] (*Tos.*).

The actual degree of dryness that invalidates the *lulav* is the subject of dispute. *Tosafos* and *Rosh* explain that *dry* means so brittle that one can crumble it with his nail. *Ravad* (quoted by *Rosh*) maintains that practical experience contradicts this definition, since a *lulav* may last many years without reaching that state. In the context of *lulav,* therefore, *Ravad* defines dryness as a total lack of greenness, where the *lulav* remains white although all its moisture is gone. The *Shulchan Aruch* (*Orach Chaim* 645:5) follows *Ravad's* view. *Rama* states that where *lulavim* were not available it was customary to rely on the more lenient view of *Tosafos* and *Rosh.*

שֶׁל אֲשֵׁרָה — *[One] from an asherah,* i.e., a tree worshiped by idolaters.

וְשֶׁל עִיר הַנִּדַּחַת — *Or from a city that was led astray.* The law of this city is outlined in *Deuteronomy* 13:13-19. In brief, if the majority of residents in a Jewish city are persuaded by local residents to worship idols, the city and all its contents must be burned (*Rambam, Hilchos Avodah Zarah* 4:2).

פָּסוּל — *Is invalid.* This invalidation is due to the failure to meet the שִׁיעוּר, [the halachically prescribed] size of the *lulav.* In the view of halachah, once an object is condemned to be burned — as are the *asherah* and the *city led astray* — it is considered as it if had already been burned and reduced to ashes. Thus it lacks the physical dimensions required for the *mitzvah.*

◆§ The Lulav

Invalidation of the *lulav* involves its three basic physical features: שִׁדְרָה, *spine;* עָלִים, *leaves;* and תִּיוֹמֶת, *twin-leaf.*

The *spine* is the thick green core which serves as the *lulav's* center. The leaves grow out of the spine and constitute the bulk of the *lulav.* According to most commentators, the *twin-leaf* refers to the uppermost double-leaf growing from the top of the *lulav* and forming its tip (*Tosafos; Rosh; Rama, Orach Chaim* 645:3). According to *Rambam* (*Lulav* 8:4) and *Shulchan Aruch* (*ibid.*), each of the *lulav's* leaves are referred to as a *twin-leaf,* for each is composed of two connected leaves.

There is a difference of opinion among the *Rishonim,* as to which leaves the mishnah refers to as ראשו, *its top:*

— *Rosh* maintains that the 'top' of the *lulav* means the top of the *majority* of its upper leaves.

— *Ran* and *Maggid Mishnah* (8:3) hold that the top of the *lulav* is the tip of the middle leaf (תִּיוֹמֶת) only, which, if broken off, is sufficient reason to invalidate the *lulav.*

— *Shulchan Aruch* (*Orach Chaim* 645:6) follows the view of *Rosh,* but *Rama* (*ibid.*) adds that we should be strict and follow the views of *Ran* and *Maggid Mishnah.*

נִפְרְצוּ עָלָיו — *[Or] its leaves severed.* The Gemara (32a) compares the leaves of this *lulav* to the leaves of a broom. According to *Rashi,* the *lulav's* leaves are completely severed from its spine and are tied to it like an old-fashioned broom (*Rav*). *Rif* and *Rambam* (8:3) understand that the leaves are partially torn from the spine but are still dangling from it, thus resembling the leaves that are used in fashioning a broom. *Shulcan Aruch* (*Orach Chaim* 645:2) follows the

יְהוּדָה אוֹמֵר: יַאֲגְדֶנּוּ מִלְמָעְלָה. צִנֵּי הַר הַבַּרְזֶל כְּשֵׁרוֹת. לוּלָב שֶׁיֵּשׁ־בּוֹ שְׁלֹשָׁה טְפָחִים, כְּדֵי לְנַעֲנֵעַ בּוֹ, כָּשֵׁר.

[ב] הֲדַס הַגָּזוּל וְהַיָּבֵשׁ פָּסוּל. שֶׁל אֲשֵׁרָה וְשֶׁל עִיר הַנִּדַּחַת פָּסוּל. נִקְטַם רֹאשׁוֹ, נִפְרְצוּ עָלָיו, אוֹ שֶׁהָיוּ עֲנָבָיו מְרֻבּוֹת מֵעָלָיו, פָּסוּל. וְאִם מִעֲטָן כָּשֵׁר, וְאֵין מְמַעֲטִין בְּיוֹם טוֹב.

[ג] עֲרָבָה גְזוּלָה וִיבֵשָׁה פְּסוּלָה. שֶׁל אֲשֵׁרָה וְשֶׁל עִיר הַנִּדַּחַת פְּסוּלָה. נִקְטַם רֹאשָׁהּ, נִפְרְצוּ עָלֶיהָ, וְהַצַּפְצָפָה, פְּסוּלָה; כְּמוּשָׁה, וְשֶׁנָּשְׁרוּ מִקְצָת עָלֶיהָ, וְשֶׁל בַּעַל, כְּשֵׁרָה.

[ד] רַבִּי יִשְׁמָעֵאל אוֹמֵר: שְׁלֹשָׁה הֲדַסִּים, וּשְׁתֵּי עֲרָבוֹת, לוּלָב אֶחָד, וְאֶתְרוֹג אֶחָד; אֲפִילוּ שְׁנַיִם קְטוּמִים וְאֶחָד אֵינוֹ קָטוּם. רַבִּי טַרְפוֹן אוֹמֵר: אֲפִלּוּ שְׁלָשְׁתָּן קְטוּמִים. רַבִּי עֲקִיבָא אוֹמֵר: כְּשֵׁם שֶׁלּוּלָב אֶחָד וְאֶתְרוֹג אֶחָד, כָּךְ הֲדַס אֶחָד וַעֲרָבָה אַחַת.

[ה] אֶתְרוֹג הַגָּזוּל וְהַיָּבֵשׁ פָּסוּל. שֶׁל אֲשֵׁרָה וְשֶׁל עִיר הַנִּדַּחַת פָּסוּל. שֶׁל עָרְלָה פָּסוּל. שֶׁל תְּרוּמָה טְמֵאָה פָּסוּל. שֶׁל תְּרוּמָה טְהוֹרָה לֹא יִטֹּל,

---

יד אברהם

view of *Rif* and *Rambam*.

פָּסוּל — *It is invalid.* In both cases it is invalid due to a lack of הָדָר, *beauty*.

נִפְרְדוּ עָלָיו — *If its leaves spread apart,* i.e., they are fully attached to the spine but are spread apart on top like the branches of a tree (*Rashi, Rav*).

צִנֵּי הַר הַבַּרְזֶל — *The thorn palms of the Iron Mountain.* The spines of these palm branches are very sparsely covered with short leaves. In some such branches, the top of the lower leaf does not reach even as far as the beginning of the one above it (*Rashi; Rav*). They are valid only if the top of one leaf reaches the base of the next one (*Gem.* 32a; *Orach Chaim* 645:4).

כְּדֵי לְנַעֲנֵעַ בּוֹ — *[Long] enough to wave.* The *lulav* must be three handbreadths long — the length of the *hadas* and *aravah* — plus another handbreadth for waving (see m. 9). Thus, in total, the *lulav* must be at least *four* handbreadths long, while the *hadas* and *aravah* need be only three.

⏴ The Hadas

2. From the Scriptural description (*Lev.* 23:40) of the *hadas* as עֲנַף עֵץ־עָבֹת, *twig of a plaited tree* (*Rambam, Lulav* 7:2), we derive the requirement that the *hadas* be covered with leaves in a fashion that resembles a plait or braid. The *Gemara* (32b) stipulates that the leaves of the *hadas* should grow in clusters of at least three — either from central points on the twig, or from three points on one level.

וְהַיָּבֵשׁ — *Or a dry one.* [See comm. to previous

mishnah, s.v. וְהִיבֵשׁ).] *Ravad* maintains that the myrtle is dried out only when it turns white. At this stage, the moisture is gone and cannot be restored. *Shulchan Aruch* (648:7) concurs.

נִקְטַם רֹאשׁוֹ — *If its top was broken off.* In the case of the *hadas*, the commentators are in almost total agreement that the top of the *stem* is meant. However, the halachah follows R' Tarfon in mishnah 4, who disagrees (*Rav*).

נִפְרְצוּ עָלָיו — *[Or] its leaves were severed,* i.e., if a *hadas* lost most of its leaves.

אוֹ שֶׁהָיוּ עֲנָבָיו מְרֻבּוֹת מֵעָלָיו, פָּסוּל — *Or its berries outnumbered its leaves, it is invalid.* Hadas twigs sometimes produce a small berry-like fruit. As long as the berries are green like the leaves, they are acceptable, but if the berries are black or red, and they outnumber the leaves, they create a spotted appearance that is inconsistent with the requirement of beauty, invalidating the *hadas* (*Rav*).

וְאִם מִעֲטָן — *If he decreased them,* i.e., he plucked off enough berries before *Yom Tov* so that they no longer outnumbered the leaves.

וְאֵין מְמַעֲטִין בְּיוֹם טוֹב — *But we may not decrease them on Yom Tov.* Since the removal is to validate the twig it is considered 'repairing,' and is prohibited on the Sabbath and *Yom Tov* (*Gemara* 33b).

⏴ The Aravah

3. נִפְרְצוּ עָלֶיהָ — *[Or] its leaves were severed.* The majority of its leaves fell off, as in the case of the *hadas* (see comm. to mishnah 2).

R' Yehudah says: He should tie them together at the top. The thorn palms of the Iron Mountain are valid. A lulav that is three handbreadths long, [long] enough to wave, is valid.

[2] A stolen myrtle twig or a dry one is invalid. [One] from an asherah or a city that was led astray is invalid. If its top was broken off, [or] its leaves were severed, or its berries outnumbered its leaves, it is invalid. If he decreased them it is valid, but we may not decrease them on Yom Tov.

[3] A stolen willow twig or a dry one is invalid. [One] from an asherah or from a city that was led astray is invalid. If its top was broken off, [or] its leaves were severed, or [it is] a tzaftzafah, it is invalid. [One whose leaves are] wilted, or part of its leaves have fallen off, or [one] from a field, is valid.

[4] R' Yishmael says: Three myrtle twigs, two willow twigs, one lulav, and one esrog [are required]; even if two are broken off and one is not broken off. R' Tarfon says: Even if all three are broken off. R' Akiva says: Just as there is one lulav and one esrog, so [there is] one myrtle twig and one willow twig.

[5] A stolen esrog or a dry one is invalid. [One] from an asherah or from a city that was led astray is invalid. [One] of orlah is invalid. [One] of contaminated terumah is invalid. [If it is] of pure terumah he should not use it,

וְהַצְפְצָפָה — Or [it is] a tzaftzafah. This is a mountain plant that resembles the aravah, but is a different species. Its stem is white rather than reddish and its leaves are rounded with serrated edges, unlike the elongated, smooth leaves of the aravah (Gem.; Rambam, Lulav 7:4).

כְּמוּשָׁה — [One whose leaves are] wilted, i.e., no longer fresh, but not dried out.

וְשֶׁנָּשְׁרוּ מִקְצָת עָלֶיהָ — Or part of its leaves have fallen off, but only a minority of them.

וְשֶׁל בַּעַל — Or [one] from a field. It grew in a rain-watered field, and not near a brook (Rav). The Gemara explains that the phrase עַרְבֵי נָחַל, willows of the stream, does not exclude willows that grew elsewhere.

רַבִּי יִשְׁמָעֵאל אוֹמֵר: שְׁלֹשָׁה הֲדַסִּים, וּשְׁתֵּי עֲרָבוֹת, .4 לוּלָב אֶחָד, וְאֶתְרוֹג אֶחָד — R' Yishmael says: Three myrtle twigs, two willow twigs, one lulav, and one esrog [are required]. The Gemara (34b) explains that he derives these numbers from the wording of the verse (Lev. 23:40).

אֲפִילוּ שְׁנַיִם קְטוּמִים וְאֶחָד אֵינוֹ קָטוּם — Even if two [hadas twigs] are broken off and one is not broken off.

רַבִּי טַרְפוֹן אוֹמֵר: אֲפִילוּ שְׁלָשְׁתָּן קְטוּמִים — R' Tarfon says: Even if all three are broken off. R' Tarfon, in opposition to mishnah 2, validates a broken hadas because he does not require הָדָר, beauty, for the hadas or aravah (Rashi; Rav). Rambam, however, explains that since the leaves cover the twig all the way to the top, the missing tip is not noticeable, and does not lack in beauty. Shulchan Aruch (Orach Chaim 646:1,10), following the opinion of Rif, Rambam, and

Rosh, validates a hadas whose top is clipped off. Rama, however, rules that wherever possible, one should not use such a hadas.

רַבִּי עֲקִיבָא אוֹמֵר — R' Akiva says that just one each of the species is necessary to fulfill the mitzvah.

◄§ The Esrog

5. Since the esrog is the only one of the Four Species that is edible, laws relating to food will apply to it. Some of these laws are among the subjects of our mishnah.

וְהַיָּבֵשׁ — Or a dry one. Ravad defines the degree of dryness which invalidates an esrog as the complete lack of moisture (Tur 648).

שֶׁל עָרְלָה — [One] of orlah. For the first three years after a tree's planting, the fruit is forbidden for consumption and no benefit may be derived from it (Leviticus 19:23). Such fruit is called 'orlah' (restricted), and it must be burned.

שֶׁל תְּרוּמָה טְמֵאָה פָּסוּל — [One] of contaminated terumah is invalid. If terumah, the tithe given to a Kohen, becomes tamei [contaminated], it must be burned. Thus, such an esrog, as well as the orlah-esrog, is not considered his property because they are forbidden to him.

שֶׁל תְּרוּמָה טְהוֹרָה לֹא יִטֹּל — [If it is] of pure terumah he should not use it. Although an uncontaminated terumah-esrog is valid according to the halachah, the Sages decreed that its use should be avoided in order to avoid the possibility that it might become contaminated.

[137]   **SUCCOS** / Its Significance, Laws, and Prayers

וְאִם נָטַל, כָּשֵׁר. שֶׁל דְּמַאי, בֵּית שַׁמַּאי פּוֹסְלִין, וּבֵית הִלֵּל מַכְשִׁירִין. שֶׁל מַעֲשֵׂר שֵׁנִי בִּירוּשָׁלַיִם, לֹא יִטֹּל, וְאִם נָטַל, כָּשֵׁר.

[ו] עָלְתָה חֲזָזִית עַל־רֻבּוֹ, נִטְּלָה פִּטְמָתוֹ, נִקְלַף, נִסְדַּק, נִקַּב וְחָסַר כָּל־שֶׁהוּא, פָּסוּל. עָלְתָה חֲזָזִית עַל־מִעוּטוֹ, נִטַּל עֻקְצוֹ, נִקַּב וְלֹא חָסַר כָּל־שֶׁהוּא, כָּשֵׁר. אֶתְרוֹג הַכּוּשִׁי פָּסוּל. וְהַיָּרֹק כְּכַרְתִּי, רַבִּי מֵאִיר מַכְשִׁיר, וְרַבִּי יְהוּדָה פּוֹסֵל.

[ז] שִׁעוּר אֶתְרוֹג הַקָּטָן — רַבִּי מֵאִיר אוֹמֵר: כָּאֱגוֹז. רַבִּי יְהוּדָה אוֹמֵר: כַּבֵּיצָה. וּבַגָּדוֹל — כְּדֵי שֶׁיֹּאחַז שְׁנַיִם בְּיָדוֹ אַחַת; דִּבְרֵי רַבִּי יְהוּדָה. רַבִּי יוֹסֵי אוֹמֵר: אֲפִילוּ אֶחָד בִּשְׁתֵּי יָדָיו.

[ח] אֵין אוֹגְדִין אֶת־הַלּוּלָב אֶלָּא בְמִינוֹ; דִּבְרֵי רַבִּי יְהוּדָה. רַבִּי מֵאִיר אוֹמֵר: אֲפִילוּ בְמִשִׁיחָה. אָמַר רַבִּי מֵאִיר: מַעֲשֶׂה בְאַנְשֵׁי יְרוּשָׁלַיִם שֶׁהָיוּ אוֹגְדִין אֶת־לוּלְבֵיהֶן בְּגִימוֹנִיּוֹת שֶׁל זָהָב. אָמְרוּ לוֹ: בְּמִינוֹ הָיוּ אוֹגְדִין אוֹתוֹ מִלְּמַטָּה.

[ט] וְהֵיכָן הָיוּ מְנַעְנְעִין? בְּ,,הוֹדוּ לַה'," תְּחִלָּה וָסוֹף, וּבְ,,אָנָּא ה',"

יד אברהם

שֶׁל דְּמַאי — [If it is] of demai. In the times of Yochanan, the High Priest, it was found that many unlearned people were careful to separate terumah, but were lax in separating ma'aser. As a result, the Sages decreed that one who buys produce from an עַם הָאָרֶץ, unlearned person, must separate ma'aser from it even if assured by the seller that he had already done so. This produce is called demai.

בֵּית שַׁמַּאי פּוֹסְלִין — Beis Shammai invalidate it. Since the demai-esrog may not be eaten until it is tithed, it lacks the necessary requirement of לָכֶם, yours (Rashi; Rav).

וּבֵית הִלֵּל מַכְשִׁירִין — And Beis Hillel validate it. Beis Hillel regard an esrog of demai as 'yours' because the Sages permitted it to the poor for consumption without re-tithing. Beis Shammai, however, forbid demai even to the poor (Ran).

שֶׁל מַעֲשֵׂר שֵׁנִי בִּירוּשָׁלַיִם — [If it is] of ma'aser sheni in Jerusalem. In addition to מַעֲשֵׂר רִאשׁוֹן, the first tithe, which must be given to the Levite, the Torah requires the owner to separate מַעֲשֵׂר שֵׁנִי, the second tithe, which belongs to the owner but can be eaten only in Jerusalem. Unlike the Levite's tithe, ma'aser sheni is holy, and thus, like terumah, may not be contaminated (Lev. 27:30). Therefore, the Sages preferred that an esrog of ma'aser sheni, like one of terumah, not be used.

וְאִם נָטַל, כָּשֵׁר — But if he used it, it is valid. However, outside Jerusalem, where ma'aser sheni fruits may not be eaten, an esrog of maaser sheni would not be valid (Rashi; Rav).

6. עַל רֻבּוֹ — On most of it. Only if the boil covers the greater portion of the esrog is it considered invalid. An esrog with such a growth lacks beauty (Rosh; Mishnah Berurah 648:37). The Gemara (35b) adds that even a small boil can invalidate the esrog if it is on its חוֹטֶם, nose, i.e., the part that narrows towards its peak. This part of the esrog is more important because any blemish there is immediately visible (Rashi).

נִטְּלָה פִּטְמָתוֹ — [Or] its pitam was removed, i.e., the short stem that protrudes from the nose of the esrog. The tip of this stem is called the שׁוֹשַׁנְתָּא, bud. An esrog whose top stem, pitam, has been removed is invalid because it is חָסֵר, deficient. Esrogim, however, that grow without a pitam obviously are not deficient (Mishnah Berurah 648:32).

נִקְלַף — [Or] it was peeled. The esrog in our mishnah is missing its thin outer peel, leaving its body intact and not altering its color (Ran). It is invalid because it lacks beauty.

נִסְדַּק — [Or] it was split. Although no part of the esrog is missing, the fact that it is split invalidates it as if it were deficient (Orach Chaim 648:5).

נִקַּב וְחָסַר כָּל שֶׁהוּא — [Or] it was punctured and is missing a slight portion. The esrog was both punctured and made partially deficient (Rashi; Ravad). According to Rambam, however, a puncture and a deficiency are two separate invalidations.

נִטַּל עֻקְצוֹ — [Or] its stem was removed, i.e., the stem at the base of the esrog, by which it was attached to the tree.

כָּשֵׁר — It is valid. In none of these latter cases

but if he used it, it is valid. [If it is] of demai, Beis Shammai invalidate it, and Beis Hillel validate it. [If it is of] ma'aser sheni in Jerusalem, he should not use it, but if he used it, it is valid.

[6] If a scab-like boil grew on most of it, [or] its pitam was removed, [or] it was peeled, [or] it was split, [or] it was punctured and is missing a slight portion, it is invalid. If a boil covered a minority of it, [or] its stem was removed, [or] it was punctured and nothing was missing, it is valid. An Ethiopian esrog is invalid. If one is green as a leek, R' Meir validates it but R' Yehudah invalidates it.

[7] The minimum size of an esrog — R' Meir says: Like a nut. R' Yehudah says: Like an egg. And the maximum — so that he can hold two [esrogim] in one hand; these are the words of R' Yehudah. R' Yose says: Even one [that must be held] in both hands.

[8] We do not bind the lulav except with its own kind; these are the words of R' Yehudah. R' Meir says: Even with cord. R' Meir said: It happened that the men of Jerusalem would bind their lulavim with gold wire. The Sages said to him [in rebuttal]: They would bind it with its own kind underneath.

[9] At which point [in the Hallel service] did they wave [the lulav]? At 'Give thanks to HASHEM,' at the beginning and end, and at 'Please HASHEM,

---

is there sufficient lack of beauty to invalidate the esrog. Nor do these deficiencies disqualify it as not being intact.

אֶתְרוֹג הַכּוּשִׁי פָּסוּל — An Ethiopian (i.e., dark) esrog is invalid. Dark esrogim are invalid only in areas like Eretz Yisrael where esrogim do not grow that color. In Ethiopia or nearby, where a dark color is natural, they are valid.

וְהַיָרֹק כְּכַרְתִי — If one is green as a leek, which resembles grass (Rosh).

רַבִּי מֵאִיר מַכְשִׁיר וְרַבִּי יְהוּדָה פּוֹסֵל — R' Meir validates it but R' Yehudah invalidates it. Rosh quotes Tosafos that a green esrog that will turn yellow eventually is valid, because the fact that it will turn yellow is sufficient indication of its ripeness. This is also the view of Orach Chaim 648:21.

7. רַבִּי יְהוּדָה אוֹמֵר: כַּבֵּיצָה — R' Yehudah says: Like an egg. The halachah follows R' Yehudah that an esrog smaller than an egg is not valid (Orach Chaim 648:22).

כְּדֵי שֶׁיֹאחֵז שְׁנַיִם בְּיָדוֹ אַחַת — So that he can hold two [esrogim] in one hand. Sometimes people inadvertently take the esrog and lulav in the wrong hands and are forced to transfer them. If an esrog is oversized, it may fall and become invalid. If it is small enough for two to fit into one hand, we do not fear its falling (Gem. 31b). The halachah, however, follows R' Yose (Orach Chaim 648:22; 651:12).

8. אֶלָא בְמִינוֹ — Except with its own kind. The mitzvah calls for the lulav to be bound together with the hadasim and aravos. Any part of the palm tree is considered material of its own kind

— even strips of the bark or the vine-like material growing around the trunk (Gem. 36b). According to R' Yehudah, the binding is considered an essential part of the mitzvah; consequently, the use of a different material would be tantamount to adding a fifth species to the four specified by the Torah (Gem. 31b; Rashi).

רַבִּי מֵאִיר אוֹמֵר — R' Meir says that one may take the four species without tying them together. Accordingly, the binding material, because it is unessential, is not part of the mitzvah, so its material cannot be considered a forbidden addition to the mitzvah.

אָמְרוּ לוֹ: בְּמִינוֹ הָיוּ אוֹגְדִין אוֹתוֹ מִלְמַטָּה — The Sages [lit., they] said to him [in rebuttal]: They would bind it with its own kind underneath. The noble Jews of Jerusalem first tied together the lulav and the other species with material of its own kind, and over that they placed gold bands to glorify the mitzvah, so the gold bands served only as adornment and were not an essential part of the mitzvah (Rashi Rav). Nevertheless, the halachah follows R' Meir (Orach Chaim 651:1).

9. וְהֵיכָן הָיוּ מְנַעְנְעִין — At which point [in the Hallel service] did they wave [the lulav]? The Rabbis instituted the procedure of נַעְנוּעִים, which involves moving and shaking the lulav in all four directions, as well as upward and downward.

בְּ,,הוֹדוּ לַה׳״,תְּחִלָּה וָסוֹף — At 'Give thanks to HASHEM,' at the beginning and end. Psalm 118 begins and ends with the verse הוֹדוּ לַה׳ כִּי טוֹב

[139]   SUCCOS / Its Significance, Laws, and Prayers

הוֹשִׁיעָה נָּא״, דִּבְרֵי בֵית הִלֵּל. וּבֵית שַׁמַּאי אוֹמְרִים: אַף בְּ״אָנָּא ה׳,
הַצְלִיחָה נָּא.״ אָמַר רַבִּי עֲקִיבָא: צוֹפֶה הָיִיתִי בְרַבָּן גַּמְלִיאֵל וְרַבִּי יְהוֹשֻׁעַ,
שֶׁכָּל־הָעָם הָיוּ מְנַעְנְעִין אֶת־לוּלְבֵיהֶן, וְהֵן לֹא נִעְנְעוּ אֶלָּא בְ״אָנָּא ה׳,
הוֹשִׁיעָה נָּא.״ מִי שֶׁבָּא בַדֶּרֶךְ וְלֹא הָיָה בְיָדוֹ לוּלָב לִטּוֹל, לִכְשֶׁיִּכָּנֵס
לְבֵיתוֹ יִטּוֹל עַל־שֻׁלְחָנוֹ. לֹא נָטַל שַׁחֲרִית יִטּוֹל בֵּין הָעַרְבַּיִם, שֶׁכָּל־הַיּוֹם
כָּשֵׁר לַלּוּלָב.

[י] מִי שֶׁהָיָה עֶבֶד, אוֹ אִשָּׁה, אוֹ קָטָן מַקְרִין אוֹתוֹ, עוֹנֶה אַחֲרֵיהֶן מַה
שֶּׁהֵן אוֹמְרִין – וּתְהִי לוֹ מְאֵרָה! אִם הָיָה גָדוֹל מַקְרֵא אוֹתוֹ, עוֹנֶה
אַחֲרָיו: ״הַלְלוּיָהּ.״

[יא] מָקוֹם שֶׁנָּהֲגוּ לִכְפּוֹל, יִכְפּוֹל; לִפְשׁוֹט, יִפְשׁוֹט; לְבָרֵךְ אַחֲרָיו, יְבָרֵךְ
אַחֲרָיו – הַכֹּל כְּמִנְהַג הַמְּדִינָה. הַלּוֹקֵחַ לוּלָב מֵחֲבֵרוֹ בַּשְּׁבִיעִית,
נוֹתֵן לוֹ אֶתְרוֹג בְּמַתָּנָה, לְפִי שֶׁאֵין רַשַּׁאי לְלָקְחוֹ בַּשְּׁבִיעִית.

יד אברהם

כִּי לְעוֹלָם חַסְדּוֹ, *Give thanks to* HASHEM, *for He is good, for His loving-kindness is eternal.* The waving of the *lulav* corresponds to the beginning and the end of the chapter (*Rashi*).

אָמַר רַבִּי עֲקִיבָא – *Said R' Akiva.* He testified that Rabban Gamliel and R' Yehoshua, who were disciples of Beis Hillel, waved only during אָנָּא ה׳, and not during הוֹדוּ לַה׳. Thus, R' Akiva disagrees with the mishnah's version of Beis Hillel. The halachah, however, follows the *Tanna Kamma's* version of Beis Hillel, not R' Akiva's.

לִכְשֶׁיִּכָּנֵס לְבֵיתוֹ יִטּוֹל עַל שֻׁלְחָנוֹ – *When he comes* [lit., *enters*] *home he should take it at his table.* If he began his meal in violation of the Rabbinic prohibition of eating before taking the *lulav*, he should interrupt his meal to perform the *mitzvah.*

שֶׁכָּל הַיּוֹם כָּשֵׁר לַלּוּלָב – *For the entire day is valid for the lulav.* The *mitzvah* is valid only during the day, but not at night. Nevertheless, it is always preferable to perform a *mitzvah* as early as possible.

10. In the times of the Mishnah, there were periods when not everyone was educated enough to read the *Hallel*. In order to insure that everyone fulfilled his obligation, the *chazzan* would recite the *Hallel* and the congregation merely listened, in much the same way that the Reading of the Torah and the *Megillah* are performed today (*Rashi*). This is effective based on the principle of שׁוֹמֵעַ כְּעוֹנֶה, *listening is equivalent to answering,* by which one can fulfill such obligations as *Megillah* or *Kiddush* by listening to someone read for him. A prerequisite for this principle is that the reader be obligated to perform the reading just as is

the listener. Since *Hallel* is a time-related *mitzvah*, it is not obligatory for women or for non-Jewish slaves. Accordingly, they cannot discharge males of their obligations.

עוֹנֶה אַחֲרֵיהֶן מַה שֶּׁהֵן אוֹמְרִין – *He must repeat after them whatever they say.* By repeating each phrase after them, he reads the *Hallel* himself (*Rashi; Rav*).

וּתְהִי לוֹ מְאֵרָה – *And let it be a curse upon him!* If he was compelled to resort to this form of *Hallel* reading because of his ignorance, let him be cursed for being so unlearned (*Rav*).

עוֹנֶה אַחֲרָיו: ״הַלְלוּיָהּ״ – *He must respond after him, 'Halleluyah.'* The *chazzan* would recite the entire first verse of *Hallel* and the congregation would respond הַלְלוּיָהּ, *give praise to God,* and so on throughout the entire *Hallel*. However even if he does not respond with *Halleluyah,* he fulfills his obligation, for it is the listening to the *chazzan* that is essential to the *mitzvah,* not the response (*Gem.* 38b).

11. מָקוֹם שֶׁנָּהֲגוּ לִכְפּוֹל – *In a place where they are accustomed to repeat.* The custom to repeat many verses in the *Hallel* prayer stems from *Psalm* 118 — a major part of the *Hallel* — many of whose verses have a repetitive character. For example, the chapter begins with four verses that end with the phrase כִּי לְעוֹלָם חַסְדּוֹ, *for His loving-kindness is eternal;* and the first of those verses ... הוֹדוּ לַה׳, *Give thanks to* HASHEM, is repeated in its entirety at the end of the chapter. According to *Rav,* the custom was to repeat the verses in chapter 118 that do not in themselves have a repetitive content, beginning with v. 21 אוֹדְךָ כִּי עֲנִיתָנִי, *I thank You,* HASHEM, *for You have answered me.* The custom of the locality

bring salvation now'; these are the words of Beis Hillel. Beis Shammai say: Also at 'Please HASHEM, bring success now.' Said R' Akiva: As I was watching Rabban Gamliel and R' Yehoshua, all the people were waving their lulavim, but they did not wave except during 'Please HASHEM, bring salvation now.' One who arrived from a journey where he did not have a lulav at hand to use, when he comes home he should take it at his table. If he did not take it in the morning he should take it in the afternoon, for the entire day is valid for the lulav.

[10] If a [non-]Jewish] slave, or a woman, or a minor recited [Hallel] for someone, he must repeat after them whatever they say — and let it be a curse upon him! If an adult was reciting for him, he must respond after him, 'Halleluyah.'

[11] In a place where they are accustomed to repeat, he repeats; [where the custom is] to recite as is, he recites as is; [where the custom is] to recite a blessing after it, he recites a blessing after it — everything [must be done] in accord with the local custom. If one purchases a lulav from his friend during Shemittah, he must give him the esrog as a gift, because it is forbidden to purchase it during Shemittah.

---

becomes an obligatory part of the performance of the mitzvah and must be followed.

לְבָרֵךְ אַחֲרָיו, יְבָרֵךְ אַחֲרָיו — [Where the custom is] to recite a blessing after it, he recites a blessing after it. Many places had the custom, in common use today, of concluding the Hallel with a blessing that begins with יְהַלְלוּךָ, They shall praise You (Meiri).

הַכֹּל כְּמִנְהַג הַמְּדִינָה — Everything [must be done] in accord with the local custom [lit., the custom of the country]. Rama (Orach Chaim 690:17) rules that we may not nullify any customs or amend them, for they were established with good reason.

◆§ Shemittah — Sabbatical Year

One may not purchase Shemittah produce from a person who is suspected of not using the money in compliance with the laws of Shemittah, specifically, for purchasing food by a certain deadline. If, however, the price does not exceed the cost of three meals, one may pay him for he will use the funds immediately (Rambam, Shemittah 8:10, 12).

There is a distinction between fruit and vegetables concerning the reckoning of the Shemittah year: fruits that reached the stage of חֲנָטָה, budding, before Rosh Hashanah of the seventh year have the status of sixth-year produce and are not subject to Shemittah restrictions even if they were picked during Shemittah. Vegetables, however, that were picked during Shemittah — even if they were grown in the sixth year — are considered Shemittah products. There is a question, however, whether an esrog has the halachic status of a fruit or whether it is an exception

to the law of fruit and follows the law of vegetables (ibid. 4:12; see Kesef Mishnah).

הַלּוֹקֵחַ לוּלָב מֵחֲבֵרוֹ בַּשְּׁבִיעִית — If one purchases a lulav from his friend during Shemittah [lit., during the seventh]. Although the mishnah speaks of purchasing a lulav, the problem of Shemittah produce in this context applies only to the esrog that presumably was purchased with the lulav. The prohibition of Shemittah does not apply to the lulav for it has the status of a tree product, whose growth is calculated according to its חֲנָטָה, budding. Since a lulav used on Succos of Shemittah was obviously past its budding stage by Rosh Hashanah, it is considered as a product of the sixth year (Gem. 39a; Rashi). The seller here is an unlearned person [am haaretz] to whom one may not give money for Shemittah products for fear he will not use them in accordance with the halachah.

נוֹתֵן לוֹ אֶתְרוֹג בְּמַתָּנָה, — He must give him the esrog as a gift. Since the price of the esrog usually exceeds the equivalent of three meals, one may not give the am haaretz money for the purchase, for fear he will hoard it past the time of בִּיעוּר, removal, when it is forbidden to keep it (Rashi); or he will spend it on products or services that one is forbidden to purchase with money of Shemittah (Gem. 39a; Tos.). The Gemara (39a) adds that if the am haaretz refuses to give the esrog as a gift, then he may raise the price of the lulav to cover the cost of the esrog so that it is considered as if the money is only in exchange for the lulav and thus not subject to the restrictions of Shemittah. This procedure is called הַבְלָעָה, inclusion [of the esrog for the price of the lulav].

[יב] בָּרִאשׁוֹנָה הָיָה לוּלָב נִטָּל בַּמִּקְדָּשׁ שִׁבְעָה, וּבַמְּדִינָה יוֹם אֶחָד. מִשֶּׁחָרַב בֵּית הַמִּקְדָּשׁ, הִתְקִין רַבָּן יוֹחָנָן בֶּן־זַכַּאי שֶׁיְּהֵא לוּלָב נִטָּל בַּמְּדִינָה שִׁבְעָה זֵכֶר לַמִּקְדָּשׁ; וְשֶׁיְּהֵא יוֹם הָנֵף כֻּלּוֹ אָסוּר.

[יג] יוֹם טוֹב הָרִאשׁוֹן שֶׁל חַג שֶׁחָל לִהְיוֹת בַּשַּׁבָּת, כָּל־הָעָם מוֹלִיכִין אֶת־לוּלְבֵיהֶן לְבֵית הַכְּנֶסֶת. לַמָּחֳרָת מַשְׁכִּימִין וּבָאִין. כָּל אֶחָד וְאֶחָד מַכִּיר אֶת־שֶׁלּוֹ וְנוֹטְלוֹ, מִפְּנֵי שֶׁאָמְרוּ חֲכָמִים: אֵין אָדָם יוֹצֵא יְדֵי חוֹבָתוֹ בְּיוֹם טוֹב הָרִאשׁוֹן שֶׁל חַג בְּלוּלָבוֹ שֶׁל חֲבֵרוֹ; וּשְׁאָר יְמוֹת הֶחָג, אָדָם יוֹצֵא יְדֵי חוֹבָתוֹ בְּלוּלָבוֹ שֶׁל חֲבֵרוֹ.

[יד] רַבִּי יוֹסֵי אוֹמֵר: יוֹם טוֹב הָרִאשׁוֹן שֶׁל חַג שֶׁחָל לִהְיוֹת בַּשַּׁבָּת, וְשָׁכַח וְהוֹצִיא אֶת־הַלּוּלָב לִרְשׁוּת הָרַבִּים, פָּטוּר — מִפְּנֵי שֶׁהוֹצִיאוֹ בִרְשׁוּת.

[טו] מְקַבֶּלֶת אִשָּׁה מִיַּד בְּנָהּ וּמִיַּד בַּעְלָהּ וּמַחֲזִירָתוֹ לַמַּיִם בַּשַּׁבָּת. רַבִּי יְהוּדָה אוֹמֵר: בַּשַּׁבָּת מַחֲזִירִין, בְּיוֹם טוֹב מוֹסִיפִין, וּבַמּוֹעֵד מַחֲלִיפִין. קָטָן הַיּוֹדֵעַ לְנַעֲנֵעַ חַיָּב בַּלּוּלָב.

---

12. בָּרִאשׁוֹנָה — *Originally.* [In the years when the Temple stood.]

הָיָה לוּלָב נִטָּל בַּמִּקְדָּשׁ — *The lulav was taken in the Temple seven [days].* The mitzvah of lulav was performed all seven days of Succos in the Temple. This Scriptural obligation, based on the verse (*Lev.* 23:40) which is the source of the mitzvah of lulav, stems from the words: וּשְׂמַחְתֶּם לִפְנֵי ה' אֱלֹהֵיכֶם שִׁבְעַת יָמִים, *And you shall rejoice before HASHEM your God for seven days.*

וּבַמְּדִינָה — *And in the provinces.* This includes all areas outside the Temple. Even Jerusalem is considered part of 'the provinces' in this context (*Rashi* 41a; *Rav; Ran*). But in the view of the *Rambam* (*Shofar* 2:8) and *Aruch*, the entire city of Jerusalem is included in the category of the Temple, while everywhere outside of Jerusalem is referred to as the provinces.

יוֹם אֶחָד — *[It was taken] one day.* This is stated in the first segment of the same verse (ibid.): וּלְקַחְתֶּם לָכֶם בַּיּוֹם הָרִאשׁוֹן, *and you shall take for yourselves on the first day.*

זֵכֶר לַמִּקְדָּשׁ — *In remembrance of the Temple.* The *Gemara* (41a) explains that the concept of performing mitzvos in remembrance of the Temple was first expressed by Jeremiah (*Jer.* 30:17): צִיּוֹן הִיא דֹּרֵשׁ אֵין לָהּ, *she is Zion; she has no one inquiring about her.* The way to show concern for Zion, the Sages determined, was to perform mitzvos in remembrance of the Temple.

וְשֶׁיְּהֵא יוֹם הָנֵף כֻּלּוֹ אָסוּר — *And that the entire Day of Waving be forbidden.* The Day of Waving refers to the Omer offering which was brought in the Temple on the sixteenth of Nissan. When the Temple stood, no new grain crop was permitted to be eaten until after the Omer service was complete. Following the destruction, Rabban Yochanan decreed that new crops not be eaten until the sixteenth of Nissan was over (see *Rosh Hashanah* 4:3).

13. — יוֹם טוֹב הָרִאשׁוֹן שֶׁל חַג שֶׁחָל לִהְיוֹת בַּשַּׁבָּת — *On the first day of the Festival that fell on the Sabbath.* As explained in *Rosh Hashanah* (4:1), the Rabbis chose to nullify the mitzvah on the Sabbath, for fear that a person might inadvertently carry his lulav in the street to a learned person that he may teach him how to perform the mitzvah, thus violating the prohibition of carrying in a public domain. When the first day of Succos occurred on a Sabbath, however, the Rabbis placed no restrictions on the mitzvah of lulav, for on the first day the mitzvah is מְדְאוֹרַיְיתָא, of Scriptural origin. [The *Gemara* (43a) adds, however, that since the destruction of the Temple, the lulav is never taken on the Sabbath, even on the first day.]

כָּל הָעָם מוֹלִיכִין אֶת לוּלְבֵיהֶן לְבֵית הַכְּנֶסֶת — *All the people would bring their lulavim to the synagogue.* They would do this on Friday before the commencement of the Sabbath, because carrying the Four Species in a public domain (or from a private domain to a public domain) does not override the Sabbath (*Rashi*).

MISHNAYOS SUCCAH *Chapter Three* / מִשְׁנָיוֹת סוכה   [142]

[12] *Originally the lulav was taken in the Temple seven [days], and in the*
provinces [it was taken] one day. After the Temple was destroyed,
Rabban Yochanan ben Zakkai instituted that the lulav be taken in the
provinces seven [days] in remembrance of the Temple; and that the entire
Day of Waving be forbidden.

[13] *On the first day of the Festival that fell on the Sabbath, all the people*
would bring their lulavim to the synagogue. On the morrow they would
awaken early and come. Everyone would recognize his own [lulav] and take
it, for the Sages said: A man cannot fulfill his obligation on the first day
of Succos with a lulav belonging to his friend; but on the other days of Succos
a man can fulfill his obligation with a lulav belonging to his friend.

[14] *R' Yose says: If the first day of Succos fell on the Sabbath, and one*
forgot and carried the lulav out into the public domain, he is exempt
—· for he carried it out with permission.

[15] *A woman may accept [a lulav] from her son or from her husband and*
return it to the water on the Sabbath. R' Yehudah says: On the Sabbath
we return [it], on the Festival we add [water], and during [the Intermediate
Days of] the Festival we change [the water]. A minor who knows how to
wave is obligated to take the lulav.

אֵין אָדָם יוֹצֵא יְדֵי חוֹבָתוֹ בְּיוֹם טוֹב הָרִאשׁוֹן שֶׁל חַג
— *A man cannot fulfill his obligation on the first*
day of Succos, the day on which the taking of
the *lulav* is דְּאוֹרַיְתָא, a Scriptural obligation,
with a *lulav* belonging to someone else, as
explained above, 3:1.

14. וְשָׁכַח — *And one forgot.* Involved in the
detail of this *mitzvah* he forgot that the day was
also the Sabbath (*Rashi*).

וְהוֹצִיא אֶת הַלּוּלָב לִרְשׁוּת הָרַבִּים — *And carried*
the lulav out into the public domain. Thereby
unintentionally performing the forbidden labor
of transporting an object from a private domain
to the public domain.

פָּטוּר — *He is exempt.* Ordinarily when one
violates the Sabbath unintentionally, he is
obligated to bring a sin-offering (*Shabbos* 7:1).
But in this case R' Yose holds that his
involvement in the present *mitzvah* frees him
from the need for expiation. Thus the performance of the *mitzvah* 'permitted' the uninten-
tional transgression (*Rashi*). *Rambam* (*She-*
gagos 2:10) rules according to R' Yose. The
Gemara (42a) adds that R' Yose exempts one
from a sin-offering only if his action was done
in the course of fulfilling the *mitzvah*, not after
the *mitzvah* was already fulfilled.

15. מְקַבֶּלֶת אִשָּׁה מִיַּד בְּנָהּ וּמִיַּד בַּעְלָהּ — *A woman*
may accept [a lulav] from her son or from her
husband. This mishnah addresses the question
of *muktzeh* [lit., *set aside*], the category of

objects that, for various reasons, were forbidden
by the Rabbis to be moved. Although a woman
is exempt from the *mitzvah* of *lulav*, the *lulav*
is not *muktzeh* and a woman may take the *lulav*
from her husband or son and return it to its
place in the water. *Rashi* explains that since men
are obligated to perform the *mitzvah*, it is not
muktzeh for anyone; as long as something is
useful to some people it is not *muktzeh* to others
either.

וּמַחֲזִירָתוֹ לַמַּיִם בְּשַׁבָּת — *And return it to the*
water on the Sabbath, i.e., to the same water
from which it was removed, in order to keep
it from withering (*Rashi; Rav*). Nowadays,
since the *lulav* is not taken on the Sabbath, it
is *muktzeh* and may not even be handled on
the Sabbath. Consequently, if the *lulav* was
inadvertently removed from the water on the
Sabbath, it is forbidden to replace it (*Orach*
Chaim 658:2).

בְּיוֹם טוֹב מוֹסִיפִין — *On the Festival we add* water
to the vase where the *lulav* is kept, but may
not replace the old water with fresh water. This
is considered undue exertion, which is prohibited on *Yom Tov* (*Rashi; Rav*).

קָטָן הַיּוֹדֵע לְנַעֲנֵעַ — *A minor who knows how to*
wave. He knows how the *lulav* should be raised
and lowered, and waved back and forth.

חַיָּב בְּלוּלָב — *Is obligated to take the lulav,* i.e.,
at this point in his son's development, a father
is obligated to train his son in the performance
of *mitzvos* (*Rashi; Rav*).

[א] לוּלָב וַעֲרָבָה שִׁשָּׁה וְשִׁבְעָה. הַהַלֵּל וְהַשִּׂמְחָה שְׁמוֹנָה. סֻכָּה וְנִסּוּךְ הַמַּיִם שִׁבְעָה. וְהֶחָלִיל חֲמִשָּׁה וְשִׁשָּׁה.

[ב] לוּלָב שִׁבְעָה כֵּיצַד? יוֹם טוֹב הָרִאשׁוֹן שֶׁל חַג שֶׁחָל לִהְיוֹת בַּשַּׁבָּת, לוּלָב שִׁבְעָה; וּשְׁאָר כָּל־הַיָּמִים, שִׁשָּׁה.

[ג] עֲרָבָה שִׁבְעָה כֵּיצַד? יוֹם שְׁבִיעִי שֶׁל עֲרָבָה שֶׁחָל לִהְיוֹת בַּשַּׁבָּת, עֲרָבָה שִׁבְעָה; וּשְׁאָר כָּל־הַיָּמִים, שִׁשָּׁה.

[ד] מִצְוַת לוּלָב כֵּיצַד? יוֹם טוֹב הָרִאשׁוֹן שֶׁל חַג שֶׁחָל לִהְיוֹת בַּשַּׁבָּת, מוֹלִיכִין אֶת־לוּלְבֵיהֶן לְהַר הַבַּיִת, וְהַחַזָּנִין מְקַבְּלִין מֵהֶן וְסוֹדְרִין אוֹתָן עַל־גַּב הָאִצְטַבָּא—וְהַזְּקֵנִים מַנִּיחִין אֶת־שֶׁלָּהֶן בַּלִּשְׁכָּה—וּמְלַמְּדִים אוֹתָם לוֹמַר: „כָּל־מִי שֶׁמַּגִּיעַ לוּלָבִי בְיָדוֹ, הֲרֵי הוּא לוֹ בְמַתָּנָה." לְמָחָר מַשְׁכִּימִין וּבָאִין. וְהַחַזָּנִין זוֹרְקִין אוֹתָם לִפְנֵיהֶם וְהֵן מְחַטְּפִין, וּמַכִּין אִישׁ

יד אברהם

CHAPTER FOUR

The first mishnah introduces this chapter and the first four *mishnayos* of chapter 5. Each law mentioned here is reviewed in a subsequent mishnah and elaborated upon.

1. וַעֲרָבָה — *And the willow branch.* This refers to the ceremony of ringing the Altar with willow branches and then marching around it as described in mishnah 5 below (*Rav; Rashi* to 42b).

שִׁשָּׁה וְשִׁבְעָה — *[Are performed] six or seven [days].* Since Succos is seven days long (*Lev.* 23:39), one of the days must always be a Sabbath. Our mishnah teaches that in some years the commandments of *lulav* and *aravah* are performed even on the Sabbath and are thus fulfilled for seven days. In other years, though, neither is performed on the Sabbath, and is thus performed on only six days. *Mishnayos* 2 and 3 explain these variations in detail (*Rashi; Rav*).

הַהַלֵּל — *The [recitation of] the Hallel.* On the seven days of Succos and *Shemini Atzeres*, the entire *Hallel* (*Psalms* 113-118) is recited [see mishnah 8], in contrast to *Pesach* when the entire *Hallel* is recited only on the first day (and on the first two days outside of *Eretz Yisrael*). The *Talmud* (*Arachin* 10a,b) explains that this distinction is based on the difference between their respective *mussaf* offerings (*Numbers* 28:19-25; 29:13-34). During *Pesach*, the *mussaf* offering is the same every day, while on Succos each day's is different. *Rashi* and *Tosafos* (*Taanis* 28b) explain that this changing number of offerings demonstrates that Succos should be considered a set of seven one-day festivals, each of which requires its own recitation of the *Hallel*, whereas all seven days of *Pesach* should be regarded as a single festival spread out over a

seven-day period, for which a single *Hallel* at the beginning of the festival is sufficient.

וְהַשִּׂמְחָה — *And the [mitzvah of] rejoicing.* This refers to the eating of the *shlomim* [peace-offerings] (or of other sacrifices; see *Chagigah* 8a and *Rambam, Hil. Chagigah* 2:9) on each day of the festival (see m. 8).

Rambam (*Yom Tov* 6:17-18), however, in codifying our mishnah lists various forms of 'rejoicing' without mentioning sacrificial meat: children are given candies, women are given clothing and jewelry, and men are served meat and wine.

שְׁמוֹנָה — *[Are performed] eight [days].* These *mitzvos* are observed on the seven days of Succos and on Shemini Atzeres.

סֻכָּה — *The [mitzvos of] succah,* i.e., the commandment to dwell in the *succah.*

וְנִסּוּךְ הַמַּיִם — *And the water libation.* In a ceremony performed only during Succos, water was poured on the Altar as explained below in m. 8 and 9.

וְהֶחָלִיל — *And the flute [is played].* Musical instruments were played to accompany the jubilation that preceded the ceremony of water-drawing, as described in 5:2-4 (*Rashi; Rav*).

2. יוֹם טוֹב הָרִאשׁוֹן שֶׁל חַג שֶׁחָל לִהְיוֹת בַּשַּׁבָּת, לוּלָב שִׁבְעָה — *If the first day of the Festival falls on the Sabbath, the lulav [is taken] seven [days].* In the Temple era, if the first day fell on the Sabbath, the Four Species were taken — even in the provinces, where the Torah ordained the *mitzvah* for only one day (see above 3:13; *Gem.*).

וּשְׁאָר כָּל־הַיָּמִים, שִׁשָּׁה — *But [if it falls] on any of the other days, [it is taken] six [days].* If the first day of the Festival fell on a weekday, one of the

[1] **לוּלָב** The [mitzvos of] lulav and the willow branch [are performed] six or seven [days]. The [recitation of] Hallel and the [mitzvah of] rejoicing [are performed] eight [days]. The [mitzvos of] succah and the water libation [are performed] seven [days]. And the flute [is played] five or six [days].

[2] How is [the mitzvah of] lulav [performed] seven [days]? If the first day of the Festival falls on the Sabbath, the lulav [is taken] seven [days]; but [if it falls] on any of the other days, [it is taken] six [days].

[3] How is [the mitzvah of the] willow branch [performed] seven [days]? If the seventh day of [the] willow [ceremony] falls on the Sabbath, the willow [ceremony] is seven [days]; but [if it falls] on any of the other days, [the ceremony is performed] six [days].

[4] How is the mitzvah of lulav [performed]? If the first day of Succos falls on the Sabbath, they bring their lulavim to the Temple Mount, and the attendants receive [the lulavim] from them and arrange them upon the bench — but the elderly place theirs in a chamber — and they teach them to say, 'My lulav is presented as a gift to whomever it may come.' On the morrow they arise early and come. The attendants throw [the lulavim] before them and they would snatch them, striking one another. When

---

YAD AVRAHAM

Intermediate Days would fall on the Sabbath, and the *lulav* would not be taken. Thus it would be taken only six days (*Rashi; Rav*).

Because the *mitzvah* on the first day applies in both the Temple and the provinces [and is therefore to be considered of greater importance (*Meiri*)], the Sages did not wish to hinder the performance of this *mitzvah*. Nowadays, the *lulav* is not taken on the Sabbath even on the first day of the Festival (*Orach Chaim* 658:2).

3. יוֹם שְׁבִיעִי שֶׁל עֲרָבָה שֶׁחָל לִהְיוֹת בְּשַׁבָּת, עֲרָבָה שִׁבְעָה — *If the seventh day of [the] willow [ceremony] fell on the Sabbath, the willow [ceremony] is seven [days].* The *mitzvah* of circling the altar with the willow-branch is not performed on the Sabbath unless it is the seventh day of Succos, Hoshana Rabbah.

Why is this *mitzvah*, which involves no labor, prohibited on the Sabbath at all? The *Gemara* (43b) replies that if the *mitzvah* of *aravah* were permitted on the Sabbath while the taking of the *lulav* were not, unknowing people would come to the erroneous conclusion that the *mitzvah* of *lulav* was not done on the Sabbath because it was less important than the *mitzvah* of *aravah*. The Sages did not wish the *mitzvah* of *lulav* to be held in such low regard. Nowadays, since the advent of a fixed calendar, the question is academic because the seventh day of Succos (21 Tishrei) can never fall on the Sabbath.

4. מוֹלִיכִין אֶת לוּלְבֵיהֶן לְהַר הַבַּיִת — *They bring their lulavim to the Temple Mount.* The populace bring their *lulavim* to the Temple Mount on the afternoon before the Sabbath (*Rashi* to 42b;

Rav), since it is forbidden to carry them four cubits in the public domain or from a private domain to the public domain on the Sabbath. [The *lulav* could be carried on the Temple Mount which was considered רְשׁוּת הַיָּחִיד, *a private domain* — even though it was open to the public — because it was surrounded by a wall (see *Middos* 1:3).]

וְהַחַזָּנִין מְקַבְּלִין מֵהֶן וְסוֹדְרִין אוֹתָן עַל גַּב הָאִצְטַבָּא — *And the attendants receive [the lulavim] from them and arrange them [i.e., the lulavim] upon the bench.* Two long benches were built on the Temple Mount, one higher and closer to the Temple than the other. These benches were covered by pillared canopies so that people could rest in the shade. The masses of *lulavim* were placed on the benches so that the roofs would shade them from the sun (*Rashi* 45a).

וְהַזְּקֵנִים — *But the elderly.* They were provided with a special room to prevent injury the next day when everyone was jostling for his *lulav* (*Rashi; Rav*).

וּמְלַמְּדִים אוֹתָם לוֹמַר — *And they teach them to say.* The *beis din* taught the entire populace to make this declaration, because one cannot fulfill the *mitzvah* of *lulav* on the first day with a *lulav* that belongs to someone else (3:13), whether borrowed or stolen (see 3:1). As a result of this statement, every *lulav* became the property of whoever had it (*Rashi; Rav*).

וְהֵן מְחַטְפִין, וּמַכִּין אִישׁ אֶת חֲבֵרוֹ — *And they would snatch them [i.e., the lulavim], striking one another.* [In their eagerness to retrieve their *lulavim*.]

אֶת־חֲבֵרוֹ. וּכְשֶׁרָאוּ בֵית דִּין שֶׁבָּאוּ לִידֵי סַכָּנָה, הִתְקִינוּ שֶׁיְּהֵא כָל־אֶחָד וְאֶחָד נוֹטֵל בְּבֵיתוֹ.

[ה] מִצְוַת עֲרָבָה כֵּיצַד? מָקוֹם הָיָה לְמַטָּה מִירוּשָׁלַיִם וְנִקְרָא מוֹצָא. יוֹרְדִין לְשָׁם, וּמְלַקְּטִין מִשָּׁם מֻרְבִּיּוֹת שֶׁל עֲרָבָה, וּבָאִין וְזוֹקְפִין אוֹתָן בְּצִדֵּי הַמִּזְבֵּחַ, וְרָאשֵׁיהֶן כְּפוּפִין עַל־גַּבֵּי הַמִּזְבֵּחַ. תָּקְעוּ, וְהֵרִיעוּ, וְתָקְעוּ. בְּכָל־יוֹם מַקִּיפִין אֶת־הַמִּזְבֵּחַ פַּעַם אַחַת וְאוֹמְרִים: ,,אָנָּא ה' הוֹשִׁיעָה נָּא, אָנָּא ה' הַצְלִיחָה נָּא!" רַבִּי יְהוּדָה אוֹמֵר: ,,אֲנִי וָהוֹ, הוֹשִׁיעָה נָּא!" וְאוֹתוֹ הַיּוֹם מַקִּיפִין אֶת־הַמִּזְבֵּחַ שִׁבְעָה פְעָמִים. בִּשְׁעַת פְּטִירָתָן מָה הֵן אוֹמְרִים? ,,יֹפִי לָךְ, מִזְבֵּחַ! יֹפִי לָךְ, מִזְבֵּחַ!" רַבִּי אֱלִיעֶזֶר אוֹמֵר: ,,לְיָהּ וְלָךְ, מִזְבֵּחַ! לְיָהּ וְלָךְ, מִזְבֵּחַ!"

[ו] כְּמַעֲשֵׂהוּ בַחֹל, כָּךְ מַעֲשֵׂהוּ בַשַּׁבָּת, אֶלָּא שֶׁהָיוּ מְלַקְּטִין אוֹתָן מֵעֶרֶב שַׁבָּת וּמַנִּיחִים אוֹתָן בְּגִיגִיּוֹת שֶׁל זָהָב כְּדֵי שֶׁלֹּא יִכְמֹשׁוּ. רַבִּי יוֹחָנָן בֶּן בְּרוֹקָה אוֹמֵר: חֲרִיּוֹת שֶׁל דֶּקֶל הָיוּ מְבִיאִין וְחוֹבְטִין אוֹתָן בַּקַּרְקַע בְּצִדֵּי הַמִּזְבֵּחַ. וְאוֹתוֹ הַיּוֹם נִקְרָא יוֹם חִבּוּט חֲרִיּוֹת.

[ז] מִיָּד הַתִּינוֹקוֹת שׁוֹמְטִין אֶת־לוּלְבֵיהֶן וְאוֹכְלִין אֶתְרוֹגֵיהֶן.

יד אברהם

הִתְקִינוּ שֶׁיְּהֵא כָל־אֶחָד וְאֶחָד נוֹטֵל בְּבֵיתוֹ — *They ordained that everyone should take [his lulav] at home* [lit., *in his house*]. One should perform the *mitzvah* at home, rather than bring his *lulav* to the Temple Mount on Friday.

5. **מִצְוַת עֲרָבָה כֵּיצַד?** — *How was the mitzvah of the willow [performed]?* I.e., how was the special *aravah* ceremony performed in the Temple? Although not stated explicitly in the Torah, this precept has the status of a Scriptural commandment, because it was transmitted to Moses at Sinai.

מוֹצָא — *Motza.* Willows grew there (*Rav*).

יוֹרְדִין לְשָׁם — *They descended there.* The emissaries of *beis din* would go to Motza to bring the willows. This procedure survives in the custom that the synagogue attendant (שַׁמָּשׁ) brings willows for the congregants for Hoshana Rabbah (*Ran*).

וּבָאִין וְזוֹקְפִין אוֹתָן — *And came and stood them up.* Some say they held the willow while they walked around the Altar, and the branches were set up after a circuit had been made around the Altar (*Tosafos*). Others say that first the willows were set up next to the Altar and then the circuit was made (*Tos. Yom Tov*).

בְּצִדֵּי הַמִּזְבֵּחַ — *Against the sides of the Altar.* They were placed on the base of the Altar, leaning against its sides (*Gem.* 45a).

וְרָאשֵׁיהֶן כְּפוּפִין עַל־גַּבֵּי הַמִּזְבֵּחַ — *With their tops drooping over the top of the Altar.* The Gemara

(45a) explains that in order for the willows to reach that far and droop down one cubit they had to be eleven cubits tall and be standing on the base of the Altar.

תָּקְעוּ, וְהֵרִיעוּ, וְתָקְעוּ — *They blew [on a trumpet] a tekiah, a teruah, and a tekiah.* Rambam (*Klei HaMikdash* 7:21) states that the trumpet was blown during the procession of bringing the willow branches and while arranging them around the Altar. The blowing created an atmosphere of joy and happiness (*Tosafos*).

בְּכָל יוֹם מַקִּיפִין אֶת הַמִּזְבֵּחַ פַּעַם אַחַת — *Each day they would circle the Altar one time.* Only the *Kohanim* would walk around the Altar, not the general public, because in order to circuit the Altar one had to pass between the אוּלָם, *antechamber of the Temple,* and the Altar, and only *Kohanim* were allowed to enter this part of the Temple (see *Keilim* 1:8,9).

רַבִּי יְהוּדָה אוֹמֵר: אֲנִי וָהוֹ, הוֹשִׁיעָה נָּא! — *R' Yehudah says: [They would say] 'ANI VAHO, bring salvation now!'* Instead of saying אָנָּא ה', *Please HASHEM, the Kohanim* said the words אֲנִי וָהוֹ, *ANI VAHO.* The numerical value of both phrases is identical — 78 [which is three times the numerical value of HASHEM]. Furthermore, ANI and VAHO are two of the seventy-two Divine Names which are secreted in three verses in *Exodus* (14:19-21).

וְאוֹתוֹ הַיּוֹם — *But on that day,* i.e., the seventh day of Succos, Hoshana Rabbah.

מַקִּיפִין אֶת הַמִּזְבֵּחַ שִׁבְעָה פְעָמִים — *They circled*

the beis din saw that they were endangered, they ordained that everyone should take [his lulav] at home.

[5] How was the mitzvah of the willow [performed]? There was a place below Jerusalem called Motza. They descended there, gathered from there large willow branches, and came and stood them up against the sides of the Altar, with their tops drooping over the top of the Altar. They blew [on a trumpet] a tekiah, a teruah, and a tekiah. Each day they would circle the Altar one time and say, 'Please HASHEM bring salvation now, please HASHEM bring success now!' R' Yehudah says: [They would say] 'ANI VAHO, bring salvation now!' But on that day they circled the Altar seven times. When they left what did they say? 'Beauty is yours, O Altar! Beauty is yours, O Altar!' R' Eliezer says: [They said,] 'To YAH and to you, O Altar! To YAH and to you, O Altar!'

[6] Just as it was performed on the weekdays, so it was performed on the Sabbath, except they gathered them on the eve of the Sabbath and placed them in golden vessels so that they should not wilt. R' Yochanan ben Berokah says: They brought date-palm branches and beat them on the ground at the sides of the Altar. That day was called the day of the beating of the [date-palm] branches.

[7] Immediately the children loosened their lulavim and ate their esrogim.

---

the Altar seven times. Yerushalmi (4:3) states that this is in commemoration of the conquest of Jericho. Each day the Jewish People walked around the city one time, and on the seventh day they walked around it seven times.

בִּשְׁעַת פְּטִירָתָן — When they left. When they finished the circuits and left the Altar.

רַבִּי אֱלִיעֶזֶר אוֹמֵר: ,,לְיָה וְלָךְ, מִזְבֵּחַ! לְיָה וְלָךְ, מִזְבֵּחַ!" — R' Eliezer says: [They said,] 'To YAH and to you, O Altar! To YAH and to you, O Altar,' i.e., we believe in HASHEM and do not deny that He is our God, and we praise the Altar, which is so dear to God since it serves to atone for us (Rashi).

6. כָּךְ מַעֲשֵׂהוּ בַּשַּׁבָּת — So it was performed on the Sabbath. The ceremony is conducted in exactly the same manner when the seventh day falls on the Sabbath.

וּמַנִּיחִים אוֹתָן בְּגִיגִיּוֹת שֶׁל זָהָב כְּדֵי שֶׁלֹּא יִכְמְשׁוּ — And placed them in golden vessels so that they should not wilt. These vessels were filled with water to prevent the leaves from withering (Rav).

רַבִּי יוֹחָנָן בֶּן בְּרוֹקָה אוֹמֵר: חֲרִיּוֹת שֶׁל דֶּקֶל הָיוּ מְבִיאִין — R' Yochanan ben Berokah says: They brought date-palm branches. Not willow branches, as is the view of the first Tanna.

וְחוֹבְטִין אוֹתָן — And beat them, [i.e., the date-palm branches]. [It would seem that according to the first Tanna the same was done

with the willow branches.]

וְאוֹתוֹ הַיּוֹם נִקְרָא יוֹם חִבּוּט חֲרִיּוֹת — That day was called the day of the beating of the [date-palm] branches. Rashi, Tosafos and Rav maintain that R' Yochanan ben Berokah disagrees with the first Tanna regarding weekdays as well as the Sabbath. Accordingly, each day of the Festival was called "the day of the beating of the palm branches."

7. מִיָּד — Immediately, i.e., as soon as the mitzvos of the lulav and the willow branch had been performed [on the seventh day] (Rosh).

הַתִּינוֹקוֹת שׁוֹמְטִין אֶת לוּלְבֵיהֶן — The children loosened their lulavim. They untied the festive bindings of the lulav (Meiri).

וְאוֹכְלִין אֶתְרוֹגֵיהֶן — And ate their esrogim. Even though the esrog may not be used for any purpose but the mitzvah of the Four Species, because it was set aside for mitzvah use for the whole seven-day period, nevertheless, the children ignored this law (Rambam). Rashi (46b) suggests that the esrogim of children, unlike those of adults, were not set aside for a מִצְוָה גְמוּרָה, complete mitzvah. [Presumably, since children take the Four Species only because of their parents' obligation to train them, their esrogim are not considered to be totally dedicated for the purpose of a mitzvah.] Therefore, the children were allowed to eat theirs on the seventh day, but the adults did not eat theirs.

[ח] הַהַלֵּל וְהַשִּׂמְחָה שְׁמוֹנָה כֵּיצַד? מְלַמֵּד שֶׁחַיָּב אָדָם בַּהַלֵּל, וּבַשִּׂמְחָה, וּבִכְבוֹד יוֹם טוֹב הָאַחֲרוֹן שֶׁל חַג, כִּשְׁאָר כָּל־יְמוֹת הֶחָג. סֻכָּה שִׁבְעָה כֵּיצַד? גָּמַר מִלֶּאֱכוֹל, לֹא יַתִּיר סֻכָּתוֹ, אֲבָל מוֹרִיד אֶת־הַכֵּלִים מִן־הַמִּנְחָה וּלְמַעֲלָה, מִפְּנֵי כְבוֹד יוֹם טוֹב הָאַחֲרוֹן שֶׁל חַג.

[ט] נִסּוּךְ הַמַּיִם כֵּיצַד? צְלוֹחִית שֶׁל זָהָב מַחֲזֶקֶת שְׁלֹשֶׁת לֻגִּים, הָיָה מְמַלֵּא מִן־הַשִּׁלּוֹחַ. הִגִּיעוּ לְשַׁעַר הַמַּיִם תָּקְעוּ, וְהֵרִיעוּ, וְתָקְעוּ. עָלָה בַכֶּבֶשׁ וּפָנָה לִשְׂמֹאלוֹ. שְׁנֵי סְפָלִים שֶׁל כֶּסֶף הָיוּ שָׁם. רַבִּי יְהוּדָה אוֹמֵר: שֶׁל סִיד הָיוּ, אֶלָּא שֶׁהָיוּ מֻשְׁחָרִין פְּנֵיהֶם מִפְּנֵי הַיָּיִן. וּמְנֻקָּבִין כְּמִין שְׁנֵי חֳטָמִין דַּקִּין, אֶחָד מְעֻבֶּה וְאֶחָד דַּק, כְּדֵי שֶׁיְּהוּ שְׁנֵיהֶם כָּלִין בְּבַת אַחַת. מַעֲרָבִי שֶׁל מַיִם; מִזְרָחִי שֶׁל יָיִן. עֵרָה שֶׁל מַיִם לְתוֹךְ שֶׁל יַיִן, וְשֶׁל יַיִן לְתוֹךְ שֶׁל מַיִם, יָצָא. רַבִּי יְהוּדָה אוֹמֵר: בַּלֹּג הָיָה מְנַסֵּךְ כָּל־שְׁמוֹנָה. וְלַמְנַסֵּךְ אוֹמְרִים לוֹ: ,,הַגְבַּהּ יָדֶךָ!״ שֶׁפַּעַם אַחַת נִסֵּךְ אֶחָד עַל־גַּבֵּי רַגְלָיו, וּרְגָמוּהוּ כָל־הָעָם בְּאֶתְרוֹגֵיהֶן.

יד אברהם

8. וּבַשִּׂמְחָה — *(And) in the [mitzvah of] rejoicing.* 'Rejoicing' here means eating the meat of the *shlomim*, peace-offerings (*Rashi* to 48a).

וּבִכְבוֹד יוֹם טוֹב הָאַחֲרוֹן שֶׁל חַג — *And in [the] honor of the last Festival day of Succos.* Succos proper is only seven days, but Shemini Atzeres is considered the last day of the Festival *season*, even though it is not part of Succos. Thus the eighth day for *Hallel* and rejoicing is Shemini Atzeres.

כִּשְׁאָר כָּל־יְמוֹת הֶחָג — *Like all the other days of Succos.* The *Gemara* (48a) derives the obligation of rejoicing on Shemini Atzeres from *Deut.* (16:15): וְהָיִיתָ אַךְ שָׂמֵחַ, *and you shall be only joyful.* This verse teaches that the *mitzvah* of rejoicing applies to the night of Shemini Atzeres as a continuation of the first seven days of Succos.

גָּמַר מִלֶּאֱכוֹל — *When one has finished eating.* On the seventh day of Succos, Hoshana Rabbah (*Rashi*).

לֹא יַתִּיר סֻכָּתוֹ — *He may not take apart* [lit., *undo*] his succah. Because the *mitzvah* of *succah* is still in force the entire day (*Rav*).

Rashi emphasizes that there is always the possibility that he will eat another meal that day — and it will have to be eaten in the *succah*.

מִן־הַמִּנְחָה וּלְמַעֲלָה — *From Minchah time and later,* i.e., from two and a half hours before the end of the day (*Ritva*). One may not take his utensils back into the home until the time stated by the mishnah (*Rashi*; *Rav*).

9. נִסּוּךְ הַמַּיִם כֵּיצַד — *How is the water libation done?* This special libation was performed only

during the seven days of Succos. All other libations in the Temple were of wine poured on the Altar, but during the seven days of Succos water was poured simultaneously with the wine libation as part of the daily burnt offering in the morning.

This water libation was commanded to Moses orally on Sinai [הֲלָכָה לְמֹשֶׁה מִסִּינַי] (*Gemara* 44a), and has the force of Scriptural law. However, R' Yehudah ben Besaira noted that the Torah alluded to the superfluous word מַיִם, *water,* in the section (*Numb.* 29) describing the *mussaf* sacrifices of Succos. In referring to the libations of Succos, the Torah generally uses the word וְנִסְכָּה. However, verse 19 uses the word וְנִסְכֵּיהֶם; thus, there is an extra ם. The Torah uses וְנִסְכֶּיהָ in verse 31, providing an extra י. And in verse 33, the Torah uses the word כְּמִשְׁפָּט rather than the word כַּמִּשְׁפָּט which appears on all the other days. Thus, again, an extra ם. The three extra letters spell מַיִם, *water,* an allusion to the Succos water-libation (*Taanis* 2b).

צְלוֹחִית שֶׁל זָהָב מַחֲזֶקֶת שְׁלֹשֶׁת לֻגִּים הָיָה מְמַלֵּא — *He filled a golden flagon holding three lugim.* *Numbers* 15:5 describes this libation as רְבִיעִית הַהִין, *a quarter of a hin.* A hin is twelve *lugim*; thus three *lugim* mentioned in our mishnah are one quarter of a *hin*. Depending on the various opinions regarding the size of a *log*, it is at least approximately 30.6 fluid ounces; according to others it is much more.

מִן־הַשִּׁלּוֹחַ — *From the Shiloach,* a fresh-water spring near the Temple Mount (*Rashi*; *Rav*).

הִגִּיעוּ לְשַׁעַר הַמַּיִם — *When they reached the Water Gate.* The Water Gate was one of the southern gates of the Temple Courtyard. It was

[8] How are [the recitation of] the Hallel and the [mitzvah of] rejoicing [done for] eight [days]? This teaches that a man is obligated in [the recitation of] the Hallel, in the [mitzvah of] rejoicing, and in [the] honor of the last Festival day of Succos, like all the other days of Succos. How is [the mitzvah of] succah [observed for] seven [days]? When one has finished eating, he may not take apart his succah, but he may take down his utensils from Minchah time and later, in honor of the last day of Succos.

[9] How is the water libation done? He filled a golden flagon holding three lugim, from the Shiloach. When they reached the Water Gate they sounded a tekiah, a teruah, and a tekiah. He went up the ramp and turned to his left. There were two silver bowls there. R' Yehudah says: They were of plaster, but their surfaces were darkened from wine. Each had a hole like a thin nostril, one wider and the other narrower, so that both would drain out at the same time. The western one was for water; the eastern one was for wine. If he poured [the flagon] of water into [the bowl] for wine, or [the flagon] of wine into [the bowl] for water, he fulfilled the obligation. R' Yehudah says: He would pour with one log all eight [days]. To the pourer they would say, 'Raise your hand!' For once someone poured it over his feet, and all the people pelted him with their esrogim.

---

given this name because the flagon for the water libation was brought into the Courtyard through it (Rashi; Rav).

בֶּכֶבֶשׁ — The ramp. The Kohen chosen to carry the flagon went up the ramp to the Altar in the Temple Courtyard (Rashi; Rav).

שְׁנֵי סְפָלִים שֶׁל כֶּסֶף הָיוּ שָׁם — There were two silver bowls there, [on the southwestern corner] permanently cemented to the Altar (Tosafos 48a s.v. שְׁנֵי), one for wine and the other for water (Tif. Yis.).

וּמְנֻקָּבִין כְּמִין שְׁנֵי חֹטָמִין דַּקִּין — Each had a hole like a thin nostril. Beneath each bowl was a thin projection through which the liquid flowed. The Kohen would pour the wine and the water simultaneously into their respective bowls. The liquids would then flow through the projections onto the top of the Altar, and then through a hole in the top of the Altar, down into a deep cavity beneath the Altar called the shissin (Rashi 48b; Rav; Tif. Yis.).

כְּדֵי שֶׁיְּהוּ שְׁנֵיהֶם כָּלִין בְּבַת אַחַת — So that both would drain out at the same time. Since water flows more freely than wine, the hole of the wine bowl was made wider and that of the water bowl narrower, so that both bowls would empty at the same time (Rashi; Rav).

יָצָא — He fulfilled the obligation. Although this is not the proper manner of fulfilling the mitzvah, as long as both libations were made, the mitzvah is considered fulfilled.

רַבִּי יְהוּדָה אוֹמֵר: בְּלֹג הָיָה מְנַסֵּךְ כָּל שְׁמוֹנָה — R'

Yehudah says: He would pour with one log all eight [days]. R' Yehudah argues with the first Tanna on two points: He maintains that the amount of water used in the water libation was one log, while the first Tanna holds three lugim. In addition, R' Yehudah says the water-libation ceremony was performed all eight days — seven of Succos and one of Shemini Atzeres, but the first Tanna holds that it was performed only during the seven days of Succos (Rashi; Rav).

The halachah does not follow R' Yehudah (Rav).

וְלַמְנַסֵּךְ אוֹמְרִים לוֹ: ,,הַגְבֵּהַּ יָדְךָ!'' — To the pourer they would say, 'Raise your hand!' They would ask the Kohen who performed the water-libation to keep his hands high as he poured so that all could see that he was pouring it into the bowl. During the Second Temple era there arose a heretical sect called the Sadducees who rejected any law not stated explicitly in the Torah. This sect found adherents among Jerusalem's upper class, even among the Kohanim. Since the water libation is an oral tradition transmitted to Moses and is not explicit in the Torah, the Sadducean Kohanim denied its validity and refused to perform it properly (Rashi; Rav).

שֶׁפַּעַם אַחַת נִסֵּךְ אֶחָד עַל גַּבֵּי רַגְלָיו — For once someone poured it over his feet. The Kohen performing the rite at that time was a Sadducee and, instead of pouring the water into the proper bowl, he poured it over his feet (Rashi; Rav).

[יז] כְּמַעֲשֵׂהוּ בַחֹל, כָּךְ מַעֲשֵׂהוּ בַשַּׁבָּת, אֶלָּא שֶׁהָיָה מְמַלֵּא מֵעֶרֶב שַׁבָּת חָבִית שֶׁל זָהָב שֶׁאֵינָהּ מְקֻדֶּשֶׁת מִן־הַשִּׁלּוֹחַ, וּמַנִּיחָהּ בַּלִּשְׁכָּה. נִשְׁפְּכָה אוֹ נִתְגַּלְּתָה, הָיָה מְמַלֵּא מִן־הַכִּיּוֹר, שֶׁהַיַּיִן וְהַמַּיִם הַמְגֻלִּין פְּסוּלִים לְגַבֵּי הַמִּזְבֵּחַ.

פרק חמישי

[א] **הֶחָלִיל** חֲמִשָּׁה וְשִׁשָּׁה, זֶהוּ הֶחָלִיל שֶׁל בֵּית הַשּׁוֹאֵבָה, שֶׁאֵינוֹ דּוֹחֶה לֹא אֶת־הַשַּׁבָּת וְלֹא אֶת־יוֹם טוֹב. אָמְרוּ: „כָּל־מִי שֶׁלֹּא רָאָה שִׂמְחַת בֵּית הַשּׁוֹאֵבָה לֹא רָאָה שִׂמְחָה מִיָּמָיו."

[ב] בְּמוֹצָאֵי יוֹם טוֹב הָרִאשׁוֹן שֶׁל חַג יָרְדוּ לְעֶזְרַת נָשִׁים, וּמְתַקְּנִין שָׁם תִּקּוּן גָּדוֹל. וּמְנוֹרוֹת שֶׁל זָהָב הָיוּ שָׁם וְאַרְבָּעָה סְפָלִים שֶׁל זָהָב בְּרָאשֵׁיהֶן, וְאַרְבָּעָה סֻלָּמוֹת לְכָל אֶחָד וְאֶחָד, וְאַרְבָּעָה יְלָדִים מִפִּרְחֵי כְהֻנָּה וּבִידֵיהֶם כַּדִּים שֶׁל שֶׁמֶן שֶׁל מֵאָה וְעֶשְׂרִים לֹג, שֶׁהֵן מַטִּילִין לְכָל סֵפֶל וָסֵפֶל.

[ג] מִבְּלָאֵי מִכְנְסֵי כֹהֲנִים וּמֵהֶמְיָנֵיהֶן מֵהֶן הָיוּ מַפְקִיעִין וּבָהֶן הָיוּ מַדְלִיקִין. וְלֹא הָיָה חָצֵר בִּירוּשָׁלַיִם שֶׁאֵינָהּ מְאִירָה מֵאוֹר בֵּית הַשּׁוֹאֵבָה.

יד אברהם

10. אֶלָּא שֶׁהָיָה מְמַלֵּא מֵעֶרֶב שַׁבָּת חָבִית שֶׁל זָהָב שֶׁאֵינָהּ מְקֻדֶּשֶׁת — *Except that he would fill an unconsecrated golden barrel on the eve of the Sabbath.* To draw water on the Sabbath from the Shiloach would have required carrying it from a public domain into the Temple era, a private domain. Such carrying is forbidden on the Sabbath.

Why was a consecrated vessel not used to store the water until the following morning? A consecrated vessel sanctifies what is put into it, but sanctified matter becomes invalid by being left overnight. Since they drew the water on Friday for use the next morning, they stored the vessel in an unconsecrated golden barrel so that it could remain overnight (*Gem.* 50a; *Rav; Rashi*).

נִשְׁפְּכָה אוֹ נִתְגַּלְּתָה, הָיָה מְמַלֵּא מִן הַכִּיּוֹר — *If they were spilled or uncovered, he would refill it from the laver.* The laver, situated in the Temple Court, was a consecrated vessel that held water. Even though the laver was a consecrated vessel, a special device was invented by a *Kohel Gadol* named Ben-Katin to keep its water from being disqualified by remaining overnight (*Yoma* 3:10). He devised a wheel which lowered the entire laver into a well. There the water of the well and the water of the laver merged and became one, so that the water in the laver was considered part of the well rather than separate water stored in the laver. Since the laver water was not disqualified, it could be used for the

libation (*Rashi* 48b; *Rav*).

שֶׁהַיַּיִן וְהַמַּיִם הַמְגֻלִּין פְּסוּלִים לְגַבֵּי הַמִּזְבֵּחַ — *For uncovered wine and water are unfit for the Altar.* But the laver was a *covered* vessel, and its water was therefore fit for the Altar. Wine and water left uncovered, for the amount of time it would take a snake to emerge from a nearby hole and drink, may not be drunk for fear that a snake may have drunk from them and left some of its venom behind (*Terumos* 8:4 and *Rav* ibid.). They are then surely unfit for Temple service.

CHAPTER FIVE

1. זֶהוּ הֶחָלִיל שֶׁל בֵּית הַשּׁוֹאֵבָה — *This is the flute of Beis HaSho'evah* [lit., *the place of Water Drawing*]. The water drawing is described in 4:9. The festivities that preceded the water drawing are discussed below (mishnayos 2-4). Many other instruments besides the flute were played during the festivities. However, since the flute was the main instrument and its sound was heard above that of the other instruments, it was singled out (*Rav; Rambam, Comm.*).

שֶׁאֵינוֹ דּוֹחֶה לֹא אֶת הַשַּׁבָּת וְלֹא אֶת יוֹם טוֹב — *Which overrides neither Sabbath nor Festival.* If the first day of Succos fell on the Sabbath, the flute would be played each of the remaining six days. If the first day of Succos fell on a weekday, one of the Intermediate Days would be a Sabbath and the flute would only be played for five days (*Rashi* 50a; *Rav*).

---

[10] *Just as it is performed on a weekday, so it is performed on the Sabbath,
except that he would fill an unconsecrated golden barrel on the eve of
the Sabbath from the Shiloach, and place it in a chamber. If they were spilled
or uncovered, he would refill it from the laver, for uncovered wine and water
are unfit for the Altar.*

CHAPTER FIVE

[1] הֶחָלִיל *The flute [is played] five or six [days], this is the flute of Beis
HaSho'evah, which overrides neither Sabbath nor Festival. They
said, 'Whoever did not see the rejoicing of Beis HaSho'evah never saw rejoicing
in his lifetime.'*

[2] *At the conclusion of the first Festival day of Succos they descended to the
Women's Courtyard, where they made a great improvement. There were
golden candelabra there with four golden bowls atop them, four ladders for each
[candelabrum], and four youths from [among] the young Kohanim each holding
a thirty-log pitcher of oil — for a total of one hundred and twenty log — which
he poured into one of the bowls.*

[3] *From the worn-out trousers of the Kohanim and their belts they made wicks
and they would kindle them. There was not a courtyard in Jerusalem that
was not illuminated by the light of the Beis HaSho'evah.*

YAD AVRAHAM

כָּל מִי שֶׁלֹּא רָאָה שִׂמְחַת בֵּית הַשּׁוֹאֵבָה לֹא רָאָה שִׂמְחָה
מִיָּמָיו. — *Whoever did not see the rejoicing of
the Beis HaSho'evah never saw rejoicing in his
lifetime.*

Rashi (50a) points out that these extraordinarily joyous festivities fulfilled the verse in *Isaiah*
(12:3): וּשְׁאַבְתֶּם מַיִם בְּשָׂשׂוֹן — *And you shall draw
water joyously.*

2. יָרְדוּ לְעֶזְרַת נָשִׁים — *They descended to the
Women's Courtyard.* The *Kohanim* and Levites
would descend from the Temple Courtyard to
the Women's Courtyard which was situated
lower down on the slope of the Temple Mount
(*Rashi* 51a).

Adjoining the Courtyard (עֲזָרָה) surrounding
the Temple was the עֶזְרַת נָשִׁים, *Women's
Courtyard.* This court, occupying an area of
135x135 cubits, was situated on the east side of
the Temple Courtyard. Its width (135 cubits)
corresponded to the width of the Temple
Courtyard, and the wall surrounding the
Temple Courtyard separated it from the
Women's Courtyard. Since the Temple stood on
a mountain, the Temple Courtyard was higher
than the Women's Courtyard. One had to
ascend fifteen steps to go from one to the other
(*Middos* 2:5).

וּמְתַקְּנִין שָׁם תִּקּוּן גָּדוֹל — *Where they made a great
improvement. Rashi* explains that projecting
brackets were built into the walls all around the
Courtyard. Each year they would arrange
planks of wood on the brackets [with a railing
(*Tif. Yis.*)] to create a balcony from which the
women could view the festivities without
mingling with the men, thereby preventing
frivolity. It was this great improvement that was

made every year. *Rambam (Comm.)* comments
that the balcony was built to keep the men from
looking at the women.

The *mechitzah* or dividing wall separating
the men and the women in synagogues is based
on the separate courtyards for men and women
in the Temple. The galleries of the large
synagogues derive from the great improvement
enacted in the Temple.

וּמְנוֹרוֹת שֶׁל זָהָב הָיוּ שָׁם — *There were golden
candelabra there.* [In the Women's Courtyard
stood candelabra that were used only for the
water-drawing festivities.]

וְאַרְבָּעָה סְפָלִים שֶׁל זָהָב בְּרָאשֵׁיהֶן — *With four
golden bowls atop them.* Into these bowls were
placed very thick wicks (*Tif. Yis.*).

וְאַרְבָּעָה סֻלָּמוֹת לְכָל אֶחָד וְאֶחָד — *Four ladders
for each [candelabrum].* The ladders were
needed because the candelabra were fifty cubits
high (*Gemara* 52b).

וְאַרְבָּעָה יְלָדִים מִפִּרְחֵי כְהֻנָּה — *And four youths
from [among] the young Kohanim.* Each youth
was assigned a ladder which he climbed to light
a wick in one bowl. Consequently, four youths
were assigned for each candelabrum.

3. מִבְּלָאֵי מִכְנְסֵי כֹהֲנִים וּמֵהֶמְיָנֵיהֶן — *From the
worn-out trousers of the Kohanim and their
belts.* Both these garments were purchased from
communal funds and were worn by the
Kohanim when they performed the Temple
service (*Rashi* 51a; see *Yoma* 7:5).

וְלֹא הָיָה חָצֵר בִּירוּשָׁלַיִם שֶׁאֵינָהּ מְאִירָה מֵאוֹר בֵּית
הַשּׁוֹאֵבָה — *There was not a courtyard in
Jerusalem that was not illuminated by the light
of the Beis HaSho'evah.* Since the fifty-cubit-

[ד] חֲסִידִים וְאַנְשֵׁי מַעֲשֶׂה הָיוּ מְרַקְּדִים לִפְנֵיהֶם בַּאֲבוּקוֹת שֶׁל אוֹר שֶׁבִּידֵיהֶן, וְאוֹמְרִים לִפְנֵיהֶן דִּבְרֵי שִׁירוֹת וְתִשְׁבָּחוֹת; וְהַלְוִיִּם בְּכִנּוֹרוֹת, וּבִנְבָלִים, וּבִמְצִלְתַּיִם, וּבַחֲצוֹצְרוֹת, וּבִכְלֵי שִׁיר בְּלֹא מִסְפָּר עַל־חֲמֵשׁ עֶשְׂרֵה מַעֲלוֹת הַיּוֹרְדוֹת מֵעֶזְרַת יִשְׂרָאֵל לְעֶזְרַת נָשִׁים – כְּנֶגֶד חֲמִשָּׁה עָשָׂר שִׁיר הַמַּעֲלוֹת שֶׁבַּתְּהִלִּים. שֶׁעֲלֵיהֶן לְוִיִּם עוֹמְדִין בִּכְלֵי שִׁיר וְאוֹמְרִים שִׁירָה. וְעָמְדוּ שְׁנֵי כֹהֲנִים בַּשַּׁעַר הָעֶלְיוֹן שֶׁיּוֹרֵד מֵעֶזְרַת יִשְׂרָאֵל לְעֶזְרַת נָשִׁים, וּשְׁתֵּי חֲצוֹצְרוֹת בִּידֵיהֶן. קָרָא הַגֶּבֶר, תָּקְעוּ, וְהֵרִיעוּ, וְתָקְעוּ. הִגִּיעוּ לְמַעֲלָה עֲשִׂירִית, תָּקְעוּ, וְהֵרִיעוּ, וְתָקְעוּ. הִגִּיעוּ לָעֲזָרָה, תָּקְעוּ, וְהֵרִיעוּ, וְתָקְעוּ. הָיוּ תּוֹקְעִין וְהוֹלְכִין עַד שֶׁמַּגִּיעִין לְשַׁעַר הַיּוֹצֵא מִזְרָח. הִגִּיעוּ לְשַׁעַר הַיּוֹצֵא מִזְרָחָה, הָפְכוּ פְּנֵיהֶן לַמַּעֲרָב וְאָמְרוּ: "אֲבוֹתֵינוּ שֶׁהָיוּ בַּמָּקוֹם הַזֶּה אֲחֹרֵיהֶם אֶל־הֵיכַל קַדְמָה, וּפְנֵיהֶם קַדְמָה, וְהֵמָּה מִשְׁתַּחֲוִים קַדְמָה לַשָּׁמֶשׁ. וְאָנוּ – לְיָהּ עֵינֵינוּ." רַבִּי יְהוּדָה אוֹמֵר: הָיוּ שׁוֹנִין וְאוֹמְרִין "אָנוּ לְיָהּ, וּלְיָהּ עֵינֵינוּ."

[ה] אֵין פּוֹחֲתִין מֵעֶשְׂרִים וְאַחַת תְּקִיעוֹת בַּמִּקְדָּשׁ, וְאֵין מוֹסִיפִין עַל־אַרְבָּעִים וּשְׁמוֹנֶה. בְּכָל־יוֹם הָיוּ שָׁם עֶשְׂרִים וְאַחַת תְּקִיעוֹת בַּמִּקְדָּשׁ: שָׁלֹשׁ לִפְתִיחַת שְׁעָרִים; וְתֵשַׁע לְתָמִיד שֶׁל שַׁחַר; וְתֵשַׁע לְתָמִיד שֶׁל בֵּין הָעַרְבָּיִם. וּבַמּוּסָפִין הָיוּ מוֹסִיפִין עוֹד תֵּשַׁע וּבְעֶרֶב שַׁבָּת הָיוּ מוֹסִיפִין עוֹד שֵׁשׁ: שָׁלֹשׁ לְהַבְטִיל הָעָם מִמְּלָאכָה; וְשָׁלֹשׁ לְהַבְדִּיל

יד אברהם

high candelabra rose up above the eastern wall of the Temple, and the Temple Mount was higher than the rest of Jerusalem, the light shone out over the whole city (Rashi 51a; Rav).

4. וְאַנְשֵׁי מַעֲשֶׂה — And men of [good] deeds, who occupy themselves in communal matters, such as the collection of charity, raising orphans, helping poor brides and so on.

הָיוּ מְרַקְּדִים לִפְנֵיהֶם — Would dance before them. The outstanding scholars of Israel, the heads of the yeshivos, the Sanhedrin, and the pious men and men of good deeds, would dance and clap and sing and act joyously in the Temple during the days of Succos. The general populace, both men and women, would come to watch and listen (Rambam Lulav 8:4).

בַּאֲבוּקוֹת שֶׁל אוֹר שֶׁבִּידֵיהֶן — With the flaming torches [that were] in their hands. They would throw them up in the air and then catch them. Some were expert enough to juggle four torches and some could juggle eight (Rashi 51b; Rav).

וְאוֹמְרִים לִפְנֵיהֶן דִּבְרֵי שִׁירוֹת וְתִשְׁבָּחוֹת — And would utter before them words of songs and praises. Those elders who had led fully righteous lives would praise God by saying, 'Happy is our youth that has not shamed our old age' — i.e., we did not transgress in our youth and, as such, are not ashamed in our old age.

Penitents would say, 'Happy is our old age

which has atoned for our youth.'

All of them would say together, 'Happy is he who did not sin, but if he has sinned let him repent and He will forgive him.'

עַל חֲמֵשׁ עֶשְׂרֵה מַעֲלוֹת — [Stood] on the fifteen steps. The Levites stood on these steps while they played their instruments during the Beis HaSho'evah festivities. Throughout the rest of the year when they sang and played for the daily sacrifices, they stood on a דּוּכָן, platform, near the Altar (Rashi 51b; Rav).

The steps ran across the width of the Courtyard. Each step ran across the width of the Courtyard. Each step was half a cubit deep and half a cubit high (Rashi 51b; Middos 2:3).

כְּנֶגֶד חֲמִשָּׁה עָשָׂר שִׁיר הַמַּעֲלוֹת שֶׁבַּתְּהִלִּים — Corresponding to the fifteen Songs of Ascent in Psalms. The fifteen steps corresponded to the fifteen Songs of Ascent (Psalms 120-134), each of which begins with the words שִׁיר הַמַּעֲלוֹת, A Song of Ascents, or Steps.

קָרָא הַגֶּבֶר — [When] the crier called out. Gevini, the Temple Crier (Shekalim 5:1), called out every morning at daybreak (or at some time prior to it), 'Arise Kohanim to perform your service; Levites to your platform; and Israelites to your stations' (Yoma 20b).

תָּקְעוּ, וְהֵרִיעוּ, וְתָקְעוּ — They sounded a tekiah, a teruah, and a tekiah. The two Kohanim sounded a tekiah, a teruah, and a tekiah [on

[4] *Devout men and men of [good] deeds would dance before them with the flaming torches [that were] in their hands and would utter before them words of songs and praises; and the Levites with harps, lyres, cymbals, trumpets, and countless musical instruments [stood] on the fifteen steps that descend from the Courtyard of the Israelites to the Women's Courtyard — corresponding to the fifteen Songs of Ascent in Psalms. Upon them the Levites would stand with musical instruments and chant songs. Two Kohanim stood at the Upper Gate that descends from the Courtyard of the Israelites to the Women's Courtyard, with two trumpets in their hands. [When] the crier called out, they sounded a tekiah, a teruah, and a tekiah. [When] they reached the tenth step, they sounded a tekiah, a teruah, and a tekiah. When they reached the Courtyard, they sounded a tekiah, a teruah, and a tekiah. They would continue sounding tekiah until they reached the gate leading out [to the] east. When they reached the gate leading out to the east, they turned to the west and said, 'Our forefathers who were in this place [had] their backs toward the Sanctuary and their faces toward the east, and they bowed eastward toward the sun. But as for us — our eyes are toward YAH.' R' Yehudah says: They repeated and said, 'We are for YAH and toward YAH are our eyes.'*

[5] *They make no fewer than twenty-one trumpet blasts in the Temple, and no more than forty-eight. Every day there were twenty-one trumpet blasts in the Temple: three for the opening of the gates; nine for the morning tamid-offering; and nine for the afternoon tamid offering. With the mussaf offerings they added another nine. And on the eve of the Sabbath they added another six: three to stop the people from work; and three to distinguish*

---

their trumpets] as a signal to proceed toward the Shiloach spring to draw the water for the libation (*Rashi* 51b; *Rav*).

עַד שֶׁמַּגִּיעִין לְשַׁעַר הַיּוֹצֵא מִזְרָח — *Until they reached the gate leading out [to the] east.* The gate led from the Women's Courtyard to the eastern slope of the Temple Mount. This gate faced the Upper Gate mentioned above. Their route of descent was from west to east. When they entered the Temple, they ascended from east to west (*Rashi* 51b).

הָפְכוּ פְּנֵיהֶן לַמַּעֲרָב — *They turned to the west,* i.e., the entire group [which was about to exit] turned toward the Temple Courtyard and the more sanctified portions of the Temple (*Rashi* 51b; *Rav*).

וְאָמְרוּ: אֲבוֹתֵינוּ שֶׁהָיוּ בַּמָּקוֹם הַזֶּה — *And said, 'Our forefathers who were in this place.'* Some of the Jews at the end of the First Temple era were sun worshipers (see *Ezekiel* 8:16) and would deliberately turn their backs to the Temple in an obscene gesture of derision (see *Yoma* 77a) while bowing down eastward toward the rising sun (*Rashi* 51b).

וְאָנוּ לְיָה עֵינֵינוּ — *But as for us — our eyes are toward YAH.* In the First Temple period the sin of idol worship was prevalent, but in the Second Temple period this temptation was removed. [So they could truly state, 'Our eyes are toward God'] (*Yoma* 9b).

5. אֵין פּוֹחֲתִין מֵעֶשְׂרִים וְאַחַת תְּקִיעוֹת בַּמִּקְדָּשׁ — *They make no fewer than twenty-one trumpet blasts in the Temple.* Every sounding of the trumpet was a set of three blasts — a *tekiah,* a *teruah* and another *tekiah.* On any given day in the Temple, a minimum of twenty-one blasts was sounded in the Temple, and on specific occasions there were as many as forty-eight. The mishnah proceeds to explain.

וְתֵשַׁע לְתָמִיד שֶׁל שַׁחַר — *Nine for the morning tamid-offering.* Each morning when they poured the wine libation as part of the morning *tamid-*offering, the Levites would chant the Song of the Day. This daily psalm was divided into three parts. Before each part, the Kohanim sounded a *tekiah-teruah-tekiah* on their trumpets and the people bowed, for a total of nine blasts (*Tamid* 7:3; *Rashi* 53b; *Rav*).

הָיוּ מוֹסִיפִין עוֹד תֵּשַׁע — *They added another nine.* Consequently, on a day when there was a *mussaf* offering, the sum total of blasts was thirty: the daily twenty-one plus the additional nine.

The Gemara (55a) concludes that even when there is more than one additional offering (e.g., when a festival falls on the Sabbath — one for the festival and one for the Sabbath), they blew only nine blasts for all of them.

עוֹד שֵׁשׁ — *Another six.* Thus on most Fridays there would be twenty-seven blasts: the daily

---

בֵּין קֹדֶשׁ לְחֹל. עֶרֶב שַׁבָּת שֶׁבְּתוֹךְ הֶחָג, הָיוּ שָׁם אַרְבָּעִים וּשְׁמוֹנָה: שָׁלֹשׁ
לִפְתִיחַת שְׁעָרִים; שָׁלֹשׁ לְשַׁעַר הָעֶלְיוֹן, וְשָׁלֹשׁ לְשַׁעַר הַתַּחְתּוֹן; וְשָׁלֹשׁ
לְמִלּוּי הַמַּיִם; וְשָׁלֹשׁ עַל־גַּבֵּי מִזְבֵּחַ; תֵּשַׁע לַתָּמִיד שֶׁל שַׁחַר; וְתֵשַׁע
לַתָּמִיד שֶׁל בֵּין הָעַרְבַּיִם; וְתֵשַׁע לַמּוּסָפִין; שָׁלֹשׁ לְהַבְטִיל אֶת־הָעָם
מִן־הַמְּלָאכָה; וְשָׁלֹשׁ לְהַבְדִּיל בֵּין קֹדֶשׁ לְחֹל.

[ו] יוֹם טוֹב הָרִאשׁוֹן שֶׁל חַג הָיוּ שָׁם שְׁלֹשָׁה עָשָׂר פָּרִים, וְאֵילִים שְׁנַיִם,
וְשָׂעִיר אֶחָד; נִשְׁתַּיְּרוּ שָׁם אַרְבָּעָה עָשָׂר כְּבָשִׂים לִשְׁמוֹנָה מִשְׁמָרוֹת.
בַּיּוֹם הָרִאשׁוֹן שִׁשָּׁה מַקְרִיבִין שְׁנַיִם שְׁנַיִם, וְהַשְּׁאָר אֶחָד אֶחָד. בַּשֵּׁנִי
חֲמִשָּׁה מַקְרִיבִין שְׁנַיִם שְׁנַיִם, וְהַשְּׁאָר אֶחָד אֶחָד. בַּשְּׁלִישִׁי אַרְבָּעָה מַקְרִיבִין
שְׁנַיִם שְׁנַיִם, וְהַשְּׁאָר אֶחָד אֶחָד. בָּרְבִיעִי שְׁלֹשָׁה מַקְרִיבִין שְׁנַיִם שְׁנַיִם,
וְהַשְּׁאָר אֶחָד אֶחָד. בַּחֲמִישִׁי שְׁנַיִם מַקְרִיבִין שְׁנַיִם שְׁנַיִם, וְהַשְּׁאָר אֶחָד
אֶחָד. בַּשִּׁשִּׁי אֶחָד מַקְרִיב שְׁנַיִם, וְהַשְּׁאָר, אֶחָד אֶחָד. בַּשְּׁבִיעִי כֻּלָּן שָׁוִין.
בַּשְּׁמִינִי חָזְרוּ לְפַיִס כָּבָּרְגָלִים. אָמְרוּ: ,,מִי שֶׁהִקְרִיב פָּרִים הַיּוֹם לֹא יַקְרִיב
לְמָחָר;" אֶלָּא חוֹזְרִין חֲלִילָה.

[ז] בִּשְׁלֹשָׁה פְרָקִים בַּשָּׁנָה הָיוּ כָל־מִשְׁמָרוֹת שָׁווֹת בְּאֵמוּרֵי הָרְגָלִים
וּבְחִלּוּק לֶחֶם הַפָּנִים. בָּעֲצֶרֶת אוֹמְרִים לוֹ: ,,הֵילָךְ מַצָּה; הֵילָךְ

יד אברהם

twenty-one plus the additional six. When a *mussaf* offering was brought on a Friday, e.g., on Rosh Chodesh, the total was thirty-six.

שָׁלֹשׁ לְהַבְטִיל הָעָם מִמְּלָאכָה — *Three to stop the people from work.* The first *tekiah* signaled the stoppage of all work in the fields; the second blast, a *teruah*, was a signal for all the shops to close and lock up; the third blast, a second *tekiah*, was the signal to remove all the boiling pots from the fire, to store the hot food in the oven, to seal the oven, and to light the Sabbath candles (*Shabbos* 35b).

וְשָׁלֹשׁ לְהַבְדִּיל בֵּין קֹדֶשׁ לְחֹל — *And three to distinguish between the sacred and the secular.* After pausing long enough to roast a small fish or to attach an unbaked bread to the side of an oven, they sounded a second set of *tekiah-teruah-tekiah*. This set signaled the arrival of the holy Sabbath. All work was forbidden from that moment on (*Shabbos* 35b).

וְשָׁלֹשׁ לְשַׁעַר הַתַּחְתּוֹן — *Three for the Lower Gate.* [This was the gate which led out from the Women's Courtyard to the eastern slope of the Temple Mount.] The mishnah states that the blasts were made as soon as the procession reached the floor of the Courtyard, which was before they arrived at the Lower Gate. However, they prolonged the blasts until they reached the gate of the Women's Courtyard, which was known as the Lower Gate. Because this series of blasts was stretched out until the *Kohanim* arrived at the gate, the blasts are identified with the Lower Gate (*Rashi* 53b; *Rav*).

The *Gemara* (54a) notes that the *Tanna* of this mishnah disagrees with the *Tanna* of mishnah 4 and therefore omits the three blasts which the latter said were sounded on the tenth step; the *Tanna* of that mishnah disagrees with the *Tanna* of this mishnah and therefore omits the three blasts which the latter said (below) were sounded at the Altar.

וְשָׁלֹשׁ לְמִלּוּי הַמַּיִם — *Three at the filling of the water.* After filling the gold flask with water they returned to the Temple and entered the Courtyard through the Water Gate as described in 4:9. It was at this gate that they sounded three blasts (*Rashi* 53b; *Rav*)

וְשָׁלֹשׁ עַל גַּבֵּי מִזְבֵּחַ — *Three on top of the Altar.* This took place when the willow branches were set up against the side of the Altar as described in 4:5 (*Rashi; Rav*).

6. Samuel and David divided the *Kohanim* into twenty-four watches, each of which would be in charge of the Temple service for one week after which another watch would take its place. This continued until each of the twenty-four had a turn and then the rotation would begin again (*Rambam, K'lei HaMikdash* 4:3).

On the three pilgrimage festivals of Pesach, Shavuos, and Succos, however, all the watches shared in the service of the festival *mussaf* offering (*Deut.* 18:7-8 with *Rashi*; mishnah 7; *Rambam, ibid.* 4). However, the regular daily service, as well as sacrifices offered by individuals, belonged to the *Kohanim* in whose watch the festival fell. Our mishnah explains how the

between the sacred and the secular. On the eve of the Sabbath during Succos, there were forty-eight: three for the opening of the gates; three for the Upper Gate; three for the Lower Gate; three at the filling of the water; three on top of the Altar; nine for the daily morning burnt offering; nine for the daily afternoon burnt offering; and nine for the mussaf offerings; three to stop the people from work; and three to distinguish between the sacred and the secular.

[6] *On the first festival day of Succos there were thirteen bulls, two rams, and one he-goat; there remained fourteen sheep in their first year for eight watches. On the first day six [of the watches] offered up two each, and the rest [offered] one each. On the second [day] five offered up two each, and the rest one each. On the third [day] four offered up two each, and the rest one each. On the fourth [day] three offered up two each, and the rest one each. On the fifth [day] two offered up two each, and the rest one each. On the sixth [day] one offered up two, and the rest, one each. On the seventh [day] all were equal. On the eighth [day] they reverted to [casting] lots as on the [other] festivals. [The Sages] said, 'Whoever offered up bulls today should not offer them tomorrow;' but they took turns in rotation.*

[7] *During three periods of the year all [twenty-four] watches were equal in the prescribed offerings of the Festival and in the division of the Panim Bread. On Shavuos they would say to him, 'Here is matzah for you; here*

mussaf offerings were divided among the watches on Succos.

יוֹם טוֹב הָרִאשׁוֹן שֶׁל חַג הָיוּ שָׁם שְׁלֹשָׁה עָשָׂר פָּרִים, וְאֵילִים שְׁנַיִם, וְשָׂעִיר אֶחָד — *On the first festival day of Succos there were thirteen bulls, two rams, and one he-goat.* The entire *mussaf* offering specified for the first day of Succos (*Numbers* 29:12-16) is: *And on the fifteenth day of the seventh month ... you shall offer [as] a burnt offering ... thirteen bulls, two rams, fourteen first-year sheep and one he-goat for a sin offering.* Our mishnah lists sixteen of them, which were offered by sixteen different watches, leaving fourteen first-year sheep not accounted for (*Rashi* 55b; *Rav*).

בַּיּוֹם הָרִאשׁוֹן — *On the first day.* [The eight watches divided the fourteen lambs as follows:]

בַּשֵּׁנִי — *On the second [day].* Scripture (*Num.* 29:13-32) requires one bull less on each successive day of Succos: twelve for the second day, eleven for the third day, and so on, together with the constant two rams and single he-goat. Thus on the second day there was a total of fifteen animals requiring fifteen watches. That left nine watches to offer the fourteen lambs (*Rashi* 55b; *Rav*).

כֻּלָּן שָׁוִין — *All were equal.* Since each of the remaining fourteen watches offered one lamb, every one of the twenty-four watches offered only one animal that day (*Rashi; Rav*).

חָזְרוּ לְפַיִס — *They reverted to [casting] lots.* For Shemini Atzeres the Torah (*Numbers* 29:25-38) requires one bull, one ram, one he-goat, and seven lambs to be offered. Since there were only

ten offerings that day, all twenty-four watches participated in the lots to determine which ones would bring the ten offerings (*Rashi* 55b; *Rav*).

R' Elazar said: To what do those seventy bulls offered during the seven days of Succos correspond? To the seventy nations (*Gem.* 55b). These offerings were brought on behalf of the seventy nations to atone for their sins so that they would merit proper rainfall throughout the year [cf. *Zechariah* 14:17-18]. For it is on Succos that the world is judged on the year's water supply (*Rashi*).

To what does the single bull offered on Shemini Atzeres correspond? To the unique nation [Israel]. This may be compared to a mortal king who said to his servants, 'Prepare for me a great banquet.' But on the next day he said to his favorite, 'Prepare for me a simple feast, so that I may derive pleasure from you. [I can have pleasure and satisfaction only from you (Israel) and not from them]' (*Rashi, ibid.*).

7. וּבְחִלּוּק לֶחֶם הַפָּנִים —*And in the division of the Panim Bread.* Every Sabbath, twelve fresh breads, the *Panim* Breads, were arranged on the Table in the Sanctuary (*Lev.* 24:5-9), and the previous week's breads were removed and divided between the incoming and the outgoing watches, for it was on the Sabbath that the watches would relieve each other (mishnah 8). The mishnah informs us here that on a festival Sabbath the *Panim* Bread was divided equally among all twenty-four watches.

בַּעֲצֶרֶת — *On Shavuos.* When Shavuos falls on the Sabbath (*Rashi; Rav*), all watches shared not only the *Panim* Bread, but also the שְׁתֵּי

חָמֵץ!" מִשְׁמָר שֶׁזְּמַנּוּ קָבוּעַ — הוּא מַקְרִיב תְּמִידִין, נְדָרִים, וּנְדָבוֹת,
וּשְׁאָר קָרְבְּנוֹת צִבּוּר, וּמַקְרִיב אֶת־הַכֹּל. יוֹם טוֹב הַסָּמוּךְ לַשַּׁבָּת,
בֵּין מִלְּפָנֶיהָ בֵּין לְאַחֲרֶיהָ, הָיוּ כָל־הַמִּשְׁמָרוֹת שָׁווֹת בְּחִלּוּק לֶחֶם
הַפָּנִים.

[ח] חָל לִהְיוֹת יוֹם אֶחָד לְהַפְסִיק בֵּינָתַיִם, מִשְׁמָר שֶׁזְּמַנּוּ קָבוּעַ הָיָה
נוֹטֵל עֶשֶׂר חַלּוֹת, וְהַמִּתְעַכֵּב נוֹטֵל שְׁתַּיִם. וּבִשְׁאָר יְמוֹת הַשָּׁנָה,
הַנִּכְנָס נוֹטֵל שֵׁשׁ וְהַיּוֹצֵא נוֹטֵל שֵׁשׁ. רַבִּי יְהוּדָה אוֹמֵר: הַנִּכְנָס
נוֹטֵל שֶׁבַע וְהַיּוֹצֵא נוֹטֵל חָמֵשׁ. הַנִּכְנָסִין חוֹלְקִין בַּצָּפוֹן וְהַיּוֹצְאִין
בַּדָּרוֹם. בִּלְגָּה לְעוֹלָם חוֹלֶקֶת בַּדָּרוֹם, וְטַבַּעְתָּהּ קְבוּעָה, וְחַלּוֹנָהּ
סְתוּמָה.

יד אברהם

הַלֶּחֶם, *Two Loaves*, that were brought as a special offering from the חָדָשׁ, *new wheat* that grew after Pesach (Lev. 23:16; Menachos 9:1). While the *Panim* Bread was *matzah* [unleavened], the Two Loaves were *chametz* [leavened bread] (Lev. 23:17; Menachos 5:1). Thus, on a Shavuos-Sabbath, the service included both *chametz* and *matzah* (Rambam, Comm.).

אוֹמְרִים לוֹ — *They would say to him.* Those who distributed portions from these two kinds of breads would say when they gave a *Kohen* his portions of the *Panim* Bread and the Two Loaves (Rashi; Rav).

מִשְׁמָר שֶׁזְּמַנּוּ קָבוּעַ — *The watch whose time [of service] was fixed.* The watch whose turn it was to serve in the Temple on the week of the festival brings all the offerings listed below that were not brought specifically because of the festival (Rashi; Rav)

נְדָרִים וּנְדָבוֹת — *Vow offerings, freewill offerings.* Various personal offerings were pledged during the year and brought to the Temple in fulfillment of the pledges during the festival. The watches whose turns were not fixed for this week did not share in these offerings, for they were entitled to share only in offerings that were directly connected with the festival (Rashi 55b; Rav).

A נֶדֶר, *vow offering*, is an obligation undertaken when a man vows to bring an offering without designating a specific animal. A נְדָבָה, *freewill offering*, is an obligation when a person designates a specific animal and states, 'This one is an offering,' without, however, explicitly obligating *himself* to bring an offering. Accordingly, in the case of the vow offering if the eventually chosen animal dies or is stolen, it must be replaced, because the obligation to bring an offering is a personal one and remains incumbent upon him. In the case of a freewill offering, however, if the animal

dies or is stolen, its owner is exempt from offering a different one, because his sole obligation was to offer the specifically designated animal (Kinnim 1:1).

וּשְׁאָר קָרְבְּנוֹת צִבּוּר — *The remaining public offerings.* This term includes the bull brought by each tribe in the rare instance when a majority of the entire Jewish People sinned following an erroneous ruling of the *Beis Din* which permitted a transgression whose deliberate violation would result in *kares* [spiritual excision]. If the *Beis Din* erred in permitting idol worship, then a he-goat must accompany the bull (Gem. 56a; Rambam, Shegagos 12:1; Rashi 56a; Rav).

יוֹם טוֹב הַסָּמוּךְ לַשַּׁבָּת בֵּין מִלְּפָנֶיהָ — *If a festival fell near a Sabbath, either before it.* For example, if a festival fell on Friday so that all the *Kohanim* who were not part of the regular watch could not leave for home until after the Sabbath (Gem. 56a and Rashi; Rav).

בֵּין לְאַחֲרֶיהָ — *Or after it.* If a festival fell on Sunday, all the *Kohanim* coming to serve during the festival had to arrive before the Sabbath (Gem. 56 and Rashi; Rav).

8. חָל לִהְיוֹת יוֹם אֶחָד לְהַפְסִיק בֵּינָתַיִם — *If one day intervened between them.* If the festival was to begin on Monday, many *Kohanim* would arrive on Friday instead of Sunday, and if the festival ended Thursday, many *Kohanim* would remain for the Sabbath rather than leave for home on Friday (Rashi 56a; Rav).

וְהַמִּתְעַכֵּב — *And the one that stayed behind.* Those were the *Kohanim* who came to the Temple on Friday and remained over the Sabbath, even though they could have come on Sunday, or the *Kohanim* who could have gone home on Friday but decided to stay over the Sabbath (Rashi; Rav).

וּבִשְׁאָר יְמוֹת הַשָּׁנָה — *But during the rest of the*

*is chametz for you!' The watch whose time [of service] was fixed — [only]
it offers the daily burnt offerings, vow offerings, freewill offerings, the
remaining public offerings, and [this watch] offers everything. If a festival
fell near a Sabbath, either before it or after it, all the watches shared equally
in the division of the Panim Bread.*

[8] *If one day intervened between them, the watch whose time was fixed
took ten loaves, and the one that stayed behind took two. But during the
rest of the year, the incoming [watch] took six [loaves] and the outgoing [watch]
took six. R' Yehudah says: The incoming [watch] took seven and the outgoing
[watch] took five. The incoming [watch] divided [the bread] in the north and
the outgoing [watch] in the south. [The watch of] Bilgah always divided [the
bread] in the south, its ring was permanently affixed, and its window was
sealed.*

---

year, i.e., on Sabbaths that were not festival
days.

רַבִּי יְהוּדָה אוֹמֵר: הַנִּכְנָס נוֹטֵל שֶׁבַע — *R' Yehudah
says: The incoming [watch] took seven.* The
incoming watch is entitled to seven of the
breads. The *Gemara* (56b) explains that it
receives an extra loaf because that evening it
will close the Temple gates which had been
opened that morning by the outgoing watch.
Rashi (56b s.v. בשכר) implies that those who
opened the gates in the morning should have
had the duty of completing their task by closing
them at night. Since the incoming watch closed
them, its seems as though it were doing the
work of the outgoing watch. Therefore the
outgoing watch must yield one of its loaves in
payment of this service.

הַנִּכְנָסִין חוֹלְקִין בַּצָּפוֹן — *The incoming [watch]
divided [the bread] in the north.* They divided
their loaves among themselves ... in the section
of the Courtyard north of the Altar (see *Yoma*
36a).

בִּלְגָּה — *[The watch of] Bilgah.* Because of the
following incident that brought the watch of
Bilgah into disrepute, the Sages punished it in
the three ways discussed in the mishnah below:
A woman named Miriam from the family of
Bilgah became an apostate and married a Greek
officer. When the Greeks entered the Sanctuary
during the time of Mattisyahu the son of
Yochanan, she stamped with her sandal upon
the Altar crying out, 'Lukos, Lukos, [wolf,
wolf,] how long will you consume Israel's
money and yet not stand by them in the time
of oppression!'
[*Maharsha* explains Miriam's outburst as an
allusion to the daily offerings. Wolves are
known to eat sheep, and the Altar 'ate' the two
sheep of the *tamid*-offering every day.]
When the Sages heard of this they punished
Bilgah.
Others say that the reason for the penalties
was the fact that Bilgah's watch was once tardy

in coming and so Yeshevav, one of its fellow
watches, replaced it.
The *Gemara* (56b) notes that according to the
view that the whole watch was tardy, it is
understandable that the whole watch was
penalized. But according to the view that only
one of its daughters left the fold, why was the
whole watch penalized?
Abaye explained: "The child's statement in
the marketplace is either of his father or of his
mother. Moreover, 'Woe to the wicked and woe
to his neighbor.' Thus, Miriam would not have
degraded the Altar unless she had heard her
family speak that way."

לְעוֹלָם חוֹלֶקֶת בַּדָּרוֹם — *Always divided [the
bread] in the south.* Even when it was the
incoming watch, Bilgah was required to divide
its share in the southern part of the Courtyard;
consequently, Bilgah always seemed to be
leaving the Temple (*Rabbeinu Chananel*). This
was the first fine imposed upon the Bilgah
watch.

וְטַבַּעְתָּהּ קְבוּעָה — *Its ring was permanently
affixed.* Twenty-four rings were affixed to the
floor of the Temple Courtyard where the
slaughtering was done. The rings were stapled
to the floor at one point, and were raised so that
the animal's head could be inserted in them and
locked in place during the slaughterings. The
ring assigned to Bilgah, however, was permanently stapled to the floor at two points so that
it could not be raised. This forced Bilgah to use
the ring of another watch and thus suffer
embarrassment.

וְחַלּוֹנָהּ סְתוּמָה — *And its [Bilgah's] window was
sealed.* The אוּלָם, *antechamber*, of the Temple
was thirty cubits wider than the Temple proper,
and there were rooms at its northern and
southern extremities. These were called בֵּית
הַחֲלִיפוֹת, *the knife room(s).* Each of the watches
had a window through which it would deposit
its knives in the room. Bilgah's window was
permanently sealed (*Rav; Rashi;* see *Meiri*).

❦ קֹהֶלֶת ❧

Koheles is read before the Torah reading on the Sabbath of Chol HaMoed.
In the event there is no Sabbath during Chol HaMoed, it is read on Shemini Atzeres.

פרק א

א דִּבְרֵי קֹהֶלֶת בֶּן־דָּוִד מֶלֶךְ בִּירוּשָׁלָ͏ִם: ב הֲבֵל הֲבָלִים אָמַר קֹהֶלֶת הֲבֵל הֲבָלִים הַכֹּל הָבֶל: ג מַה־יִּתְרוֹן לָאָדָם בְּכָל־עֲמָלוֹ שֶׁיַּעֲמֹל תַּחַת הַשָּׁמֶשׁ: ד דּוֹר הֹלֵךְ וְדוֹר בָּא וְהָאָרֶץ לְעוֹלָם עֹמָדֶת: ה וְזָרַח הַשֶּׁמֶשׁ וּבָא הַשָּׁמֶשׁ וְאֶל־מְקוֹמוֹ שׁוֹאֵף זוֹרֵחַ הוּא שָׁם: ו הוֹלֵךְ אֶל־דָּרוֹם וְסוֹבֵב אֶל־צָפוֹן סוֹבֵב ׀ סֹבֵב הוֹלֵךְ הָרוּחַ וְעַל־סְבִיבֹתָיו שָׁב הָרוּחַ: ז כָּל־הַנְּחָלִים הֹלְכִים אֶל־הַיָּם וְהַיָּם אֵינֶנּוּ מָלֵא אֶל־מְקוֹם שֶׁהַנְּחָלִים הֹלְכִים שָׁם הֵם שָׁבִים לָלָכֶת: ח כָּל־הַדְּבָרִים יְגֵעִים לֹא־יוּכַל אִישׁ לְדַבֵּר לֹא־תִשְׂבַּע עַיִן לִרְאוֹת וְלֹא־תִמָּלֵא אֹזֶן מִשְּׁמֹעַ: ט מַה־שֶּׁהָיָה הוּא שֶׁיִּהְיֶה וּמַה־

◆§ Koheles on Succos

Succos is זְמַן שִׂמְחָתֵנוּ, *the time of our gladness.* In *Eretz Yisrael,* the harvest is complete. For everyone, the stressful period of the Days of Awe is over and we prepare to celebrate and express our gratitude for God's blessing, bounty, and protection. Unfortunately, unrestrained joy does not bring out the best in people. We may forget ourselves and fail to live up to our responsibilities as servants of God. To help us retain our perspectives during this season of happiness, major segments of the Jewish people have adopted the custom of reading the sobering Book of *Koheles.* Thinking people cannot be carried away to excess frivolity after listening carefully to Solomon, the wisest of men, proclaiming, 'Futility of futilities! All is futile!'

Indeed, *Avudraham* writes that Solomon first proclaimed *Koheles* to the Jewish people during Succos, precisely to serve as an antidote to the danger of light-headedness on Succos.

According to *Ramban (Sermon on Koheles),* the book has three main themes: 1. Man should not strive after the pleasures of this world, because — for all their allures — they are fleeting and without value. 2. Man's spiritual essence is eternal and he has a vital role in God's master plan. 3. Human intelligence cannot comprehend God's ways or assimilate all the situations and calculations upon which His justice is based. Only when the Messiah leads the world to perfection will we know why the righteous seem to suffer while the wicked seem to prosper.

Seen this way, *Koheles* hardly dampens the festivity of Succos; rather, it deepens our enjoyment of the festival because it helps us focus on what our goals in life should be. And, as in many areas, a clear knowledge of one's goal is half the job of getting there.

CHAPTER ONE

1. The *Talmud* notes that King Hezekiah and his colleagues committed themselves to writing the Books of *Isaiah, Proverbs, Song of Songs,* and *Koheles (Bava Basra* 15a).

Seder Olam Rabba [by the *Tanna,* Rabbi Yose ben Chalafta, student of Rabbi Akiva] mentions that: 'in Solomon's old age — shortly before his death — the Divine Spirit rested upon him and he "uttered" the three Books: *Proverbs, Song of Songs,* and *Koheles.*'

The Sages of the *Mishnah (Shabbos* 30b) considered whether to conceal [לִגְנוֹ] *Koheles* because it contained *apparent* contradictions [ibid.] and *seemingly* heretical statements (*Midrash*) [i.e., expressions which ignorant people might misinterpret (*Akeidas Yitzchak*)]. They decided to canonize it as part of the Scriptures because its beginning and conclusion indisputably demonstrate that the entire book is dedicated to the fear of God and is an expression of His Word. Thus the danger of misinterpretation is mitigated. (See *Overview to ArtScroll Koheles.*)

דִּבְרֵי — *The words of.* This expression always introduces דִּבְרֵי תוֹכֵחָה, words of reproof or admonition (*Rashi*).

קֹהֶלֶת — *Koheles.* He was called by three names: Yedidyah [*II Samuel* 12:25], Koheles, and Solomon.

He was called '*Koheles*' because of the wisdom שֶׁנִּקְהֲלָה בּוֹ, 'which was assembled within him' (*Ibn Ezra*), or because שֶׁקִּיהֵל חָכְמוֹת הַרְבֵּה, 'he assembled many branches of wisdom' (*Rashi*).

מֶלֶךְ בִּירוּשָׁלָ͏ִם — *King in Jerusalem.* The city of wisdom (*Rashi*). As king of an illustrious city famed for its wise men, Koheles had ample opportunity to delve deeply into the knowledge of the world and to investigate his theories first hand (*Sforno, Metzudos David*).

2. הֲבֵל הֲבָלִים — *Futility of futilities!* [lit. 'breath of breaths'; 'vapor of vapors', i.e., something empty of substance, utterly futile].

Koheles cries that everything created during the seven days of creation is futile. The seven

---

Koheles is read before the Torah reading on the Sabbath of Chol HaMoed.
In the event there is no Sabbath during Chol HaMoed, it is read on Shemini Atzeres.

CHAPTER ONE

¹*The words of Koheles son of David, King in Jerusalem:*
² *Futility of futilities! — said Koheles — Futility of futilities! All is futile!*
³ *What profit does man have for all his labor which he toils beneath the sun?* ⁴ *A generation goes and a generation comes, but the earth endures forever.* ⁵ *And the sun rises and the sun sets — then to its place it rushes; there it rises again.* ⁶ *It goes toward the south and veers toward the north; the wind goes round and round, and on its rounds the wind returns.* ⁷ *All the rivers flow into the sea, yet the sea is not full; to the place where the rivers flow there they flow once more.*

⁸ *All words are wearying, one becomes speechless; the eye is never sated with seeing, nor the ear filled with hearing.* ⁹ *Whatever has been, is what will be, and*

---

references in this verse to הֶבֶל, *futility*, [the word הֶבֶל appears three times; and the plural הֲבָלִים, each of which connotes at least two, appears twice, making a total of seven] correspond to the seven days of creation (*Rashi; Midrash*).

All man's actions [see next verse] are futile and fruitless — unless they are motivated by lofty Torah ideals. Nothing will remain of his earthly labors; only his spiritual labor — his righteousness and Torah learning — will yield everlasting fruits (*Rabbeinu Yonah*).

3. מַה יִּתְרוֹן לָאָדָם — *What profit does man have ...?* i.e., 'what reward or gains' (*Rashi*).

The verse does not read מַה יִּתְרוֹן לָעוֹלָם, 'what profit does the *world* have?' Indeed the world *does* gain from man's physical toil; as *Rambam* notes: 'Were it not for foolish people who hoard money and who build houses to last a hundred years, the earth would never be developed!' Rather, the verse questions what real gain does *man himself* have from such labor (*Kol Yaakov*).

תַּחַת הַשָּׁמֶשׁ — *Beneath the sun.* The phrase means 'this earth where the sun shines' (*Metzudos David*).

4. וְהָאָרֶץ לְעוֹלָם עֹמָדֶת — *But the earth endures forever,* i.e., unlike man's temporary existence wherein one generation perishes and makes room for the next, the earth itself is enduring and unchanging (*Lekach Tov*).

5. וְזָרַח הַשָּׁמֶשׁ וּבָא הַשָּׁמֶשׁ — *And the sun rises and the sun sets.* Verses 5-7 elaborate on the phrase 'but the earth endures forever' by citing the daily motions of the natural world. The sun follows a monotonously regular course in order to ensure the orderly continuity of life on earth.

The Midrash perceives a deeper meaning in this phrase: Rav Berachiah said in the name of Rav Abba bar Kahana: Do we not know that the sun rises and sets! Rather the verse [using the rising and setting sun to symbolize the life-death cycle] tells us that before the 'sun' of one righteous man sets, He causes the 'sun' of another righteous man to rise. On the day Rabbi

Akiva died, Rabbi Yehudah HaNasi was born ... Before the sun of Sarah set, He caused the sun of Rebeccah to rise. Before the sun of Moses set, He caused the sun of Joshua to rise ... and so on, generation after generation. [The same thought has been applied to the birth of Rashi which coincided with the death of Rabbeinu Gershom Meor HaGolah.]

Harav Mordechai Gifter adds that this concept is fundamental in Jewish life, and was apparent in the last generation, during the Holocaust. 'Before the sun of Europe set, He caused the sun of America to rise,' for God had prepared for the continuity of Torah.

6. This verse refers allegorically to the wicked. Although their 'sun' shines and they prosper — their 'sun' will ultimately set and they will return to their stench. 'From filth they come and to filth they shall return' (*Rashi*).

7. All physical endeavors are futile. Even primal elements engage in a constant, futile path, unable to break away from their monotonous course. Since there is no lasting value to toil in this world, why should man strive aimlessly for material gain? (*Ibn Ezra*).

8. כָּל־הַדְּבָרִים יְגֵעִים — *All words are wearying.* This translation follows *Rashi* who connects this verse to verse 3. If one gives up Torah study to engage in idle talk, such topics *are wearying*, and he will be unable to attain anything. If he seeks to indulge himself visually, his eyes will not be sated; if he seeks aural gratification, his ears will never be satisfied.

One who engages in idle talk transgresses a prohibition, for it is said, *all words are wearying, man cannot* [i.e., 'ought not'] *speak.* (*Yoma 19b*).

9. מַה־שֶּׁהָיָה הוּא שֶׁיִּהְיֶה — *Whatever has been, is what will be,* etc. God's creation is perfect and complete, and lacks nothing. Whatever we see as new has already been provided for in His infinite wisdom. As part of Creation, God created the resources, conditions, and concepts for all discoveries and inventions until the end of

שֶׁנַּעֲשָׂה הוּא שֶׁיֵּעָשֶׂה וְאֵין כָּל־חָדָשׁ תַּחַת הַשָּׁמֶשׁ: י יֵשׁ דָּבָר שֶׁיֹּאמַר רְאֵה־זֶה חָדָשׁ הוּא כְּבָר הָיָה לְעֹלָמִים אֲשֶׁר הָיָה מִלְּפָנֵנוּ: יא אֵין זִכְרוֹן לָרִאשֹׁנִים וְגַם לָאַחֲרֹנִים שֶׁיִּהְיוּ לֹא־יִהְיֶה לָהֶם זִכָּרוֹן עִם שֶׁיִּהְיוּ לָאַחֲרֹנָה: יב אֲנִי קֹהֶלֶת הָיִיתִי מֶלֶךְ עַל־יִשְׂרָאֵל בִּירוּשָׁלָָם: יג וְנָתַתִּי אֶת־לִבִּי לִדְרוֹשׁ וְלָתוּר בַּחָכְמָה עַל כָּל־אֲשֶׁר נַעֲשָׂה תַּחַת הַשָּׁמָיִם הוּא ׀ עִנְיַן רָע נָתַן אֱלֹהִים לִבְנֵי הָאָדָם לַעֲנוֹת בּוֹ: יד רָאִיתִי אֶת־כָּל־הַמַּעֲשִׂים שֶׁנַּעֲשׂוּ תַּחַת הַשָּׁמֶשׁ וְהִנֵּה הַכֹּל הֶבֶל וּרְעוּת רוּחַ: טו מְעֻוָּת לֹא־יוּכַל לִתְקֹן וְחֶסְרוֹן לֹא־יוּכַל לְהִמָּנוֹת: טז דִּבַּרְתִּי אֲנִי עִם־לִבִּי לֵאמֹר אֲנִי הִנֵּה הִגְדַּלְתִּי וְהוֹסַפְתִּי חָכְמָה עַל כָּל־אֲשֶׁר־הָיָה לְפָנַי עַל־יְרוּשָׁלָָם וְלִבִּי רָאָה הַרְבֵּה חָכְמָה וָדָעַת: יז וָאֶתְּנָה לִבִּי לָדַעַת חָכְמָה וְדַעַת הֹלֵלוֹת וְשִׂכְלוּת יָדַעְתִּי שֶׁגַּם־זֶה הוּא רַעְיוֹן רוּחַ: יח כִּי בְּרֹב חָכְמָה רָב־כָּעַס וְיוֹסִיף דַּעַת יוֹסִיף מַכְאוֹב:

פרק ב

א אָמַרְתִּי אֲנִי בְּלִבִּי לְכָה־נָּא אֲנַסְּכָה בְשִׂמְחָה וּרְאֵה בְטוֹב וְהִנֵּה גַם־הוּא הָבֶל: ב לִשְׂחוֹק אָמַרְתִּי מְהוֹלָל וּלְשִׂמְחָה מַה־זֶּה עֹשָׂה: ג תַּרְתִּי בְלִבִּי לִמְשׁוֹךְ בַּיַּיִן אֶת־בְּשָׂרִי וְלִבִּי נֹהֵג בַּחָכְמָה וְלֶאֱחֹז בְּסִכְלוּת עַד אֲשֶׁר־אֶרְאֶה אֵי־זֶה טוֹב לִבְנֵי הָאָדָם אֲשֶׁר יַעֲשׂוּ תַּחַת הַשָּׁמַיִם מִסְפַּר יְמֵי חַיֵּיהֶם: ד הִגְדַּלְתִּי מַעֲשָׂי בָּנִיתִי לִי בָּתִּים נָטַעְתִּי לִי כְּרָמִים: ה עָשִׂיתִי לִי

---

time. Therefore, when any generation witnesses an unusual phenomenon and takes it as 'new', they are mistaken; it is new only to them.

11: וְגַם לָאַחֲרֹנִים שֶׁיִּהְיוּ — *So too the latter ones that are yet to be.* Those who live after us will not be remembered by the generations that succeed them (Rashi).

Therefore, whatever 'profit' [verse 3] transient man thinks he has gained from his toil beneath the sun is only of temporal value and is in reality vanity and worthless (Akeidas Yitzchak).

15. לֹא יוּכַל לִתְקֹן — *Can not be made straight.* The Rabbis [Chagigah 9a] interpret this phrase as referring to the case of one who had illicit relations and begat a mamzer. The result of his sin lives on, unlike one who steals and can always return the theft. Alternately, the verse refers to a sage who abandoned the Torah — from a good beginning he became 'crooked' (Rashi).

וְחֶסְרוֹן לֹא יוּכַל לְהִמָּנוֹת — *And what is not there cannot be numbered.* This refers to the case of one whose comrades formed a group to perform a mitzvah and he absented himself; once the mitzvah is performed he can not count himself among them to share their reward (Rashi; Berachos 26a).

18. כִּי בְּרֹב חָכְמָה רָב כָּעַס — *For with much wisdom comes much grief* [lit. 'anger']. Rashi explains that Solomon had always relied heavily

on his exceptional wisdom to protect him from sin. He was confident that his amassing of horses would *not* cause the people to return to Egypt and that his many wives would *not* lead him astray as the Torah warns [comp. *Deut.* 17:16, 17]. But in the final analysis it is recorded of him (*I Kings* 11:3) 'and his wives turned away his heart.' When one relies too much on his own wisdom and does not avoid prohibitions — *much grief comes to the Holy One blessed is He.* [Rashi thus interprets *God* as the subject of grief in this verse.]

A wise man perceives more than the ignorant man, and is more affected by it (Lekach Tov).

וְיוֹסִיף דַּעַת יוֹסִיף מַכְאוֹב — *And he who increases knowledge increases pain.* Similarly, the extra awareness caused by increased knowledge — of the futility of mankind's strivings — will only increase the wise man's pain at this realization (Metzudos David).

[Solomon is not advocating that 'ignorance is bliss.' He is acknowledging that the accumulation of רֹב חָכְמָה, *much* wisdom, is the main source of unhappiness (see verse 16). As the Kotzker Rabbi said, 'For with much wisdom comes much grief — וְאַף עַל פִּי כֵן, but nevertheless, it is still man's obligation to acquire wisdom!']

CHAPTER TWO

1. אָמַרְתִּי אֲנִי בְּלִבִּי — *I [therefore] said to myself.* Having achieved little lasting satisfaction with

whatever has been done is what will be done. There is nothing new beneath the sun! ^{10} *Sometimes there is something of which one says: 'Look, this is new!' — It has already existed in the ages before us.* ^{11} *As there is no recollection of the former ones; so too, of the latter ones that are yet to be, there will be no recollection among those of a still later time.*

^{12} *I, Koheles, was King over Israel in Jerusalem.* ^{13} *I applied my mind to seek and probe by wisdom all that happens beneath the sky — it is a sorry task that God has given to the sons of man with which to be concerned.* ^{14} *I have seen all the deeds done beneath the sun, and behold all is futile and a vexation of the spirit.* ^{15} *A twisted thing can not be made straight; and what is not there cannot be numbered.*

^{16} *I said to myself: Here I have acquired great wisdom, more than any of my predecessors over Jerusalem, and my mind has had much experience with wisdom and knowledge.* ^{17} *I applied my mind to know wisdom and to know madness and folly. I perceived that this, too, is a vexation of the spirit.* ^{18} *For with much wisdom comes much grief, and he who increases knowledge increases pain.*

CHAPTER TWO

^{1} *I said to myself: Come, I will experiment with joy and enjoy pleasure. That, too, turned out to be futile.* ^{2} *I said of laughter, 'It is mad!' And of joy, 'what does it accomplish!'*

^{3} *I ventured to stimulate my body with wine — while my heart is involved with wisdom — and to grasp folly, until I can discern which is best for mankind to do under the heavens during the brief span of their lives.* ^{4} *I acted in grand style: I built myself houses, I planted vineyards;* ^{5} *I made for myself*

his previous pursuits, Solomon seeks new areas of experimentation.

וְהִנֵּה גַם הוּא הָבֶל — *That, too, turned out to be futile.* Because I saw prophetically that much evil is caused by light-hearted frivolity (Rashi); i.e., this obsession with worldly pleasure is itself futility (Sforno; Metzudas David).

2. לִשְׂחוֹק אָמַרְתִּי מְהוֹלָל — *I said of laughter, 'It is mad!'* i.e., I said of laughter born of joy that it is madness (Metzudas David); and it does not lead to worthwhile objectives (Sforno).

The *Talmud* relates the word to מְהוֹלָל, *praiseworthy*, and translates: *I said of laughter it is praiseworthy* — this refers to the mirth with which the Holy One, Blessed is He, rejoices with the righteous in the World to Come (Shabbos 30b).

וּלְשִׂמְחָה מַה זֹה עֹשָׂה — *And of joy, 'What does it accomplish?'* Taalumos Chachmah comments that Solomon says: 'I never understood what harm could come from joy — until I indulged in it and found myself succumbing to temptations induced by light-headedness.'

The *Talmud* comments that joy is useless only if it is שִׂמְחָה שֶׁאֵינָה שֶׁל מִצְוָה, *joy not connected with a mitzvah.* This teaches that the Shechinah [Divine Presence] does not rest upon man through gloom, nor through sloth, nor through frivolity, nor through levity, nor through talk nor through vain pursuits, אֶלָּא מִתּוֹךְ דְּבַר שִׂמְחָה

שֶׁל מִצְוָה, only as a result of a matter of joy connected with a mitzvah (Shabbos 30b).

3. תַּרְתִּי בְלִבִּי — *I ventured.* [lit., 'I probed my heart' (as in 1:13 וְלָתוּר בַּחָכְמָה, 'and to probe wisdom')], i.e., I resolved to attempt to have everything: merry-making, wisdom, and folly, and to stimulate and pamper my flesh by imbibing wine (Rashi).

Having found pure wisdom a source of pain [1:18] and merriment futile [2:1], he resolves to explore a life of pleasure, yet not remain neglectful of wisdom (Ibn Ezra).

וְלֶאֱחֹז בְּסִכְלוּת — *And to grasp folly,* i.e., the commandments of God that the heathens ridiculed as 'folly,' such as the prohibition against mixtures of wool and linen, and other Divine decrees for which we are not given a reason. Comp. 7:18 (Rashi).

Metzudas David explains 'folly' in this case as referring to the externalities that entice man: fine houses, musical instruments, etc. Since they do not enter the body [i.e., the body receives no direct nourishment from them], they are called 'folly'.

4. In order to accomplish the experiment outlined in verses 1-3, Solomon not only 'lived like a king,' he even exceeded the normal self-indulgence of royalty, as the following verses relate. [He bemoans the outcome in verse 11.]

גַּנּוֹת וּפַרְדֵּסִים וְנָטַעְתִּי בָהֶם עֵץ כָּל־פֶּרִי: ו עָשִׂיתִי לִי בְּרֵכוֹת מָיִם לְהַשְׁקוֹת מֵהֶם יַעַר צוֹמֵחַ עֵצִים: ז קָנִיתִי עֲבָדִים וּשְׁפָחוֹת וּבְנֵי־בַיִת הָיָה לִי גַּם מִקְנֶה בָקָר וָצֹאן הַרְבֵּה הָיָה לִי מִכֹּל שֶׁהָיוּ לְפָנַי בִּירוּשָׁלָ͏ִם: ח כָּנַסְתִּי לִי גַּם־כֶּסֶף וְזָהָב וּסְגֻלַּת מְלָכִים וְהַמְּדִינוֹת עָשִׂיתִי לִי שָׁרִים וְשָׁרוֹת וְתַעֲנוּגוֹת בְּנֵי הָאָדָם שִׁדָּה וְשִׁדּוֹת: ט וְגָדַלְתִּי וְהוֹסַפְתִּי מִכֹּל שֶׁהָיָה לְפָנַי בִּירוּשָׁלָ͏ִם אַף חָכְמָתִי עָמְדָה לִּי: י וְכֹל אֲשֶׁר שָׁאֲלוּ עֵינַי לֹא אָצַלְתִּי מֵהֶם לֹא־מָנַעְתִּי אֶת־לִבִּי מִכָּל־שִׂמְחָה כִּי־לִבִּי שָׂמֵחַ מִכָּל־עֲמָלִי וְזֶה־הָיָה חֶלְקִי מִכָּל־עֲמָלִי: יא וּפָנִיתִי אֲנִי בְּכָל־מַעֲשַׂי שֶׁעָשׂוּ יָדַי וּבֶעָמָל שֶׁעָמַלְתִּי לַעֲשׂוֹת וְהִנֵּה הַכֹּל הֶבֶל וּרְעוּת רוּחַ וְאֵין יִתְרוֹן תַּחַת הַשָּׁמֶשׁ: יב וּפָנִיתִי אֲנִי לִרְאוֹת חָכְמָה וְהוֹלֵלוֹת וְסִכְלוּת כִּי ו מֶה הָאָדָם שֶׁיָּבוֹא אַחֲרֵי הַמֶּלֶךְ אֵת אֲשֶׁר־כְּבָר עָשׂוּהוּ: יג וְרָאִיתִי אָנִי שֶׁיֵּשׁ יִתְרוֹן לַחָכְמָה מִן־הַסִּכְלוּת כִּיתְרוֹן הָאוֹר מִן־הַחֹשֶׁךְ: יד הֶחָכָם עֵינָיו בְּרֹאשׁוֹ וְהַכְּסִיל בַּחֹשֶׁךְ הוֹלֵךְ וְיָדַעְתִּי גַם־אָנִי שֶׁמִּקְרֶה אֶחָד יִקְרֶה אֶת־כֻּלָּם: טו וְאָמַרְתִּי אֲנִי בְּלִבִּי כְּמִקְרֵה הַכְּסִיל גַּם־אֲנִי יִקְרֵנִי וְלָמָּה חָכַמְתִּי אֲנִי אָז יוֹתֵר וְדִבַּרְתִּי בְלִבִּי שֶׁגַּם־זֶה הָבֶל: טז כִּי אֵין זִכְרוֹן לֶחָכָם עִם־הַכְּסִיל לְעוֹלָם בְּשֶׁכְּבָר הַיָּמִים הַבָּאִים הַכֹּל נִשְׁכָּח וְאֵיךְ יָמוּת הֶחָכָם עִם־הַכְּסִיל: יז וְשָׂנֵאתִי אֶת־הַחַיִּים כִּי רַע עָלַי הַמַּעֲשֶׂה שֶׁנַּעֲשָׂה תַּחַת הַשָּׁמֶשׁ כִּי־הַכֹּל הֶבֶל וּרְעוּת רוּחַ: יח וְשָׂנֵאתִי אֲנִי אֶת־כָּל־עֲמָלִי שֶׁאֲנִי עָמֵל תַּחַת הַשָּׁמֶשׁ שֶׁאַנִּיחֶנּוּ לָאָדָם שֶׁיִּהְיֶה אַחֲרָי: יט וּמִי יוֹדֵעַ הֶחָכָם יִהְיֶה אוֹ סָכָל וְיִשְׁלַט בְּכָל־עֲמָלִי שֶׁעָמַלְתִּי וְשֶׁחָכַמְתִּי תַּחַת הַשָּׁמֶשׁ גַּם־זֶה הָבֶל: כ וְסַבּוֹתִי אֲנִי לְיַאֵשׁ אֶת־לִבִּי עַל כָּל־הֶעָמָל שֶׁעָמַלְתִּי תַּחַת הַשָּׁמֶשׁ: כא כִּי־יֵשׁ אָדָם שֶׁעֲמָלוֹ בְּחָכְמָה וּבְדַעַת וּבְכִשְׁרוֹן וּלְאָדָם שֶׁלֹּא עָמַל־בּוֹ יִתְּנֶנּוּ חֶלְקוֹ גַּם־זֶה הֶבֶל וְרָעָה רַבָּה: כב כִּי מֶה־הֹוֶה לָאָדָם בְּכָל־עֲמָלוֹ וּבְרַעְיוֹן לִבּוֹ שֶׁהוּא עָמֵל תַּחַת הַשָּׁמֶשׁ: כג כִּי כָל־יָמָיו מַכְאֹבִים וָכַעַס עִנְיָנוֹ גַּם־בַּלַּיְלָה לֹא־שָׁכַב לִבּוֹ גַּם־זֶה הֶבֶל הוּא:

---

10. [Determined to ensure the success of the experiment, Koheles catered to his every whim and desire, denying himself nothing.]

וְזֶה הָיָה חֶלְקִי מִכָּל עֲמָלִי — *And this was my reward for all my endeavors.* All these efforts yielded me nothing more than this (*Rashi*); i.e., this fleeting satisfaction, alone, was my only reward for all my endeavors (*Ibn Ezra*).

11. וְאֵין יִתְרוֹן תַּחַת הַשָּׁמֶשׁ — *And there is no real profit under the sun.* None of my endeavors was capable of yielding benefit *in this world beneath the sun* (*Metzudas David*). [The Mishnah in *Peah* lists good deeds for which there is some reward in This World, but in all cases the primary reward is bestowed in the World to Come.]

12. [Having realized the futility of all the above, Solomon sets out to establish whether there is an advantage to wisdom over folly and madness, and, as *Rashi* interprets, to contemplate the Torah and perceive madness and folly, i.e., the punishment of sins.]

כִּי מֶה הָאָדָם שֶׁיָּבוֹא אַחֲרֵי הַמֶּלֶךְ — *For what can man who comes after the king do?* Since God has created *folly,* how can man presume to detest it seeing that it already exists. Would, then, God have created it for naught? (*Metzudas David*).

What more could anyone hope to accomplish than the king has already done? (*Ibn Ezra*). [I.e., since the king is best equipped to institute the comparison between wisdom and folly on the basis of personal experience, there is no need for anyone to follow him and repeat the experiment.]

13. One can perceive the advantage of wisdom only by comparison with folly, just as one can

gardens and orchards and planted in them every kind of fruit tree; ⁶ I constructed pools from which to irrigate a grove of young trees; ⁷ I bought slaves — male and female — and I acquired stewards; I also owned more possessions, both cattle and sheep, than all of my predecessors in Jerusalem; ⁸ I amassed even silver and gold for myself, and the treasure of kings and the provinces; I provided myself with various musical instruments, and with every human luxury — chests and chests of them. ⁹ Thus, I grew and surpassed any of my predecessors in Jerusalem; still, my wisdom stayed with me. ¹⁰ Whatever my eyes desired I did not deny them; I did not deprive myself of any kind of joy. Indeed, my heart drew joy from all my activities, and this was my reward for all my endeavors.

¹¹ Then I looked at all the things that I had done and the energy I had expended in doing them; it was clear that it was all futile and a vexation of the spirit — and there is no real profit under the sun.

¹² Then I turned my attention to appraising wisdom with madness and folly — for what can man who comes after the king do? It has already been done. ¹³ And I perceived that wisdom excels folly as light excels darkness. ¹⁴ The wise man has his eyes in his head, whereas a fool walks in darkness. But I also realized that the same fate awaits them all. ¹⁵ So I said to myself: The fate of the fool will befall me also; to what advantage, then, have I become wise? But I concluded that this, too, was futility, ¹⁶ for there is no comparison between the remembrance of the wise man and of the fool at all, for as the succeeding days roll by, is all forgotten? How can the wise man die like the fool?

¹⁷ So I hated life, for I was depressed by all that goes on under the sun, because everything is futile and a vexation of the spirit.

¹⁸ Thus I hated all my achievements laboring under the sun, for I must leave it to the man who succeeds me. ¹⁹ — and who knows whether he will be wise or foolish? — and he will control of all my possessions for which I toiled and have shown myself wise beneath the sun. This, too, is futility. ²⁰ So I turned my heart to despair of all that I had achieved by laboring under the sun, ²¹ for there is a man who labored with wisdom, knowledge and skill, yet he must hand on his portion to one who has not toiled for it. This, too, is futility and a great evil. ²² For what has a man of all his toil and his stress in which he labors beneath the sun? ²³ For all his days are painful, and his business is a vexation; even at night his mind has no rest. This, too, is futility!

---

appreciate light only by comparison with darkness.

14. Solomon now elaborates on the factors that distinguish the sage from the fool.

בְּרֹאשׁוֹ — *In his head.* The wise man realizes that God put eyes high up on his body so he could see far and study his route well in advance. Figuratively, the wise man looks ahead to chart the proper course for himself (*Metzudas David*).

וְיָדַעְתִּי גַם אָנִי ... — *But I also realized ... them all.* Even though I praise the superiority of the wise man over the fool, nevertheless, I cannot overlook the fact that death will overtake אֶת כֻּלָּם, *them all,* i.e., the wise man and fool equally (*Rashi*).

16. The remembrance of a wise man is praised but that of the fool is degraded (*Metzudas David*) [as Solomon declared in *Proverbs* 10:7: *'The memory of the righteous is for a blessing, but the name of the wicked shall rot'*].

וְאֵיךְ יָמוּת הֶחָכָם עִם הַכְּסִיל — *How can the wise man die like the fool?* How can one even suggest that the deaths of the wise man and fool are similar! [The former's fame lives; the latter leaves nothing worth remembering.] (*Metzudas David; Alshich*)

18-23. Koheles is further distressed by the fact that even the fruits of man's strenuous *physical* efforts to accumulate wealth will ultimately go to heirs, whose prudence and wisdom are questionable.

כד אֵין־טוֹב בָּאָדָם שֶׁיֹּאכַל וְשָׁתָה וְהֶרְאָה אֶת־נַפְשׁוֹ טוֹב בַּעֲמָלוֹ גַּם־זֹה רָאִיתִי אָנִי כִּי מִיַּד הָאֱלֹהִים הִיא: כה כִּי מִי יֹאכַל וּמִי יָחוּשׁ חוּץ מִמֶּנִּי: כו כִּי לְאָדָם שֶׁטּוֹב לְפָנָיו נָתַן חָכְמָה וְדַעַת וְשִׂמְחָה וְלַחוֹטֶא נָתַן עִנְיָן לֶאֱסֹף וְלִכְנוֹס לָתֵת לְטוֹב לִפְנֵי הָאֱלֹהִים גַּם־זֶה הֶבֶל וּרְעוּת רוּחַ:

פרק ג

א לַכֹּל זְמָן וְעֵת לְכָל־חֵפֶץ תַּחַת הַשָּׁמָיִם:

עֵת לָטַעַת וְעֵת לַעֲקוֹר נָטוּעַ:	ב עֵת לָלֶדֶת וְעֵת לָמוּת
עֵת לִפְרוֹץ וְעֵת לִבְנוֹת:	ג עֵת לַהֲרוֹג וְעֵת לִרְפּוֹא
עֵת סְפוֹד וְעֵת רְקוֹד:	ד עֵת לִבְכּוֹת וְעֵת לִשְׂחוֹק
עֵת לַחֲבוֹק וְעֵת לִרְחֹק מֵחַבֵּק:	ה עֵת לְהַשְׁלִיךְ אֲבָנִים וְעֵת כְּנוֹס אֲבָנִים
עֵת לִשְׁמוֹר וְעֵת לְהַשְׁלִיךְ:	ו עֵת לְבַקֵּשׁ וְעֵת לְאַבֵּד
עֵת לַחֲשׁוֹת וְעֵת לְדַבֵּר:	ז עֵת לִקְרוֹעַ וְעֵת לִתְפּוֹר
עֵת מִלְחָמָה וְעֵת שָׁלוֹם:	ח עֵת לֶאֱהֹב וְעֵת לִשְׂנֹא

ט מַה־יִּתְרוֹן הָעוֹשֶׂה בַּאֲשֶׁר הוּא עָמֵל: י רָאִיתִי אֶת־הָעִנְיָן אֲשֶׁר נָתַן אֱלֹהִים לִבְנֵי הָאָדָם לַעֲנוֹת בּוֹ: יא אֶת־הַכֹּל עָשָׂה יָפֶה בְעִתּוֹ גַּם אֶת־הָעֹלָם נָתַן בְּלִבָּם מִבְּלִי אֲשֶׁר לֹא־יִמְצָא הָאָדָם אֶת־הַמַּעֲשֶׂה אֲשֶׁר־עָשָׂה הָאֱלֹהִים מֵרֹאשׁ וְעַד־סוֹף: יב יָדַעְתִּי כִּי אֵין טוֹב בָּם כִּי אִם־לִשְׂמוֹחַ

---

24. .... אֵין טוֹב בָּאָדָם שֶׁיֹּאכַל וְשָׁתָה — *Is it not good for man that he eats and drinks.* This translation follows *Rashi* who understands the phrase interrogatively, and according to whom the verse continues: 'and guides his soul to perform righteousness and charity with this food and drink?'

כִּי מִיַּד הָאֱלֹהִים הִיא — *That ... is from the hand of God.* I perceived that he who accumulates wealth must view himself only as its guardian, who does not have permission to dispense it without Divine sanction. [Man must act only according to the ideals of charity and justice, because his wealth is not simply the result of his labor; it is a gift of God (*Kol Yaakov*).]

25. [This verse apparently modifies the previous one: If all my property will eventually pass on to strangers, is it not right that I should view my possessions as a Divine gift and perform lofty spiritual deeds with them while I am still alive? Why should only others benefit from my wealth (next verse)? This is all part of God's Master Plan.]

26. גַּם־זֶה הֶבֶל — *That, too, is futility.* Since God will, in any event, transfer the wealth to whomever pleases Him, it is futile to strive madly for its accumulation (*Ibn Ezra*).

CHAPTER THREE

1-15. Solomon elaborates on a theme that recurs throughout the Book: '*What profit does man have for all his labor which he toils beneath the*

sun? — the sun symbolizes time which is governed by the rising and setting sun (see 1:3). Man has no power over the laws which control the world. Moreover, he cannot fathom God's scheme for the world, nor can he change the fixed order of natural phenomena. He can only live in awe of time, witnessing the endless procession of events following one another in an unbroken circle.

2. וְעֵת לָמוּת — *And a time to die.* The Midrash notes: Is then all the wisdom which Solomon uttered simply that there is '*A time to be born and a time to die?*' Rather, the meaning is: Happy is the man whose hour of death is like the hour of his birth; just as he was pure in the hour of his birth, so should he be pure in the hour of his death.

3. עֵת לַהֲרוֹג — *A time to kill.* The reference is to killing in war time (*Midrash*) or, according to some, to the legal execution of criminals (*Michlol Yofi*).

4. עֵת לִבְכּוֹת — *A time to weep.* Tishah b'Av (*Rashi*).

וְעֵת לִשְׂחוֹק — *And a time to laugh* — in the time to come [when Israel is redeemed] as it is written (*Psalms 126:2*): אָז יִמָּלֵא שְׂחוֹק פִּינוּ, *Then our mouth will be filled with laughter* (*Midrash; Lekach Tov*).

5. עֵת לְהַשְׁלִיךְ אֲבָנִים — *A time to scatter stones.* *Midrash Lekach Tov* explains this as prophetic reference to the Destruction of the Temple, and

²⁴ *Is it not good for man that he eats and drinks and shows his soul satisfaction in his labor? And even that, I perceived, is from the hand of God. —* ²⁵ *For who should eat and who should make haste except me? —* ²⁶*To the man who pleases Him He has given wisdom, knowledge and joy; but to the sinner He has given the urge to gather and amass — that he may hand it on to one who is pleasing to God. That, too, is futility and a vexation of the spirit.*

CHAPTER THREE

¹*Everything has its season, and there is a time for everything under the heaven:*
² *A time to be born*   *and a time to die;*
    a time to plant   *and a time to uproot the planted.*
³ *A time to kill*   *and a time to heal;*
    a time to wreck   *and a time to build.*
⁴ *A time to weep*   *and a time to laugh;*
    a time to wail   *and a time to dance.*
⁵ *A time to scatter stones*   *and a time to gather stones;*
    a time to embrace   *and a time to shun embraces.*
⁶ *A time to seek*   *and a time to lose;*
    a time to keep   *and a time to discard.*
⁷ *A time to rend*   *and a time to mend;*
    a time to be silent   *and a time to speak.*
⁸ *A time to love*   *and a time to hate;*
    a time for war   *and a time for peace.*
⁹ *What gain, then, has the worker by his toil?*
¹⁰ *I have observed the task which God has given the sons of man to be concerned with:* ¹¹ *He made everything beautiful in its time; He has also put an enigma into their minds so that man cannot comprehend what God has done from beginning to end.*
¹² *Thus I perceived that there is nothing better for them than to rejoice and do*

---

to the ultimate Rebuilding.

7. עֵת לִקְרוֹעַ — *A time to rend* — garments over the dead; וְעֵת לִתְפּוֹר, *and a time to mend* — new clothes for a wedding (*R' Saadiah Gaon*).

8. עֵת לֶאֱהֹב וְעֵת לִשְׂנֹא — *A time to love and a time to hate.* Even *love/hate* is regulated by time (*Ibn Ezra*); one may love something today and detest that same object tomorrow (*Metzudas David*).

9. מַה יִּתְרוֹן — *What gain, then, has the worker?* Since all is governed by seasons and time — over which man has no control — what hope is there for him to retain mastery over his efforts? (*Ibn Ezra*). The *'time'* of the evildoer will come and all his ill-gotten gains will be forfeited (*Rashi*). [Solomon is not simply speaking rhetorically. Having himself amassed fortunes (2:4-11) and having concluded it was all *'futility'*, he includes his *personal* experiences in this query.]

10. לַעֲנוֹת בּוֹ — *To be concerned with.* [See 1:3.] *Sforno* translates: 'to be afflicted with': I perceive that God caused man to toil in order to keep him subservient lest he rebel against Him, as did Adam.

11. גַּם אֶת־הָעֹלָם נָתַן בְּלִבָּם — *He has also put an enigma into their minds.* This translation follows *Rashi*: Although God instilled worldly wisdom into the hearts of man, He did not instill all wisdom into all men. Rather, He dispensed small amounts to each person so no one would grasp fully the workings of God, or foresee the future. This is to ensure that, not knowing when they will die or what would befall them, people will indulge in repentance.

Therefore, continues Rashi: הָעֹלָם is spelled without a *vav*, so the word can be read as meaning הֶעְלֵם, *hidden*, for if man knew that his day of death was near, he would neither build a house nor plant a vineyard. Thus Solomon exclaims that 'it is a good thing that . . . God has kept things hidden from man.'

מֵרֹאשׁ וְעַד־סוֹף — *From beginning to end*, i.e., the full plan and purpose of God.

12. בָּם — *For them*, i.e., for mankind. 'Since [as mentioned in the previous verse] people's "time of remembrance" [i.e., day of death] is hidden, there is nothing better for them than to rejoice in their lot and do what is right in God's eyes while they are yet alive' (*Rashi*).

וְלַעֲשׂוֹת טוֹב בְּחַיָּיו: יג וְגַם כָּל־הָאָדָם שֶׁיֹּאכַל וְשָׁתָה וְרָאָה טוֹב
בְּכָל־עֲמָלוֹ מַתַּת אֱלֹהִים הִיא: יד יָדַעְתִּי כִּי כָּל־אֲשֶׁר יַעֲשֶׂה הָאֱלֹהִים
הוּא יִהְיֶה לְעוֹלָם עָלָיו אֵין לְהוֹסִיף וּמִמֶּנּוּ אֵין לִגְרֹעַ וְהָאֱלֹהִים עָשָׂה
שֶׁיִּרְאוּ מִלְּפָנָיו: טו מַה־שֶּׁהָיָה כְּבָר הוּא וַאֲשֶׁר לִהְיוֹת כְּבָר הָיָה וְהָאֱלֹהִים
יְבַקֵּשׁ אֶת־נִרְדָּף: טז וְעוֹד רָאִיתִי תַּחַת הַשָּׁמֶשׁ מְקוֹם הַמִּשְׁפָּט שָׁמָּה
הָרֶשַׁע וּמְקוֹם הַצֶּדֶק שָׁמָּה הָרָשַׁע: יז אָמַרְתִּי אֲנִי בְּלִבִּי אֶת־הַצַּדִּיק
וְאֶת־הָרָשָׁע יִשְׁפֹּט הָאֱלֹהִים כִּי־עֵת לְכָל־חֵפֶץ וְעַל כָּל־הַמַּעֲשֶׂה שָׁם:
יח אָמַרְתִּי אֲנִי בְּלִבִּי עַל־דִּבְרַת בְּנֵי הָאָדָם לְבָרָם הָאֱלֹהִים וְלִרְאוֹת
שְׁהֶם־בְּהֵמָה הֵמָּה לָהֶם: יט כִּי מִקְרֶה בְנֵי־הָאָדָם וּמִקְרֶה הַבְּהֵמָה וּמִקְרֶה
אֶחָד לָהֶם כְּמוֹת זֶה כֵּן מוֹת זֶה וְרוּחַ אֶחָד לַכֹּל וּמוֹתַר הָאָדָם מִן־הַבְּהֵמָה
אָיִן כִּי הַכֹּל הָבֶל: כ הַכֹּל הוֹלֵךְ אֶל־מָקוֹם אֶחָד הַכֹּל הָיָה מִן־הֶעָפָר וְהַכֹּל
שָׁב אֶל־הֶעָפָר: כא מִי יוֹדֵעַ רוּחַ בְּנֵי הָאָדָם הָעֹלָה הִיא לְמָעְלָה וְרוּחַ
הַבְּהֵמָה הַיֹּרֶדֶת הִיא לְמַטָּה לָאָרֶץ: כב וְרָאִיתִי כִּי אֵין טוֹב מֵאֲשֶׁר יִשְׂמַח
הָאָדָם בְּמַעֲשָׂיו כִּי־הוּא חֶלְקוֹ כִּי מִי יְבִיאֶנּוּ לִרְאוֹת בְּמֶה שֶׁיִּהְיֶה אַחֲרָיו:

פרק ד

א וְשַׁבְתִּי אֲנִי וָאֶרְאֶה אֶת־כָּל־הָעֲשֻׁקִים אֲשֶׁר נַעֲשִׂים תַּחַת הַשָּׁמֶשׁ וְהִנֵּה
וְדִמְעַת הָעֲשֻׁקִים וְאֵין לָהֶם מְנַחֵם וּמִיַּד עֹשְׁקֵיהֶם כֹּחַ וְאֵין לָהֶם מְנַחֵם:
ב וְשַׁבֵּחַ אֲנִי אֶת־הַמֵּתִים שֶׁכְּבָר מֵתוּ מִן־הַחַיִּים אֲשֶׁר הֵמָּה חַיִּים עֲדֶנָה:
ג וְטוֹב מִשְּׁנֵיהֶם אֵת אֲשֶׁר־עֲדֶן לֹא הָיָה אֲשֶׁר לֹא־רָאָה אֶת־הַמַּעֲשֶׂה
הָרָע אֲשֶׁר נַעֲשָׂה תַּחַת הַשָּׁמֶשׁ: ד וְרָאִיתִי אֲנִי אֶת־כָּל־עָמָל וְאֵת
כָּל־כִּשְׁרוֹן הַמַּעֲשֶׂה כִּי הִיא קִנְאַת־אִישׁ מֵרֵעֵהוּ גַּם־זֶה הֶבֶל וּרְעוּת רוּחַ:

In this connection, R' David Feinstein points
out that Jeremiah [9:22-23] prophesies that man
should not praise himself for wisdom, strength,
or wealth; but only for understanding and
knowing God. This means that man's intelligence, strength, or wealth — which are unearned
gifts of God — are not praiseworthy. Only for
harnessing his ability and resources and turning
them toward knowledge of God — achievements that he has *earned* — man is rightly
praised.

14. Unlike man's actions, which are transient
and vain, God's creation is eternal, except for
those changes He purposely made to instill His
fear in man.

15. מַה־שֶּׁהָיָה כְּבָר הוּא — *What has been, already
exists*, i.e., history repeats itself.

וְהָאֱלֹהִים יְבַקֵּשׁ אֶת־נִרְדָּף — *And God always
seeks* [i.e., to be on the side of] *the pursued*, and
to exact retribution from the pursuer. Therefore,
of what benefit are the evil ways in which one
toils? Ultimately man will be held to account for
his deeds (*Rashi*).

16-22. [Koheles now enters into a discussion on

corruption in the administration of justice,
eventual Divine retribution against the wicked,
and the seeming similarity between man and
beast.]

מְקוֹם הַמִּשְׁפָּט שָׁמָּה הָרֶשַׁע — *In the place of justice
there is wickedness.* In the courts of law one
expects to find justice; instead he finds injustice
and perversion (*Alshich; Ibn Yachya*).

17. וְעַל כָּל־הַמַּעֲשֶׂה — *And for every deed* — that
man does on this world, שָׁם, *there*, will he be
judged (*Ibn Yachya*).

Akeidas Yitzchak discusses the question of
why, if certain evil acts are pre-ordained, man is
punished for committing them, when, in effect,
the perpetrator is merely carrying out God's will.
He cites the example of the Egyptians who were
punished for enslaving the Jews although it was
the Jews' lot to be enslaved. He concludes that
God reckons retribution *for every deed* because
human beings possess free will. Neither the
Egyptians nor other evildoers were motivated by
the knowledge that they were carrying out
God's will. The Divine plan had no effect on
their actions; they committed evil because they
wanted to.

good in his life. [13] Indeed every man who eats and drinks and finds satisfaction in all his labor — it is a gift of God.

[14] I realized that whatever God does will endure forever: Nothing can be added to it and nothing can be subtracted from it, and God has acted so that [man] should stand in awe of Him. [15] What has been, already exists, and what is still to be, has already been, and God always seeks the pursued.

[16] Furthermore, I have observed beneath the sun: In the place of justice there is wickedness, and in the place of righteousness there is wickedness. [17] I mused: God will judge the righteous and the wicked, for there is a time for everything and for every deed, there.

[18] Then I said to myself concerning men: 'God has chosen them out, but only to see that they themselves are as beasts.' [19] For the fate of men and the fate of beast — they have one and the same fate: as one dies, so dies the other, and they all have the same spirit. Man has no superiority over beast, for all is futile. [20] All go to the same place; all originate from dust and all return to dust. [21] Who perceives that the spirit of man is the one that ascends on high while the spirit of the beast is the one that descends down into the earth? [22] I therefore observed that there is nothing better for man than to be happy in what he is doing, for that is his lot. For who can enable him to see what will be after him?

CHAPTER FOUR

[1] I returned and contemplated all the acts of oppression that are committed beneath the sun: Behold! Tears of the oppressed with none to comfort them, and their oppressors have the power — with none to comfort them. [2] So I consider more fortunate the dead who have already died, than the living who are still alive; [3] but better than either of them is he who has not yet been, and has never witnessed the evil that is committed beneath the sun.

[4] And I saw that all labor and all skillful enterprise spring from man's rivalry with his neighbor. This, too, is futility and a vexation of the spirit!

---

18. שֶׁהֶם־בְּהֵמָה הֵמָּה לָהֶם — *That they themselves are as beasts.* [This is the general sense of this ambiguous phrase (lit., 'they are a beast, they are to them'). The translation, rendering כִּבְהֵמָה as beasts, follows *Targum* and most commentators. The sense of the verse is clear. Although men are vain about their supposed superiority, God has selected the most eminent among them to demonstrate that they are not superior at all, that even kings and officers are as selfish and short sighted as any other animal or beast.]

19. כִּי הַכֹּל הָבֶל — *For all is futile,* i.e., mankind perceives no difference between man and beast; or that the sin of Man has caused him to share the same physical death as the beast.

21. מִי יוֹדֵעַ — *Who perceives,* i.e., who is of sufficient intellect to grasp ... (*Akeidas Yitzchak*):

R' Saadiah comments that should anyone infer from these concluding verses of the chapter that Solomon truly doubts the superiority of man over beast or spirit over pleasure, his final certainty is made clear by his statement: 'And the spirit returns to God' [12:7] and by

his pronouncement: 'But know that for all these things God will bring you into judgment' [11:9.]

הָעֹלָה הִיא לְמַעְלָה — *Is the one that ascends on high* — and, unlike the beast, must stand trial for his actions (*Rashi*).

CHAPTER FOUR

2-3. Koheles resolves, therefore, that the dead, who are no longer exposed to social injustices, are more fortunate than the living. But most fortunate of all are the unborn who were never exposed to any form of human cruelty (R' Yosef Kara).

4. Now Koheles turns to those whose toil is not motivated by criminal motives. He concludes that even though most people are basically sincere, they are impelled by competition, greed, and jealousy. These factors are themselves 'futility and a vexation of the spirit' (Ibn Latif).

כִּי הִיא קִנְאַת־אִישׁ מֵרֵעֵהוּ — *Spring from man's rivalry with his neighbor.* Everyone wants to outdo his neighbor in status, living quarters, clothing, children, food, wisdom, and reputation (Ibn Ezra).

ה הַכְּסִיל חֹבֵק אֶת־יָדָיו וְאֹכֵל אֶת־בְּשָׂרוֹ: ו טוֹב מְלֹא כַף נָחַת מִמְּלֹא חָפְנַיִם עָמָל וּרְעוּת רוּחַ: ז וְשַׁבְתִּי אֲנִי וָאֶרְאֶה הֶבֶל תַּחַת הַשָּׁמֶשׁ: ח יֵשׁ אֶחָד וְאֵין שֵׁנִי גַּם בֵּן וָאָח אֵין־לוֹ וְאֵין קֵץ לְכָל־עֲמָלוֹ גַּם־עֵינוֹ לֹא־תִשְׂבַּע עֹשֶׁר וּלְמִי l אֲנִי עָמֵל וּמְחַסֵּר אֶת־נַפְשִׁי מִטּוֹבָה גַּם־זֶה הֶבֶל וְעִנְיַן רָע הוּא: ט טוֹבִים הַשְּׁנַיִם מִן־הָאֶחָד אֲשֶׁר יֵשׁ־לָהֶם שָׂכָר טוֹב בַּעֲמָלָם: י כִּי אִם־יִפֹּלוּ הָאֶחָד יָקִים אֶת־חֲבֵרוֹ וְאִילוֹ הָאֶחָד שֶׁיִּפּוֹל וְאֵין שֵׁנִי לַהֲקִימוֹ: יא גַּם אִם־יִשְׁכְּבוּ שְׁנַיִם וְחַם לָהֶם וּלְאֶחָד אֵיךְ יֵחָם: יב וְאִם־יִתְקְפוֹ הָאֶחָד הַשְּׁנַיִם יַעַמְדוּ נֶגְדּוֹ וְהַחוּט הַמְשֻׁלָּשׁ לֹא בִמְהֵרָה יִנָּתֵק: יג טוֹב יֶלֶד מִסְכֵּן וְחָכָם מִמֶּלֶךְ זָקֵן וּכְסִיל אֲשֶׁר לֹא־יָדַע לְהִזָּהֵר עוֹד: יד כִּי־מִבֵּית הָסוּרִים יָצָא לִמְלֹךְ כִּי גַּם בְּמַלְכוּתוֹ נוֹלַד רָשׁ: טו רָאִיתִי אֶת־כָּל־הַחַיִּים הַמְהַלְּכִים תַּחַת הַשָּׁמֶשׁ עִם הַיֶּלֶד הַשֵּׁנִי אֲשֶׁר יַעֲמֹד תַּחְתָּיו: טז אֵין־קֵץ לְכָל־הָעָם לְכֹל אֲשֶׁר־הָיָה לִפְנֵיהֶם גַּם הָאַחֲרוֹנִים לֹא יִשְׂמְחוּ־בוֹ כִּי־גַם־זֶה הֶבֶל וְרַעְיוֹן רוּחַ: יז שְׁמֹר רַגְלְךָ כַּאֲשֶׁר תֵּלֵךְ אֶל־בֵּית הָאֱלֹהִים וְקָרוֹב לִשְׁמֹעַ מִתֵּת הַכְּסִילִים זָבַח כִּי־אֵינָם יוֹדְעִים לַעֲשׂוֹת רָע:

פרק ה

א אַל־תְּבַהֵל עַל־פִּיךָ וְלִבְּךָ אַל־יְמַהֵר לְהוֹצִיא דָבָר לִפְנֵי הָאֱלֹהִים כִּי הָאֱלֹהִים בַּשָּׁמַיִם וְאַתָּה עַל־הָאָרֶץ עַל־כֵּן יִהְיוּ דְבָרֶיךָ מְעַטִּים: ב כִּי בָּא הַחֲלוֹם בְּרֹב עִנְיָן וְקוֹל כְּסִיל בְּרֹב דְּבָרִים: ג כַּאֲשֶׁר תִּדֹּר נֶדֶר

---

5. הַכְּסִיל חֹבֵק אֶת־יָדָיו — *The fool folds* ['hugs'] *his hands.* The fool sits, 'with his arms folded,' and eats what is readily available (Ibn Ezra).

וְאֹכֵל אֶת בְּשָׂרוֹ — *And eats his own flesh.* He destroys himself and eventually dies of starvation (Ibn Ezra). He allegorically 'lives off his fat' (Metzudas David).

6. טוֹב מְלֹא כַף נָחַת — *Better is one handful of pleasantness.* It is better for man to earn less, but with pleasantness and quiet, than to earn more — handfuls more — through difficult labor and aggravation (Metzudas David).

8. יֵשׁ אֶחָד וְאֵין שֵׁנִי — *A lone and solitary man.* He has no heirs (Almosnino).

Rashi interprets the verse [as a reference to people in varying situations who share the same flaw: they do not bring companionship into their lives]: He is utterly alone. If he is a scholar, he seeks no student to be like a son and no friend to be like a brother; if a bachelor, he seeks no wife; if an entrepreneur, no partner. He goes his way alone.

גַּם זֶה הֶבֶל — *This, too, is futility.* The indolent 'fool' in verse 5, who folds his hands, and the miser who strives aimlessly — both are equally foolish. The proper approach is the middle path between laziness and over-aggressiveness (R' Galico; Ibn Ezra; Metzudas David).

9. In this verse, Koheles addresses the fool who toils utterly alone, and advises him of the advantages of companionship, someone with whom to toil and share (Ibn Ezra).

מִן־הָאֶחָד — *Than one.* Therefore man should find a comrade and get married (Rashi).

Two who study Torah are better than one who studies alone, for if one errs, his partner will correct him (Midrash; see also Makkos 10a). As the *Talmud* notes: 'Knowledge of Torah can be acquired only in association with others' (Berachos 63b).

10. כִּי אִם־יִפֹּלוּ — *For should they fall* — physically; or should one of them err in Torah learning or in judgment, his comrade will correct him and set him on the proper path (R' Saadiah Gaon).

11. Solomon cites another example of the benefits of association.

Alshich explains the verse in a spiritual sense: If two people fall into spiritual slumber and neglect their religious observances, their hearts will stir within them with the 'fire of God,' and each one will 'warm the heart' of his comrade to 'awaken' and serve God in the proper manner.

12. [And the final example of mutual security:] וְהַחוּט הַמְשֻׁלָּשׁ לֹא בִמְהֵרָה יִנָּתֵק — *A three-ply*

⁵ *The fool folds his hands and eats his own flesh.* ⁶ *Better is one handful of pleasantness than two fistfuls of labor and vexation of the spirit.*

⁷ *Then I returned and contemplated [another] futility beneath the sun:* ⁸ *a lone and solitary man who has neither son nor brother, yet there is no end to his toil, nor is his eye ever sated with riches, [nor does he ask himself,] 'For whom am I toiling and depriving myself of goodness.' This, too, is futility; indeed, it is a sorry task.*

⁹ *Two are better than one, for they get a greater return for their labor.* ¹⁰ *For should they fall, one can raise the other; but woe to him who is alone when he falls and there is no one to raise him!* ¹¹ *Also, if two sleep together they keep warm, but how can one be warm alone?* ¹² *Where one can be overpowered, two can resist attack: A three-ply cord is not easily severed!*

¹³ *Better is a poor but wise youth than an old and foolish king who no longer knows how to take care of himself;* ¹⁴ *because from the prison-house he emerged to reign, while even in his reign he was born poor.* ¹⁵ *I saw all the living that wander beneath the sun throng to the succeeding youth who steps into his place.* ¹⁶ *There is no end to the entire nation, to all that was before them; similarly the ones that come later will not rejoice in him. For this, too, is futility and a vexation of the spirit.*

¹⁷ *Guard your foot when you go to the House of God; better to draw near and hearken than to offer the sacrifices of fools, for they do not consider that they do evil.*

CHAPTER FIVE

¹*Be not rash with your mouth, and let not your heart be hasty to utter a word before God; for God is in heaven and you are on earth, so let your words be few.* ² *For a dream comes from much concern, and foolish talk from many words.*

---

cord is not easily severed! If the companionship of one friend yields such benefits, (above, verse 10-11) imagine the value of *two* companions! A three-ply cord is stronger than one or two plies! [as if to say: *Two are better than one; but three are better than two.*]

Rashi refers to the Talmudic dictum [*Bava Metzia* 85a]: If someone is a scholar, and his son and grandson are scholars as well, the Torah will nevermore cease from his seed [see *Isaiah* 59:21]. These three generations of scholarship are alluded to by the strength of the *three-ply cord* in our verse. Henceforth, (*Kesubos* 62b) the Torah 'seeks its home' [i.e., the family which has been its host for three generations].

13. Solomon now proceeds to extol the reign of wisdom, but concludes that it, too, is impermanent and ultimately futile.

15-16. The structure of these two verses is difficult and ambiguous, but the theme emerges: Although droves of people flocked around this new young king, he himself ultimately fell into disfavor because popularity is short lived and is itself *futility and a vexation of the spirit.*

Solomon bemoans this series of events — commonplace even in our day, as *futility and a vexation of the spirit!*

17. Having stated the main theme of his philosophy and remonstrated against the futilities of life, *Koheles* now turns to a more optimistic series of thoughts: the proper path a man should take in this world. In the following verses he exhorts man to serve God with dignity and respect — even in such commonplace acts as walking and talking. He begins with prayer, man's most intimate form of communication with God, and concludes that hearkening to God's Word is preferable to insincere sacrifice.

CHAPTER FIVE

1. לְהוֹצִיא דָבָר לִפְנֵי הָאֱלֹהִים — *To utter a word before God,* i.e., to speak critically of Him (*Rashi*).

כִּי הָאֱלֹהִים בַּשָׁמַיִם וְאַתָּה עַל-הָאָרֶץ — *For God is in heaven and you are on earth. Rashi* quotes the Midrash: 'If the weak one is above and the strong one below, the fear of the weak one is upon the strong one; how much more so when it is the strong One [God] Who is above and the weak one [mortal man] below [we should surely be in awe of Him and not speak rashly of Him.].'

2. כִּי בָּא הַחֲלוֹם בְּרֹב עִנְיָן — *For a dream comes from much concern.* [Solomon employs the simile of dreams to lend cogency to the earlier

לֵאלֹהִים אַל־תְּאַחֵר לְשַׁלְּמוֹ כִּי אֵין חֵפֶץ בַּכְּסִילִים אֵת אֲשֶׁר־תִּדֹּר שַׁלֵּם: ד טוֹב אֲשֶׁר לֹא־תִדֹּר מִשֶּׁתִּדּוֹר וְלֹא תְשַׁלֵּם: ה אַל־תִּתֵּן אֶת־פִּיךָ לַחֲטִיא אֶת־בְּשָׂרֶךָ וְאַל־תֹּאמַר לִפְנֵי הַמַּלְאָךְ כִּי שְׁגָגָה הִיא לָמָּה יִקְצֹף הָאֱלֹהִים עַל־קוֹלֶךָ וְחִבֵּל אֶת־מַעֲשֵׂה יָדֶיךָ: ו כִּי בְרֹב חֲלֹמוֹת וַהֲבָלִים וּדְבָרִים הַרְבֵּה כִּי אֶת־הָאֱלֹהִים יְרָא: ז אִם־עֹשֶׁק רָשׁ וְגֵזֶל מִשְׁפָּט וָצֶדֶק תִּרְאֶה בַמְּדִינָה אַל־תִּתְמַהּ עַל־הַחֵפֶץ כִּי גָבֹהַּ מֵעַל גָּבֹהַּ שֹׁמֵר וּגְבֹהִים עֲלֵיהֶם: ח וְיִתְרוֹן אֶרֶץ בַּכֹּל הִיא מֶלֶךְ לְשָׂדֶה נֶעֱבָד: ט אֹהֵב כֶּסֶף לֹא־יִשְׂבַּע כֶּסֶף וּמִי־אֹהֵב בֶּהָמוֹן לֹא תְבוּאָה גַּם־זֶה הָבֶל: י בִּרְבוֹת הַטּוֹבָה רַבּוּ אוֹכְלֶיהָ וּמַה־כִּשְׁרוֹן לִבְעָלֶיהָ כִּי אִם־רְאוּת עֵינָיו: יא מְתוּקָה שְׁנַת הָעֹבֵד אִם־מְעַט וְאִם־הַרְבֵּה יֹאכֵל וְהַשָּׂבָע לֶעָשִׁיר אֵינֶנּוּ מַנִּיחַ לוֹ לִישׁוֹן: יב יֵשׁ רָעָה חוֹלָה רָאִיתִי תַּחַת הַשָּׁמֶשׁ עֹשֶׁר שָׁמוּר לִבְעָלָיו לְרָעָתוֹ: יג וְאָבַד הָעֹשֶׁר הַהוּא בְּעִנְיַן רָע וְהוֹלִיד בֵּן וְאֵין בְּיָדוֹ מְאוּמָה: יד כַּאֲשֶׁר יָצָא מִבֶּטֶן אִמּוֹ עָרוֹם יָשׁוּב לָלֶכֶת כְּשֶׁבָּא וּמְאוּמָה לֹא־יִשָּׂא בַעֲמָלוֹ שֶׁיֹּלֵךְ בְּיָדוֹ:

---

exhortation against excess verbiage.] Dreams reflect an overabundance of thoughts and preoccupation during the day. Similarly, excessive chatter [often as incoherent and unrelated as in a dream (*Akeidas Yitzchak*)] betrays the fool. Therefore 'let your words be few' (*Rashi*).

3. אֲשֶׁר תִּדֹּר נֶדֶר לֵאלֹהִים — *When you make a vow to God,* to perform a righteous deed (*Metzudas David*). [Quoted almost verbatim from Deut. 23:22.]

Just as you are exhorted to guard your tongue in the House of God, and speak little, so should you exercise caution in every utterance you make before Him [as when you make vows] and not be like the fools for whom He has no use (*Ibn Ezra*).

אַל־תְּאַחֵר לְשַׁלְּמוֹ — *Do not delay paying it.* Alshich cautions that one, who made a vow to give charity as a result of being subjected to great suffering, should fulfill the vow immediately without waiting for the suffering to end. Proper belief in God dictates that the vow be discharged immediately.

4. טוֹב אֲשֶׁר לֹא־תִדֹּר — *Better that you do not vow at all.* Rav Meir said: It is preferable not to vow at all than to vow and not pay, or even to vow and pay. Rather let the man bring his lamb to the Temple [without previously making a vow to bring it], dedicate it, and then have it offered (*Midrash*).

If you don't have the money, why vow? Wait until the money is in your hand and give it then (*Ibn Yachya*).

[However, in time of trouble, it is commendable to make vows for charity, or vows to do good deeds, as we find 'and Jacob vowed a vow' (Genesis 28:20; *Tosafos, Chullin* 2b). It is also commendable to made a vow to strengthen one's resolve to perform good deeds (*Nedarim* 8a).]

מִשֶּׁתִּדּוֹר וְלֹא תְשַׁלֵּם — *Than that you vow and not pay.* [Hence the praiseworthy custom of saying בְּלִי נֶדֶר, 'without a vow.' Thereby, although the speaker still obligates himself to keep his word, he avoids the transgression of breaking a vow in the event he is unable to do so.]

5. וְאַל־תֹּאמַר לִפְנֵי הַמַּלְאָךְ — *And do not tell the messenger.* The representative of the congregation who comes to collect the proceeds of the vow (*Midrash; Rashi; Kara*).

6. . . . . כִּי בְרֹב חֲלֹמוֹת — *In spite of all dreams,* futility and idle chatter, rather: Fear God. The verse is difficult in syntax and the translation follows most commentators who counsel that one should ignore all contrary influences (dreams, vain prophets and idle chatter) and, instead, *Fear God.*

7. בַמְּדִינָה — *In the State.,* i.e., open and brazen oppression, rather than stealthy and clandestine (*Ibn Ezra*).

אַל־תִּתְמַהּ עַל־הַחֵפֶץ — *Do not be astonished at the fact* [or: 'at the will']. Do not be astonished that God *seems* to approve of this, and is 'slow' in exacting retribution (*Almosnino*).

כִּי גָבֹהַּ מֵעַל גָּבֹהַּ — *For* [have faith that:] *there is One higher than high,* i.e., God. Do not despair at the impunity and freedom from retribution with which unscrupulous wielders of power oppress the helpless. Know that the most august of all beings, God, who is *Higher than High,* sees what they do and will avenge the victims when the proper time comes (*R' Saadiah Gaon; Sforno*).

8. וְיִתְרוֹן אֶרֶץ בַּכֹּל הִיא — *The advantage of land* [i.e., of agriculture] *is supreme; even a king is indebted* [i.e., subject] *to the soil.* The phrase is obscure and the translation follows *Ibn Ezra,* who comments: Having discoursed on the fear of God, Solomon reverts to the theme of which

³ *When you make a vow to God, do not delay paying it, for He has no liking for fools; what you vow, pay.* ⁴ *Better that you do not vow at all than that you vow and not pay.* ⁵ *Let not your mouth bring guilt on your flesh, and do not tell the messenger that it was an error. Why should God be angered by your speech and destroy the work of your hands?* ⁶ *In spite of all dreams, futility and idle chatter, rather: Fear God!*

⁷ *If you see oppression of the poor, and the suppression of justice and right in the State, do not be astonished at the fact, for there is One higher than high Who watches and there are high ones above them.*

⁸ *The advantage of land is supreme; even a king is indebted to the soil.*

⁹ *A lover of money will never be satisfied with money; a lover of abundance has no wheat. This, too, is futility!* ¹⁰ *As goods increase, so do those who consume them; what advantage, then, has the owner except what his eyes see?* ¹¹ *Sweet is the sleep of the laborer, whether he eats little or much; the satiety of the rich does not let him sleep.*

¹² *There is a sickening evil which I have seen under the sun: riches hoarded by their owner to his misfortune,* ¹³ *and he loses those riches in some bad venture. If he begets a son, he has nothing in hand.* ¹⁴ *As he had come from his mother's womb, naked will he return, as he had come; he can salvage nothing*

---

occupation is best and most sin-free. Agriculture yields the most reward, for even a king is sustained by the soil . . .

And whoever tills the land, living a righteous life and providing honestly for his own sustenance, is assured a life of dignity likened to a king, who must himself by sustained by the produce of the earth. The miser in the next verse, however, loves money — rather than honest work — and steals to satisfy his lust for it. לֹא־יִשְׂבַּע כֶּסֶף — *he will never be* satisfied with money (*Alshich*).

9. אֹהֵב כֶּסֶף לֹא־יִשְׂבַּע כֶּסֶף — *A lover of money will never be satisfied with money.* Money will never still a rich man's hunger, for who can eat money? (*Akeidas Yitzchak*).

וּמִי־אֹהֵב . . . — *A lover of abundance has no wheat.* One who surrounds himself with an abundance of non-productive servants in order to impress his friends will 'have no wheat', i.e., will not be able to feed and sustain them and, what is more, he will have nothing left for himself as explained in the next verse (*Kara; Sforno*).

Rashi comments: He who loves to accumulate [inedible] money, rather than nourishing wheat, indulges in futility.

10. בִּרְבוֹת הַטּוֹבָה רַבּוּ אוֹכְלֶיהָ — *As goods increase, so do those who consume them.* A wealthier household acquires a larger stock of food and supplies and attracts more relatives, friends, and paupers. The owner sees before him a larger supply of provisions, speedily to be consumed. Thus, he is often in a worse position than he was before (*Ibn Yachya; Kara*).

11. מְתוּקָה שְׁנַת הָעֹבֵד — *Sweet is the sleep of the laborer.* This verse extols the man who is not indolent, and does not work only in order to hoard riches, but who tills the ground earnestly to support his family. Such a person has few concerns. He has no large estates or fortunes over which to worry constantly. Whether he eats little or much, he is able to sleep undisturbed by business worries (*Rav Yosef Kara*).

וְהַשָּׂבָע לֶעָשִׁיר אֵינֶנּוּ מַנִּיחַ לוֹ לִישׁוֹן — *The satiety of the rich does not let him sleep.* [Koheles does not refer to *physical* satiety; that would affect the rich and poor alike.] The reference is to the abundant *possessions* of the rich (*Ibn Ezra*): It fills him with worry and anxious cares which deprive him of his sleep (*Rashi; Lekach Tov*).

The Sages similarly expounded this concept in the *Mishnah* [*Avos* 2:7]: מַרְבֶּה נְכָסִים מַרְבֶּה דְאָגָה, *the more possessions the more worry* (*Rav Yosef Kara*).

12-13. רָעָה חוֹלָה — *A sickening evil* [i.e., an unusually grievous injustice]. This verse continues extolling the benefits of owning real property rather than hoarding money (*Ibn Ezra*).

וְהוֹלִיד בֵּן — *If he begets a son.* The further irony is that when he possessed the treasure he had no heir; only now that he is penniless is a child born (*Akeidas Yitzchak*).

14. וּמְאוּמָה לֹא־יִשָּׂא בַעֲמָלוֹ שֶׁיֹּלֵךְ בְּיָדוֹ — *He can salvage nothing from his labor to take with him.* When a person enters this world his hands are clenched as if to say: 'The whole world is mine, I shall inherit it'; but when he takes leave of the world, his hands are spread open as if to say: 'I have inherited nothing from the world' (*Midrash*).

טו וְגַם־זֹה רָעָה חוֹלָה כָּל־עֻמַּת שֶׁבָּא כֵּן יֵלֵךְ וּמַה־יִּתְרוֹן לוֹ שֶׁיַּעֲמֹל
לָרוּחַ: טז גַּם כָּל־יָמָיו בַּחֹשֶׁךְ יֹאכֵל וְכָעַס הַרְבֵּה וְחָלְיוֹ וָקָצֶף: יז הִנֵּה
אֲשֶׁר־רָאִיתִי אָנִי טוֹב אֲשֶׁר־יָפֶה לֶאֱכוֹל־וְלִשְׁתּוֹת וְלִרְאוֹת טוֹבָה
בְּכָל־עֲמָלוֹ | שֶׁיַּעֲמֹל תַּחַת־הַשֶּׁמֶשׁ מִסְפַּר יְמֵי־חַיָּו אֲשֶׁר־נָתַן־לוֹ
הָאֱלֹהִים כִּי־הוּא חֶלְקוֹ: יח גַּם כָּל־הָאָדָם אֲשֶׁר נָתַן־לוֹ הָאֱלֹהִים עֹשֶׁר
וּנְכָסִים וְהִשְׁלִיטוֹ לֶאֱכֹל מִמֶּנּוּ וְלָשֵׂאת אֶת־חֶלְקוֹ וְלִשְׂמֹחַ בַּעֲמָלוֹ זֹה
מַתַּת אֱלֹהִים הִיא: יט כִּי לֹא הַרְבֵּה יִזְכֹּר אֶת־יְמֵי חַיָּו כִּי הָאֱלֹהִים מַעֲנֶה
בְּשִׂמְחַת לִבּוֹ:

פרק ו

א יֵשׁ רָעָה אֲשֶׁר רָאִיתִי תַּחַת הַשָּׁמֶשׁ וְרַבָּה הִיא עַל־הָאָדָם: ב אִישׁ
אֲשֶׁר יִתֶּן־לוֹ הָאֱלֹהִים עֹשֶׁר וּנְכָסִים וְכָבוֹד וְאֵינֶנּוּ חָסֵר לְנַפְשׁוֹ | מִכֹּל
אֲשֶׁר־יִתְאַוֶּה וְלֹא־יַשְׁלִיטֶנּוּ הָאֱלֹהִים לֶאֱכֹל מִמֶּנּוּ כִּי אִישׁ נָכְרִי
יֹאכְלֶנּוּ זֶה הֶבֶל וָחֳלִי רָע הוּא: ג אִם־יוֹלִיד אִישׁ מֵאָה וְשָׁנִים רַבּוֹת יִחְיֶה
וְרַב | שֶׁיִּהְיוּ יְמֵי־שָׁנָיו וְנַפְשׁוֹ לֹא־תִשְׂבַּע מִן־הַטּוֹבָה וְגַם־קְבוּרָה
לֹא־הָיְתָה לּוֹ אָמַרְתִּי טוֹב מִמֶּנּוּ הַנָּפֶל: ד כִּי־בַהֶבֶל בָּא וּבַחֹשֶׁךְ יֵלֵךְ
וּבַחֹשֶׁךְ שְׁמוֹ יְכֻסֶּה: ה גַּם־שֶׁמֶשׁ לֹא־רָאָה וְלֹא יָדָע נַחַת לָזֶה מִזֶּה:
ו וְאִלּוּ חָיָה אֶלֶף שָׁנִים פַּעֲמַיִם וְטוֹבָה לֹא רָאָה הֲלֹא אֶל־מָקוֹם אֶחָד
הַכֹּל הוֹלֵךְ: ז כָּל־עֲמַל הָאָדָם לְפִיהוּ וְגַם־הַנֶּפֶשׁ לֹא תִמָּלֵא: ח כִּי
מַה־יּוֹתֵר לֶחָכָם מִן־הַכְּסִיל מַה־לֶּעָנִי יוֹדֵעַ לַהֲלֹךְ נֶגֶד הַחַיִּים:
ט טוֹב מַרְאֵה עֵינַיִם מֵהֲלָךְ־נָפֶשׁ גַּם־זֶה הֶבֶל וּרְעוּת רוּחַ: י מַה־שֶּׁהָיָה

---

16. גַּם כָּל־יָמָיו בַּחֹשֶׁךְ יֹאכֵל — *Indeed, all his life he eats in darkness.* Being obsessively overcome with accumulating riches, he sits down to eat only at night. He thus lives a life of rigorous self-denial, fear of robbery, and exposes himself to many trying experiences (*Ibn Ezra; Akeidas Yitzchak*).

17-18. These two verses are essentially a restatement of the conclusion Solomon reached in earlier discourses: (2:24; 3:12,22) Since man must depart exactly as he came, I concluded that financial pursuits are worthless. Let man rather involve himself in Torah pursuits (*Rashi*), and let him eat of God's bounty and be content (*Ibn Yachya; Ibn Ezra*).

לֶאֱכוֹל וְלִשְׁתּוֹת — *To eat and drink.* Note the *Midrash:* All the eating and drinking mentioned in this Book refers to Torah and good deeds. The most clear proof is in 8:15. Do, then, food and drink accompany men to the grave? What does accompany him? Torah and good deeds.

כִּי־הוּא חֶלְקוֹ — *For that is his lot.* God bequeathed these few pleasures to man, so it is only proper that man harness them and, by utilizing them for the proper spiritual goals, lift himself up to the greater service of God (*Almosnino*).

נָתַן לוֹ הָאֱלֹהִים עֹשֶׁר וּנְכָסִים — *To whom God has given riches and possessions.* 'Why should God give you more than you need unless He intended to make you the administrator of this blessing for others; the treasurer of His treasures? Every penny you can spare is not yours, but should become a tool for bringing blessing to others. Would you close your hand on something that is not yours?' (Rabbi S. R. Hirsch, *Horeb*).

CHAPTER SIX

1. Solomon now bemoans those who have wealth, but whom God has denied the opportunity of enjoying it. In contrast to 5:12-14, which speaks of a man who begat children but lost his wealth, here the verse describes a man who has everything but is prevented by circumstances from enjoying it.

2. לֶאֱכֹל מִמֶּנּוּ — *The power to enjoy it.* Instead, He instilled in him miserly tendencies (*Metzudas David*) [in contrast to 5:18].

3. According to most commentators, this verse introduces a new case in distinction to the previous one of a childless person whom 'a stranger will inherit.' Here Solomon describes the futility of someone blessed with a large family, longevity and every opportunity to

from his labor to take with him. ¹⁵*This, too, is a sickening evil: Exactly as he came he must depart, and what did he gain by toiling for the wind?* ¹⁶ *Indeed, all his life he eats in darkness; he is greatly grieved, and has illness and anger.*

¹⁷ *So what I have seen to be good is that it is suitable to eat and drink and enjoy pleasure with all one's labor that he toils beneath the sun during the brief span of his life that God has given him, for that is his lot.* ¹⁸ *Furthermore, every man to whom God has given riches and possessions and has given him the power to enjoy them, possess his share and be happy in his work: this is the gift of God.* ¹⁹ *For he shall remember that the days of his life are not many, while God provides him with the joy of his heart.*

CHAPTER SIX

¹*There is an evil I have observed beneath the sun, and it is prevalent among mankind:* ² *a man to whom God has given riches, wealth and honor, and he lacks nothing that the heart could desire, yet God did not give him the power to enjoy it; instead, a stranger will enjoy it. This is futility and an evil disease.* ³ *If a man begets a hundred children and lives many years — great being the days of his life — and his soul is not content with the good — and he even is deprived of burial; I say: the stillborn is better off than he.* ⁴ *Though its coming is futile and it departs in darkness, though its very name is enveloped in darkness,* ⁵ *though it never saw the sun nor knew it; it has more satisfaction than he.* ⁶ *Even if he should live a thousand years twice over, but find no contentment — do not all go to the same place?*

⁷ *All man's toil is for his mouth, yet his wants are never satisfied.* ⁸ *What advantage, then, has the wise man over the fool? What [less] has the pauper who knows how to conduct himself among the living?* ⁹ *Better is what the eyes see than what is imagined. That, too, is futility and a vexation of the spirit.*

---

enjoy goodness. But he lacks the capacity to derive joy from his blessings, and ultimately dies without even proper burial. A stillborn, declares Solomon, is better than he.

5. נַחַת לָזֶה מִזֶּה — *It has more satisfaction than he.* The stillborn does not anguish over what he never had, unlike the wealthy man who *'begat a hundred children, etc.'* but now grieves because everything was taken from him (*Metzudas David*).

6. [The subject of this verse is again the rich man described in verse 3.] Even if he lives to two thousand years, of what benefit is this longevity to him since וְטוֹבָה לֹא רָאָה, *'he found no contentment'?* Ultimately he will return to the dust, just like all paupers! (*Rashi*).

7-9. Man labors incessantly to satisfy his cravings, which, alas, remain unappeased. What, then, is the advantage of wisdom, especially when, despite intelligence and ability, one remains poor? It is of no advantage. It is better that we should enjoy the little we have than the futile quest of unsatisfied longing.

8. מַה־יּוֹתֵר לֶחָכָם — *What advantage then has the wise man* from his wisdom, מִן הַכְּסִיל — *over* what he would have if he were a fool? (*Rashi*). [A rhetorical question. There is no advantage to

the wise. Both must toil for what they achieve. The difference lies in how the fruits of the labor are utilized and appreciated.]

מַה לֶּעָנִי יוֹדֵעַ לַהֲלֹךְ נֶגֶד הַחַיִּים — *What [less] has the pauper who knows how to conduct himself among the living?* A difficult phrase, the translation of which follows *Rashi, Kara, Ibn Ezra:* how is a pauper, who has the intelligence to get along in this world, worse off than the wise man who has wealth but finds no contentment?

The Midrash asks: What is a poor man to do regarding business transactions? Is he to sit idle? Let him learn a handicraft and the Holy One, blessed is He, will support him with a livelihood.

9. טוֹב מַרְאֵה עֵינַיִם מֵהֲלָךְ נָפֶשׁ — *Better is what the eyes see than what is imagined.* Man should utilize the little that is available to him (*'that which the eyes see'*), rather than yearn in vain for riches that may elude him (*R' Saadiah Gaon*).

R' Yosef Kara and *Rashi*, however, view this verse as the rationale of the miser: it is a great evil that many people would rather gaze upon a treasury full of gold and silver, enjoying *what the eyes see* and contenting themselves with that lustful vision, than to diminish their wealth by investing it to nourish their souls. Such a trait, is *'futility and a vexation of the spirit.'*

כְּבָר נִקְרָא שְׁמוֹ וְנוֹדָע אֲשֶׁר־הוּא אָדָם וְלֹא־יוּכַל לָדִין עִם שֶׁתַּקִּיף מִמֶּנּוּ: יא כִּי יֵשׁ־דְּבָרִים הַרְבֵּה מַרְבִּים הָבֶל מַה־יֹּתֵר לָאָדָם: יב כִּי מִי־יוֹדֵעַ מַה־טּוֹב לָאָדָם בַּחַיִּים מִסְפַּר יְמֵי־חַיֵּי הֶבְלוֹ וְיַעֲשֵׂם כַּצֵּל אֲשֶׁר מִי־יַגִּיד לָאָדָם מַה־יִּהְיֶה אַחֲרָיו תַּחַת הַשָּׁמֶשׁ:

פרק ז

א טוֹב שֵׁם מִשֶּׁמֶן טוֹב וְיוֹם הַמָּוֶת מִיּוֹם הִוָּלְדוֹ: ב טוֹב לָלֶכֶת אֶל־בֵּית־אֵבֶל מִלֶּכֶת אֶל־בֵּית מִשְׁתֶּה בַּאֲשֶׁר הוּא סוֹף כָּל־הָאָדָם וְהַחַי יִתֵּן אֶל־לִבּוֹ: ג טוֹב כַּעַס מִשְּׂחֹק כִּי־בְרֹעַ פָּנִים יִיטַב לֵב: ד לֵב חֲכָמִים בְּבֵית אֵבֶל וְלֵב כְּסִילִים בְּבֵית שִׂמְחָה: ה טוֹב לִשְׁמֹעַ גַּעֲרַת חָכָם מֵאִישׁ שֹׁמֵעַ שִׁיר כְּסִילִים: ו כִּי כְקוֹל הַסִּירִים תַּחַת הַסִּיר כֵּן שְׂחֹק הַכְּסִיל וְגַם־זֶה הָבֶל: ז כִּי הָעֹשֶׁק יְהוֹלֵל חָכָם וִיאַבֵּד אֶת־לֵב מַתָּנָה: ח טוֹב אַחֲרִית דָּבָר מֵרֵאשִׁיתוֹ טוֹב אֶרֶךְ־רוּחַ מִגְּבַהּ־רוּחַ: ט אַל־תְּבַהֵל בְּרוּחֲךָ לִכְעוֹס כִּי כַעַס בְּחֵיק כְּסִילִים יָנוּחַ: י אַל־תֹּאמַר מֶה הָיָה שֶׁהַיָּמִים הָרִאשֹׁנִים הָיוּ טוֹבִים מֵאֵלֶּה כִּי לֹא מֵחָכְמָה שָׁאַלְתָּ עַל־זֶה:

---

10. The verse cautions that man should perceive the limits of his essence as predetermined by God. He is אָדָם, *mortal man*, and his limitations as a human being have been imposed on him from Creation. He cannot contend with his Creator Who formed him thus (*Ibn Latif*). But he should be thankful for however God formed him (*Midrash Lekach Tov*). Nor can he hope to overpower the angel of death; he should submit to his mortality.

Rashi (as amplified by *Metzudas David*) explains the verse differently. Man's greatness was established and well known during his lifetime. His death, however, makes it manifestly clear that he is essentially אָדָם, *mortal*. Ultimately he dies, unable to resist the Angel of Death, who is more powerful than he.

11. כִּי יֵשׁ־דְּבָרִים הַרְבֵּה מַרְבִּים הָבֶל — *There are many things that increase futility*. Man becomes involved in many activities during his lifetime [such as the accumulation of wealth, power or pleasures (*Ibn Ezra*)]. Later he realizes that they were futile (*Kara; Rashi*).

12. מַה־יִּהְיֶה אַחֲרָיו תַּחַת הַשָּׁמֶשׁ — *What will be after him beneath the sun*. Can anyone guarantee that the fortune which he accumulated unjustly will endure with his children on this world? (*Rashi*).

Koheles displays the same intellectual remorse which he developed in 2:3-21, and with which he culminated 3:22, regarding the uncertainty of the future. The best course, therefore, is to store up *spiritual fortunes* which will definitely live on beyond him (*Alshich*) — as the *Midrash* concludes: I will tell you what is best of all [next verse] טוֹב שֵׁם מִשֶּׁמֶן טוֹב, *a good name is better than good oil*.

CHAPTER SEVEN

1. טוֹב שֵׁם מִשֶּׁמֶן טוֹב — *A good name is better than good oil*. A fine reputation — acquired with diligence and good deeds (*Sforno*) — is a more valuable possession than precious oil (*Rashi*) [which was used in ancient times to preserve the body from disintegration]. Thus, notes the *Alshich*, a fine reputation will preserve a dead person's memory more effectively than precious oils will preserve his body.

It has been taught: 'A man is called by three names: one which his father and mother call him, a second which other persons call him, and a third which he gains for himself as the result of his conduct in life (*Midrash*).

וְיוֹם הַמָּוֶת מִיּוֹם הִוָּלְדוֹ — *And the day of death* [is better] *than the day of birth*. Because the man who has lived an exemplary life and acquired a *good name* views his death as a culmination of a life well spent and as a transition to the world of peace and reward, unlike the time of his birth, 'for man is born to toil' when he is uncertain of how his life will unfold (*Akeidas Yitzchak; Ibn Ezra*).

2. טוֹב לָלֶכֶת אֶל־בֵּית־אֵבֶל — *It is better to go to the house of mourning*. The commentators explain that by visiting the house of mourning and listening to the eulogies and lamentations, one will be stimulated to think about the beauty of life, and be inspired to repent and lead a religiously observant life. When the virtues of the deceased are recounted, the listener realizes that the only good thing of lasting value is a good reputation, and will resolve to assure himself an untarnished name by the time he dies and others visit *his* house of mourning.

בַּאֲשֶׁר הוּא סוֹף כָּל־הָאָדָם — *For that is the end*

Koheles / קהלת **[174]**

¹⁰ What has been was already named, and it is known that he is but a man. He cannot contend with one who is mightier than he. ¹¹ There are many things that increase futility; how does it benefit man? ¹² Who can possibly know what is good for man in life, during the short span of his futile existence which he should consider like a shadow; who can tell a man what will be after him beneath the sun?

CHAPTER SEVEN

¹A good name is better than good oil, and the day of death than the day of birth.

² It is better to go to the house of mourning than to go to a house of feasting, for that is the end of all man, and the living should take it to heart.

³ Grief is better than gaiety — for through a sad countenance the heart is improved. ⁴ The thoughts of the wise turn to the house of mourning, but the thoughts of a fool to the house of feasting.

⁵ It is better to listen to the rebuke of a wise man than for one to listen to the song of fools, ⁶ for like the crackling of thorns under a pot, so is the laughter of the fool; ⁷ for oppression makes the wise foolish, and a gift corrupts the heart.

⁸ The end of a matter is better than its beginning; patience is better than pride. ⁹ Do not be hastily upset, for anger lingers in the bosom of fools.

¹⁰ Do not say, 'How was it that former times were better than these?' For that is not a question prompted by wisdom.

---

of all man. Death is the inevitable fate of everyone and if he does not attend the funeral now, when then? A feast is different — if a person could not attend one celebration, he will be able to attend another in that family at some later time (*Rashi*).

וְהָחַי יִתֵּן אֶל־לִבּוֹ — *And the living should take it to heart.* Do a kindness so that one will be done to you; attend a funeral so that people should attend your funeral; mourn for others so that others should mourn for you; bury others so that others should concern themselves with your burial; act benevolently so that benevolence should be done to you (*Midrash*).

3. טוֹב כַּעַס מִשְּׂחוֹק — *Grief is better than gaiety.* [In this context, many commentators understand כַּעַס not in its usual sense of 'anger', but as the *grief* aroused by the laments in the *'house of mourning.'*] Such 'grief' brings about רַע פָּנִים, a sad face, i.e. a brooding, reflective countenance; which in turn יִיטַב לֵב, will cause *'his heart to be improved'*, i.e., turn his heart to try and better his ways — because such reflection will cause him to take stock of his own situation. He will repent and thus bring on his own redemption. שְׂחוֹק, 'gaiety', however, is not conducive to such serious contemplation (*Rav Yosef Kara*).

5. טוֹב לִשְׁמוֹעַ גַּעֲרַת חָכָם — *It is better to listen to the rebuke of a wise man* — although criticism hurts, it is beneficial because it brings about moral improvement (*Metzudas David*).

7. כִּי הָעֹשֶׁק יְהוֹלֵל חָכָם — *For oppression makes the wise foolish.* The provocations of fools cause the wise man's wisdom to depart from him —

until even he may eventually provoke the Holy One, blessed is He (*Rashi; Midrash*).

8. טוֹב אַחֲרִית דָּבָר מֵרֵאשִׁיתוֹ — *The end of a matter is better than its beginning* — since only by the outcome can a matter be properly evaluated (*Rashi*). A wise man should always try to foresee any of the result of his every action and proceed accordingly (*Ibn Ezra*).

9. כִּי כַעַס בְּחֵיק כְּסִילִים יָנוּחַ — *For anger lingers in the bosom of fools* — eager to burst forth at the slightest provocation (*Sforno*).

10. This verse cautions the wise to be satisfied with their lot. If they suffer an adverse turn of fortune they should not complain about their lot and be jealous of those who are better and attribute their own decline to a changing world. Every understanding person is aware that life remains the same — man is given whatever has been ordained for him (*Ibn Ezra*).

The *Talmud* remarks that one should not deprecate the leaders of his time by comparing them to great personalities of the past. Rather Jerubaal in his generation is like Moses in his generation ... Yiftach in his generation is like Samuel in his ... one must be content with the judge who is in his days, and not look back at former times (*Rosh Hashanah* 25b).

The *Kobriner Rebbe* said: Some people feel that 'Nowadays it is difficult to serve God. In former times it was easier; there were more *tzadikim* whose example could be imitated.' This is absurd. Has anyone ever endeavored to seek God to no avail? Endeavor to seek Him in the manner of those in former days and you too will find Him, just as they did.

יא טוֹבָה חָכְמָה עִם־נַחֲלָה וְיֹתֵר לְרֹאֵי הַשָּׁמֶשׁ: יב כִּי בְּצֵל הַחָכְמָה בְּצֵל
הַכֶּסֶף וְיִתְרוֹן דַּעַת הַחָכְמָה תְּחַיֶּה בְעָלֶיהָ: יג רְאֵה אֶת־מַעֲשֵׂה הָאֱלֹהִים
כִּי מִי יוּכַל לְתַקֵּן אֵת אֲשֶׁר עִוְּתוֹ: יד בְּיוֹם טוֹבָה הֱיֵה בְטוֹב וּבְיוֹם רָעָה רְאֵה
גַּם אֶת־זֶה לְעֻמַּת־זֶה עָשָׂה הָאֱלֹהִים עַל־דִּבְרַת שֶׁלֹּא יִמְצָא הָאָדָם
אַחֲרָיו מְאוּמָה: טו אֶת־הַכֹּל רָאִיתִי בִּימֵי הֶבְלִי יֵשׁ צַדִּיק אֹבֵד בְּצִדְקוֹ וְיֵשׁ
רָשָׁע מַאֲרִיךְ בְּרָעָתוֹ: טז אַל־תְּהִי צַדִּיק הַרְבֵּה וְאַל־תִּתְחַכַּם יוֹתֵר לָמָּה
תִּשּׁוֹמֵם: יז אַל־תִּרְשַׁע הַרְבֵּה וְאַל־תְּהִי סָכָל לָמָּה תָמוּת בְּלֹא עִתֶּךָ:
יח טוֹב אֲשֶׁר תֶּאֱחֹז בָּזֶה וְגַם־מִזֶּה אַל־תַּנַּח אֶת־יָדֶךָ כִּי־יְרֵא אֱלֹהִים יֵצֵא
אֶת־כֻּלָּם: יט הַחָכְמָה תָּעֹז לֶחָכָם מֵעֲשָׂרָה שַׁלִּיטִים אֲשֶׁר הָיוּ בָּעִיר: כ כִּי
אָדָם אֵין צַדִּיק בָּאָרֶץ אֲשֶׁר יַעֲשֶׂה־טּוֹב וְלֹא יֶחֱטָא: כא גַּם לְכָל־הַדְּבָרִים
אֲשֶׁר יְדַבֵּרוּ אַל־תִּתֵּן לִבֶּךָ אֲשֶׁר לֹא־תִשְׁמַע אֶת־עַבְדְּךָ מְקַלְלֶךָ: כב כִּי
גַּם־פְּעָמִים רַבּוֹת יָדַע לִבֶּךָ אֲשֶׁר גַּם־אַתְּ קִלַּלְתָּ אֲחֵרִים: כג כָּל־זֹה נִסִּיתִי
בַחָכְמָה אָמַרְתִּי אֶחְכָּמָה וְהִיא רְחוֹקָה מִמֶּנִּי: כד רָחוֹק מַה־שֶּׁהָיָה וְעָמֹק
עָמֹק מִי יִמְצָאֶנּוּ: כה סַבּוֹתִי אֲנִי וְלִבִּי לָדַעַת וְלָתוּר וּבַקֵּשׁ חָכְמָה וְחֶשְׁבּוֹן
וְלָדַעַת רֶשַׁע כֶּסֶל וְהַסִּכְלוּת הוֹלֵלוֹת: כו וּמוֹצֵא אֲנִי מַר מִמָּוֶת אֶת־הָאִשָּׁה
אֲשֶׁר־הִיא מְצוֹדִים וַחֲרָמִים לִבָּהּ אֲסוּרִים יָדֶיהָ טוֹב לִפְנֵי הָאֱלֹהִים יִמָּלֵט

11. טוֹבָה חָכְמָה עִם־נַחֲלָה — *Wisdom is good with an inheritance.* It is good for the scholar to be self-supporting and free from financial worries so he can immerse himself in his studies (*Alshich*).

וְיֹתֵר לְרֹאֵי הַשָּׁמֶשׁ — *And a boon to those who see the sun.* Such wisdom benefits all mankind. רֹאֵי הַשָּׁמֶשׁ, *'those who see the sun'*, is an all-encompassing phrase embracing all those who benefit from the sun and not only those with sight (*Rashi*).

13. Man must contemplate why God gave him life. Obviously, only to perform His commandments and act righteously — for who can right his wrongs after death? Therefore submit to God and accept the vicissitudes of life (*Tuv Taam*).

14. בְּיוֹם טוֹבָה הֱיֵה בְטוֹב — *Be pleased when things go well.* Enjoy the good that is granted you and derive pleasure to your heart's content (*Metzudas David*), seeking to acquire eternal perfection which is the greatest 'good' (*Sforno*). But while enjoying the good, וּבְיוֹם רָעָה רְאֵה *anticipate the inevitability of bad times,* and act accordingly (*Ibn Ezra*).

Rashi interprets the phrase: when you are in a position to do good, be among those who do good — וּבְיוֹם רָעָה רְאֵה, and when evil comes upon the wicked, be among the observers only, not among the afflicted.

גַּם אֶת־זֶה לְעֻמַּת־זֶה עָשָׂה הָאֱלֹהִים — *God has made the one as well as the other* [i.e., one parallel to the other] — good with its reward, and evil with its ensuing punishment (*Rashi*).

שֶׁלֹּא יִמְצָא הָאָדָם אַחֲרָיו מְאוּמָה — *Man should find nothing after Him.* Man can have no just cause to complain to God because all punishment is clearly in response to man's deeds (*Rashi; Ibn Ezra; Alshich; Sforno*).

15. יֵשׁ צַדִּיק אֹבֵד בְּצִדְקוֹ — *Sometimes a righteous man perishes for all his righteousness.* In spite of his righteousness, God will be more exacting with him and punish him immediately for a minor infraction. Were he not righteous, he might not have been punished at all, because better behavior could not be expected of him (*Metzudas David*). [See *Overview* to ArtScroll edition of *Koheles*, and *Overview* to ArtScroll edition of *Ruth*, pp. 23-26.]

וְיֵשׁ רָשָׁע מַאֲרִיךְ בְּרָעָתוֹ — *And sometimes a wicked man endures for all his wickedness.* *Alshich* explains this as the paradox of צַדִּיק וְרַע — לוֹ רָשָׁע וְטוֹב לוֹ — *righteous people who suffer while wicked are fortunate.* God deals strictly with the righteous to atone for their sins, so that they will not require punishment in the Hereafter, but He is seemingly lax in punishing the wicked. In reality, however, He is waiting for them to repent, or He may be rewarding their good deeds in This World so that they will not enjoy the bliss of the World to Come.

17. אַל־תִּרְשַׁע הַרְבֵּה — *Be not overly wicked.* Even if you have done something wicked, do not persist in your wickedness [mistakenly thinking that there is no hope of repentance] (*Rashi*).

אַל־תְּהִי סָכָל — *Nor be a fool.* Upon realizing that excessive wisdom is a cause of desolation, do

¹¹ *Wisdom is good with an inheritance, and a boon to those who see the sun,* ¹² *for to sit in the shelter of wisdom is to sit in the shelter of money, and the advantage of knowledge is that wisdom preserves the life of its possessors.*

¹³ *Observe God's doing! For who can straighten what He has twisted?* ¹⁴ *Be pleased when things go well, but in a time of misfortune reflect: God has made the one as well as the other so that man should find nothing after Him.*

¹⁵ *I have seen everything during my futile existence: Sometimes a righteous man perishes for all his righteousness, and sometimes a wicked man endures for all his wickedness.* ¹⁶ *Do not be overly righteous or excessively wise: why be left desolate?* ¹⁷ *Be not overly wicked nor be a fool: why die before your time?* ¹⁸ *It is best to grasp the one and not let go of the other; he who fears God performs them all.* ¹⁹ *Wisdom strengthens the wise more than ten rulers who are in the city.* ²⁰ *For there is no man so wholly righteous on earth that he [always] does good and never sins.*

²¹ *Moreover, pay no attention to everything men say, lest you hear your own servant disparaging you,* ²²*for your own conscience knows that many times you yourself disparged others.*

²³ *All this I tested with wisdom; I thought I could become wise, but it is beyond me.* ²⁴ *What existed is elusive; and so very deep, who can fathom it?* ²⁵*So I turned my attention to study and probe and seek wisdom and reckoning, and to know the wickedness of folly, and the foolishness which is madness:*

²⁶ *And I have discovered more bitter than death: the woman whose heart is snares and nets; her arms are chains. He who is pleasing to God escapes*

---

not take the opposite course and become a fool! (Kara).

18. . . . בֶּה וְגַם מִזֶּה בָּזֶה תֶּאֱחֹז אֲשֶׁר טוֹב — It is best to grasp the one and not let go of the other. Ibn Ezra comments that one should grasp both worlds — the spiritual and physical — and scrupulously follow the ideals of the Torah.

According to R' Yosef Kara, the verse refers to 'righteousness' and 'wisdom' in verse 16, and advises that one should tread a middle path between these two virtues and cling to both.

19. לֶחָכָם תָּעֹז הַחָכְמָה — Wisdom strengthens the wise. Having recommended that excessive, conceitful wisdom be shunned, Solomon adds that, nevertheless, wisdom in its proper measure — neither carried to extremes nor obsessive — is one's surest protection [because it leads him to repent (Rashi)] (Ibn Ezra).

20. יֶחֱטָא וְלֹא טוֹב יַעֲשֶׂה אֲשֶׁר — That he [always] does good and never sins. Therefore the wise man should not be over confident. Even Moses sinned! (Michlol Yofi). Let him rather search out and improve his ways (Rashi).

Therefore, if you see a righteous man who perishes notwithstanding all his righteousness [verse 16], know that his punishment is probably the result of some infraction for which he received retribution in this world, because no man is so righteous on earth that he never sinned (R' Saadiah Gaon).

21-22. יְדַבֵּרוּ אֲשֶׁר הַדְּבָרִים לְכָל גַּם — Moreover, pay not attention to everything [men] say. Do

not be receptive to the evil talk of others about yourself (Rashi).

מְקַלְלֶךָ עַבְדְּךָ אֶת תִשְׁמַע לֹא אֲשֶׁר — Lest you hear your [own] servant disparaging you. If you pay attention to what others say about you, you will discover that even your own servant speaks disparagingly of you. Therefore, ignore such talk and spare yourself anger and vexation (Ibn Ezra; Kehilas Yaakov).

24. יִמְצָאֶנּוּ מִי עָמֹק וְעָמֹק שֶׁהָיָה מַה רָחוֹק — What existed is elusive; and so very deep, who can fathom it? Everything is elusive: what pre-existed creation; what is above and below, who can fathom? Man is helpless — in his limited intellect — before the infinite greatness of God's Creation.

25. When it became clear to Koheles that comprehension of the deeper workings of the world was beyond his intellectual grasp, he shifted his attention to pursuing his observations on life as they flowed from his own practical wisdom. He tried to perceive which is the worst of all evils and most foolish of all follies, and he reveals them in the following verses (Kara).

26. מִמָּוֶת מַר אֲנִי וּמוֹצֵא — And I have discovered more bitter than death. Because she demands of man things which are beyond his power, such a woman ultimately kills him with a bitter death (Midrash). Given a choice, one should prefer death (Metzudas David).

[It is abundantly clear that Solomon refers

מִמֶּנָּה וְחוֹטֵא יִלָּכֶד בָּהּ: כז רְאֵה זֶה מָצָאתִי אָמְרָה קֹהֶלֶת אַחַת לְאַחַת לִמְצֹא חֶשְׁבּוֹן: כח אֲשֶׁר עוֹד־בִּקְשָׁה נַפְשִׁי וְלֹא מָצָאתִי אָדָם אֶחָד מֵאֶלֶף מָצָאתִי וְאִשָּׁה בְכָל־אֵלֶּה לֹא מָצָאתִי: כט לְבַד רְאֵה־זֶה מָצָאתִי אֲשֶׁר עָשָׂה הָאֱלֹהִים אֶת־הָאָדָם יָשָׁר וְהֵמָּה בִקְשׁוּ חִשְּׁבֹנוֹת רַבִּים:

פרק ח

א מִי כְּהֶחָכָם וּמִי יוֹדֵעַ פֵּשֶׁר דָּבָר חָכְמַת אָדָם תָּאִיר פָּנָיו וְעֹז פָּנָיו יְשֻׁנֶּא: ב אֲנִי פִּי־מֶלֶךְ שְׁמֹר וְעַל דִּבְרַת שְׁבוּעַת אֱלֹהִים: ג אַל־תִּבָּהֵל מִפָּנָיו תֵּלֵךְ אַל־תַּעֲמֹד בְּדָבָר רָע כִּי כָּל־אֲשֶׁר יַחְפֹּץ יַעֲשֶׂה: ד בַּאֲשֶׁר דְּבַר־מֶלֶךְ שִׁלְטוֹן וּמִי יֹאמַר־לוֹ מַה־תַּעֲשֶׂה: ה שׁוֹמֵר מִצְוָה לֹא יֵדַע דָּבָר רָע וְעֵת וּמִשְׁפָּט יֵדַע לֵב חָכָם: ו כִּי לְכָל־חֵפֶץ יֵשׁ עֵת וּמִשְׁפָּט כִּי־רָעַת הָאָדָם רַבָּה עָלָיו: ז כִּי־אֵינֶנּוּ יֹדֵעַ מַה־שֶּׁיִּהְיֶה כִּי כַּאֲשֶׁר יִהְיֶה מִי יַגִּיד לוֹ: ח אֵין אָדָם שַׁלִּיט בָּרוּחַ לִכְלוֹא אֶת־הָרוּחַ וְאֵין שִׁלְטוֹן בְּיוֹם הַמָּוֶת וְאֵין מִשְׁלַחַת בַּמִּלְחָמָה וְלֹא־יְמַלֵּט רֶשַׁע אֶת־בְּעָלָיו: ט אֶת־כָּל־זֶה רָאִיתִי וְנָתוֹן אֶת־לִבִּי לְכָל־מַעֲשֶׂה אֲשֶׁר נַעֲשָׂה תַּחַת הַשָּׁמֶשׁ עֵת אֲשֶׁר שָׁלַט הָאָדָם בְּאָדָם לְרַע לוֹ: י וּבְכֵן רָאִיתִי רְשָׁעִים קְבֻרִים וָבָאוּ וּמִמְּקוֹם קָדוֹשׁ יְהַלֵּכוּ וְיִשְׁתַּכְּחוּ בָעִיר אֲשֶׁר כֵּן־עָשׂוּ גַּם־זֶה הָבֶל:

---

only to evil, licentious women, who trap man into evil ways. This is not a wholesale condemnation of all woman. His praise of the God-fearing women in *Proverbs* 18:22 מָצָא אִשָּׁה מָצָא טוֹב *he who has found a wife found good*; ibid. 31:10 ff (the famous *Aishes Chayil*); and his statement in 9:9 leave no room for doubt.]

27. [Solomon assures us that he formulated this discovery only after careful investigation.]

אָמְרָה קֹהֶלֶת — *Said Koheles.* The verb here is in the feminine form. *Rashi* explains that here *Koheles* means 'a collection of wisdom', rather than the name of Solomon. Thus, the noun *Koheles* is feminine in this sense.

28. אָדָם אֶחָד מֵאֶלֶף מָצָאתִי — *One man in a thousand I have found* — I was able to find a small number of worthy men, aloof from sin; who could collaborate in my investigation; *but one woman among them* — i.e., from all my thousand wives [700 wives, 300 concubines (*I Kings* 11:3)] *I could not find* (*Kara; Ralbag*) [because Solomon was ultimately led into sin by his wives (*Ibn Yachya*)].

[It is clear, as was pointed out earlier, that Solomon is not suggesting that righteous women did not exist at all — but, in his personal experience, they were even a greater rarity than righteous men.]

29. בִּקְשׁוּ חִשְּׁבֹנוֹת רַבִּים — *Sought many intrigues.* Many commentators apply this verse to mankind as a whole: *God created mankind upright* — i.e., with a perfect nature capable of high attainments. Man's perversions spring from

his own devices, which, in turn, cause his downfall (*Rambam*). [God has provided man with all his needs — but man is not satisfied; he always tries to 'improve' nature, thus causing his own complications].

CHAPTER EIGHT

1. מִי כְּהֶחָכָם — *Who is like the wise man?* [A rhetorical question:] Who in this world is as important as the man of wisdom (*Rashi*)?

חָכְמַת אָדָם תָּאִיר פָּנָיו — *A man's wisdom lights up his face.* Because of his wisdom man gains the admiration of all who know him. This gladdens one's heart and causes his countenance to beam (*Metzudas David*).

See the difference between wealth and wisdom. Wealth increases anxieties and robs one of his sleep [2:23]; wisdom, however, brightens up his face (*Kara*).

2. פִּי־מֶלֶךְ שְׁמֹר — *Obey the king's command.* [lit. 'guard the king's mouth']. The commentators differ regarding the identity of this *king*: the King of the Universe or a mortal king. *Rashi* offers both interpretations.

וְעַל דִּבְרַת שְׁבוּעַת אֱלֹהִים — *And that in the manner of an oath of God.* [An ambiguous phrase which can be variously interpreted:] Because of the oath of allegiance to God's commandments that we took at Horeb (*Rashi*).

Obey the king's orders if only because of the oath of allegiance taken in God's Name at the time of coronation (*Kara*).

The king's command must be obeyed — but only when his command is in consonance with

her but the sinner is caught by her.

²⁷ See, this is what I found, said Koheles, adding one to another to reach a conclusion, ²⁸ which yet my soul seeks but I have not found. One man in a thousand I have found, but one woman among them I have not found. ²⁹ But, see, this I did find: God has made man simple, but they sought many intrigues.

CHAPTER EIGHT

¹Who is like the wise man? and who knows what things mean? A man's wisdom lights up his face, and the boldness of his face is transformed.

² I counsel you: Obey the king's command, and that in the manner of an oath of God. ³ Do not hasten to leave his presence, do not persist in an evil thing; for he can do whatever he pleases. ⁴ Since a king's word is law, who dare say to him, 'What are you doing?' ⁵ He who obeys the commandment will know no evil; and a wise mind will know time and justice. ⁶ For everything has its time and justice, for man's evil overwhelms him. ⁷ Indeed, he does not know what will happen, for when it happens, who will tell him?

⁸ Man is powerless over the spirit — to restrain the spirit; nor is there authority over the day of death; nor discharge in war; and wickedness cannot save the wrongdoer.

⁹ All this have I seen; and I applied my mind to every deed that is done under the sun: there is a time when one man rules over another to his detriment.

¹⁰ And then I saw the wicked buried and newly come while those who had done right were gone from the Holy place and were forgotten in the city. This, too, is futility! ¹¹ Because the sentence for wrong-doing is not executed quickly — that is why men are encouraged to do evil, ¹² because a sinner does what is

---

שְׁבוּעַת אֱלֹהִים, the Oath to God, i.e., that his requests are not contrary to the Laws of the Torah (Metzudas David).

3. אַל-תַּעֲמֹד בְּדָבָר רָע — Do not persist [lit., 'stand'] in an evil thing, i.e., something that is evil in his eyes, for he can do as he pleases [and exact retribution] (Ibn Ezra).

This phrase is cited as the reason that in the synagogal reading of the Torah, the reader does not conclude an individual aliyah with an inauspicious phrase, because אַל תַּעֲמֹד בְּדָבָר רָע, 'Do not stand [i.e., pause] during a bad thing [an inauspicious verse]' (cf. Midrash; Poras Yosef).

5. וְעֵת וּמִשְׁפָּט יֵדַע לֵב חָכָם — And a wise mind will know time and justice. A wise man will perceive that there is a predetermined time during which God will exact justice from the wicked (Rashi). [לֵב, heart, is used interchangeably throughout Scriptures to represent both the seats of intellect and emotion.]

8. אֵין אָדָם שַׁלִּיט בָּרוּחַ — Man is powerless over the spirit. Even if man were to know his day of death, how would it avail him? He has no control over God's emissary [the Angel of Death who is referred to as a 'spirit' (Midrash)], לִכְלוֹא אֶת-הָרוּחַ, to restrain the spirit, i.e., to lock his soul within his body where it is 'imprisoned' and not release it (Rashi, Ibn Ezra, Metzudas David).

וְאֵין שִׁלְטוֹן בְּיוֹם הַמָּוֶת — Nor is there authority over the day of death, as the Midrash comments: A man cannot say to the Angel of Death, 'Wait until I finish my business and then I will come.'
Rashi and Ibn Ezra translate: Royalty is of no avail on the day of death [i.e., kings, too, are subject to death and their royalty is not recognized by the Angel of Death].

וְלֹא יְמַלֵּט רֶשַׁע אֶת-בְּעָלָיו — And wickedness cannot save the wrongdoer. Evildoers will not escape punishment for their deeds — their wickedness will not be their salvation (Kara).

10. וּבְכֵן רָאִיתִי — And then I saw. This is one of the most semantically difficult verses in the entire book and several interpretations are offered. Our translation, which follows the written text, is based on Ibn Ezra. The subject of the verse is the wicked of the previous verse 'who rule over their fellow man'. Those evildoers are קְבֻרִים, buried peacefully in their graves, i.e., they died without anguish. He understands וָבָאוּ as meaning "they came into the world a second time" (i.e., their children carry on after them)...
The phrase וּמִמְּקוֹם קָדוֹשׁ יְהַלֵּכוּ, while those who... were gone from the holy place, refers to the righteous, the holy ones who, because they die without children, become forgotten in the city where they were ...
Ironically, these are the ones אֲשֶׁר כֵּן-עָשׂוּ, who

יא אֲשֶׁר אֵין־נַעֲשָׂה פִתְגָם מַעֲשֵׂה הָרָעָה מְהֵרָה עַל־כֵּן מָלֵא לֵב בְּנֵי־
הָאָדָם בָּהֶם לַעֲשׂוֹת רָע: יב אֲשֶׁר חֹטֶא עֹשֶׂה רָע מְאַת וּמַאֲרִיךְ לוֹ כִּי
גַם־יוֹדֵעַ אָנִי אֲשֶׁר יִהְיֶה־טּוֹב לְיִרְאֵי הָאֱלֹהִים אֲשֶׁר יִירְאוּ מִלְּפָנָיו: יג
וְטוֹב לֹא־יִהְיֶה לָרָשָׁע וְלֹא־יַאֲרִיךְ יָמִים כַּצֵּל אֲשֶׁר אֵינֶנּוּ יָרֵא מִלִּפְנֵי
אֱלֹהִים: יד יֶשׁ־הֶבֶל אֲשֶׁר נַעֲשָׂה עַל־הָאָרֶץ אֲשֶׁר ׀ יֵשׁ צַדִּיקִים אֲשֶׁר
מַגִּיעַ אֲלֵהֶם כְּמַעֲשֵׂה הָרְשָׁעִים וְיֵשׁ רְשָׁעִים שֶׁמַּגִּיעַ אֲלֵהֶם כְּמַעֲשֵׂה
הַצַּדִּיקִים אָמַרְתִּי שֶׁגַּם־זֶה הָבֶל: טו וְשִׁבַּחְתִּי אֲנִי אֶת־הַשִּׂמְחָה אֲשֶׁר
אֵין־טוֹב לָאָדָם תַּחַת הַשֶּׁמֶשׁ כִּי אִם־לֶאֱכֹל וְלִשְׁתּוֹת וְלִשְׂמוֹחַ וְהוּא
יִלְוֶנּוּ בַעֲמָלוֹ יְמֵי חַיָּיו אֲשֶׁר־נָתַן־לוֹ הָאֱלֹהִים תַּחַת הַשָּׁמֶשׁ: טז כַּאֲשֶׁר
נָתַתִּי אֶת־לִבִּי לָדַעַת חָכְמָה וְלִרְאוֹת אֶת־הָעִנְיָן אֲשֶׁר נַעֲשָׂה עַל־הָאָרֶץ
כִּי גַם בַּיּוֹם וּבַלַּיְלָה שֵׁנָה בְּעֵינָיו אֵינֶנּוּ רֹאֶה: יז וְרָאִיתִי אֶת־כָּל־מַעֲשֵׂה
הָאֱלֹהִים כִּי לֹא יוּכַל הָאָדָם לִמְצוֹא אֶת־הַמַּעֲשֶׂה אֲשֶׁר נַעֲשָׂה תַחַת־
הַשֶּׁמֶשׁ בְּשֶׁל אֲשֶׁר יַעֲמֹל הָאָדָם לְבַקֵּשׁ וְלֹא יִמְצָא וְגַם אִם־יֹאמַר
הֶחָכָם לָדַעַת לֹא יוּכַל לִמְצֹא:

פרק ט

א כִּי אֶת־כָּל־זֶה נָתַתִּי אֶל־לִבִּי וְלָבוּר אֶת־כָּל־זֶה אֲשֶׁר הַצַּדִּיקִים
וְהַחֲכָמִים וַעֲבָדֵיהֶם בְּיַד הָאֱלֹהִים גַּם־אַהֲבָה גַם־שִׂנְאָה אֵין יוֹדֵעַ הָאָדָם
הַכֹּל לִפְנֵיהֶם: ב הַכֹּל כַּאֲשֶׁר לַכֹּל מִקְרֶה אֶחָד לַצַּדִּיק וְלָרָשָׁע לַטּוֹב
וְלַטָּהוֹר וְלַטָּמֵא וְלַזֹּבֵחַ וְלַאֲשֶׁר אֵינֶנּוּ זֹבֵחַ כַּטּוֹב כַּחֹטֶא הַנִּשְׁבָּע כַּאֲשֶׁר

---

had acted righteously (כֵּן meaning 'right' as in
Numbers 27:7].

The anomaly is how the good deeds of the
righteous are forgotten, but the wicked die
peacefully and leave a legacy of evil behind
them. This is a great futility.

11. Koheles attributes the flourishing of wickedness to the delay in retribution which tends to
strengthen the tendency toward evil.

12-13. These verses continue the thought of the
previous verse. They elaborate on what the
wicked see that encourages them to sin with
impunity. Nevertheless, Solomon disavows this
evidence and affirms his faith in the Divine
Justice which rewards the righteous and pun-
ishes the sinner.

כִּי גַם־יוֹדֵעַ אָנִי — *Yet, nevertheless, I am aware*
[lit. *'for also I know'*]. Let no one think that I
[Koheles] share the sinner's view. Just as every
man of intellect perceives God's justice, so do I
know that in the Eternal World it will go well
only for those who fear Him, and that in the
Hereafter the wicked will find no goodness, but
their souls will be cut off (*Metzudas David*).

Even to the righteous God is 'patient' in
granting his reward, but just as I believe that in
the end the sinner will receive his due, I also

believe that the righteous will ultimately receive
his reward (*Tuv Taam*).

14. [The following verses until 9:12 form a
cohesive unit discussing the dilemma presented
by the prosperity of the wicked and the suffering of the righteous.]

שֶׁגַּם־זֶה הָבֶל — *This, too, is vanity.* The mainte-
nance of Free Will — a necessary ingredient of
God's plan — requires a certain amount of
suffering for the righteous and prosperity for the
wicked. For if all wickedness were to be punished immediately, there would be no room for
choice and everyone would be righteous. Thus,
the wicked often prosper, but they misinterpret
this prosperity as sanction to continue their
wicked ways. They should realize that it is
futility — that in reality there is justice, but that
God allows them to flourish in order to confuse
mankind (*R' Saadiah Gaon*).

15. וְשִׁבַּחְתִּי אֲנִי אֶת הַשִּׂמְחָה — *So I praised
enjoyment.* Not enjoyment for its own sake but
שֶׁיְהֵא שָׂמֵחַ בְּחֶלְקוֹ, that a person should be
satisfied with his lot and be involved in performing 'righteous precepts which gladden the heart'
[*Psalms* 19:9] from that which God has bestowed
upon him (*Rashi*).

לֶאֱכֹל וְלִשְׁתּוֹת וְלִשְׂמֹחַ — *To eat, drink, and be*

wrong a hundred times and He is patient with him, yet nevertheless I am aware that it will be well with those who fear God that they may fear Him, [13] and that it will not be well with the wicked, and he will not long endure — like a shadow — because he does not fear God.

[14] There is a futility that takes place on earth: Sometimes there are righteous men who are treated as if they had done the deeds of the wicked; and there are wicked men who are treated as if they had done the deeds of the righteous. I declared, this, too, is vanity.

[15] So I praised enjoyment, for man has no other goal under the sun but to eat, drink and be joyful; and this will accompany him in his toil during the days of his life which God has given him beneath the sun.

[16] When I set my mind to know wisdom and to observe the activity which takes place on earth — for even day or night its eyes see no sleep. — [17] And I perceived all the work of God. Indeed, man cannot fathom the events that occur under the sun, inasmuch as man tries strenuously to search, but cannot fathom it. And even though a wise man should presume to know, he cannot fathom it.

CHAPTER NINE

[1] For all this I noted and I sought to ascertain all this: that the righteous and the wise together with their actions are in the hand of God; whether love or hate man does not know; all preceded them.

[2] All things come alike to all; the same fate awaits the righteous and the wicked, the good and the clean and the unclean, the one who brings a sacrifice and the one who does not. As is the good man, so is the sinner; as is the one who swears, so is the one who fears an oath.

---

joyful. The Midrash notes that all 'eating and drinking' mentioned in this Book signify Torah and good deeds. For just as eating and drinking sustain the body, Torah and good deeds sustain the soul (*Torah Temimah* based on *Zohar*).

The proof of this [continues the *Midrash*] is our verse: *this will accompany him in his toil during the days of his life* — to the grave. בְּעֲמָלוֹ, *in his toil* should be homiletically read בְּעַלְמוֹ, *in his world.* Are there, then, food and drink which accompany man to the grave? — It means Torah and good deeds that a man performs.

16-17. בַּאֲשֶׁר נָתַתִּי אֶת-לִבִּי. — *When I set my mind,* Solomon proceeds to explain why he came to the conclusion set forth in the last verse praising enjoyment: When I mustered up every ounce of my God-given superior wisdom to understand why the righteous suffer while the wicked prosper — even to the extent of going without sleep day and night — I became convinced that man cannot fathom these matters. Although he may feel he has nearly grasped it, he will ultimately fail in his quest. It is beyond the realm of his intellect. (*Divrei Chefetz; Kara; Rashi; Ralbag; Taalumos Chochmah*).

[Although Koheles opened this chapter implying that the wise man 'knows what all things mean,' — he concludes that certain divine matters remain hidden even from the wisest of men.]

CHAPTER NINE

1. [Continuing his theme of the righteous and wicked, Divine Providence and Fate, Solomon affirms his conclusion that God's plan for the universe is unfathomable by mortal man, who bases his conclusions on empirical observations alone.]

גַּם-אַהֲבָה גַּם-שִׂנְאָה אֵין יוֹדֵעַ הָאָדָם — *Whether love or hate, man does not know.* Man cannot even comprehend what inspires him to love or hate something (*Metzudas David*). The execution of man's desire is in the realm of man's Free Will. However, the final determination of the true success of man's efforts is in God's hand: often one achieves what he seeks — only to find that the object of his love is detrimental to him, or that the object of his hate would have been beneficial to him.

2. מִקְרֶה אֶחָד — *The same fate awaits them all.* Everyone knows that death, the common equalizer, is the fate that awaits all men in this world. Nevertheless intelligent people choose the proper path because they realize that there is a distinction between good and evil people in the Hereafter (*Rashi*).

שְׁבוּעָה יָרֵא: ג זֶה ן רָע בְּכֹל אֲשֶׁר־נַעֲשָׂה תַּחַת הַשֶּׁמֶשׁ כִּי־מִקְרֶה אֶחָד לַכֹּל וְגַם לֵב בְּנֵי־הָאָדָם מָלֵא־רָע וְהוֹלֵלוֹת בִּלְבָבָם בְּחַיֵּיהֶם וְאַחֲרָיו אֶל־הַמֵּתִים: ד כִּי־מִי אֲשֶׁר יְחֻבַּר אֶל כָּל־הַחַיִּים יֵשׁ בִּטָּחוֹן כִּי־לְכֶלֶב חַי הוּא טוֹב מִן־הָאַרְיֵה הַמֵּת: ה כִּי הַחַיִּים יוֹדְעִים שֶׁיָּמֻתוּ וְהַמֵּתִים אֵינָם יוֹדְעִים מְאוּמָה וְאֵין־עוֹד לָהֶם שָׂכָר כִּי נִשְׁכַּח זִכְרָם: ו גַּם אַהֲבָתָם גַּם־שִׂנְאָתָם גַּם־קִנְאָתָם כְּבָר אָבָדָה וְחֵלֶק אֵין־לָהֶם עוֹד לְעוֹלָם בְּכֹל אֲשֶׁר־נַעֲשָׂה תַּחַת הַשֶּׁמֶשׁ: ז לֵךְ אֱכֹל בְּשִׂמְחָה לַחְמֶךָ וּשֲׁתֵה בְלֶב־טוֹב יֵינֶךָ כִּי כְבָר רָצָה הָאֱלֹהִים אֶת־מַעֲשֶׂיךָ: ח בְּכָל־עֵת יִהְיוּ בְגָדֶיךָ לְבָנִים וְשֶׁמֶן עַל־רֹאשְׁךָ אַל־יֶחְסָר: ט רְאֵה חַיִּים עִם־אִשָּׁה אֲשֶׁר־אָהַבְתָּ כָּל־יְמֵי חַיֵּי הֶבְלֶךָ אֲשֶׁר נָתַן־לְךָ תַּחַת הַשֶּׁמֶשׁ כֹּל יְמֵי הֶבְלֶךָ כִּי הוּא חֶלְקְךָ בַּחַיִּים וּבַעֲמָלְךָ אֲשֶׁר־אַתָּה עָמֵל תַּחַת הַשָּׁמֶשׁ: י כֹּל אֲשֶׁר תִּמְצָא יָדְךָ לַעֲשׂוֹת בְּכֹחֲךָ עֲשֵׂה כִּי אֵין מַעֲשֶׂה וְחֶשְׁבּוֹן וְדַעַת וְחָכְמָה בִּשְׁאוֹל אֲשֶׁר אַתָּה הֹלֵךְ שָׁמָּה: יא שַׁבְתִּי וְרָאֹה תַחַת־הַשֶּׁמֶשׁ כִּי לֹא לַקַּלִּים הַמֵּרוֹץ וְלֹא לַגִּבּוֹרִים הַמִּלְחָמָה וְגַם לֹא לַחֲכָמִים לֶחֶם וְגַם לֹא לַנְּבֹנִים עֹשֶׁר וְגַם לֹא לַיֹּדְעִים חֵן כִּי־עֵת וָפֶגַע יִקְרֶה אֶת־כֻּלָּם: יב כִּי גַּם לֹא־יֵדַע הָאָדָם אֶת־עִתּוֹ כַּדָּגִים שֶׁנֶּאֱחָזִים בִּמְצוֹדָה רָעָה וְכַצִּפֳּרִים הָאֲחֻזוֹת בַּפָּח כָּהֵם יוּקָשִׁים בְּנֵי הָאָדָם לְעֵת רָעָה כְּשֶׁתִּפּוֹל עֲלֵיהֶם פִּתְאֹם: יג גַּם־זֹה רָאִיתִי חָכְמָה תַּחַת הַשֶּׁמֶשׁ וּגְדוֹלָה הִיא אֵלָי: יד עִיר קְטַנָּה וַאֲנָשִׁים בָּהּ מְעָט

---

3. כִּי־מִקְרֶה אֶחָד לַכֹּל — *That the same fate awaits them all* [i.e., that תַּחַת הַשֶּׁמֶשׁ, *in this world*, death comes to all, and no distinction is made 'beneath the sun' between the righteous and the wicked. All distinction comes in the Hereafter].

This is what confuses the wicked (*Taalumos Chochmah*).

4. ... כִּי־מִי אֲשֶׁר יְחֻבַּר — *For he who is attached to all the living has hope.* As long as he lives, there is hope that even the sinner will repent (*Rashi*).

5. וְאֵין־עוֹד לָהֶם שָׂכָר — *There is no more reward for them.* Once they die they no longer perform *mitzvos* worthy of reward, and 'if one has not prepared on the eve of the Sabbath, what shall he eat on Sabbath?' (*Rashi*).

6. [According to *Rashi* this verse refers to *the dead* who died without having repented, and who are forgotten.]

7-10. [There is a difference of opinion among the commentators concerning the interpretation of verses 3-10. In general, we follow the interpretation of *Rashi* and most commentators who understand these verses as describing the wicked man's inability to perceive beyond what his empirical experience allows him to comprehend. He therefore becomes a fatalist and feels that all is governed by chance. The wicked thus become emboldened to sin. Solomon bemoans this fact

and praises life, for while life exists there is hope that the wicked will repent. Once they reach the grave, however, it is too late for regrets.

Now (in verses 7-10) Solomon advises the righteous — whose deeds God has already approved, and who are destined for the World to Come — to enjoy what God has granted them and not fear death but rather 'wear white', i.e., do good deeds and always stand in spiritual readiness for eventual death and their imminent reward, and in general, spend life in God's service.

8. בְּכָל־עֵת יִהְיוּ בְגָדֶיךָ לְבָנִים — *Let your garments always be white.* The Talmud interprets this verse allegorically that one should always be in a state of spiritual preparedness.

In a very beautiful homiletical interpretation of this verse, *Olelos Ephraim* comments that a white garment stains easily and even a small spot is readily noticeable, and hard to remove... Therefore, Solomon exhorts man to conduct his life constantly as if he were wearing white garments and carrying a full pitcher of oil on his head. He must concentrate on keeping his balance and not approach anything that can soil the whiteness of his garments. Man must live with spiritual and moral purity, always on guard lest he besmirch himself with a careless sin, for man, like a white garment, is easy to soil and hard to cleanse.

9. There is no contradiction between this verse

³ *This is an evil about all things that go on under the sun: that the same fate awaits all. Therefore, the heart of man is full of evil; and madness is in their heart while they live; and after that, they go to the dead.*

⁴ *For he who is attached to all the living has hope, a live dog being better than a dead lion.* ⁵ *For the living know that they will die, but the dead know nothing at all; there is no more reward for them, their memory is forgotten.* ⁶ *Their love, their hate, their jealousy have already perished — nor will they ever again have a share in whatever is done beneath the sun.*

⁷ *Go, eat your bread with joy and drink your wine with a glad heart, for God has already approved your deeds.* ⁸ *Let your garments always be white, and your head never lack oil.*

⁹ *Enjoy life with the wife you love through all the fleeting days of your life that He has granted you beneath the sun, all of your futile existence; for that is your compensation in life and in your toil which you exert beneath the sun.*
¹⁰ *Whatever you are able to do with your might, do it. For there is neither doing nor reckoning nor knowledge nor wisdom in the grave where you are going.*

¹¹ *Once more I saw under the sun that the race is not won by the swift; nor the battle by the strong, nor does bread come to the wise, riches to the intelligent, nor favor to the learned; but time and death will happen to them all.* ¹²*For man does not even know his hour: like fish caught in a fatal net, like birds seized in a snare, so are men caught in the moment of disaster when it falls upon them suddenly.*

¹³ *This, too, have I observed [about] wisdom beneath the sun, and it affected me profoundly:*

¹⁴ *There was a small town with only a few inhabitants; and a mighty king*

---

and Solomon's harsh estimate of women in 7:26,28. There he condemns *the woman whose heart is snares and nets;* here his sober admonition is directed to *the wife you love.*

כָּל אֲשֶׁר תִּמְצָא יָדְךָ לַעֲשׂוֹת בְּכֹחֲךָ עֲשֵׂה **.10** — *Whatever you are able to do with your might, do it.* In fulfilling the Will of your Creator do whatever you can; while you still possess your strength, use it properly (*Rashi*).

Repent while you have the ability. While the wick is still lit, add oil to keep it kindled. Once the light is extinguished, oil no longer helps (*Yalkut Shimoni*).

11. Solomon affirms his principles that this world is transitory and man is governed by God (*Rashi*).

וְגַם לֹא לַחֲכָמִים לֶחֶם — *Nor does bread come to the wise.* One would think that the wise man would rule over fools. But the matter is usually reversed (*Ibn Ezra*). Being wise does not guarantee one's food (*Metzudas David*).

וְגַם לֹא לַיֹּדְעִים חֵן — *Nor favor to the learned.* Knowledge does not always win one the acclaim of his fellow man (*Metzudas David*).

An example of unappreciated knowledge is given in verses 14-17 (*Kara*).

אֶת־עִתּוֹ **.12** — *His hour.* The time when misfortune suddenly descends upon him (*Rashbam*); so he can take precautions against it (*Sforno*).

This is a rebuke to men who always postpone repentance by rationalizing that death is far off, with the result that even if they live to seventy it does not suffice — death will still catch them unprepared (*Alshich*).

כָּהֵם יוּקָשִׁים בְּנֵי הָאָדָם לְעֵת רָעָה — *Like* (them)... *so are men caught in the moment of disaster.* Like fish who cause their own death, and later attribute it to the bait, not to the hook hidden within, so men attribute their death to sickness, not to their sins (*Alshich*).

[Thus, man — with all his intellect, power and skill — is not even superior to fish when it comes to knowing his life span; all Creation is subject to God's government of the Universe.]

גַּם־זוֹ רָאִיתִי חָכְמָה תַּחַת הַשָּׁמֶשׁ **.13-14** — *This, too, have I observed [about] wisdom beneath the sun.* Having earlier deprecated wisdom [verse 11], Solomon now relates a story complimentary to wisdom (*Ibn Ezra; Sforno; Metzudas David*).

14. According to the *Talmud* [*Nedarim* 32b], *Midrash*, and many commentators, the story is an allegory:

There was a small town, refers to the body; *with only a few inhabitants:* the limbs; *and a mighty king ... surrounded it:* the יֵצֶר הָרָע, Evil Inclination; — *Why is it called 'mighty'?* Because it is thirteen years older than the יֵצֶר הַטוֹב, Good Inclination, since man is born with selfishness

וּבָא־אֵלֶיהָ מֶלֶךְ גָּדוֹל וְסָבַב אֹתָהּ וּבָנָה עָלֶיהָ מְצוֹדִים גְּדֹלִים: טו וּמָצָא בָהּ אִישׁ מִסְכֵּן חָכָם וּמִלַּט־הוּא אֶת־הָעִיר בְּחָכְמָתוֹ וְאָדָם לֹא זָכַר אֶת־הָאִישׁ הַמִּסְכֵּן הַהוּא: טז וְאָמַרְתִּי אָנִי טוֹבָה חָכְמָה מִגְּבוּרָה וְחָכְמַת הַמִּסְכֵּן בְּזוּיָה וּדְבָרָיו אֵינָם נִשְׁמָעִים: יז דִּבְרֵי חֲכָמִים בְּנַחַת נִשְׁמָעִים מִזַּעֲקַת מוֹשֵׁל בַּכְּסִילִים: יח טוֹבָה חָכְמָה מִכְּלֵי קְרָב וְחוֹטֶא אֶחָד יְאַבֵּד טוֹבָה הַרְבֵּה:

פרק י

א זְבוּבֵי מָוֶת יַבְאִישׁ יַבִּיעַ שֶׁמֶן רוֹקֵחַ יָקָר מֵחָכְמָה מִכָּבוֹד סִכְלוּת מְעָט: ב לֵב חָכָם לִימִינוֹ וְלֵב כְּסִיל לִשְׂמֹאלוֹ: ג וְגַם־בַּדֶּרֶךְ כְּשֶׁסָּכָל הֹלֵךְ לִבּוֹ חָסֵר וְאָמַר לַכֹּל סָכָל הוּא: ד אִם־רוּחַ הַמּוֹשֵׁל תַּעֲלֶה עָלֶיךָ מְקוֹמְךָ אַל־תַּנַּח כִּי מַרְפֵּא יַנִּיחַ חֲטָאִים גְּדוֹלִים: ה יֵשׁ רָעָה רָאִיתִי תַּחַת הַשָּׁמֶשׁ כִּשְׁגָגָה שֶׁיֹּצָא מִלִּפְנֵי הַשַּׁלִּיט: ו נִתַּן הַסֶּכֶל בַּמְּרוֹמִים רַבִּים וַעֲשִׁירִים בַּשֵּׁפֶל יֵשֵׁבוּ: ז רָאִיתִי עֲבָדִים עַל־סוּסִים וְשָׂרִים הֹלְכִים כַּעֲבָדִים עַל־הָאָרֶץ: ח חֹפֵר גּוּמָּץ בּוֹ יִפּוֹל וּפֹרֵץ גָּדֵר יִשְּׁכֶנּוּ נָחָשׁ: ט מַסִּיעַ אֲבָנִים יֵעָצֵב בָּהֶם בּוֹקֵעַ עֵצִים יִסָּכֶן בָּם: י אִם־קֵהָה הַבַּרְזֶל וְהוּא לֹא־פָנִים קִלְקַל וַחֲיָלִים יְגַבֵּר וְיִתְרוֹן הַכְשֵׁיר חָכְמָה: יא אִם־יִשֹּׁךְ הַנָּחָשׁ בְּלוֹא־לָחַשׁ וְאֵין יִתְרוֹן לְבַעַל הַלָּשׁוֹן: יב דִּבְרֵי פִי־חָכָם חֵן וְשִׂפְתוֹת כְּסִיל תְּבַלְּעֶנּוּ: יג תְּחִלַּת דִּבְרֵי־פִיהוּ סִכְלוּת וְאַחֲרִית פִּיהוּ הוֹלֵלוּת רָעָה: יד וְהַסָּכָל יַרְבֶּה דְבָרִים לֹא־יֵדַע הָאָדָם מַה־שֶׁיִּהְיֶה וַאֲשֶׁר יִהְיֶה מֵאַחֲרָיו מִי יַגִּיד לוֹ: טו עֲמַל הַכְּסִילִים תְּיַגְּעֶנּוּ אֲשֶׁר לֹא־יָדַע לָלֶכֶת אֶל־עִיר: טז אִי־לָךְ אֶרֶץ

and the makings of future greed, passion, and lust; *and built great siege works over it:* guiding it to do evil. The next verse continues, *Present was a poor wise man:* The Good Inclination — Why is it called *'poor'?* Because most people ignore it; *who by his wisdom saved the town:* for whoever obeys the Good Inclination escapes punishment; *yet no one remembers that poor man:* no one holds the Good Inclination in any kind of esteem, and when the Evil Inclination gains dominion, no one remembers the Good Inclination.

In the following verses, according to this interpretation, Solomon praises the Good Inclination as being superior to the Evil Inclination.

CHAPTER TEN

1. [This verse continues the theme of the last verse: *A single rogue can ruin a great deal of good.*]

יָקָר מֵחָכְמָה מִכָּבוֹד סִכְלוּת מְעָט — *A little folly outweighs wisdom and honor.* All of man's wisdom and honor can be nullified in the eyes of people by one foolish act, just as one sin can outweigh much good (*Ibn Ezra*)

2. [There follows a series of one sentence proverbs.]

לֵב חָכָם לִימִינוֹ — *A wise man's mind* [*tends*] *to his right.* His wisdom is always prepared to lead him in the correct path for his benefit (*Rashi*); and his intellect is always at hand when he needs it (*Metzudas David*).

4. כִּי מַרְפֵּא יַנִּיחַ חֲטָאִים גְּדוֹלִים — *For deference* ['weakness'] *appeases great offenses.* Deference to his rule — rather than flagrant flight from him — will make him more kindly disposed towards clemency and will avoid a penalty for great offenses (*Ibn Yachya*).

5. כִּשְׁגָגָה — *As if it were an error.* I.e., like a royal decree made in error, which is irreversible, so are the Heavenly decrees described in verses 6 and 7 (*Rashi*).

Ibn Ezra and *Metzudas David* comment that this verse continues the thought in verse 4 in describing the potential evils of a rise to power. A ruler sometimes finds it politically expedient to commit an injustice and say it was done in error.

6. נִתַּן הַסֶּכֶל בַּמְּרוֹמִים רַבִּים — *Folly is placed on lofty heights.* This is one of the evils referred to in the previous verse: The rich who presumably deserve honor are arbitrarily shunted, while fools are elevated to high positions. It appears to

came upon it and surrounded it, and built great siege works over it. [15] Present in the city was a poor wise man who by his wisdom saved the town. Yet no one remembered that poor man. [16] So I said: Wisdom is better than might, although a poor man's wisdom is despised and his words go unheeded.

[17] The gentle words of the wise are heard above the shouts of a king over fools, [18] and wisdom is better than weapons, but a single rogue can ruin a great deal of good.

CHAPTER TEN

[1] Dead flies putrefy the perfumer's oil; a little folly outweighs wisdom and honor.

[2] A wise man's mind [tends] to his right; while a fool's mind [tends] to his left. [3] Even on the road as the fool walks, he lacks sense, and proclaims to all that he is a fool.

[4] If the anger of a ruler flares up against you, do not leave your place, for deference appeases great offenses.

[5] There is an evil which I have observed beneath the sun as if it were an error proceeding from the ruler: [6] Folly is placed on lofty heights, while rich men sit in low places. [7] I have seen slaves on horses and nobles walking on foot like slaves.

[8] He who digs a pit will fall into it, and he who breaks down a wall will be bitten by a snake. [9] He who moves about stones will be hurt by them; he who splits logs will be endangered by them.

[10] If an axe is blunt and one has not honed the edge, nevertheless it strengthens the warriors. Wisdom is a more powerful skill.

[11] If the snake bites because it was not charmed, then there is no advantage to the charmer's art.

[12] The words of a wise man win favor, but a fool's lips devour him. [13] His talk begins as foolishness and ends as evil madness. [14] The fool prates on and on, but man does not know what will be; and who can tell what will happen after him?

[15] The toil of fools exhaust them, as one who does not know the way to town.

[16] Woe to you, O land, whose king acts as an adolescent, and whose ministers

---

be an error from On High, but it is no error [it is part of God's unrevealed plan of governing the Universe] (*Metzudas David*).

8. [In the following proverbs *Koheles* enjoins care in all undertakings. These verses may also be interpreted as additional examples of the 'evils' described in vss. 6-7, in the sense that man should not put faith in his control of events: Every act is the result, not of human planning, but of Divine Providence (*Alshich*)

חֹפֵר גּוּמָץ בּוֹ יִפּוֹל — *He who digs a pit will fall into it.* He who plots against his fellow man, will himself fall into the trap (*Rashi*).

9. The fool will place himself in danger, while the wise man will guard himself. Also, nothing in this world is acquired without toil and some inherent danger (*Ibn Ezra*).

11. וְאֵין יִתְרוֹן לְבַעַל הַלָּשׁוֹן — *Then there is no advantage to the charmer's art*, There is no advantage in knowing how to exercise a charm

and not making use of it (*Rashbam*).

Similarly, there is no advantage to wisdom if, while his fellow men sin, the wise man maintains his silence, and does not teach them Torah (*Rashi*).

14. לֹא־יֵדַע הָאָדָם מַה־שֶׁיִּהְיֶה — *But man does not know what will be.* Only a fool will presume to make irresponsible plans for the near or distant future.

15. A traveler could be guided properly were he to ask directions. Conversely, the fool persists in his folly to the point of exhaustion, because he refuses to consult with the wise and seek proper guidance.

16. וְשָׂרַיִךְ בַּבֹּקֶר יֹאכֵלוּ — *And whose ministers dine in the morning.* Because their prime concern is not the welfare of the State but their own satiety. They indulge in revelry when they should attend to the duties of the State (*Ibn Latif*).

שֶׁמַּלְכֵּךְ נָ֑עַר וְשָׂרַ֖יִךְ בַּבֹּ֥קֶר יֹאכֵֽלוּ: יז אַשְׁרֵ֣יךְ אֶ֔רֶץ שֶׁמַּלְכֵּ֖ךְ בֶּן־חוֹרִ֑ים
וְשָׂרַ֙יִךְ֙ בָּעֵ֣ת יֹאכֵ֔לוּ בִּגְבוּרָ֖ה וְלֹ֥א בַשְּׁתִֽי: יח בַּעֲצַלְתַּ֖יִם יִמַּ֣ךְ הַמְּקָרֶ֑ה
וּבְשִׁפְל֥וּת יָדַ֖יִם יִדְלֹ֥ף הַבָּֽיִת: יט לִשְׂחוֹק֙ עֹשִׂ֣ים לֶ֔חֶם וְיַ֖יִן יְשַׂמַּ֣ח חַיִּ֑ים
וְהַכֶּ֖סֶף יַעֲנֶ֥ה אֶת־הַכֹּֽל: כ גַּ֣ם בְּמַדָּעֲךָ֗ מֶ֚לֶךְ אַל־תְּקַלֵּ֔ל וּבְחַדְרֵי֙ מִשְׁכָּ֣בְךָ֔
אַל־תְּקַלֵּ֖ל עָשִׁ֑יר כִּ֣י ע֤וֹף הַשָּׁמַ֙יִם֙ יוֹלִ֣יךְ אֶת־הַקּ֔וֹל וּבַ֥עַל כְּנָפַ֖יִם יַגֵּ֥יד דָּבָֽר:

פרק יא

א שַׁלַּ֥ח לַחְמְךָ֖ עַל־פְּנֵ֣י הַמָּ֑יִם כִּֽי־בְרֹ֥ב הַיָּמִ֖ים תִּמְצָאֶֽנּוּ: ב תֶּן־חֵ֜לֶק
לְשִׁבְעָ֖ה וְגַ֣ם לִשְׁמוֹנָ֑ה כִּ֚י לֹ֣א תֵדַ֔ע מַה־יִּהְיֶ֥ה רָעָ֖ה עַל־הָאָֽרֶץ:
ג אִם־יִמָּלְא֨וּ הֶעָבִ֥ים גֶּ֙שֶׁם֙ עַל־הָאָ֣רֶץ יָרִ֔יקוּ וְאִם־יִפּ֥וֹל עֵ֛ץ בַּדָּר֖וֹם וְאִ֣ם
בַּצָּפ֑וֹן מְק֛וֹם שֶׁיִּפּ֥וֹל הָעֵ֖ץ שָׁ֥ם יְהֽוּא: ד שֹׁמֵ֥ר ר֛וּחַ לֹ֥א יִזְרָ֖ע וְרֹאֶ֥ה בֶעָבִ֖ים
לֹ֥א יִקְצֽוֹר: ה כַּאֲשֶׁ֨ר אֵֽינְךָ֤ יוֹדֵ֙עַ֙ מַה־דֶּ֣רֶךְ הָר֔וּחַ כַּעֲצָמִ֖ים בְּבֶ֣טֶן הַמְּלֵאָ֑ה
כָּ֗כָה לֹ֤א תֵדַע֙ אֶת־מַעֲשֵׂ֣ה הָֽאֱלֹהִ֔ים אֲשֶׁ֥ר יַעֲשֶׂ֖ה אֶת־הַכֹּֽל: ו בַּבֹּ֙קֶר֙ זְרַ֣ע
אֶת־זַרְעֶ֔ךָ וְלָעֶ֖רֶב אַל־תַּנַּ֣ח יָדֶ֑ךָ כִּ֣י אֵֽינְךָ֤ יוֹדֵע֙ אֵ֣י זֶ֣ה יִכְשָׁ֔ר הֲזֶ֥ה אוֹ־זֶ֖ה
וְאִם־שְׁנֵיהֶ֥ם כְּאֶחָ֖ד טוֹבִֽים: ז וּמָת֖וֹק הָא֑וֹר וְט֥וֹב לַֽעֵינַ֖יִם לִרְא֥וֹת
אֶת־הַשָּֽׁמֶשׁ: ח כִּ֣י אִם־שָׁנִ֥ים הַרְבֵּ֛ה יִֽחְיֶ֥ה הָאָדָ֖ם בְּכֻלָּ֣ם יִשְׂמָ֑ח וְיִזְכֹּר֙
אֶת־יְמֵ֣י הַחֹ֔שֶׁךְ כִּֽי־הַרְבֵּ֥ה יִהְי֖וּ כָּל־שֶׁבָּ֥א הָֽבֶל: ט שְׂמַ֧ח בָּח֣וּר בְּיַלְדוּתֶ֗יךָ
וִֽיטִֽיבְךָ֤ לִבְּךָ�֙ בִּימֵ֣י בְחוּרוֹתֶ֔יךָ וְהַלֵּךְ֙ בְּדַרְכֵ֣י לִבְּךָ֔ וּבְמַרְאֵ֖ה עֵינֶ֑יךָ וְדָ֕ע כִּ֧י
עַל־כָּל־אֵ֛לֶּה יְבִֽיאֲךָ֥ הָאֱלֹהִ֖ים בַּמִּשְׁפָּֽט: י וְהָסֵ֥ר כַּ֙עַס֙ מִלִּבֶּ֔ךָ וְהַעֲבֵ֥ר רָעָ֖ה
מִבְּשָׂרֶ֑ךָ כִּֽי־הַיַּלְד֥וּת וְהַֽשַּׁחֲר֖וּת הָֽבֶל:

---

19. וְהַכֶּסֶף יַעֲנֶה אֶת־הַכֹּל — *But money answers everything.* Money is needed by all and makes everything possible. In the previous verse slothfulness is deprecated; here man is encouraged toward industry. Lazy people do not earn the money required for living (Rashi; Metzudas David).

Yalkut HaGershuni comments that יַעֲנֶה can be related to עִינוּי, *affliction:* 'money afflicts all.' [Its abundance as well as its absence causes suffering.]

On an ethical level, the verse is interpreted: 'money makes everyone respond' — for money, people will accede to your every request (Kedushas Levi).

20. כִּי עוֹף הַשָּׁמַיִם יוֹלִיךְ אֶת הַקּוֹל — *For a bird of the skies may carry the sound.* An idiomatic phrase to imply that your utterance will quickly spread and reach the ears of government officials (Metzudas David).

CHAPTER ELEVEN

1. שַׁלַּח לַחְמְךָ עַל־פְּנֵי הַמָּיִם — *Send your bread upon the waters.* Most commentators explain this verse as urging that charity be given even to strangers who will never be seen again. The generosity will not go unrewarded; the favor will be repaid.

2. The commentators explain this verse also as referring to charity, specifically its wider distribution.

לְשִׁבְעָה וְגַם לִשְׁמוֹנָה — *To seven, or even to eight,* i.e., abundantly, without pause (Ralbag). Thus, the verse admonishes: Give charity constantly.

Avudraham quotes the Midrash that this verse alludes to *Succos,* a *seven*-day festival followed by *Shimini Atzeres,* the *eighth* festival day. This may be why Koheles is read on Succos.

כִּי לֹא תֵדַע — *For you never know what calamity* will strike the land. If you are thrust into poverty and require the assistance of others, you will be saved by virtue of your former charitable acts (Rashi).

3. אִם־יִמָּלְאוּ הֶעָבִים — *If the clouds are filled.* Clouds filled with rain-water do not keep it to themselves, but they beneficently pour it upon the earth. In turn, the earth receives moisture which, by the natural moisture-cycle, returns to the clouds [cf. 1:7]. Similarly, a man who is blessed by God and 'filled' with wealth is bidden not to hoard his wealth but should dispense a portion of it as charity to those less fortunate. If the wheel turns and he finds himself in need, he will be sustained by others (Metzudas David).

4. One must perform the tasks required of him

dine in the morning. [17] Happy are you, O land, whose king is a man of dignity, and whose ministers dine at the proper time — in strength and not in drunkenness.

[18] Through slothfulness the ceiling sags, and through idleness of the hands the house leaks.

[19] A feast is made for laughter, and wine gladdens life, but money answers everything.

[20] Even in your thoughts do not curse a king, and in your bed-chamber do not curse the rich, for a bird of the skies may carry the sound, and some winged creature may betray the matter.

CHAPTER ELEVEN

[1] Send your bread upon the waters, for after many days you will find it. [2] Distribute portions to seven, or even to eight, for you never know what calamity will strike the land.

[3] If the clouds are filled they will pour down rain on the earth; if a tree falls down in the south or the north, wherever the tree falls, there it remains. [4] One who watches the wind will never sow, and one who keeps his eyes on the clouds will never reap. [5] Just as you do not know the way of the wind, nor the nature of the embryo in a pregnant stomach, so can you never know the work of God Who makes everything. [6] In the morning sow your seed and in the evening do not be idle, for you cannot know which will succeed: this or that; or whether both are equally good.

[7] Sweet is the light, and it is good for the eyes to behold the sun! [8] Even if a man lives many years, let him rejoice in all of them, but let him remember that the days of darkness will be many. All that comes is futility. [9] Rejoice, young man, in your childhood; let your heart cheer you in the days of your youth; follow the path of your heart and the sight of your eyes — but be aware that for all these things God will call you to account. [10] Rather, banish anger from your heart and remove evil from your flesh — for childhood and youth are futile.

---

and have faith that God will bless his works.

שֹׁמֵר רוּחַ לֹא יִזְרָע – One who watches the wind will never sow. One who forever waits for ideal conditions will never get his work done (Ibn Latif). Similarly in matters of dispensing charity, one should not be over-suspicious and over-prudent; he should follow his inclination and dispense it as it is required (Nachal Eshkol).

5. אֶת־מַעֲשֵׂה הָאֱלֹהִים – The work of God. Similarly, God's decrees concerning wealth and poverty are sealed to man. Therefore, one must never recoil from charity out of fear that he will become poor; nor refrain from Torah study out of fear that he will neglect his business and grow poor; nor rationalize that he should not marry because he will then have to support children (Rashi).

7. וּמָתוֹק הָאוֹר – Sweet is the light. Metzudas David explains that 'light' refers metaphorically to life: Sweet is the life of man while he is still permitted to enjoy the light of day! In the second part of the verse, the thought is rephrased forming an effective parallel.

The Midrash explains 'light' as Torah: 'Sweet

is the light of Torah ... and happy is he whose study enlightens him like the sun [leaving him free of doubts and perplexities.] ... Rav Acha said: Sweet is the light of the World to Come; happy is he who is worthy to behold that light!'

8. וְיִזְכֹּר אֶת־יְמֵי הַחֹשֶׁךְ – But let him remember [i.e., ponder] the days of darkness. But at the same time it is imperative that one keep in mind the transitory nature of this world and strive to improve his ways, for the days of darkness — an allusion to death and the judgment of the wicked — will be many. Those days are more eternal than the short duration of life on this world (Rashi).

This verse is reminiscent of an incident recorded in the Talmud: Rav Chisda's daughter asked him if he wished to take a nap. He answered: The time will come when there will be long days in the grave where Torah study and observance will be impossible. We will sleep much there. Meanwhile, we must exert ourselves and be involved with Torah and the commandments (Eruvin 65a).

9. שְׂמַח בָּחוּר בְּיַלְדוּתֶךָ – Rejoice, young man, in your childhood. [As evidenced by the end of the

א וּזְכֹר' אֶת־בּוֹרְאֶיךָ בִּימֵי בְּחוּרֹתֶיךָ עַד אֲשֶׁר לֹא־יָבֹאוּ יְמֵי הָרָעָה וְהִגִּיעוּ
שָׁנִים אֲשֶׁר תֹּאמַר אֵין־לִי בָהֶם חֵפֶץ: ב עַד אֲשֶׁר לֹא־תֶחְשַׁךְ הַשֶּׁמֶשׁ
וְהָאוֹר וְהַיָּרֵחַ וְהַכּוֹכָבִים וְשָׁבוּ הֶעָבִים אַחַר הַגָּשֶׁם: ג בַּיּוֹם שֶׁיָּזֻעוּ שֹׁמְרֵי
הַבַּיִת וְהִתְעַוְּתוּ אַנְשֵׁי הֶחָיִל וּבָטְלוּ הַטֹּחֲנוֹת כִּי מִעֵטוּ וְחָשְׁכוּ הָרֹאוֹת
בָּאֲרֻבּוֹת: ד וְסֻגְּרוּ דְלָתַיִם' בַּשּׁוּק בִּשְׁפַל קוֹל הַטַּחֲנָה וְיָקוּם לְקוֹל הַצִּפּוֹר
וְיִשַּׁחוּ כָּל־בְּנוֹת הַשִּׁיר: ה גַּם מִגָּבֹהַּ יִרָאוּ וְחַתְחַתִּים בַּדֶּרֶךְ וְיָנֵאץ הַשָּׁקֵד
וְיִסְתַּבֵּל הֶחָגָב וְתָפֵר הָאֲבִיּוֹנָה כִּי־הֹלֵךְ הָאָדָם' אֶל־בֵּית עוֹלָמוֹ וְסָבְבוּ
בַשּׁוּק הַסֹּפְדִים: ו עַד אֲשֶׁר לֹא־יֵרָתֵק' חֶבֶל הַכֶּסֶף וְתָרֻץ גֻּלַּת הַזָּהָב
וְתִשָּׁבֶר כַּד' עַל־הַמַּבּוּעַ וְנָרֹץ הַגַּלְגַּל אֶל־הַבּוֹר: ז וְיָשֹׁב הֶעָפָר עַל־הָאָרֶץ
כְּשֶׁהָיָה וְהָרוּחַ תָּשׁוּב אֶל־הָאֱלֹהִים אֲשֶׁר נְתָנָהּ: ח הֲבֵל הֲבָלִים אָמַר
הַקּוֹהֶלֶת הַכֹּל הָבֶל: ט וְיֹתֵר שֶׁהָיָה קֹהֶלֶת חָכָם עוֹד לִמַּד־דַּעַת אֶת־
הָעָם וְאִזֵּן וְחִקֵּר תִּקֵּן מְשָׁלִים הַרְבֵּה: י בִּקֵּשׁ קֹהֶלֶת לִמְצֹא דִּבְרֵי־חֵפֶץ
וְכָתוּב יֹשֶׁר דִּבְרֵי אֱמֶת: יא דִּבְרֵי חֲכָמִים כַּדָּרְבֹנוֹת וְכְמַשְׂמְרוֹת נְטוּעִים

---

verse, this is in no way to be interpreted as a hedonistic *carte-blanche* to run amok with one's passion.] It is clearly to be understood as words of warning to those rebellious youths who wallow in sin [and who would not accept his words if they were said in such negative terms as: 'Do *not* rejoice . . . do *not* follow your heart']. Rather, Solomon said: I know full well that fools tend to sin in their youth, but beware! Judgment is forthcoming (*Midrash Lekach Tov*).

CHAPTER TWELVE

1. Having warned recalcitrant youth to *'be aware that for all these things God will call you to account'* (11:9) and that *'childhood and youth are futile,'* (11:10), Solomon continues that man should spend his vigorous youth in the service of his Creator.

וּזְכֹר אֶת־בּוֹרְאֶיךָ — *So remember your Creator,* and try — in spirit and deed — to honor Him (*Sforno*).

בִּימֵי בְּחוּרֹתֶיךָ — *In the days of your youth.* While in the possession of your strength (*Midrash*).

Man should take advantage of vigorous youth to serve God, before old age sets in and service becomes more difficult (*Metzudas David*).

יְמֵי הָרָעָה — *The evil days,* i.e., old age with its infirmities (*Rashi*).

2. [The following verses, as explained by the commentators, poetically conjure an image of the fading of life as old age approaches. The allegory refers to the waning powers of the organs of the body, as will be explained.

The Talmud relates an incident in which a man described his old age as follows: 'The mountain is snowy, it is surrounded by ice, the

dog does not bark, and the grinders do not grind' [i.e., my head is snowy white, my beard likewise; my voice is feeble and my teeth do not function;] (*Shabbos* 152a).

הַשֶּׁמֶשׁ וְהָאוֹר וְהַיָּרֵחַ וְהַכּוֹכָבִים — *The sun, the light, the moon and the stars,* i.e., the forehead, the nose, the soul, and the cheeks (*Midrash*).

וְשָׁבוּ הֶעָבִים אַחַר הַגָּשֶׁם — *And the clouds return after the rain.* The eyesight which is weakened by weeping, i.e., the weeping of old age, caused by trouble and sickness, destroys the eyesight; crying, puffy eyes are compared to clouds (*Torah Temimah*)] (*Shabbos* 151b).

3. שֹׁמְרֵי הַבַּיִת — *The guards of the house.* [Koheles compares the aged human body to a house in ruins:] The 'guards of the house' are the hands and arms which protect the body from threat and injury (*Ibn Ezra*) [but now are enfeebled].

אַנְשֵׁי הֶחָיִל — *The powerful men,* i.e., the legs that support the bodily structure (*Rashi*); הַטֹּחֲנוֹת, *the grinders,* the teeth that have fallen out in old age (*Rashi*).

הָרֹאוֹת בָּאֲרֻבּוֹת — *The gazers through windows.* I.e., the eyes (*Talmud*, ibid.).

4. וְיָקוּם לְקוֹל הַצִּפּוֹר — *When one rises up at the voice of a bird.* Even the chirping of a bird will wake the aged from sleep (*Talmud* ibid.; *Rashi*, et al).

5. גַּם מִגָּבֹהַּ יִרָאוּ — *[When] they even fear a height.* Even a small knoll looks to him like the highest mountains (*Talmud* ibid.); and he is liable to stumble (*Rashi*).

CHAPTER TWELVE

¹So remember your Creator in the days of your youth, before the evil days come, and those years arrive of which you will say, 'I have no pleasure in them;' ² before the sun, the light, the moon and the stars grow dark, and the clouds return after the rain; ³ in the day when the guards of the house will tremble, and the powerful men will stoop, and the grinders are idle because they are few, and the gazers through windows are dimmed; ⁴ when the doors in the street are shut; when the sound of the grinding is low; when one rises up at the voice of the bird, and all the daughters of song grow dim; ⁵ when they even fear a height and terror in the road; and the almond tree blossoms and the grasshopper becomes a burden and the desire fails — so man goes to his eternal home, while the mourners go about the streets.

⁶ Before the silver cord snaps, and the golden bowl is shattered, and the pitcher is broken at the fountain, and the wheel is smashed at the pit. ⁷ Thus the dust returns to the ground, as it was, and the spirit returns to God Who gave it. ⁸ Futility of futilities — said Koheles — All is futile!

⁹ And besides being wise, Koheles also imparted knowledge to the people; he listened, and sought out; and arranged many proverbs.

¹⁰ Koheles sought to find words of delight, and words of truth recorded properly. ¹¹The words of the wise are like goads, and the nails well driven are the

---

הַשָּׁקֵד — *The almond tree.* The whiteness of the hair in old age (*Ibn Ezra*).

כִּי־הֹלֵךְ הָאָדָם אֶל־בֵּית עוֹלָמוֹ — *So man goes to his eternal home,* i.e., the grave where he will dwell forever (*Ibn Ezra*).

6. [The following verse also amplifies upon verse 1, exhorting man to repent before the arrival of old age, and offers another metaphor for the *final* dissolution of life.]

חֶבֶל הַכֶּסֶף — *The silver cord,* i.e., the spinal cord (*Rashi*). [The metaphor is as follows: The body — near death — is likened to the malfunctioning machinery of a well: cord, wheel and pitcher. The cord (spine) snaps; the skull shatters; the stomach breaks; and the body is smashed.]

7. וְיָשֹׁב הֶעָפָר — *Thus the dust returns.* 'Dust' refers to the body of man, which was formed from dust.

עַל־הָאָרֶץ כְּשֶׁהָיָה — *To the ground, as it was* [i.e., as it was at Creation]. The body rejoins the earth from which it was formed (*Almosnino*).

וְהָרוּחַ תָּשׁוּב אֶל־הָאֱלֹהִים — *And the spirit returns to God.* But the soul returns to its Source from which it was taken; unto God Who gave it at birth as it is written (*Gen.* 2:7); *'And [God] breathed into his nostrils the breath of life'.*

8. Epilogue

Thus begins the epilogue of the Book. Having discoursed on the life and trials of man, and described the vicissitudes that man experiences *'under the sun'* until death, Koheles reiterates the recurring refrain of his conclusions: *'All is futile'* (*Rashbam; Kehillas Yaakov*).

הַקּוֹהֶלֶת — *Koheles.* The Hebrew has the definite article ה, 'the' Koheles, because, as pointed out, Koheles is not a proper name but a title [see *comm.* to 1.1] (*Ibn Ezra*).

9. עוֹד לִמַּד־דַּעַת אֶת הָעָם — *(He) also imparted knowledge to the people.* ... Unlike many geniuses who cannot distill their wisdom in a manner that the masses can comprehend, the verse stresses that Solomon, *'the wisest of all men'* [*I Kings* 5:11], was blessed with this ability, and he utilized it by publicly expounding his knowledge in popular form (*R' Yaakov Chagiz*).

10. בִּקֵּשׁ קֹהֶלֶת לִמְצֹא דִּבְרֵי־חֵפֶץ — *Koheles sought to find words of delight.* Koheles sought in his quests to achieve supreme wisdom; he exerted himself to find Truth (*Ibn Ezra; Metzudas David*).

The commentators explain that Solomon sought to comprehend God's government of the Universe.

וְכָתוּב יֹשֶׁר דִּבְרֵי אֱמֶת — *And words of truth recorded properly.* This refers to the Bible (*Rashi*).

He sought to insure that people would find his proverbs to be a 'delight of God', and he later discovered that all his thoughts were already recorded in the Word of Truth [i.e., that his wisdom reflected the Truth of Torah] (*Rashi*).

11. כַּדָּרְבֹנוֹת — *Like goads.* Used by shepherds to prod their animals (*Metzudas David*).

As *Rashi* explains: Just as the goad directs the heifer along its proper path, so do words of the wise lead men along the paths of life (*Chagigah* 3b).

בַּעֲלֵי אֲסֻפּוֹת נִתְּנוּ מֵרֹעֶה אֶחָד: יב וְיֹתֵר מֵהֵמָּה בְּנִי הִזָּהֵר עֲשׂוֹת סְפָרִים הַרְבֵּה֙ אֵין קֵץ וְלַהַג הַרְבֵּה יְגִעַת בָּשָׂר: יג סוֹף דָּבָר הַכֹּל נִשְׁמָע אֶת־הָאֱלֹהִים יְרָא֙ וְאֶת־מִצְוֺתָיו שְׁמוֹר כִּי־זֶה כָּל־הָאָדָם: יד כִּי אֶת־כָּל־מַעֲשֶׂה הָאֱלֹהִים יָבִא בְמִשְׁפָּט עַל כָּל־נֶעְלָם אִם־טוֹב וְאִם־רָע:

סוֹף דָּבָר הַכֹּל נִשְׁמָע
אֶת־הָאֱלֹהִים יְרָא֙ וְאֶת־מִצְוֺתָיו שְׁמוֹר
כִּי־זֶה כָּל־הָאָדָם:

---

12. וְיֹתֵר מֵהֵמָּה בְּנִי הִזָּהֵר — *Beyond these, my son, beware.* The verse is couched in a term of endearment [as if addressing a pupil] (*Metzudas David*).

עֲשׂוֹת סְפָרִים הַרְבֵּה אֵין קֵץ — *The making of many books is without limit,* Lest you say, 'If it is necessary to obey wise men, why are their words not published?' The answer is — 'the making of many books is without limit'; it is not possible to commit everything to writing (*Rashi*).

Rav Yisrael Salanter, when discussing publishing books, would homiletically cite this verse and say: King Solomon cautioned us that not

everything that man thinks must he say; not everything he says must he write, but, most important, not everything that he has written must he publish.

וְלַהַג הַרְבֵּה יְגִעַת בָּשָׂר — *And much study is weariness of the flesh.* The total accumulation of Torah knowledge is more than man can absorb. If so, you may ask, 'Why indulge in so much wearying effort?' The answer is given in the following verse.

13. Solomon said: Although I have expounded many esoteric and difficult concepts in this Book, nevertheless סוֹף דָּבָר, *the summation of the*

sayings of the masters of collections, coming from one Shepherd.

[12] Beyond these, my son, beware: the making of many books is without limit, and much study is weariness of the flesh.

[13] The sum of the matter, when all has been considered: Fear God and keep His commandments, for that is man's whole duty. [14] For God will judge every deed — even everything hidden — whether good or evil.

> *The sum of the matter, when all has been considered:*
> *fear God and keep His commandments,*
> *for that is man's whole duty.*

---

matter, הַכֹּל נִשְׁמָע, *is obvious to all and unquestionable: Fear God with your every limb and organ, for this is all of man* (Derech Chaim).

אֶת־הָאֱלֹהִים יְרָא וְאֶת־מִצְוֹתָיו שְׁמוֹר — *Fear God and keep His commandments.* 'Fear God' in your heart; 'and keep His commandments' by deed (Ramban).

Do your utmost [and direct] your heart to Heaven (Rashi).

כִּי־זֶה כָּל־הָאָדָם — *For that is man's whole duty.* It was for this that all men were created (Rashi).

This is the essence of man (Ibn Ezra); and 'the entire world was created only for such a man' (Shabbos 30b).

14. עַל כָּל־נֶעְלָם — *Even everything hidden —* even unwillful transgressions (Rashi).

Even transgressions done in privacy [concealed from your fellow man and hence not punishable by human courts of law] (Ralbag).

אִם־טוֹב וְאִם רָע — *Whether good or evil.* Whether the deed was good and deserving of reward; or evil and deserving of punishment (Sforno).

סוֹף דָּבָר — *The sum of the matter.* It is customary, during public-readings of Koheles, to repeat verse 13 rather than end with the word רָע, *evil,* in verse 14. We act similarly at the end of *Isaiah, Malachi* and *Lamentations,* and thus end these books on a positive note.

MW00453190